T0372695

Asian Americans in an Anti-Black World

Where do Asian Americans fit into the U.S. racial order? Are they subordinated comparably to Black people or permitted adjacency to whiteness? The racial reckoning prompted by the police murder of George Floyd and the surge in anti-Asian hate during the COVID-19 pandemic raise these questions with new urgency. *Asian Americans in an Anti-Black World* is a groundbreaking study that will shake up scholarly and popular thinking on these matters. Theoretically innovative and based on rigorous historical research, this provocative book tells us we must consider *both* anti-Blackness and white supremacy – and the articulation of the two forces – in order to understand U.S. racial dynamics. The construction of Asian Americans as not-white *but above all not-Black* has determined their positionality for nearly two centuries. How Asian Americans choose to respond to this status will help to define racial politics in the U.S. in the twenty-first century.

Claire Jean Kim is Professor of Political Science and Asian American Studies at University of California, Irvine. Her writing has appeared in the *Los Angeles Times*, *The Nation*, and *Ms. Magazine*. Her two previous books, *Bitter Fruit: The Politics of Black–Korean Conflict* and *Dangerous Crossings: Race, Species and Nature in a Multicultural Age*, have both won best book awards from the American Political Science Association. Kim has been a fellow at the Institute of Advanced Study and the University of California Humanities Research Institute.

Asian Americans in an Anti-Black World

CLAIRE JEAN KIM
University of California, Irvine

CAMBRIDGE
UNIVERSITY PRESS

Shaftesbury Road, Cambridge CB2 8EA, United Kingdom

One Liberty Plaza, 20th Floor, New York, NY 10006, USA

477 Williamstown Road, Port Melbourne, VIC 3207, Australia

314–321, 3rd Floor, Plot 3, Splendor Forum, Jasola District Centre,
New Delhi – 110025, India

103 Penang Road, #05–06/07, Visioncrest Commercial, Singapore 238467

Cambridge University Press is part of Cambridge University Press & Assessment,
a department of the University of Cambridge.

We share the University's mission to contribute to society through the pursuit of
education, learning and research at the highest international levels of excellence.

www.cambridge.org
Information on this title: www.cambridge.org/9781009222259

DOI: 10.1017/9781009222280

First published 2023

Printed in the United Kingdom by TJ Books Limited, Padstow Cornwall

A catalogue record for this publication is available from the British Library

Library of Congress Cataloging-in-Publication Data
NAMES: Kim, Claire Jean, author.
TITLE: Asian Americans in an anti-Black world / Claire Jean Kim, University
of California, Irvine.
DESCRIPTION: Cambridge, United Kingdom ; New York, NY : Cambridge
University Press, [2023] | Includes bibliographical references and
index.
IDENTIFIERS: LCCN 2023002722 | ISBN 9781009222259 (hardback)
| ISBN 9781009222280 (ebook)
SUBJECTS: LCSH: Asian Americans – Race identity. | African
Americans – Relations with Asian Americans. | Asian Americans – Social
conditions. | African Americans – Social conditions. | Racism – United
States – History. | United States – Race relations – History.
CLASSIFICATION: LCC E184.A75 K528 2023 | DDC 305.895/073–dc23/eng/20230126
LC record available at https://lccn.loc.gov/2023002722

ISBN 978-1-009-22225-9 Hardback

For Sam,
heart of my heart

Contents

Acknowledgments

My sincere appreciation to friends and colleagues for their encouragement and feedback.

Thanks to Michael Dawson, Stephen Lee, Robert Gooding-Williams, Rogers Smith, and Jane Junn for constructive comments on parts of the manuscript.

Special thanks to Reuel Schiller, David Levine, and Vincent Moyer, librarian at Hastings College of Law, for their generous assistance.

Gratitude to Brian Williams, law librarian at University of California, Irvine, whose years of assistance, support, and good cheer made this a better book.

Thank you to my editor at Cambridge University Press, Robert Dreesen, for his commitment to this project.

And love to my family, human and more than human, for keeping me company on the journey.

Introduction

Better Asians than Blacks

[N]on-Black oppressed people in this country are both impacted by racism and domination, and simultaneously BENEFIT from anti-black racism.

Alicia Garza

The global scope of COVID-19 tempts us to think "we are all in this together," but the pandemic in fact shows us—like the ecological crisis does at a slower tempo—that we are not all in this together, or, more precisely, that we are all in this together very differently. Due to the pre-existing fault lines of race and class, the pandemic has landed unevenly upon various groups. Nor does intervention by the neoliberal state necessarily mitigate these inequalities. On April 28, 2020, as COVID-19 rates soared among U.S. meatpacking plant employees, President Donald Trump declared the plants to be "critical infrastructure" and ordered them to stay open, thus endangering their largely Black female workforce. Workers had to choose between losing their jobs and possibly losing their lives. Trump then indemnified plant owners from the legal repercussions of exposing workers to deadly harm. There was little pretense about who was disposable and who was not, who was grievable and who was not, who mattered and who did not. Articulated with capitalism, racism is, in Ruth Wilson Gilmore's words, the "production and exploitation of group-differentiated vulnerability to premature death."[1]

For low-income Black communities in the U.S., a perfect storm of conditions set the stage for COVID-19's devastating impact. Neoliberal austerity policies, together with systemic discrimination, segregation,

---

[1] Gilmore 2007, 247.

I

overpolicing, and mass incarceration, have created widespread economic precarity and poverty. The stresses inflicted by these traumatic experiences, along with disproportionate exposure to environmental harms and inadequate access to medical care, compromised health outcomes well before the pandemic. In addition, employment in low-wage, temporary work and entanglement in carceral institutions heightened exposure to the virus. As a result, Black people, according to the American Public Media's report *The Color of Coronavirus*, have one of the highest COVID-19 mortality rates in the U.S. One *Guardian* reporter wondered if Blackness should be considered a "pre-existing condition" for the disease.[2]

It was in this context that the murder of a Black man, George Floyd, by four Minneapolis police officers on May 25, 2020, sparked the largest uprising in U.S. history. The *New York Times* estimates that between 15 million and 26 million people in the U.S. participated in demonstrations over the next several months. The unbearable confluence of epidemiological violence, neoliberal economic violence, and anti-Black violence on the part of the state generated this dramatic resurgence in the Black Lives Matter movement. The protest cry "I can't breathe"—first raised after the police murdered Eric Garner via chokehold in New York City in 2014—took on new layers of meaning, referring at once to Black people's relatively high rates of asthma, a pulmonary disease that is linked to poverty and is a possible risk factor for COVID-19; the disproportionate impact of COVID-19, a respiratory disease, upon Black communities; and the murder by asphyxiation of George Floyd, who cried "I can't breathe" more than twenty times during the 9 minutes 29 seconds that Derek Chauvin kneeled on his neck.

Within a few months, the reenergized Black Lives Matter movement transformed "defund the police" into a legitimate topic of public discussion, tying this goal to a broader vision of a society in which people would be liberated from fear, oppression, violence, and want. Legislators introduced the George Floyd Justice in Policing Bill, which aimed to curb discriminatory actions by the police, in the U.S. House of Representatives. The families of the victims of several high-profile police murders—including George Floyd, Breonna Taylor, Michael Brown, and Philando Castile—worked with racial justice organizations to petition

---

[2] I use the phrase "Black people" throughout the book, except when preserving the terminology used by those whose views or actions I am discussing. Similarly for the term "Latinx."

the United Nations Human Rights Council to appoint a Commission of Inquiry into police violence against Black people in the U.S. When the U.S. government used its power to thwart this request, an international group of judges, lawyers, professors, and other human rights experts formed their own Commission of Inquiry on the subject.[3] Meanwhile, Black-led demonstrations sprang up around the world, as activists in Brazil, the United Kingdom, Belgium, Australia, and elsewhere rose to challenge the legacies of slavery and colonialism in their own societies.

But if the pandemic has (re)illuminated the singular status of Black people in the U.S. (and beyond), it has not brought a similar clarity to the status of Asian Americans, who at times seem precariously perched in the category of "people of color."[4] On the one hand, the pandemic has reminded us of Asian Americans' vulnerability to racial harm. After President Trump described COVID-19 as "kung flu" and "the Chinese flu," incidents of anti-Asian harassment and violence surged across the nation. The nineteenth-century notion of Asian immigrants as a "yellow peril" riddled with contagious afflictions retains its hold on the white imagination. Long accustomed to daily microaggressions, Asian Americans now report being yelled at, spat upon, denied service, and attacked in the street. Their sense of safety in public spaces has diminished. Like the bombing of Pearl Harbor, the pandemic has brought to the surface the enduring undercurrent of anti-Asian animus in U.S. culture.

At the same time, Asian Americans continue to stand apart from other not-white groups in noticeable ways. On the whole, they fare better in socioeconomic terms than other not-white groups. They are not persistently segregated in urban ghettos, or barrios, or reservations. They are not disproportionately targeted by police violence or carceral institutions. Their children do not endure caging and family separation at the border. There is no epidemic of thousands of Asian American women who have disappeared.

The American Public Media's report *The Color of Coronavirus* reveals that Asian Americans have a lower COVID-19 mortality rate than any other group, including whites. The contrast with Black Americans is worth noting: Asian Americans are 5.6 percent of the U.S. population

---

[3] In March 2021, they released a report entitled *Report of the International Commission of Inquiry on Systemic Racist Police Violence against People of African Descent in the United States*. See Part Three for further discussion.

[4] C. Kim 2001; 2004.

and have experienced 3.6 percent of all COVID-19 deaths of known race, whereas Black people, who are 12.4 percent of the population, have experienced 14.9 percent of all COVID-19 deaths of known race.[5] What explains this gap? We would expect COVID-19 mortality rates to vary by socioeconomic status, and indeed Asian Americans are doing well relative to Black people, whether we look at median household income, wealth accumulation, educational attainment, or occupational attainment. Of course, this just raises the question of why Asian Americans as a group are enjoying greater educational, social, and economic mobility than Black people as a group.[6]

Do Asian Americans, as a whole, have different class investments than many Black people? On May 25, 2020, as Derek Chauvin kneeled on George Floyd's neck and two other officers sat on Floyd's torso and legs, Tou Thao, a Hmong American police officer, held back the crowd of distressed bystanders and deflected their anguished appeals. Like NYPD officer Peter Liang's fatal shooting of Akai Gurley in 2014, Thao's actions are symbolically loaded. What does it mean for an Asian American to don a police uniform and murder a Black person? Does this tell us something about where Asian Americans stand in relation to the regimes of private property, policing, and incarceration that subtend racial capitalism? What about the many Asian Americans who joined Black Lives Matter protests in memory of George Floyd? In the paradigmatic scene where the white officer commands the Black person to assume the position, what exactly is the Asian American doing?

It has been decades since Gary Okihiro observed that Asian Americans were "neither black nor white" and Mari Matsuda warned they were

---

[5] See at: www.apmresearchlab.org/covid/deaths-by-race#counts-new (as of January 22, 2022). Indigenous people are the only group in the U.S. that has a higher mortality rate from COVID-19 than Black people.

[6] All of this is not to say that Asian Americans are becoming white. Whiteness in the U.S. expanded from the early twentieth century onward to incorporate many European immigrant groups previously considered liminal, including Jews, the Irish, Slavs, Poles, and Italians. Blackness was the foil against which this occurred. See Jacobson 1998; Ignatiev 2009 [1995]; Roediger 2007 [1991]. With this historical precedent in mind, scholars have drawn on recent data on intermarriage rates and socioeconomic status to argue that whiteness is expanding again, this time to incorporate Asian Americans and Latinos. See Gans 1999; Lee and Bean 2007; Warren and Twine 1997; Yancey 2004. Yet the evidence is also consistent with the view that these groups are being allowed some of the privileges of whiteness while still being kept outside of it. I argue in this book that Asian Americans' "minority" status makes them useful to whites in the project of stabilizing structural anti-Blackness. In other words, it benefits whites to maintain Asian Americans in a position where they are near-white but still a "minority."

becoming a "racial bourgeoisie."[7] In this book, I build on these insights and propose a new theoretical approach for understanding where Asian Americans fit into the U.S. racial order. It is an approach that can account for the apparently contradictory evidence that has always made Asian American positionality a conundrum. It is not only a better understanding of Asian Americans' status or experiences per se that is on offer here. Looking at how this group gets positioned over time can teach us a great deal about how not-white, not-Black groups are recruited to the project of maintaining white supremacy and Black abjection—that is, about how the system as a whole operates.

~~~~

I have been thinking about these issues for some time. My first published article, "The Racial Triangulation of Asian Americans,"[8] argued that the U.S. racial order was constructed in the late 1800s as a two-dimensional plane defined by two axes: the superior–inferior scale (y axis) and the insider–outsider scale (x axis). Whites, who are positioned at the top of the superior–inferior scale and the inside of the insider–outsider scale, sit at the apex of the equilateral triangle. Black people, who are positioned at the bottom of the superior–inferior scale but also on the inside of the insider–outsider scale (because of their formal inclusion in the polity during the postbellum period), occupy the bottom point of the triangle. Asian Americans, who are positioned between Black people and white people on the superior–inferior scale but also on the outside of the insider–outsider scale (because of their formal exclusion from citizenship during the postbellum period), occupy the third, outermost point of the triangle. Two types of practices stabilize Asian Americans in this triangulated location: relative valorization (rendering them superior to Black people) and civic ostracism (rendering them unassimilable and unfit for inclusion in the body politic). Racial triangulation, I argued, gives whites a certain flexibility, whereby they can racialize Asians variably, as circumstances warranted, while also disciplining Black people as the most inferior group.

Two years later, in "Playing the Racial Trump Card: Asian Americans in Contemporary U.S. Politics,"[9] I addressed the differential in status and power between Asian Americans and Black people more directly. I

[7] See Okihiro 1994 and Matsuda 1993.
[8] C. Kim 1999.
[9] C. Kim 2001.

argued that Asian American scholars and activists sometimes make rhetorical and discursive choices that undermine the Black struggle, albeit
inadvertently. When they claim that Asian Americans are minorities,
too, deserving of equal consideration with Black people, they abstract
from history and disavow the ways in which Asian Americans are, on the
whole, advantaged relative to Black people. By asserting formal interminority equivalences in the face of persistent interminority differentials in
status, privilege, and power, they enable conservative whites to charac-
terize Black demands that (appear to) impinge on Asian Americans—for
example, in race-conscious admissions—as "reverse discrimination" that
is presumptively illegitimate. After all, if all minority groups are viewed
as formal equivalents, it seems unfair that one would burden another in
its efforts to advance.

Some years later, in "The Afro-Asian Analogy" (2008), Colleen
Lye mentioned the theory of racial triangulation as an example of
how "the foundational status of antiblackness in conceptualizations
of racism obstructs Asian Americanist endeavors to elaborate the
nonderivative nature of Asian racialization."[10] I did not in fact discuss the concept of anti-Blackness in my 1999 piece, but I believe Lye
meant that Asian Americanists should stop trying to link the racialization of Asian Americans to that of Black people. They should instead
treat Asian Americans as *sui generis*. Who indeed does not want to be
"nonderivative?"

Ironically, Lye was reaching this conclusion just as I was reaching
the opposite one, based upon reading scholarship in Black studies that
draws upon Frantz Fanon's discussions of "negrophobia" to elaborate
foundational or structural anti-Blackness—a concept that names the
way in which our collective psychic and institutional lives are organized
around the phobic hatred and avoidance of Blackness.[11] Unlike the
generic concept of racism, the concept of anti-Blackness addresses the
historical specificity of the status of Black people as it has been shaped
by racial slavery and colonialism.[12] Here was a language that could help
to deconstruct the interminority differentials in status and power that I

---

[10] Lye 2008, 1733.
[11] See, for example, Marriott 2000; Gordon 1997; Wilderson 2010; Sexton 2010b; Sharpe
2016.
[12] Articulated with global capitalism in manifold, historically contingent ways, structural
anti-Blackness helps to define who matters and who does not, who is deserving and who
is not, who should live and who should die. On racial capitalism, see Robinson 1983;
Dawson 2016; Melamed 2015; Burden-Stelly 2020.

had discussed in my 2001 piece. *Pace* Lye, I soon concluded that anti-Blackness is not overemphasized in Asian American studies scholarship. To the contrary, it is not uncommon for Asian Americanists to focus exclusively on white-on-Asian domination and redact anti-Blackness (both the concept and the reality to which it refers) altogether. What would happen, I wondered, if we brought structural anti-Blackness *back into* the narrative(s) of Asian American history? This is the question that animates this book.

To begin with, the theory of racial triangulation would have to be rethought.[13] The premise that Black people came to occupy an "insider" position after the Civil War would be undermined, destabilizing the entire geometric structure. It is true, of course, that Black people were granted new citizenship, voting, and naturalization rights after the Civil War, but these were promises honored in the breach. If we want to look at how the U.S. government actually imagined and treated freed-people during and after Reconstruction, an indispensable text is *Scenes of Subjection: Terror, Slavery, and Self-Making in Nineteenth-Century America*.[14] Hartman shows that the freedperson's "rights" were viti-ated in the very way they were conceived, at the very moment of their conception, and even in the eyes of the their putative champion, the Freedmen's Bureau. In fact, it was the Freedmen's Bureau that sealed the freedman's fate by imagining him as a highly burdened, debt-bound individual obligated to stay on the plantation and "bend [his] back joy-fully and hopefully" to labor, rather than as a (white) liberal political subject enjoying freedom of movement, freedom of contract, and the protection of the state.[15] Hartman observes: "[E]mancipation appears less the grand event of liberation than a point of transition between modes of servitude and racial subjection."[16] Reflecting on "the afterlife of slavery," she shows how historical continuity (in this case, the ongo-ing nature of Black subjection) can occur not despite historical change but *because of it and through it*.

How, then, do we theorize Asian American existence in an anti-Black world? How do we think about Asian American life and death, thriving and suffering, enjoyment and loss in the "afterlife" of slavery? How do we understand anti-Asian racism in relation to structural anti-Blackness?

---

[13] See also Davies forthcoming.
[14] Hartman 1997.
[15] Hartman 1997, 135.
[16] Hartman 1997, 6.

In the past few decades, and especially since the emergence of Black Lives Matter in 2013, a growing number of scholars in and around Asian American studies are producing work directly relevant to these questions. They have, among other things, traced the histories of anti-Blackness in Asian homelands, illuminated the relation between Chinese coolies and African slaves, analyzed the comparative evaluation of Japanese Americans and Black Americans in the Cold War era, provided new perspectives on the Los Angeles rebellion of 1992, embedded with Chinese American activists defending NYPD officer Peter Liang, and cautioned against the anti-Black ramifications of recent organizing around anti-Asian violence.[17] Simultaneously, Asian American grassroots groups like Asians4BlackLives (which emerged in 2014 to support Black Lives Matter) and the Committee Against Anti-Asian Violence (CAAAV) Organizing Asian Communities (which emerged after the murder of Vincent Chin in 1982) are challenging structural anti-Blackness on the ground in new and creative ways. Together, these scholars and activists are pushing the theoretical and political envelope in pursuit of historical truth and racial justice, broadly conceived. This book owes a debt to all of them.

~~~~

In *Her Majesty's Other Children: Sketches of Racism From a Neocolonial Age* (1997), philosopher Lewis Gordon writes of Blackness as "a point from which the greatest distance must be forged."[18] Nearness or farness from Blackness—not whiteness—is the overriding determinant of racial status, which means that the key categorical divide is not that between whites and everyone else, but *that between Black people and everyone else*. Displacing the concept of white supremacy, the concept of anti-Blackness sees the degradation of Blackness, rather than the exaltation of whiteness, as the fulcrum of the racial order. In an anti-Black order, the reproduction of power arrangements means promoting practices that secure Black abjection and suppressing practices that challenge it. Robin Kelley notes: "[T]o say that anti-Blackness is foundational to Western

---

[17] M. Jung 2008; Yang 2020; Aarim-Heriot 2003; E. Wong 2015; Wu 2014; Nopper 2012; W. Liu 2018; Kuo 2019; Leroy 2017; Chen 2017; Hong 2017; Kim and Jung 2021; Kim and Jung 2019; J. Kim 2015. Significantly, the two main journals in the field—*Amerasia Journal* and *Journal of Asian American Studies*—have recently published issues exploring Asian Americans' connections to Black Lives Matter.
[18] Gordon 1997, 53.

civilization is not to say that it is fixed or permanent [but rather that] it is incredibly fragile and must be constantly remade."[19]

This does not mean we should discard the concept of white supremacy. There is more than one gravitational force in the racial universe. Consider that astronomers have long attributed the continuous movement of the Local Group (the cluster of galaxies that includes the Milky Way) to the gravitational pull of the Shapley Supercluster 650 million light-years away. But they have always wondered if there was more to the story. In space, being or presence attracts, while a void repels. Since the universe contains "under-dense regions of dark matter that repel mass, and over-dense regions of luminous galaxies that attract it," astronomers wondered if there could also be an under-dense region *pushing* the Local Group away.[20] In 2017, they found it and named it the Dipole Repeller. Using a 3D map of the "galaxy flow field," which tracks the paths galaxies are taking through the universe, an international team of scientists confirmed that galaxies move toward the Shapley Supercluster and, at the same time, move *away from the Dipole Repeller*.[21] The repulsive force of the latter has been estimated to be at least as powerful as (and perhaps more powerful than) the attractive force of the former. One needs both to understand the movement of galaxies through space.

Blackness repels and whiteness attracts, and together these two forces govern the movement of bodies in the racial universe. It is a matter of *both* anti-Blackness *and* white supremacy, then, rather than either/or. The U.S. racial order, Lewis Gordon argues, is shaped by two principles: "1) be white, but above all 2) don't be black."[22] "But above all" indicates that anti-Blackness is, despite the order of presentation, the first principle, the core logic that defines the parameters of white supremacy's operations. Indeed the historical record indicates that whites sometimes compromise the cause of white supremacy to achieve the *summum bonum* of reinforcing structural anti-Blackness. They may relax the boundary between themselves and Asian Americans, for example, when doing so strengthens the boundary between Black people and everyone else.

White supremacy and anti-Blackness are seen here not as fixed, transhistorical structures but as kinetic forces or energy flows that have shaped and been shaped by the structural regimes of slavery, colonialism,

[19] Kelley 2015, 334.
[20] Irving 2017.
[21] Irving 2017; Rzetelny 2017.
[22] Gordon 1997, 63.

capitalism, settler colonialism, and empire across the globe. White supremacy exalts whiteness and debases not-whiteness. If we imagine this in mechanical terms, it lifts up one group while pushing down all others. Similarly, anti-Blackness abjects Blackness and elevates not-Blackness. It pushes down one group while lifting up all others. It is this latter phenomenon—*of anti-Blackness lifting up not-Black groups, specifically, Asian Americans*—that is the special focus of this book.

Whites, then, are lifted up by both white supremacy and anti-Blackness, and Black people are pushed down by both. All other groups, including Asian Americans, are simultaneously *pushed down by white supremacy and lifted up by anti-Blackness*. They are located, that is, at the turbulent juncture where the two forces meet.[23] To say Asian Americans are "in-between" whites and Black people suggests a static intermediate position on a single vertical scale. It is more precise to say that Asian Americans are dynamically constituted as *not-white, but above all not-Black*. Condensing Lewis Gordon's two principles—"be white, but above all, don't be black"—into one axiom, we arrive at *white is best but the most important thing is not-Blackness*. And its corollary: *better Asians than Blacks*. The status and experience of Asian Americans are indelibly shaped by the fact that they are always already understood to be *the lesser of two evils*. I refer to this discrepant positioning of Asian Americans and Black people in the racial order as the *Asian–Black gap*. The creation of differentiated groups with differential investments in the status quo stabilizes the racial order against a variety of threats.[24]

---

[23] This book is about Asian Americans, but the theoretical approach advanced here can also shed light on the ways in which other not-Black groups—including but not limited to Latinx people, Indigenous peoples, and Arabs/Muslims—negotiate an anti-Black order. It would be optimal for a book to consider each group in its irreducible specificity *and* analyze the interactions of all groups at once, but the logistical difficulties are daunting. The alternative is to piece together, as best we can, fragments of a whole picture, knowing they are fragments and hoping that they nevertheless help to illuminate the whole. *Asian Americans in an Anti-Black World* is offered in this spirit.

[24] In "People-of-Color-Blindness: Notes on the Afterlife of Slavery" (2010b), Jared Sexton argues that the concept "people of color," which implies a rough comparability or equivalence among not-white groups, reflects a "refusal to admit to significant differences of structural position born of discrepant histories between blacks and their political allies" (2010b, 47–48). In other words, the concept disavows structural anti-Blackness as the framework of action, "presum[ing] or insist[ing] upon the monolithic character of victimization under white supremacy—thinking (the afterlife of) slavery as a form of exploitation or colonization or a species of racial oppression among others" (2010b, 48).

The archive of official and popular discourses in the mid-nineteenth century shows how the first sizeable cohorts of Asian immigrants to the U.S., Chinese laborers, were located in the racial order through systematically unfavorable comparisons to whites *and* systematically favorable comparisons to Black people. Even as they were imagined as diseased, rat-eating, inscrutable aliens who threatened white civilization, they were also seen, *in relation to Africans*, as bearers of an ancient culture who were members of the Family of Man and ineligible for enslavement. When Africans became slaves, all other groups experienced a critical upgrade in status. Which is to say, anti-Blackness, forged in the crucible of racial slavery, endowed even the despised Chinaman with not-Blackness, rescuing him from the abyss. With important variations and qualifications, the position of the Asiatic—constituted as not-white, but above all not-Black—has endured to this day. This is not to say that it has been impervious to history. Racial formation processes are dynamic and contingent, and the status of Asian Americans has shifted in important ways across the centuries. At the same time, in other respects, their status has been uncannily persistent across time, and this has happened not despite but because of and through historical change.

Not-Blackness is a vital form of property in an anti-Black world.[25] If Asian Americans don't possess whiteness, at least they have not-Blackness. James Baldwin observed that even the worst-off whites have "something to save" in a negrophobic society, and something similar can be said about all not-Black groups, including Asian Americans.[26] W. E. B. Du Bois noted that white workers enjoy the public and psychic "wage of whiteness," and Asian Americans, too, despite the perpetual shadow of foreignness, enjoy the public and psychic "wage of not-Blackness," which helps them to secure better access than many Black people to good housing, good schools, good jobs, good healthcare, and good credit. Asian immigrants and their descendants have been constituted through various forms of violence under global white supremacy (and U.S. imperialism in the Pacific), but because they are seen as the lesser of two evils, they are also at least partially exempted from the forms of state and private

---

[25] Warren and Twine 1997, 208: "[P]recisely because Blacks represent the 'other' against which Whiteness is constructed, the backdoor to Whiteness is open to non-Blacks." See Ellen Wu's (2014) discussion of "not-blackness" and Thomas Joo's (2008) discussion of "nonBlackness." Also see Cheryl Harris's (1993) notion of "whiteness as property."

[26] James Baldwin, "The Black Boy Looks at the White Boy" in *Nobody Knows My Name: More Notes of a Native Son* (New York: Dell, 1961), 172, quoted in Wilderson 2010, 12.

violence that afflict Black people. Even as the pandemic-related uptick in verbal and physical assaults against Asian Americans attests to their not-whiteness, the self-limiting quality of this violence and the strong response it elicited from the U.S. state attest just as clearly to their not-Blackness.[27] It is the reliably phobic response to Blackness that allows Asian Americans to gain a foothold against the downward pressure of white supremacy. Which is to say, anti-Blackness is less an analogue to anti-Asian racism than a structural force that curbs and delimits it.

The positionality of Asian Americans is intimately tied to their *political functionality* in the ongoing struggle between the U.S. state and the Black freedom movement. Maintaining structural anti-Blackness while claiming to be a liberal democracy, the U.S. state faces a never-ending public relations problem at home and abroad. Over time, the state has developed the practice of weaponizing Asian Americans against the Black freedom struggle, or invoking them as a false alibi for American society: *Anyone can succeed here if they work hard enough. A good minority can't be held down.* Note the sleight of hand whereby the state responds to *Black* critique by pointing to *Asian American* "success," thus denying the singular force of anti-Blackness. Sometimes the state takes steps against anti-Asian racism *instead of* taking steps against anti-Blackness and then celebrates these moves as a repudiation of (a genericized) "racism." The Asian–Black gap is denied, the better to reproduce it.

At this point, some Asian Americanists might be inclined to mention "the model minority myth." For several decades, scholars have critiqued the trope that praises Asian Americans for having the right cultural stuff to succeed, on the grounds that it exaggerates Asian American thriving in order to divide and conquer Asian Americans and Black people, two groups oppressed under white supremacy.[28] It is true that the depiction of Asian Americans is ideologically distorted and that the state weaponizes the group for political purposes. But because the critique pays attention to white supremacy and not anti-Blackness, it overlooks the structural advantage Asian Americans have in relation to Black people. So when the media says "Asian Americans are more successful than Black people because of their cultural traits," Asian Americanists say "Asian Americans are not really that successful"—instead of saying "Asian Americans are successful to the degree they are because of structural favoritism relative to Black people." What the critique fails to grasp,

[27] See Part Three for elaboration.
[28] Some of my work belongs in this category, notably C. Kim 1999.

then, is that the system does not just tell stories about Asian American thriving, it actually *helps to create it* as a material reality. By focusing on the discursive trope instead of social structure, the critique misses the forest for the trees. In an important sense, this book offers *a critique of the critique of the model-minority idea* and its centrality in Asian American scholarship and discourse.

Until the movement era of the 1960s and 1970s, many if not most Asian Americans embraced the boon of not-Blackness. Like other immigrants, they achieved socioeconomic progress in part by "stepping on the backs" of Black people, in Toni Morrison's unforgettable phrase. When the Asian American movement emerged in the 1960s, though, Asian Americans stopped distancing from Blackness, declared war on white supremacy, and announced their solidarity with Black people under the Third World rubric. This, in any case, is the conventional narrative about the movement. Bringing anti-Blackness back into the picture, however, shows us that movement activists produced a political critique that was only *half-finished*, one that *theorized white supremacy but not anti-Blackness*. Asian Americans' structural disadvantage relative to whites was named but their structural advantage relative to Black people was not.

The half-finished critique has shaped Asian American politics and thought for the past half-century. Disavowing structural anti-Blackness has generated one interpretive impasse after another around real-world conflicts where Asian American interests clash with Black interests—for example, the Los Angeles rebellion of 1992, the anti-affirmative action lawsuit *Brian Ho v. SFUSD* (1996), the controversy around NYPD Officer Peter Liang's shooting of Akai Gurley in 2014, and the anti-affirmative action lawsuit *Students for Fair Admissions* v. *Harvard*, which was heard by the U.S. Supreme Court in Fall 2022. (Notably, all but the first of these conflicts involved conservative, relatively affluent Chinese immigrant groups joining forces with right-wing whites to promote the racialized ideologies of "meritocracy" and "law and order" against the claims of the Black freedom struggle. More on this in Part Three.) Each of these conflicts pointed to the *ethical-political crisis* that has always faced Asian Americans but is often ignored or suppressed: how to reckon with and respond to their implicatedness in foundational anti-Blackness.[29]

---

[29] Scholarship that breaks from the premise of interminority equivalence tends to provoke anxieties about an "oppression Olympics." If all not-white groups suffer under white

Asian Americans in an Anti-Black World identifies and explores key racial dynamics that run as threads through the tapestry of U.S. history. Like every story, though, it illuminates some phenomena by allowing others to remain in shadow. Asian Americans of East Asian descent are the main characters here, raising the question of how applicable these arguments are to other Asian American groups. Indigenous and Latinx peoples are mentioned here and there in textual sources, but their role(s) in this story remain unexplored. Historical formations such as settler colonialism, colonialism, and imperialism are alluded to in passing, but their various modes of articulation with structural anti-Blackness are not investigated in depth. All of these unexplored themes are promising topics for future research.

~~~~

The book is divided into three parts, with each part written as a long narrative arc that permits a sustained consideration of Asian Americans, structural anti-Blackness, and white supremacy within a specific temporal frame. Chronologically, each part overlaps with the next. Part One examines Chinese immigrants from 1850 to 1940; Part Two examines Japanese immigrants from 1900 to 1970; and Part Three looks at Asian American identity and politics from the 1960s to the present.

Part One, "Exclusion/Belonging," traces the construction of the nineteenth-century Chinese immigrant laborer as the original Asiatic/Mongolian, a figure who was not-white but above all not-Black, a wage worker who was degraded but nonetheless categorically superior to the slave. If we examine the Chinese immigrant laborer in relation to the white worker, Chinese foreignness was a site of dispossession, persecution, and exclusion. But if we reexamine the Chinese immigrant laborer in relation to the slave, we discover that Chinese foreignness was also, paradoxically, a site of plenitude, standing, and belonging. The exclusion movement expelled the Chinese immigrant from the nation, but not

supremacy, why do we need to parse who suffers most? Will this not undermine the kind of coalition-building that we need to mount a concerted challenge to white supremacy? Why not focus on what unites us rather than on what divides us? While I understand and respect these concerns, I have a different vantage point. Repressing or sidestepping inconvenient and uncomfortable truths about how the system works invariably backfires in the realm of coalition building. Put simply, solidarity requires trust, and trust requires (historical) truthfulness and candor. Counterintuitively, then, a candid exploration of differentials in status and power among not-white groups may help to open up space for new forms of solidarity and relationality to emerge and take root.

from the Family of Man. For their part, Chinese immigrants grasped the value of their not-Blackness and developed strategies to take advantage of it, from displacing freedpeople on plantations during Reconstruction to refusing to allow their children to attend "colored" schools in the Mississippi Delta in the interwar years.

Part Two, "Ostracism/Initiation," examines twentieth-century Japanese immigrants and their descendants in relation to structural anti-Blackness and its instantiation in a nationwide system of racial segregation and anti-Black violence. Entering the U.S. in the wake of Chinese exclusion, the Japanese inherited the mantle of the Asiatic/Mongolian, much to their dismay. Despite the burdens of this label, they soon discovered that the constitutive not-Blackness of the Asiatic/Mongolian enabled their own advancement in an anti-Black order. This remained true even during the turbulent, traumatic events of the Second World War. The wartime internment of Japanese Americans constituted not only the extreme limit of their ostracism but also, as others have noted, their symbolic initiation into the nation. From this point on, their weaponization as alibis for the U.S. state and capitalism became a routine part of public discourse. Like the Chinese before them, Japanese Americans deployed their not-Blackness to their advantage in their efforts to survive and thrive.

Part Three, "Solidarity/Disavowal," looks at how Asian Americans developed a distinct political subjectivity during the Asian American movement, against the backdrop of emergent Black Power and the nation's imminent turn toward mass incarceration. Asian American activists and thinkers denounced white supremacy and expressed solidarity with Black people under the Third World rubric, but they did not theorize structural anti-Blackness or recognize their own not-Blackness. Reproducing the fallacy of minority equivalence, the movement's half-finished critique has hampered Asian Americans' ability to understand and respond to numerous Asian–Black conflicts that have unfolded in the post-movement era. With the recent rise of a right-wing Chinese immigrant politics that seeks to roll back civil rights reforms such as affirmative action, the *ethical-political crisis* facing Asian Americans—namely, how they should respond to their structural positionality and functionality in an anti-Black order—has become even more urgent.

Finally, in the coda, I suggest that the book constitutes a departure point rather than an end point, an opening up rather than a restriction of Asian Americans' intellectual and political field of vision. The point is not to persuade Asian Americans to confess that they are complicit in anti-Blackness, so that they might be absolved. Rather, the point is for Asian Americans to understand how they are dynamically positioned and weaponized by the U.S. state as it seeks to preserve structural anti-Blackness, and second, to consider how they might resist or subvert these patterns. How can Asian Americans respond ethically to their own not-Blackness? What political possibilities might be opened up if Asian Americans completed the movement's half-finished critique? Can Asian Americanness be reimagined as a force that destabilizes, rather than stabilizes, an anti-Black world?

Part One

Exclusion/Belonging

I INTRODUCTION

The persecution and exclusion of Chinese immigrant laborers in the U.S. in the second half of the nineteenth century constituted the originary structuring of Asianness in America. White workers intent upon eliminating the competitive threat of Chinese labor cast the Asiatic or Mongolian as an obdurately fixed entity—venal, treacherous, diseased, degraded, heathen, unassimilable with whites, and altogether unfit for republican citizenship. Efforts to drive resident Chinese out and keep other Chinese from entering culminated in the "closing of the gate,"[1] the passage of the Chinese Exclusion Act of 1882, the first racially discriminatory immigration law in U.S. history.[2] For decades afterward, the Chinese and then other Asian groups were barred from entry and marked as "aliens ineligible to citizenship." Long after the legal architecture of exclusion was dismantled—through the repeal of the Exclusion Act in 1943, the removal of the racial bar on naturalization in 1952, and the removal of racial quotas in immigration law in 1965—the social and political traces of that regime can be detected in the ongoing production of Asian American bodies as incorrigibly foreign.[3] Exclusion, then, has operated not as a one-time event but rather as an ongoing structuring of relations of force and power between whites and Asian Americans.[4]

This is the classic narrative about how the idea of the Asiatic first took hold in the white American imaginary. Note that it highlights white supremacy and overlooks anti-Blackness, producing a streamlined, dyadic story of Chinese victimization by whites. In the last couple of decades, however, some important histories—including Nadia Aarim-Heriot's *Chinese Immigrants, African Americans, and Racial Anxiety in the United States, 1848–82,*[5] Moon-Ho Jung's *Coolies and Cane: Race, Labor, and Sugar in the Age of Emancipation,*[6] Edlie Wong's *Racial Reconstruction: Black Inclusion, Chinese Exclusion, and the Fictions of Citizenship,*[7] and Caroline Yang's *The Peculiar Afterlife of Slavery,*[8] among others—have brought Black people back into the analysis and situated Chinese immigrants in the broader racial, economic, and political picture of the time. Together, these works demonstrate beyond a doubt that in the context of emergent industrial capitalism in the nineteenth century, as the nation lurched through slavery, the Civil War, Reconstruction, and Jim Crow, the construction of the first Asiatics was intimately intertwined with ideas about Blackness as well as whiteness.

Building on these works, Part One brings the concept of structural anti-Blackness back into the narrative of the Chinese American experience. Interweaving strands of Chinese American history with strands of Black

---

[1] Gyory 1998.
[2] The act is referred to as the "Chinese Exclusion Act" but was actually titled "An Act to Inaugurate Certain Treaty Stipulations Relating to Chinese."
[3] Lowe 1996; Ancheta 2006.
[4] See Wolfe 2006.
[5] Aarim-Heriot 2003.
[6] M. Jung 2008.
[7] E. Wong 2015.
[8] Yang 2020.

history in a long narrative arc from the mid-nineteenth to mid-twentieth century, it shows how the Chinese immigrant was constituted as not-white, but above all and paradigmatically not-Black, a wage worker who was degraded and incapable of full freedom, but nonetheless categorically superior to the slave. The foreignness of the Chinese meant they did not belong in the U.S., but it also meant they belonged *somewhere*. While slaves were stateless in the sense of lacking any political standing whatsoever, and freedpeople and free Black people possessed only an evacuated U.S. citizenship after the Civil War, Chinese aliens were recognized as bona fide subjects of the Chinese empire, enmeshed in webs of social and political relationality and possessed of human coordinates. Thus Chinese foreignness was not only a site of dispossession, persecution, and exclusion, but also a site of plenitude, standing, and belonging. Even at the nadir of exclusion, the slave provided a floor beneath which the Chinese could not fall. The 1882 Exclusion Act expelled Chinese immigrants from the nation, but not from the Family of Man.

Global racial meanings conditioned and were reinforced by global labor flows and labor relations. In all three of the Chinese labor stories touched upon here—Chinese wage labor in California, Chinese contract labor in the U.S. South, and Chinese indentured labor in Cuba—the Chinese presence was predicated on Black absence, on the unavailability or rejection of Black labor, whether enslaved or free, and the belief that the Chinese, as workers who signed contracts and were thus capable of at least a nominal "freedom," offered something better to their employers and the economy than Black people ever could. It was because California entered the Union in 1850 as a "free" state forswearing slavery (on paper if not in practice entirely) that it initially opened the gate to Chinese labor. It was because southern planters wanted to punish freedpeople during Reconstruction that they briefly experimented with Chinese labor. And it was because of the instability of the global slave trade that Cuban sugar planters turned to Chinese coolies. By virtue of their categorical unenslavability, the Chinese stepped in where Black workers could not and thereby came to represent the progressive transition from slave labor to free labor.[9]

Structurally positioned above and apart from Black people, Chinese immigrants emphasized their own not-Blackness as a strategy for achieving social and economic mobility. On one occasion when they were lumped with Black people by the California Supreme Court, they resisted the ruling as if their identity, freedom, and future depended on it—which,

[9] M. Jung 2008; Lowe 2015; Hu-Dehart 1993.

in some respects, they did. Guided by the axiom *white is best but the most important thing is not-Blackness*, and its corollary *better Asians than Blacks*, whites held the door of progress partly open for the group they defined as the lesser of two evils, and the Chinese walked through it, raising questions about Asian American innocence and implicatedness that have yet to be put to rest.

It should be noted that reading for anti-Blackness in the historical archive requires a new methodology. At times, anti-Blackness can be perceived directly, as in the Chinese–Black comparisons that show up throughout the official record. At other times, it can only be perceived indirectly, as in the unstated partial immunities that the Chinese were granted from certain forms of anti-Black coercion and violence. Thus in addition to looking at what was said about or done to the Chinese, we must also, using slavery and its afterlife as a reference point, look at *what was not said about or done to the Chinese*—what forms of aggression and harm were foreclosed or unthought because of their not-Blackness.

II SLAVERY AND RELATIONALITY

Slavery deprived African captives of more than freedom. It took from them history, language, religion, names, kinship ties, community, place—the indices and coordinates of belonging and relationality. In *Slavery and Social Death* (1982), Orlando Patterson describes natal alienation—"the loss of ties of birth in both ascending and descending generations ... [which includes] the important nuance of a loss of native status, of deracination"—as one of the three constituent elements of slavery, along with general dishonor and the infliction of gratuitous violence.[10] After destroying captives' relational ties, slavery replaced these with just one: the tie of subjugation to the master, and through him, to the whole of the white race. "Social death" meant that the slave's existence was recognizable only in relation to the master's power.[11]

During slavery, African bodies were fungible units of commodified flesh.[12] What Saidiya Hartman calls the "savage quantification" of slavery began on the African coast, where Atlantic slavers meticulously

[10] Patterson 1982, 7. See also Spillers 2003.
[11] Those who were held as slaves (usually captives in war) within West African societies, though marginal and disempowered, "were bound in a mutually obligatory relationship to some corporate group," while captives who were part of "saltwater slavery," Stephanie Smallwood argues, went through "absolute exclusion from *any* community" (2008, 30).
[12] Spillers 2003; Hartman 1997.

calculated how many slaves they needed to transport per voyage in order to achieve the desired level of profit and how many variously sized bodies they could pack into the holds of their ships. It continued, Stephanie Smallwood observes, in the "scientific empiricism" of slaveholders, who were "always seeking to find the limits of human capacity for suffering … probing the limits up to which it is possible to discipline the body without extinguishing the life within."[13] Then there was the "syntax" of slavery Hortense Spillers identifies in a 1798 Maryland property rights law, which addressed the dispensation of "specific articles, such as slaves, working beasts, animals of any kind, stock, furniture, plates, books, and so forth."[14] "[W]e are stunned by the simultaneity of disparate items in a grammatical series," Spillers writes, by the "mix of named things, live and inanimate, collapsed by contiguity."[15] What this syntax highlighted was the contrapuntal definition of slaveness and humanness, or the banishment of the slave from the realm of human mattering. Killing slaves was not too far afield from breaking a plate, or ruining a piece of furniture, or rendering lame a working beast in the sense that this was socially and legally recognized only as an injury to the slaveowner as propertyholder, rather than to the slaves themselves.[16]

Thus the slave, whose violation could not and would not be recognized, was opened to worlds of suffering that exceed thought and description. Marked by an "infinite and indeterminately horrifying and open vulnerability," Frank Wilderson writes, the slave was "an object made available (which is to say fungible) for any subject."[17] Slaveholders exerted absolute domination guaranteed by violence and the law. They routinely whipped, raped, maimed, mutilated, and tortured slaves. They killed slaves with impunity, and other whites were only barred from killing slaves to the extent that they were prohibited from destroying another man's property. Punishing slaves brutally was business as usual on the plantation, and when it resulted in the death of a slave, this was seen as an unfortunate miscalculation and regrettable diminution of assets. A 1669 Virginia statute clarified that a master could not be prosecuted if a slave died from punishment because "it

---

[13] Smallwood 2008, 35–36.
[14] Spillers 2003, 226.
[15] Spillers 2003, 226. W. E. B. Du Bois, too, alluded to the strange Black–animal–property assemblage produced by slavery's imagination when he noted the South's "insistence that [Black] men were at once monkeys and real estate" (1998 [1935], 268).
[16] Hartman 1997.
[17] Wilderson 2010, 38.

cannot be presumed that ... malice ... should induce any man to destroy his own estate."[18] In the face of plentiful evidence that slaveholders did, in fact, kill slaves with malice at their own financial expense, the law simply stated this to be a logical impossibility. Property could be destroyed but not murdered.

In her discussion of *Celia, A Slave* (1855), a case where a nineteen-year-old female slave was convicted for killing the slaveholder who repeatedly raped her, Saidiya Hartman observes that the law recognized slave agency and sentience in only one context: that of holding a slave culpable for a crime. The slave was not legible to the law as a bearer of rights, or as a victim of violence, but only as a criminal. Celia was granted just enough sentience to be found guilty of a crime and hung, but no more, for "the degree of sentience had to be cautiously calibrated in order to avoid intensifying the antagonisms of the social order."[19] In the eyes of the law, slaves were unable to give or withhold consent and thus "both will-less and always willing" in the face of sexual violence.[20] Thus, Hartman writes, "[r]ape disappeared through the intervention of seduction—the assertion of the slave woman's complicity and willful submission."[21] In a profound and fateful inversion, Celia's resistance and self-defense were refigured as sexual aggression and murder, and the slaveholder's violence was read as a surrender to Celia's wiles. This perverse couplet of Black criminalization and white exoneration is ubiquitous in the archive of racial slavery.

As "an object made available for any subject," the slave was the antithesis of the liberal subject who possessed the freedom and autonomy to enter into contracts and secure their bodily integrity through protective rights. Throughout the nineteenth century, Amy Dru Stanley argues, the contract was seen as embodying liberal freedom as defined against the unfreedom of slavery. The contract was "a worldview" that "idealized ownership of self and voluntary exchange between individuals who were formally equal and free."[22] Slaves, she notes, lacked legal control over their persons and "being dispossessed of self, [could not] enter any binding contracts."[23] They could not enter marriage contracts, labor contracts, or the political contract of citizenship.

[18] Finkelman 2012, 114.
[19] Hartman 1997, 93.
[20] Hartman 1997, 81.
[21] Hartman 1997, 87.
[22] Stanley 1998, x.
[23] Stanley 1998, 17.

In the English common-law tradition, which strongly influenced U.S. law, the formula *protectio trahit subjectionem, et subjectio protectionem* (protection implies allegiance, and allegiance protection) meant that the subject was born into a reciprocal relation with the sovereign ruler of the territory in which the subject was born.[24] The allegiance owed by the subject to the sovereign emerged automatically (through birth) and was presumed to be permanent. During the 1600s, as the English Parliament contested monarchical authority and Lockean ideas of consent and contract gained traction, a contractual understanding of political allegiance— what James Kettner calls "volitional allegiance"—emerged alongside the older one, only to be propelled to the fore a century later by the events of the American Revolution. Neither the older framework nor the newer one was thought to pertain to the slave, however. Natally alienated, the deracinated slave lacked the legal standing of the "native-born" and thus had no relation to the sovereign. Nor could they offer volitional allegiance via a political contract. Kettner says of slaves: "Property had no national character. It was neither alien nor citizen."[25] Blackness signalled "a condition of statelessness" like no other.[26]

III FREE BLACKS AND SLAVENESS

In the antebellum South, there were high stakes in maintaining the indissociability of Blackness and slaveness. Pro-slavery arguments hinged upon the claim that Blacks could never be anything other than slaves, that the condition was inscribed by nature and God into the Black body itself. In this context, the free Black was both a feared instigator who could encourage slaves to escape or revolt and a symbolic threat, a walking, breathing reminder that Blackness and slaveness could be pulled apart. W. E. B. Du Bois wrote:

As slavery grew to a system and the Cotton Kingdom began to expand into imperial white domination, a free Negro was a contradiction, a threat and a menace. As a thief and a vagabond, he threatened society; but as an educated property holder, a successful mechanic or even professional man, he more than threatened slavery. He contradicted and undermined it. He must not be. He must be suppressed, enslaved, colonized.[27]

---

[24] *United States* v. *Wong Kim Ark* (1898), 655.
[25] Kettner 1978, 311.
[26] Wagner 2009, 2.
[27] Du Bois 1998 [1935], 7.

If Blacks were slaves by nature, the institution of slavery comported with necessity and divine will. But if they could be meaningfully free, by what right or law could they be enslaved?

Beginning in the late 1700s, and with increasing intensity in the decades before the Civil War, southern whites trained their disciplinary gaze on free Black people, progressively stripping away the rights they had exercised during the colonial period and severely constricting their freedom.[28] The web of laws passed by southern states during this period was meant not only to control the movement of free Black people and discourage their physical presence, but also to indicate that Blackness entailed immutable slaveness. Almost all southern states set up a registration system that forced free Black people to carry "freedom papers," which, ironically, indexed the bearer's unfreedom: "At any time, any white could demand proof of a free Negro's status; even if his papers were in order, an unemployed free Negro could be jailed and enslaved and his children bound out to strangers."[29] Free Black people were also sold into servitude (sometimes indistinguishable from slavery) for minor infractions and unpaid fines. While the lash was phased out as a punishment for white criminals, it was retained for use on free Black people convicted of crimes, reinforcing the latter's proximity to slaves.[30] As the Civil War approached, many southern legislatures debated laws that would expel free Black people from their states altogether, with enslavement as the proposed punishment for those who refused to leave. In the Maryland legislature, Octavius Taney (brother of U.S. Supreme Court Chief Justice Roger Taney, who authored the *Dred Scott* decision) proposed holding free Black people "to service for a term of years" in order to "prevent their absconding" while plans for their forced removal/colonization were being drawn up.[31]

Until the *Dred Scott* decision in 1857, there was no authoritative federal law clarifying whether free Black people could be citizens.[32] Missouri's bid to become a state in 1820 was a flashpoint for congressional debate on this issue.[33] Missouri's draft constitution sanctioned slavery and called for laws to prevent the admission of "free negroes and

---

[28] Fehrenbacher 1978, 62.

[29] Berlin 1974, 95.

[30] Berlin 1974.

[31] M. Jones 2018, 47.

[32] See M. Jones (2018) for legal ambiguity around this issue and Black leaders' efforts to argue for birthright citizenship during the antebellum period.

[33] See Litwack 1961 and Kettner 1978.

mulattoes." Critics argued that this latter provision violated Article IV, Section 2 of the U.S. Constitution—"The citizens of each State shall be entitled to all Privileges and Immunities of Citizens in the several States"— by denying Black citizens of other states the rights accorded to white citizens of Missouri. Their operating premise was that free Black people had become citizens of states and the U.S. as a birthright. Proponents of Missouri's draft constitution argued that free Blacks were not in fact considered citizens: very few states, they observed, allowed Blacks to vote, give evidence, marry whites, or serve in the militia. Representative Charles Pinckney of South Carolina, who claimed he was responsible for advancing the privileges and immunities clause as a delegate to the Constitutional Convention in 1787, recounted: "I perfectly knew that there did not then exist such a thing in the Union as a Black or colored citizen, nor could I then have conceived it possible such a thing could ever have existed in it; nor notwithstanding all that is said on the subject, do I now believe one does exist in it."[34] At the close of the debate, Missouri was admitted to the Union, draft constitution and all.

A few years later, the debate over Black citizenship arose again in Congress. The revolution in Haiti (Saint Domingue), which unfolded from 1791 to 1804, struck terror into the hearts of southern slaveholders by producing the first independent Black republic in the Western Hemisphere. Complaining that free Black seamen traveling along the Atlantic seaboard were spreading the word about Saint Domingue among slaves and free Blacks, southern legislators in coastal states passed Negro Seamen laws mandating that all Black sailors be imprisoned while their ships were docked at local ports.[35] South Carolina became the first state to pass such a law—to prevent Black sailors from "instigat[ing] the slave population to insurrection"[36]—after the discovery of an antislavery rebellion planned by Denmark Vesey (a free Black sailor who had lived in Haiti) in 1822. Under this law, "free colored seamen" were to be taken into custody and imprisoned, and if the captain of their vessel refused to or was unable to pay for the costs of their confinement, the seamen were to be sold into slavery for life, ostensibly to recover state costs.

[34] Litwack 1961, 36.
[35] For more on the abolitionism of Black sailors, see Sinha 2017.
[36] *Proceedings of the United States Senate, on the Fugitive Slave Bill* (1850), 29. This is Senator Jefferson Davis of Mississippi, supporter of the South Carolina law and future president of the Confederacy, speaking during the U.S. Senate debate in 1850 on Southern laws imprisoning "free colored seamen."

Northern and British shipping interests objected that the laws deprived Black seamen of their constitutionally guaranteed rights as citizens, prompting Secretary of State Edward Livingston to ask Attorney General (and future U.S. Supreme Court Chief Justice) Roger Taney for his opinion about Black citizenship in 1831.[37] In an opinion never completed or published, Taney wrote: "South Carolina or any other slaveholding state has a right to guard itself from the danger to be apprehended from the introduction of free people of colour among their slaves—and have not by the constitution of the U.S. surrendered the right to pass the laws necessary for that purpose."[38] Foreshadowing his opinion in *Dred Scott* over two decades later, Taney argued that the Framers had viewed Blacks as an inferior and degraded race, and not as citizens: "The privileges they [Black people] are allowed to enjoy, are accorded to them as a matter of kindness and benevolence rather than of right .... And where they are nominally admitted by law to the privileges of citizenship, they have no effectual power to defend them, and are permitted to be citizens by the sufferance of the white population and hold whatever rights they enjoy at their mercy."[39] Black rights were not rights at all, but charitable dispensations on the part of whites, to be granted or revoked at their discretion. Whatever whites chose to do, Blacks were, quite simply, "at their mercy."

In 1850, in an effort to protect free Black sailors, Republicans tried to attach an amendment to the Fugitive Slave Act that would require the attorney general to direct a circuit or district court to determine the lawfulness of each imprisonment or detainment made under the Negro Seamen laws. During the U.S. Senate debate, John Davis of Massachusetts, who sponsored the amendment, invoked Article IV, Section 2 of the U.S. Constitution, arguing that "free colored persons" who were citizens in Massachusetts were entitled to all of the privileges and immunities of (white) citizens in South Carolina. Robert Winthrop, also from Massachusetts, demurred from Davis's expansive reading of the clause and said the question at hand was not whether Black people could be citizens but the more modest one of what the free in "free Black" meant: "[W]here is the power in the constitution to discriminate between different classes of free persons?"[40]

---

[37] Litwack 1961.
[38] M. Jones 2018, 48.
[39] Litwack 1961, 53.
[40] *Proceedings of the United States Senate, on the Fugitive Slave Bill* (1850), 25.

Andrew Butler of South Carolina—whom Charles Sumner publicly accused of taking "a mistress ... the harlot, Slavery"—had an answer for both arguments.[41] First, he dismissed Davis's argument as leading to the "preposterous, not to say revolting" conclusion that a slave could escape from South Carolina, be granted citizenship in Massachusetts, and then return to South Carolina to claim the privileges and immunities of citizens there. To the contrary, Butler insisted, the free Black could be a citizen of Massachusetts, if Massachusetts so chose, but never a citizen of the United States, which meant that the free Black's citizenship in one state was not transferrable to another state where the law forbade it. To deflect Winthrop's argument, Butler turned to the standard southern practice of invoking northern anti-Blackness as a defense. What about Illinois and other northwestern states that denied Blacks citizenship and even residence? What about anti-miscegenation statutes in northern states, including Massachusetts? Of the amendment's supporters, he observed: "[T]hese men repudiate discrimination here when it suits their purpose to assail the South, but they preserve it at home .... The Black man is put in a much higher scale by their rhetoric than he is by their practice."[42] The Republicans' amendment was defeated and free Black seamen were left unprotected.

The Fugitive Slave Act itself tended to collapse the gap between the slave and the free Black person, evacuating the citizenship claims of the latter. The U.S. Constitution had sanctioned the capture of fugitive slaves, and Congress had passed a 1793 law clarifying slaveholders' rights in this regard. Some northern states responded by passing "personal liberty laws" to protect free Black people from the slavecatcher's net. When the U.S. Supreme Court struck down these state laws in *Prigg v. Pennsylvania* (1842), northerners dug in for the fight and southerners demanded new federal legislation on the matter. Part of a compromise legislative package patched together in an effort to avert all-out sectional war, the Fugitive Slave Act of 1850 sought to thwart northern state interference in fugitive slave captures by "completely federalizing the apprehension of runaways while denying states any power to interfere."[43] All aspects of the process were to be streamlined by a U.S. court commissioner

[41] Representative Preston Brooks, Butler's kinsman from South Carolina, caned Charles Sumner nearly to death on the Senate floor three days after Sumner gave a speech denouncing Butler and Stephen Douglas for their views on slavery.
[42] *Proceedings of the United States Senate, on the Fugitive Slave Bill* (1850), 23.
[43] Lubet 2010, 42.

(a low-level functionary); apprehended fugitives were denied the right to a jury trial, the right to appeal or seek relief from another court, and the right to give testimony on their own behalf; and the slavecatcher was merely required to furnish a certificate from a southern court (obtainable as a matter of course) to "prove" the fugitive's identity. As before, the lack of procedural safeguards meant that free Black people could be kidnapped into slavery, either mistakenly or intentionally. And the 1850 Act added a new twist: federal marshals were directed to mobilize any and all white bystanders, no matter how unwilling, to form a *posse comitatus* (literally "power of the community") to hunt down fugitive slaves. If the fugitives escaped, whites who had refused to help could be held financially liable.[44] The takeaway from the statute was that all Black people, regardless of legal status, were enslaveable, and all whites, regardless of inclination, were members of the posse.

Northern whites hated slavery, in large part because they saw it as antithetical to the interests of free white labor. But many of them also hated Black people, which is why Andrew Butler's charges of northern hypocrisy had the ring of truth. The polite negrophobia of the antebellum North involved tendering Black people bastardized forms of "equality."[45] "Equality" was parsed into three separate components (civil, political, and social), and Black people in the North were said to enjoy "equality" because they had some of the first and a little of the second, albeit none of the third. In other words, they were said to be treated equally because they were not treated entirely unequally. It was not their fault, northern lawmakers insisted, that God and nature had created an impassable difference between the Black and white races, rendering political equality difficult and social equality unthinkable. (Even dedicated white abolitionists, it must be noted, were divided on the issue of social equality.)

While their status varied widely over time and place, most Black people in the North were prohibited from voting, giving evidence, serving on a jury, serving in the militia, and marrying a white person.[46] They were also segregated in the labor market, in public facilities, in housing, and in educational facilities, and they were subjected to regular mob violence in which entire communities were assaulted and permanently

---

[44] Lubet 2010.
[45] Here I am drawing on Saidiya Hartman's (1997) discussion of how whites defined "freedom" for Black people during Reconstruction.
[46] By 1840, 93 percent of northern free Black people lived in states that denied them the right to vote (Litwack 1961, 75).

driven from their homes.[47] All northern and northwestern states considered, and some passed, anti-immigration laws designed to prohibit, discourage, or render impossible Black in-migration and residence.[48] Ohio, Illinois, and Indiana passed laws that required Black people entering the state to post prohibitively large bonds (sometimes up to $1,000) guaranteeing their good behavior, and to produce papers certifying that they were free. In the absence of such papers, they were *presumed to be slaves*. And as in the South, various infractions rendered Black people subject to expulsion or fines, nonpayment of which, in some areas, could result in being whipped or sold at public auction.[49]

When the northern free Black population increased in the early 1800s, the colonization movement gained traction, promising to ship Black people to Liberia, Central or South America, or the West Indies. While colonization had its detractors—including abolitionists, who charged its proponents with aiming to deport free Black antislavery activists—it had the virtue of speaking directly to the deepest fantasies of whites. When skeptics asked how Black people could be expected to be successful colonists abroad—a reasonable query given that they were said to lack political capacity altogether—the American Colonization Society, founded in 1816, had a ready answer: contact with whites generally, and slaveholders particularly, had elevated Black people to the point where they were ready to bring God and civilization to their benighted brethren in Africa and elsewhere.[50] Toward the end of the Civil War, President Abraham Lincoln wrote a letter to General Benjamin Butler reflecting on the possibilities for colonization: "But what shall we do with the Negroes after they are free? I can hardly believe that the South and North can live in peace unless we get rid of the Negroes."[51] The colonization movement collapsed soon thereafter, but the dream of a nation emptied of Blacks lived on.

IV *DRED SCOTT* V. *SANFORD*

Like free Black seamen who traveled through southern ports, fugitive slaves who fled to free states raised urgent questions about the (Black) body, space, and the law. Their movement across sectional boundaries exposed the contradictions between incommensurable legal regimes that

[47] Litwack 1961.
[48] Litwack 1961.
[49] Litwack 1961, 70.
[50] See Burin 2005.
[51] Du Bois 1998 [1935], 149.

coexisted side by side, uneasily and untenably, within the same polity. Crucial questions were pressed to the fore: Was slavery attached to the Black body immutably or could the proper legal and spatial conditions effect a separation of the two? Was slavery a matter of natural law or was it merely an artifact of positive law? Was there any scenario under which Black people could be citizens? The U.S. Supreme Court took up these questions in *Dred Scott* v. *Sanford* (1857). Chief Justice Roger Taney's majority decision, a disquisition on slavery that bore the heavy imprint of southern ontologics, aimed to contain sectional strife through an authoritative finding on the issues. Instead, it set the nation more firmly on the path to war.

Attorneys for Dred Scott, a Missouri slave, claimed that he was emancipated when slaveholder John Emerson took him for protracted stays in Illinois (a free state) and the Wisconsin Territory (where slavery was prohibited by the Missouri Compromise of 1820), before bringing him back to Missouri.[52] Missouri courts, accepting the *Somerset* principle (that slavery was against natural right and common law and so was operative only where positive law explicitly provided for it and nowhere else), had for decades recognized the freedom of slaves who had entered free states or territories,[53] but the Missouri Supreme Court went against precedent and ruled against Scott.[54] Scott's subsequent suit in the U.S. Circuit Court for Missouri also went against him, but left open the question of whether he had standing to sue and whether, therefore, the court had jurisdiction over the case. Thus the case proceeded to the High Court.

Chief Justice Roger Taney, writing for the majority on the U.S. Supreme Court, ruled that Scott was still a slave and therefore could not sue as a citizen of Missouri. Instead of dismissing the case for lack of jurisdiction, however, Taney, "ignoring a dozen opportunities to decide the case more narrowly," used the case as a platform to expound at length upon the impossibility of Black citizenship per se, the unconstitutionality of the Missouri Compromise, and Congress's lack of authority to prohibit slavery in any part of the territories.[55] He began with the question of whether a Black person could ever be a citizen:

---

[52] The Missouri Compromise of 1820 prohibited slavery in the former Louisiana Territory north of the parallel 36° 30'.

[53] *Somerset* v. *Stewart* (1772) was an English case where the court decided that slavery was not supported by English common law.

[54] *Scott* v. *Emerson* (1852).

[55] See R. Smith 1997, 263–272.

The question is simply this: can a negro whose ancestors were imported into this country and sold as slaves become a member of the political community formed and brought into existence by the Constitution of the United States, and as such become entitled to all the rights, and privileges, and immunities, guaranteed by that instrument to the citizen.[56]

Here and throughout the decision, Taney pointedly collapsed the distinction between slaves and free Black people, employing language such as "persons who are the descendants of Africans" and "[those] whose ancestors were negroes of the African race" to emphasize that it was racial ancestry that mattered, not the technicalities of legal status.[57] Answering his own question about Black citizenship in the negative, Taney wrote:

The words "people of the United States" and "citizens" are synonymous terms, and mean the same thing. They both describe the political body who, according to our republican institutions, form the sovereignty and who hold the power and conduct the Government through their representatives. They are what we familiarly call the "sovereign people," and every citizen is one of this people, and a constituent member of this sovereignty. The question before us is whether the class of persons described in the plea in abatement compose a portion of this people, and are constituent members of this sovereignty? We think they are not, and that they are not included, and were not intended to be included, under the word "citizens" in the Constitution, and can therefore claim none of the rights and privileges which that instrument provides for and secures to citizens of the United States. On the contrary, they were at that time considered as a subordinate and inferior class of beings who had been subjugated by the dominant race, and, whether emancipated or not, yet remained subject to their authority, and had no rights or privileges but such as those who held the power and the Government might choose to grant them.[58]

Black people could not be citizens, and, as Taney had written twenty years earlier as attorney general, their enjoyment of privileges was only ever at the "sufferance" of whites. "Whether emancipated or not"— with these four words, Taney reduced the free Black person to a slave. Emancipation could not and did not alter that which made Blacks ineligible to be part of the "people." Nothing could alter it. Taney's historical-political argument about the contingencies of the founding was at the same time, unmistakably, an ontological argument—an argument about *what kind of beings Blacks were.*

All "civilized and enlightened portions of the world" shared this opinion of the "negro African race," Taney continued:

[56] *Dred Scott v. Sanford* (1857), 403.
[57] Fehrenbacher 1978.
[58] *Dred Scott v. Sanford* (1857), 404–405.

They had for more than a century before been regarded as beings of an inferior order, and altogether unfit to associate with the white race either in social or political relations, and so far inferior that they had no rights which the white man was bound to respect, and that the negro might justly and lawfully be reduced to slavery for his benefit. He was bought and sold, and treated as an ordinary article of merchandise and traffic whenever a profit could be made by it. This opinion was at that time fixed and universal in the civilized portion of the white race. It was regarded as an axiom in morals as well as in politics which no one thought of disputing or supposed to be open to dispute, and men in every grade and position in society daily and habitually acted upon it in their private pursuits, as well as in matters of public concern, without doubting for a moment the correctness of this opinion.[59]

To show that Black abjection was an "axiom" of white life, Taney conducted a sweeping (if selective) review of colonial laws, the Declaration of Independence, the Constitution, northern state laws, and federal laws, taking pains to point out that free Black people "were governed by special legislation directed expressly to them, and always connected with provisions for the government of slaves, and not with those for the government of free white citizens."[60] Like Andrew Butler in the debate over free Black seamen, Taney tarried meaningfully over northern state laws hostile to free Black people (for example, anti-miscegenation laws in the antislavery bastion of Massachusetts), emphasizing that negrophobia was, despite the North's protestations, a thoroughly national phenomenon.

A couple of years before the court took up *Dred Scott*, Josiah Nott and George Gliddon, polygenists of the American School of Anthropology, had written in their influential *Types of Mankind* (1854): "[C]ertain savage types can be neither civilized nor domesticated …. Our Indian tribes submit to extermination, rather than wear the yoke under which our Negro slaves fatten and multiply."[61] Even savage Indians were too proud and honorable to submit to slavery. Only Negroes, mere bodies devoid of mind and character, thrived under slavery like livestock. At a historical moment when anti-Indian sentiment was running high and Indigenous peoples were being violently removed from their lands and forced onto reservations, such comparisons drove home the singularity of Black abjection with special force.[62]

---

[59] *Dred Scott* v. *Sanford* (1857), 407.
[60] *Dred Scott* v. *Sanford* (1857), 421.
[61] Nott and Gliddon 1854, 461.
[62] Thomas Jefferson was partial to making Black–Indigenous comparisons, observing in *Notes on the State of Virginia*: "[Indians] astonish you with strokes of the most sublime oratory; such as prove their reason and sentiment strong, their imagination glowing and elevated. But never yet could I find that a Black had uttered a thought above the level of plain narration" (1998 [1785], 147).

When Taney took up the comparison, his purpose was quite specific: to distinguish Indians from Negroes so that the fragile path of citizenship open to the former would be closed off to the latter.[63] In earlier jurisprudence, Taney had denied that Indian tribes were independent nations.[64] Yet the fact remained that some Indigenous persons had been naturalized through treaties, so if they were not considered aliens, or subjects of foreign governments, their classification as non-aliens who gained citizenship could set a dangerous precedent for Black people born on U.S. soil. To shut down this possibility, Taney reversed himself on the question of Indian status. Although Indians were inferior and unassimilable, he wrote, they "were yet a free and independent people, associated together in nations or tribes and governed by their own laws":[65]

These Indian Governments were regarded and treated as foreign Governments as much so as if an ocean had separated the red man from the white, and their freedom has constantly been acknowledged .... Treaties have been negotiated with them, and their alliance sought for in war, and the people who compose these Indian political communities have always been treated as foreigners not living under our Government.[66]

"[D]epart[ing] from the main thrust of Jacksonian thought and his own rulings," Rogers Smith writes, Taney "preferred to elevate the status of the tribes ... [rather] than concede that Congress might naturalize native-born Blacks."[67] Though Indians were systematically judged *not to belong* on the lands whites wished to possess, it was conceded, in comparison with Black people, that they nevertheless belonged somewhere, that they were embedded in political relationality of some sort.[68] Black people alone were stateless.

Echoing Andrew Butler on the privileges and immunities clause, Taney declared that states could confer state citizenship upon Blacks, but that

---

[63] See R. Smith 1997, ch. 9, "Dred Scott Unchained."

[64] *Cherokee Nation* v. *Georgia* (1831), in which Indians were conveniently represented as too alien to be given citizenship but not alien enough to be recognized as possessing sovereignty (Kettner 1978, 297, 300).

[65] *Dred Scott* v. *Sanford* (1857), 403.

[66] *Dred Scott* v. *Sanford* (1857), 404.

[67] R. Smith 1997, 267.

[68] Taney's argument that Indians are foreigners who can be naturalized is cited in *Elk* v. *Wilkins* (1884), which is in turn cited in *United States* v. *Wong Kim Ark* (1898), the case about Chinese birthright citizenship. In *Elk* v. *Wilkins*, the U.S. Supreme Court ruled that Indians owe immediate allegiance to an alien nation and are therefore not "subject to the jurisdiction" of the U.S. at birth, and therefore cannot be citizens per the citizenship clause of the Fourteenth Amendment—even though born on U.S. soil.

they lacked the authority to make them citizens of the United States. A state could admit a member to its own political community, but could never "introduce a new member into the political community created by the Constitution of the United States."[69] Since the privileges and immunities clause applied only to those holding national citizenship, "the rights which he [the Black person] would acquire would be restricted to the State which gave them"[70] and would not be transferrable to another state. Southern slaveholders could breathe a sigh of relief. Missouri was not obligated to abide by the laws of a free state (Illinois) which emancipated slaves who entered its jurisdiction. Furthermore, the Missouri Compromise was unconstitutional because Congress lacked the authority to forbid slavery in the territories. Taney's conclusion: Neither Dred Scott's stay in Illinois nor his stay in the Wisconsin Territory freed him. He remained a slave.

Justice Peter Daniel, in his concurring opinion, restated Taney's conclusion in even more emphatic terms:

[T]he African negro race never have been acknowledged as belonging to the family of nations; that, as amongst them, there never has been known or recognised by the inhabitants of other countries anything partaking of the character of nationality, or civil or political polity; that this race has been by all the nations of Europe regarded as subjects of capture or purchase, as subjects of commerce or traffic; and that the introduction of that race into every section of this country was not as members of civil or political society, but as slaves, as *property* in the strictest sense of the term .... [A] slave, the *peculium* or property of a master, and possessing within himself no civil nor political rights or capacities, cannot be a CITIZEN .... [I]t has been insisted in argument that the emancipation of a slave ... produces a change in the status or capacities of the slave such as will transform him from a mere subject of property into a being possessing a social, civil, and political equality with a citizen .... It is difficult to conceive by what magic the mere surcease or renunciation of an interest in a subject of property, by an individual possessing that interest, can alter the essential character of that property.[71]

It was the "essential character" of Black people, and not just the slaveholder's right of possession, that rendered them property. Even the dismantling of the institution of slavery could not elevate Black people to a civil and political standing *they never possessed in the first instance*. Only "magic" could change a thing into a human being.[72]

[69] *Dred Scott* v. *Sanford* (1857), 406.
[70] *Dred Scott* v. *Sanford* (1857), 405.
[71] Justice Peter Daniel's dissent in *Dred Scott* v. *Sanford* (1857), 475–477. Italics and capitals in original.
[72] Dissenting opinions by Justices John McLean and Benjamin Robbins Curtis pointed out that free Black people had been citizens and had exercised voting rights in some areas

If the law refused to recognize slaves as persons (except to invest them with criminal culpability), continually threatened free Black people with enslavement, and denied citizenship to both, what obligation did Black people, slave or free, have to the U.S. state? If, by virtue of their slaveness, they were denied participation in the political contract and were, additionally, persecuted and oppressed by the sovereign, were they not justified in taking up arms against the state? In his pamphlet "Walker's Appeal in Four Articles; Together with a Preamble, To the Coloured Citizens of the World, but in Particular, and Very Expressly, to Those of the United States of America" (1829), David Walker called for slaves to rise up and claim their freedom through force.[73] The pamphlet was widely circulated along the Atlantic seaboard by free Black seamen. A few decades after Walker issued his appeal, while assisting in a fugitive slave rescue in Christiana, Pennsylvania, escaped slave and abolitionist William Parker explained his resistance to the Fugitive Slave Act of 1850: "They [whites] have a country and may obey the laws, but we [Black people] have no country."[74] As if to confirm his point, the local prosecutor in Christiana charged one of the white men involved in the rescue with treason, declaring that he had used "colored people as instruments of war" against the government, but charged the Black people involved with other, less serious offenses.[75] To be treasonous, one had to be capable of giving or renouncing or changing political allegiance. One had to have "the character of nationality." One had to have a nation to betray.

To "have no country" was to be bereft but also freed from what were, for everyone else, the constraining bonds of political obligation. The *Dred Scott* decision reinforced this conviction among many abolitionists.[76]

---

at the time of the Founding, and argued that slavery was only a product of positive law, which meant that the presumption was in favor of freedom for those, like Scott, who had traveled into free states and territories. But McLean and Curtis were not champions of racial equality or even, in Curtis's case, of abolition. McLean was an antislavery Republican in step with, but not out in front of, his party on racial issues. Curtis, a "Cotton Whig" from Massachusetts, was a strong defender of the Fugitive Slave Act of 1850 and would soon publicly oppose the Emancipation Proclamation and Reconstruction. The two dissents challenged Taney's historical claims and jurisprudential reasoning about slavery but stopped well short of a robust advocacy of Black citizenship and equality (R. Smith 1997, 263–272).

[73] Walker 2015 [1830].
[74] Lubet 2010, 58.
[75] Lubet 2010, 81.
[76] See Sinha (2017) for the decision's impact on abolitionists.

In his pamphlet "No Rights, No Duties, or Slaveholders, as Such, Have No Rights; Slaves, as Such, Owe No Duties" (1860), abolitionist Henry Clark Wright exhorted slaves to resist and northerners to assist them. Turning Taney's language on its head, Wright wrote: "[I]ndividual slaveholders, as such, have no rights which any man, Black or white, enslaved or free, is bound to respect."[77] Then, inverting the Black criminalization/white exoneration couplet, he wrote of the slaveholder:

> The assassin has no claims on any one. No man owes, or can be made to owe, him any duties; for he is in a relation that is out of the pale of all law, human or divine. No power can impose on any man an obligation to respect any claim or right, which, as an assassin, he may assume. So, no power in heaven or earth can impose on you, or on any one, an obligation or duty to those who hold and use men and women as chattels.[78]

It was not the slave who stood outside "the pale of all law," but rather the slaveholder, who was a murderer and a moral pariah. His power, based upon force without right, was wholly illegitimate and thus unenforceable. Writing a year before the outbreak of civil war, Wright warned: "[N]o power, not God himself, can reconcile slavery with liberty. They are moral antagonisms .... [The] death-struggle is upon us."[79]

V SLAVERY WITHOUT END

Michel Foucault, inverting Clausewitz's famous phrase, observed that "politics is a continuation of war by other means."[80] The federal laws and constitutional amendments enacted in the postbellum period did not so much consolidate the Union's victory once and for all as create new legal-political terrain upon which the war, in the form of ordinary politics, continued to be fought. During Reconstruction, a small group of Radical Republicans promised to ferret out and eliminate the "badges and incidents" of slavery (Thirteenth Amendment), to guarantee Black people the rights of citizenship and equal protection under the law (Fourteenth Amendment), and to secure Black voting rights (Fifteenth Amendment). Many moderate Republicans had reservations about these goals, however, and southern elites simply refused to capitulate. Openly defying Reconstruction laws and the new constitutional amendments, the

---

[77] Wright 1860, 3.
[78] Wright 1860, 6.
[79] Wright 1860, 14, 25.
[80] Foucault 1997.

latter set about rebuilding the antebellum social, economic, and political order as closely as they could manage.

The heat and noise of sectional struggle concealed a deep wellspring of agreement on the necessity and naturalness of permanent Black subjugation. Most Unionists had fought the war to keep the Union intact, bring the rebel states into line, destroy the Slave Power, and bring about a free-labor/free-soil nation.[81] In the course of the war, they were pressed by military and political exigencies into taking steps they had neither anticipated nor desired—from enlisting Black soldiers in the Union army to issuing the Emancipation Proclamation in 1863—but Black advancement per se had never been their concern. Entering Reconstruction, they were decidedly less interested in a positive program of racial reform than in stabilizing the war-torn polity and shoring up their own party strength. Most had in mind for freed slaves nothing more extensive than the bastardized forms of "freedom" and "equality" enjoyed by northern Black people in the antebellum period. For them, Black "freedom" meant little more than not-slavery. What was at stake in the postbellum period, then, was not whether or not the new social order would be anti-Black but *what kind* of anti-Black order would emerge.

During the Civil War, Union officials had complained about the "contraband camps" consisting of escaped slaves who fled to Union lines. Amid the turmoil and horror of war, they had fretted that these Black people would become permanently dependent upon the government if they were not properly instructed in habits of self-sufficiency.[82] In other words, they saw them not as traumatized victims of slavery and war who needed support but as would-be parasites. The 1864 report of the American Freedmen's Inquiry Commission, which led directly to the formation of the Freedmen's Bureau, intoned that freed slaves must be "self-supporting" and treated like "any other freeman" rather than being protected by special laws.[83] Slaves were not yet out of chains, then, when federal officials started to worry that they were being pampered and would enjoy an unfair advantage in "the battle of life." The Freedmen's Bureau's intense preoccupation with Black "idlers and shirkers"[84] was an eerie reprise of the slaveholder's lament that slaves would not work unless they were whipped.

---

[81] Foner 1988; Du Bois 1998 [1935].
[82] Foner 1988.
[83] Stanley 1998, 124.
[84] Hartman 1997, 143.

At the conclusion of the war, freedpeople exercised their new free-dom of movement by leaving plantations to find loved ones and distance themselves from the scene of slavery. Resisting pressure to sign labor contracts with their former masters, many chose to look elsewhere for work or to opt out of the wage-labor relation altogether by acquiring land and/or engaging in subsistence hunting and fishing. Southern plant-ers and industrialists, hungry for cheap, controllable labor, responded by setting up a draconian contract labor system that mimicked slave law. Integral to this system were the Black Codes, which ensnared freed-people in a tightening net of vagrancy laws; breach-of-contract laws; anti-enticement laws; apprenticeship laws; laws restricting Black access to hunting, fishing, and grazing; and even laws forbidding the "disre-specting" of an employer.[85] This is how many freedpeople were forced to enter labor contracts on unfavorable terms with plantation owners—often their former masters.

The Freedmen's Bureau, ostensibly an advocate for freedpeople, rejected an early proposal to distribute confiscated Confederate lands to them and instead joined in coercing them to enter labor contracts. Amy Dru Stanley drily observed: "Stationed in the South to guarantee free labor practices, agents of the national government created a scheme of compulsory contract."[86] That Black people were seen as incapable of true "freedom" made it easier to justify the creation of a coercive labor system with no small resemblance to slavery. The Freedmen's Bureau declared ominously: "Freedom does not mean the right to live without work at other people's expense. A man who can work has no right to a support by government or by charity."[87] The instructional manuals distributed by the Bureau—with genial titles such as "Friendly Counsels for Freedmen"—told freedpeople that they owed their former masters for their freedom and must repay the debt by staying on the plantation and "bend[ing their] back[s] joyfully and hopefully to the burden" of labor.[88] Saidiya Hartman writes: "Thus the transition from slavery to freedom introduced the free agent to the circuits of exchange through this construction of already accrued debt, an abstinent present, and a mortgaged future. In short, to be free was to be a debtor—that is,

---

[85] Foner 1988.

[86] Stanley 1998, 124.

[87] *Orders Issued by the Commissioner and Assistant Commissioner of the Freedmen's Bureau*, 39th Congress, 1st Session, House Exec. Doc. 70 (1865), 155, cited in Stanley 1998, 123.

[88] Hartman 1997, 135. This quotation is from a manual entitled "Advice to Freedmen."

obliged and duty-bound to others."[89] Ironically, the only way to earn "freedom," to prove oneself worthy of it, was to acquiesce to one's virtual re-enslavement. Despite all of this, President Andrew Johnson vetoed the Freedmen's Bureau Bill in 1866 on the grounds that it pampered Black people and encouraged dependency.[90] Deprived of funding, the Freedmen's Bureau closed its doors soon after.

At the close of the war, Congress recognized Black citizenship through the Civil Rights Act of 1866, the first section of which held that "all persons born in the United States and not subject to any foreign power, excluding Indians not taxed, are hereby declared to be citizens of the United States."[91] While Democrats surprised no one by opposing this statute, Republicans (with the exception of the Radicals) showed scarcely more confidence in the fitness of freedmen for citizenship. When Republicans acted to advance Black rights during this period, many did so in the imperfect subjunctive tense—*as if* the Black were fit to vote, *as if* the Black had political capacity, *as if* some "magic" had transformed property into a man—and with the stated expectation that sooner or later the project of Black improvement would collapse upon itself.

In 1870, upon the passage of the Fifteenth Amendment, an Illinois newspaper declared: "The negro is now a voter and a citizen. Let him hereafter take his chances in the battle of life."[92] There was little daylight between this declaration and the slaveholder's insistence that slavery coddled the slave and shielded him from the maelstrom of social competition, or the writings of Herbert Spencer and William Graham Sumner, whose work applying Charles Darwin's ideas about "natural selection" and "survival of the fittest" to social life gained popularity during this period.[93] The prediction of Black failure was everywhere insinuated. *We have done all we can for them, and they must now fend for themselves.*[94]

---

[89] Hartman 1997, 131.
[90] Du Bois 1998 [1935].
[91] In 1868, the Fourteenth Amendment was ratified, in which Section I states: "All persons born or naturalized in the United States and subject to the jurisdiction thereof, are citizens of the United States and of the State wherein they reside."
[92] Quoted in Foner 1988, 449.
[93] See Horan 1972.
[94] In their view, since slavery had been good, natural, and proper for Blacks, and since Blacks were incapable of handling the burdens of freedom, it was expected that Emancipation would bring about their mental and physical degeneration and cause rising rates of mania, idiocy, and sexual madness (Haller 1972). As the Black's "essential character" increasingly asserted itself against the fading influences of slavery, he would falter in

Into the vacuum created by northern skepticism roared the ferocious drive of southern negrophobia. In the decades after Reconstruction ended, southern states devised voting restrictions that were prima facie racially neutral to circumvent the Fifteenth Amendment and maintain white political control. Poll taxes, literacy tests, grandfather clauses, and related provisions were put in place to effect near-total Black disenfranchisement, backed up by the mob violence of the Ku Klux Klan. All of these measures passed muster under the Fifteenth Amendment. Even the all-white primary was allowed to stand because the courts reasoned that the Democratic Party was a private rather than a state entity and therefore not within the purview of the amendment. Permanently tagged with slaveness, the Black person was a citizen in name only.

Postbellum southern law not only forced freedpeople into highly coercive labor relations and deprived them of political standing, it also spawned a vast and organized system of entirely involuntary Black servitude across the region—a system historians have called "slavery by another name," "slavery revisited," and "worse than slavery." The Thirteenth Amendment states: "Neither slavery nor involuntary servitude, except as a punishment for crime, whereof the party shall have been duly convicted, shall exist within the United States, or anyplace subject to their jurisdiction." *Except as a punishment for crime.* As Angela Davis notes, these six words created a fatal loophole that allowed southern legislators, planters, industrialists, sheriffs, and magistrates to conspire to organize markets for Black forced labor that escaped federal scrutiny.[95] For the better part of a century, starting in the 1860s, the convict lease system developed by southern states and counties, along with more informal practices of Black forced labor, damaged or destroyed the lives of tens of thousands of Black men and their families.[96]

Douglas Blackmon's *Slavery by Another Name: The Re-Enslavement of Black Americans From the Civil War to World War II* (2008) shows how convict leasing worked. Southern legislatures passed laws criminalizing various actions such as carrying weapons, fighting, stealing, vagrancy, riding empty freight train cars, or speaking too loudly in the presence of a white woman. Deliberately vague and sweeping, the laws

competition with whites and simply disappear. All of this was a matter of letting nature take its course. Postbellum censuses were pored over anxiously for evidence supporting this "extinction" discourse. "Emancipation," George Fredrickson writes, was seen "as a step toward genocide by natural causes" (1971, 159).

[95] Davis 1998.

[96] Some of the leased convicts were women, but the vast majority were men.

were "essentially intended to criminalize Black life" and were enforced almost exclusively against Black men.[97] Once arrested and convicted of these offenses, Black men were leased out to agricultural and industrial interests (iron, coal, steel, timber, turpentine, railroad construction) for significant fees, which enriched sheriffs, the municipality, and the state. Black prisoners in labor camps were chained, whipped, abused, starved, forced to live in degrading conditions, and worked up to and beyond the limit of human capacity. They were severely punished or killed if they tried to escape. By the second year of this system, Alabama's labor camps had a mortality rate approaching 45 percent.[98] Because no records were kept of who the prisoners were, what camps they were sent to, or the duration of their sentences, many Black men disappeared into these camps never to be heard from again. For their part, officers were "incentivized to arrest and obtain convictions of as many people as possible— regardless of their true guilt or whether a crime had been committed at all," and "[a]rrests surged and fell, not as acts of crime increased or receded, but in tandem to the varying needs of the buyers of labor."[99] For almost a century, the convict lease system powered southern industrialization and economic development and grew the wealth of white planters and industrialists in the region.

More informal practices operated alongside formal leasing arrangements. A white farmer could charge a Black man with a made-up offense and summon the local justice of the peace to his farm to convict him. The justice of the peace could charge the Black man a fine, at which point the white farmer would pay the man's fine and force him to sign a contract and work until the debt was paid off. At which point he could charge him with another offense and repeat the whole process again. Or a white landholder could charge one of his Black tenant farmers with fraud in court, act as a surety and pay his bond, and force him to sign a similar contract. And so on. All Black people were vulnerable to being caught up in this brutal vortex. For white farmers and capitalists, the possibilities for enriching themselves at the expense of Black people were practically unlimited, as long as they followed certain procedures, in particular the use of contracts to falsely signal the voluntarism and legality of the arrangements. No matter how great the degree of coercion involved, no matter how far the actual contract conditions were from the

[97] Blackmon 2008, 53.
[98] Blackmon 2008, 57.
[99] Blackmon 2008, 100, 65–66.

theoretical conditions that were supposed to pertain, the performance of signing the contract sanitized the proceedings. Whites had figured out, Douglas Blackmon observes, that they "could safely force a Black man into servitude for months or years as long as they pretended that the legal rights of those Black men had not been violated."[100]

VI FOREIGNNESS AS BELONGING

Enter the Chinese. In the mid 1800s, California entered the Union as a "free" or nonslave state, and the demand for cheap labor there brought the first substantial numbers of Asian (Chinese) immigrants to U.S. shores.[101] They quickly established a presence in various sectors of the regional economy, including mining, railroad construction, agriculture, and urban manufacturing. From that point forward, as the nation moved through the Civil War, Reconstruction, and the establishment of Jim Crow, Congress, the courts, state and local governments, and the media produced the Chinese laborer as a distinctive legal-political being who was not-white but above all not-Black. Pushed downward by white supremacy, the Chinese were even more powerfully lifted up by anti-Blackness.

By the 1870s, the anti-Chinese movement was gathering steam, rendering Chinese foreignness a site of dispossession, rejection, and exclusion. But, in relation to Blackness, Chinese foreignness was always already, and more fundamentally, a site of inclusion, plenitude, and belonging. Foreignness was, after all, a "character of nationality," a defining attribute of humanness that Justice Peter Daniel pointedly denied to Black people in *Dred Scott*. Deemed "aliens ineligible to citizenship" by the courts, the Chinese were thought not to belong in the U.S., but they were thought to belong *somewhere*. Although they were judged to be unfit for republican citizenship, they were recognized as bona fide subjects of the Chinese empire and part of the Family of Man. By the late 1800s, China was accepted as part of the Family of Nations as well.[102]

In the nineteenth century, Lisa Lowe explains, Western powers began to emphasize free trade and "the worldwide movement of goods, capital,

---

[100] Blackmon 2008, 147–148.
[101] See S. Smith (2013) for the argument that as "[a] multiracial society with multiple systems of bound and semibound labor, California complicates familiar Black–white, slave–free binaries" (2013, 4).
[102] See C. Kim (2015), for discussion of the animalization of Chinese immigrants in the 1800s.

and people" as a complement to earlier patterns of direct conquest and territorial occupation.[103] During the course of the Opium Wars (1839–1842, 1856–1860), China was forced into signing a series of "unequal treaties" that opened several major Chinese ports to British ships, granted "most favored nation" status to Britain, and accepted British stipulations about extraterritoriality. Along with France, the U.S. seized the opportunity to negotiate its own "unequal treaties" with China, increasing the profits of American merchants at the expense of Chinese sovereign power.[104] Extraterritorial jurisdiction, Lisa Lowe writes, "appeared to recognize China as a state within the international legal system, while at the same time compromising its sovereignty."[105] China gained a new kind of standing in the eyes of Western powers by entering the international community, even as it confronted new forms of coercion via treaties and international norms.

The Burlingame Treaty signed by the U.S. and China in 1868 was a watershed, emphasizing reciprocity and equality between the two nations.[106] Originally appointed by President Lincoln as minister to the Qing Empire, Anson Burlingame proved such a dedicated advocate for the Chinese empire that at the end of his term, he was hired by the Chinese as special envoy and minister plenipotentiary to negotiate treaties with the U.S. and Europe on China's behalf. Burlingame described the 1868 treaty he negotiated while holding this position:

Progress. It means that China … desires to come under the obligations of … international law …. It means that she intends to come into the brotherhood of nations. It means Commerce; it means Peace; it means a unification of her own interests with the whole human race …. This is one of the mightiest movements of modern times … the fraternal feeling of four hundred millions of people has commenced to flow through the land of Washington to the elder nations of the West, and it will flow on forever.[107]

In this triumphalist narrative, the treaty not only facilitated trade and migration between China and the U.S., but also officially symbolized

---

[103] Lowe 2015, 109.

[104] These were the Wangxia Treaty of 1844 and the Tianjin Treaty of 1858. See H. Liu 2003 and Lowe 2015.

[105] Lowe 2015, 104.

[106] Anson Burlingame, the former U.S. minister to China who negotiated the treaty as China's special envoy to Western powers, was a former Massachusetts congressman with strong antislavery credentials. After Representative Preston Brooks of South Carolina caned Charles Sumner nearly to death on the Senate floor in 1856, Burlingame made an impassioned speech condemning Brooks and prompting the latter to challenge him to a duel. Burlingame accepted the challenge but Brooks did not show up (Schrecker 2010).

[107] Quoted in Schrecker 2010, 23. Italics in original.

China's entry into the international community, uniting all of (civilized) mankind in the framework of peaceful commerce and international order and stability. Burlingame toured the capitals of Europe with this message, and in 1878, China was invited for the first time to a meeting of the Association for the Reform and Codification of the Law of Nations. China had officially joined the world.[108]

Thomas Nast's engraving "The Youngest Introducing the Oldest" (*Harper's Weekly*, July 18, 1868) memorializes the signing of the Burlingame Treaty.[109] The caption reads: "America: Brothers and Sisters, I am happy to present to you the Oldest Member of the Family, who desires our better acquaintance." Columbia (representing America) grasps the hand of a Chinese man of upper-class status and faces the world leaders (Europeans and the Turkish head of state), who bow in acknowledgment. (No African leaders are depicted.) The pope remains seated, apparently reluctant to acknowledge a heathen people, while Anson Burlingame sits unassumingly at the edge of the frame next to crates of commercial goods. As Nast indicates, this was a historic moment marking the expansion of the Family of Nations to include select non-European peoples.[110] Importantly, China is depicted not as a new member of the Family of Nations, but rather as an old member, indeed, the oldest member, who had simply not been recognized as such and was thus due a certain belated veneration. Burlingame commented: "When the oldest nation in the world, containing one-third of the human race, seeks, for the first time, to come into relations with the West, and requests the youngest nation, through its representative, to act as the medium of such change, the mission is one not to be solicited or rejected."[111]

As John Schrecker writes, the treaty "expressly connected the greater security for the Chinese community [in the U.S.] to the increase in China's international status."[112] China's membership in the Family of Nations tended to elevate the status of Chinese immigrants, even if it did not protect them from the gathering storm of exclusion. The text of the Burlingame Treaty proclaimed "the inherent and inalienable right

---

[108] Hsu 1960.
[109] http://thomasnastcartoons.com/2014/02/13/the-youngest-introduces-the-oldest.
[110] The "Family of Nations" was originally thought to include only Western European Christian states, but was expanded to include Russia, the U.S., and Turkey by the mid-1800s. The Chinese had their own distinct ideas about the familial structure of international relations. See Hsu 1960.
[111] Hsu 1960, 168.
[112] Schrecker 2010, 29.

of man to change his home and allegiance, and also the mutual advantage of the free migration and emigration of their citizens and subjects respectively from the one country to the other." It further provided that "Chinese subjects visiting or residing in the United States shall enjoy the same privileges, immunities and exemptions in respect to travel or residence as may there be enjoyed by the citizens or subjects of the most favored nation," with reciprocal protections for U.S. citizens visiting or living in China.[113] This marked a clear departure from the "unequal treaties," wherein China had granted "most favored nation" status to Western powers but had not been granted it in return. The promise that Chinese immigrants would be treated at least as well as, say, British subjects amounted to granting them proximity to whiteness in a certain respect. This, at least, was the guarantee on paper.

In reality, Chinese immigrants continued to be demeaned, harassed, and systematically persecuted through legal and extralegal action, and this trend intensified through the 1870s. Congress's decision in 1870 to restrict naturalization rights to free whites and those of African descent—and explicitly exclude the Chinese, despite Senator Charles Sumner's efforts—was an indicator of what was to come. The Burlingame Treaty did not halt these developments, but it did slow them down and force them off course at various points, and for this reason, it became the bane of exclusionists. According to Senator William Stewart of Nevada, the Civil Rights Act of 1870, which extended the civil rights protections guaranteed in the Civil Rights Act of 1866 to "all persons" (i.e., aliens as well as citizens), was passed precisely to enact the Burlingame Treaty's promise of protection to Chinese migrants.[114] Lawmakers and jurists frequently cited the treaty as a reason why discriminatory state and local laws had to be struck down or could not be crafted in the first place.[115] Ironically, then, the partial effectiveness of the treaty in protecting Chinese laborers from state and local persecution helped

---

[113] The treaty also stipulated reciprocal access to education and schooling. See Bascara 2014. The concept of "most favored nation" status derived from European trade agreements in the Middle Ages and meant that the terms of trade would be at least as favorable as those enjoyed by the nation with the most favorable terms.

[114] Torok 1996. Section 16 of the Civil Rights Act of 1870 held in part: "All persons within the jurisdiction of the United States shall have the same right in every State and Territory to make and enforce contracts, to sue, be parties, give evidence, and to the full and equal benefit of all laws and proceedings for the security of persons and property as is enjoyed by white citizens, and shall be subject to like punishment, pains, penalties, taxes, licenses, and exactions of every kind and to no other."

[115] See, for example, *In re Tiburcio Parrott* (1880) and *In re Quong Woo* (1882).

convince exclusionists of the need for national legislation banning Chinese migration altogether.

That the Chinese were inferior to Europeans and superior to Africans was a truism in nineteenth-century ethnological science. In the early 1860s, French anatomist and zoologist Louis Pierre Gratiolet, stipulating that higher mental functions were associated with the front of the brain, divided humans into three groups: *"races frontales"* (whites, with anterior and frontal brain lobes most highly developed), *"races pariétales"* (Mongolians, with parietal or mid lobes most developed), and *"races occipitales"* (Blacks, with the back of the brain being most developed).[116] Eminent French craniometrist Paul Broca was embroiled in bitter debates with Gratiolet on various other matters but concurred about the ranking of these three groups. German naturalist Ernst Haeckel suggested the same pattern in his sketch "Die Familiengruppe der Katarrhinen" (1868) or "The Catarrhine Family Group."[117] The figures here are, in Haeckel's terminology, the Indo-German, the Chinese, the Fuegian, the Australian Negro, the African Negro, the Tasmanian, the gorilla, the chimpanzee, the orangutan, the gibbon, the proboscis monkey, and the mandrill. Note the Chinese man immediately follows the European man (represented per usual by what looks like a statue of Apollo) and is separated from the Negro figures by the Fuegian (referring to Indigenous inhabitants of Tierra del Fuego, off the tip of South America). The Negro figures, meanwhile, are directly adjacent to apes.

In congressional debates during Reconstruction, Chinese superiority over Black people was treated as axiomatic. Democrats regularly called out Republicans for their hypocrisy in extending the "universal rights of man" to Black people and withholding them from the more deserving Chinese. Their motivation was not to help the Chinese but rather to derail Republican initiatives on Black rights. In the debate over the Fifteenth Amendment, Senator James Doolittle of Wisconsin opened his comments by urging the deportation of Black people to the West Indies, lest "this weak, this feeble, this inferior, this subject, this dependent race" be "trampled into the dust" in the "competition of life" with white men, which was certain to happen if the proposed amendment "force[d] him upon a footing of equality" with the latter. He continued:

---

[116] Gould 1996, 129.
[117] Published in Haeckel's *Natürliche Schöpfungsgeschichte* (1868), translated into English as *The History of Creation* in 1876. http://phylonetworks.blogspot.com/2014/06/haeckel-and-march-of-progress.html.

[T]here is another objection to this amendment …. There are one hundred thousand Chinamen now on our western coast. In ten years there may be a million …. You know that the Chinese are far in advance of the African in point of civilization. You know that, in comparison with the Chinaman, the African is inferior …. If we are to carry out the idea for which gentlemen contend of the equality of all races before the law and before the Constitution of the United States in taking part in the Government of the country, if we are to extend these privileges to the African, why should we not extend them to the Chinaman? Give me a reason, if you can …. Why not stand upon the principle one way or the other?[118]

It was the slippery slope problem: if Blacks, then why not the Chinese—and any scenario with "a million" voting Chinamen was to be avoided. Doolittle knew that his Republican colleagues would not dare to argue that Black people were more qualified to vote than the Chinese.

During the 1870 debate over the naturalization law, Senator Lyman Trumbull of Illinois, cosponsor of both the Thirteenth Amendment and Civil Rights Act of 1866, posed the "if Blacks, then why not the Chinese" question as well. Unlike Doolittle, however, he did so in good faith:

We have struck the word "white" out of the naturalization laws so far as it applies to the Hottentot, to the pagan from Africa. Now, is it proposed to deny the right of naturalization to the Chinaman, who is infinitely above the African in intelligence, in manhood, and in every respect? …. [The inclusion of those of African nativity and descent in the statute] opens [the nation to] the whole continent of Africa, where are to be found the most degraded examples of man that exist on the face of the earth, pagans, cannibals, men who worship beasts, who do not compare in intelligence at all with the Chinese. And I ask of Senators, are we now going to place ourselves in the condition of authorizing these Africans to be naturalized and become citizens of the United States, and deny that right to Chinamen?[119]

Trumbull's description of Africans was so disparaging, we could be forgiven for thinking he objected to allowing them to naturalize. But in fact his aim was simply to extend naturalization rights to the Chinese. As with Doolittle, "if x then why not y?" expressed the mathematical certainty that the Chinese deserved at least as much (and probably a good bit more) consideration than did Black people.

In 1877, as the anti-Chinese movement gathered momentum, Congress's Joint Special Committee to Investigate Chinese Immigration held public hearings in California. Senator Henry Cooper of Tennessee questioned Reverend Samuel Blakeslee, an outspoken supporter of Chinese exclusion:

---

[118] Avins 1967, 377.
[119] *Congressional Record*, 41st Congress, 2d Session, U.S. Senate, July 4, 1870, 5177.

Q.   Could it [granting the Chinese suffrage] not elevate them?

A.   No, sir; the African was compelled to become an American; he became American in taste, American in feeling, American in religion, American in habits, American in morality. Slavery compelled him to do that; but the Chinese never will, as far as human knowledge can tell.

Q.   Can you not compel them the same way?

A.   No, sir; we have got to work on Chinese entirely by moral suasion.

Q.   You are making the illustration on account of the lack of desire to work with them. Why will not the same remedy apply to laboring men here that applies in the South, where the race antagonism exists. Where you elevate the colored man, does it not do away with that antagonism?

A.   It does, but you have already made the colored man an American.

Q.   Why would it not do to make the Chinaman an American in the same way?

A.   You cannot make him an American.

Q.   Can you not make him a voter?

A.   That would not make him an American.

Q.   Did it not make the negro an American?

A.   The negro was an American before he was a voter.

Q.   Do you think the elevation of the inferior class tends to prevent this antagonism of the laboring-class to work beside them?

A.   I do not think it will much. Give the Chinaman the vote, and the laborer will despise him as much as they despise him now. Only the politicians will be more shrewd to manipulate him.

Q.   Is it not the same way with the negro?

A.   It is. There is danger of the South, and there is a greater danger with the Chinaman; for, in addition, the Chinaman has a vigor of thought that has brought the nation a character, and he believes himself superior. As soon as he would get the vote he would try politically to become superior, and we should have our Chinese judges, our Chinese justices of the peace, and they will be controlled by their Chinese prejudices.

Q.   Would not the negroes do the same?

A.   No, sir; the negro is an American with American tastes.

Q.   Can he not be made equally ambitious?

A.   Yes, sir; I think so.

Q.   Why may not the Chinese after a generation equally become citizens?

A.   Because we cannot reach them except through moral influences. The African was reached through the power of slavery, and thus Americanized, but we have no power to make the Chinaman an American.

Q.   Would not contact with our civilization have the same effect upon the Chinaman as upon the African?

A.   No, sir; because the Chinaman despises our civilization; he is proud of his own. He tells us in our face, "You are small potatoes; we were a great nation three thousand years ago."[120]

---

[120] *Report of the Joint Special Committee to Investigate Chinese Immigration* (1877), 1035–1036.

The Chinaman had to be kept out not because he was inferior to Negroes but precisely because he was superior to them—because he could not be enslaved and repurposed for American citizenship. Black people were blank slates whom slavery forcibly imprinted with Americanness. (Frantz Fanon: "The Black has no ontological resistance in the eyes of the white man.")[121] But the Chinese, arrogant and boastful about their own civilization, offered resistance, and their "vigor of thought," moreover, made them hungry for power. There was no recourse to compulsion with them. Black abjection meant anything could be done to Black people, but there were limits on what could be done to everybody else.

In an article included in the appendix of the Joint Committee's final report, Charles Wolcott Brooks, former U.S. consul to Japan, observed:

Negroes—first imported from the wilds of Africa heathen barbarians in a wild and savage state far lower in the scale of being than the Chinese were four thousand years ago, for negroes had no literature, philosophy, or cultivation— were brought here as slaves, against their will, with all the horrors of the middle-passage, to furnish involuntary labor under the lash, *a thing no Chinaman will bear.*[122]

What marked Black people as slaves, Wolcott suggested, was not the mere fact of their enslavement but that *they bore it*, as livestock would, because they stood outside the realm of human dignity and honor. The Chinese would never allow themselves to be so treated. It is not clear why Wolcott made this claim when the long historical record of Black resistance (slave revolts, fugitivity, and Black abolitionism) so obviously contradicted it, but what is clear is that he regarded slavery as a test of evolutionary fitness. It only happened to those who let it happen to them. For everyone else, it was unthinkable. *The Chinaman was ineligible for citizenship, but he was also ineligible for enslavement.*

VII *PEOPLE V. GEORGE HALL*

Immigrants arriving in nineteenth-century San Francisco's Chinatown traveled a trans-Pacific circuit of anti-Black thought and feeling. Blackness was associated with slavery in the Chinese imaginary as well as the American one, with African slaves having been transported to China as early as the ninth century. After the forced opening of China

---

[121] Fanon 1952.
[122] *Report of the Joint Special Committee to Investigate Chinese Immigration* (1877), Appendix U, 1221. Italics added.

during the Opium Wars, Western ideas about race gained greater circulation in China via missionaries, Chinese students returning from study in the West, and Japanese translations of Western philosophy.[123] For the nineteenth-century Chinese, "Blackness equaled enslavement, a fate to be avoided by the Chinese."[124] A few decades later, Frank Dikötter explains, acclaimed philosopher Kang Youwei wrote of Africans as having "iron faces, silver teeth, slanting jaws like a pig, front view like an ox, full breasts and long hair, their hands and feet dark Black, stupid like sheep or swine." According to Kang, any white or yellow who was willing to marry a "monstrously ugly" Black should be given a medal as "Improver of the Race." Both Kang and esteemed Chinese historian Liang Qichao "ordered mankind into a racial hierarchy of biological groups where 'yellows' competed with 'whites' over degenerate breeds of 'browns,' 'Blacks' and 'reds.'"[125] Thus, except for the exact placement of "yellows," Chinese racial ideas bore a resemblance to American ideas. Which is to say, Chinese immigrants did not encounter anti-Blackness for the first time upon their arrival in California; they were already bound up in its ideological frame.

San Francisco Chinatown leaders forcefully rejected any attempt by whites to liken them to slaves or Blacks by asserting their property in not-Blackness. On April 23, 1852, just a few years after the arrival of the first Chinese immigrants, California Governor John Bigler gave a speech denouncing them as "coolies" and calling upon Congress to prohibit their entry. Six days later, Chinatown leaders responded with a letter to the governor, clarifying:

The poor Chinaman does not come here as a slave. He comes because of his desire for independence, and he is assisted by the charity of his countrymen, which they bestow on him safely, because he is industrious and honestly repays them. When he gets to the mines he sets to work with patience, industry, temperance, and economy.[126]

Knowing that Bigler used the term "coolies" to associate the Chinese immigrant with the slave, Chinatown leaders defined the Chinese immigrant against the foil of the slave—as an independent free laborer who came to the U.S. voluntarily and embodied the virtues of capitalist discipline.

---

[123] Lan 2016.
[124] Shih 2013, 158.
[125] Dikötter 1994, 405, 407.
[126] *An Analysis of the Chinese Question* (1852), 6.

When California entered the Union in 1850 as a "free" state, the new state legislature sought to prevent Black in-migration by restricting Black rights. To this end, it passed a law in 1850 stating that "no Black or Mulatto person, or Indian" could testify against a white person in court. In 1854, the California Supreme Court heard the case *People* v. *George Hall*, in which a white man who had been convicted of killing a Chinese man based on the testimony of three Chinese witnesses appealed his conviction on the grounds that the testimony ban applied to the Chinese. The legislature had not considered the Chinese when it crafted the law in 1850 because so few were present in the state at that time, so it was left to the court to decide whether a statute that mentioned only "Blacks," "Mulattos," and "Indians" applied to the Chinese, too. Would whites be able to continue acting with impunity against and in the presence of the Chinese?

Chief Justice Hugh Murray ruled in George Hall's favor, stating: "[I]f it had ever been anticipated that this class of people [the Chinese] were not embraced in the prohibition [on courtroom testimony], then such specific words would have been employed as would have put the matter beyond any possible controversy."[127] After a long discursus on the ethnological proximity of the Chinese and Indians, Murray concluded:

> The word "Black" may include all negroes, but the term "negro" does not include all Black persons. By the use of the term in this connection, we understand it to mean the opposite of "white," and that it should be taken as contradistinguished from all white persons. In using the words "no Black or mulatto person, or Indian shall be allowed to give evidence for or against a white person," the Legislature, if any intention can be ascribed to it, adopted the most comprehensive terms to embrace every known class or shade of color, as the apparent design was to protect the white person from the influence of all testimony other than that of persons of the same caste. The use of the terms must, by every sound rule of construction, exclude every one who is not of white blood.[128]

"Black" was to be understood as an expansive category that included not just "negroes" but also anyone else who was not indisputably white. Black meant not-white. Though not "negroes," the Chinese were, by this definition, Black, and thus barred from testifying against whites. Even apart from the question of legislative intent, Murray averred, the court would have been independently "impelled to this decision on the grounds of

---

[127] *People* v. *George Hall* (1854), 405. The ban on Chinese testimony was removed in 1872 but reinstated by the Geary Act in 1892.
[128] *People* v. *George Hall* (1854), 403.

public policy" in order to prevent "the anomalous spectacle" of "a race of people whom nature has marked as inferior" being able to "swear away the life of a citizen" and "participat[e] with us in administering the affairs of our Government."[129] George Hall's conviction was overturned, and he was set free.

The classification of the Chinese as "Black" was anomalous. In 1863, nearly a decade later, the California legislature amended the statute in question to extend the ban on testimony to the Chinese. At the same time, they deleted Blacks from the statute, presumably out of a reformist spirit inspired by the Civil War and the imminent demise of slavery. The classification of the Chinese as "Black" with regard to courtroom testimony was thus situational and temporary, a response to the specific need to block a not-white group from testifying against whites until the legislature could set things right. As the courts adjudicated the status of the Chinese in ensuing decades, they did not classify them as "Black" but rather as "Mongolian" or "Asiatic"—a category that was understood to be constitutively not-Black.

Still, for Chinatown leaders, Murray's ruling was an insufferable threat to their status, and they mobilized with their allies to try to reverse the court's decision.[130] Reverend William Speer, an advocate for the Chinese, spoke on their behalf in an open letter entitled "An Answer to the Common Objections to Chinese Testimony; and An Earnest Appeal to the Legislature of California for Their Protection By Our Law" (1857):

It is a violation of all right to include Asiatics in the category of either Indians or negroes. They are as far removed ethnologically from either variety of the human race as we are. The relationship of the extensive Mongolian stock ... is full as close with most of the people of Europe, as with our Indian or the negro.[131]

Speer did not challenge the racial ban on testimony per se—indeed he implicitly endorsed the principle of natural racial hierarchy that informed it—but sought only to exempt the Chinese on the grounds that they were recognized by ethnologists as superior to the other groups specified in the ban. His claim that Asiatics were "full as close" with Europeans as with Indians and Negroes was unremarkable for the time, suggesting a conventional unilinear scale with Asiatics located in between Europeans, on the one hand, and Indians and Negroes, on the other. But his other claim, that Asiatics were "as far removed" from Indians and Negroes as whites

[129] *People v. George Hall* (1854), 404–405.
[130] McClain 1994.
[131] Speer 1857, 7.

were, contradicted this unilinear scale and suggested something more like an equilateral triangle. In all likelihood, Speer was simply seeking to emphasize the distance between the Chinese and Blackness. The more distance here, the less likely the Chinese were to be misread as Black.

Undeterred by the objections of Chinatown leaders, Governor Bigler continued speaking out against Chinese "coolie" laborers. In 1855, Chinatown leaders issued an open letter entitled "Remarks of the Chinese Merchants of San Francisco upon Governor Bigler's Message"(1855):

[P]rejudices existing against the Chinese generally in this State, as a kind of slaves or bondsmen, is the result of want of information. Prejudice against them upon such grounds is unfounded. When this is fully understood, their condition, as poor, friendless, inoffensive, foreigners ... will ensure them sympathy, instruction and protection from many by whom they are now avoided and contemned [sic].[132]

We are not slaves, we are foreigners. In an anti-Black order, foreignness was a form of belonging, a status deserving of sympathy and concern. Upon realizing their category error, whites would surely set aside their hostility toward Chinese immigrants and embrace them instead. In the same vein, as Najia Aarim-Heriot notes, Chinese diplomats during this period insisted that U.S. government officials treat the "Chinese question" not as a race issue but as an immigration issue to be handled through diplomatic negotiations.[133] To be race-d was to be placed into proximity with Blackness; to be seen as an immigrant was to be respected as a legitimate subject of an equal sovereign power under the rubric of international law.

Writing about the 1882 exclusion of the Chinese, Chinese American journalist and editor Wong Chin Foo opined: "We [Chinese] feel grieved and humiliated every time we behold our colored brethren, even from the wilds of African jungles, sit and eat from the National family table, while we, the descendants of the oldest race on earth, are not even allowed to pick up the crumbs from under the table!"[134] It was bad enough to be expelled from the nation, but to watch Black people enjoy membership at the same time was intolerable. It seemed the world had turned upside down. Wong was writing in 1897, twenty years after the collapse of Reconstruction left southern Black people at the mercy of vengeful whites, and one year after the U.S. Supreme Court nailed down Jim Crow

---

[132] Remarks of the Chinese Merchants (1855), 16.
[133] Aarim-Heriot 2003.
[134] "A Chinese League," *San Francisco Call*, May 26, 1897, 6, cited in E. Wong 2015, 118.

in *Plessy* v. *Ferguson*, so it is not clear what he means by Blacks sitting and eating "from the National family table." In any case, we can see that negrophobia was not limited to whites. In their efforts to negotiate the anti-Black order, Chinese immigrants helped to reproduce it.[135]

VIII FOREIGNNESS AS EXCLUSION

When the anti-Chinese movement gathered steam in the 1870s, fueled largely by white workers' racialized resentment of Chinese immigrant labor, its organizers faced a conundrum. How to argue for the exclusion of a national-racial group who possessed a certain standing, as recognized by the Burlingame Treaty, and was also considered manifestly superior to the group being incorporated into the polity at that historical moment? They could not plausibly argue that the Chinese were the most abject group and thus uniquely deserving of exclusion. Black people already occupied that position. Since Chinese superiority was axiomatic, with regard to both ethnological science and racial common sense, what, then, was the rationale for granting citizenship, naturalization, and voting rights to Black people and withholding these from the Chinese? How could one argue "x but not y" when y was widely considered more worthy than x?

Thomas Nast's drawing *The Civilization of Blaine* (1879) raised these questions as the storm clouds of Chinese exclusion were gathering.[136] Nast intended to call out the hypocrisy of Senator James Blaine, Republican of Maine and presidential contender, who was the leading proponent of Chinese exclusion on the national political stage. Blaine, the imposing statesman, is shown physically supporting a diminutive, child-like Black man whose gentlemanly clothes cannot disguise his cringing, servile aspect. The Black man tenders a piece of paper inscribed with the word "vote" to Blaine, who, in turn, tramples a copy of the Burlingame Treaty under his feet. Importuning Blaine from behind is a Chinese gentleman of upper-class status, arms open, surrounded by the artifacts of Chinese civilizational accomplishment and commercial power. The caption expresses his query: "Am I not a man and a Brother?" Nast's audience would have immediately recognized the slogan that had been used to great effect by British and U.S. abolitionists in

---

[135] See Bow (2010), Koshy (2001), and Jun (2011) for discussion of how much and what kind of choice the Chinese could be said to have had in dissociating from Blackness.

[136] https://thomasnastcartoons.com/2014/04/08/civilization-of-blaine-8-march-1879

their fight against slavery. Nast's message was clear: Blaine had taken a position—favoring Black inclusion and Chinese exclusion—that was so contrary to reason (and treaty obligations), it could only be explained by his political ambition.

It was under this specific pressure of justifying the demand for Chinese exclusion in the context of granting Black people unprecedented political rights (on paper) that the Chinese had to be made out not just as different from whites but as *the most unassimilable people on the face of the earth*. The Chinese were so unassimilable, the argument would go, that even the lowly Black was more assimilable than them. Assimilability and worth, in other words, were treated as *inversely related concepts*. It was precisely because the basic considerability of the Chinese was taken for granted that Chinese foreignness had to be represented as a monumental liability. If they couldn't be enslaved, they could still be judged to be too different and sent back home.

In May 1869, journalist Henry George wrote a letter to the editor of *The New York Tribune* laying out the difference between "Mongolians" and "negroes":

[Mongolians] differ from our race by as strongly marked characteristics as do the negroes, while they will not as readily fall into our ways as the negroes. The difference between the two races in this respect is as the difference between an ignorant but docile child, and a grown man, sharp but narrow minded, opinionated and set in character. The negro when brought to this country was a simple barbarian with nothing to unlearn; the Chinese have a civilization and history of their own, a vanity which causes them to look down on all other races.[137]

Here the distinguishing virtue of the Chinese—their venerable culture and civilization—was recast as a fatal vice. They were culturally fixed and thus unable to assimilate, whereas Black people's lack of civilization and history made them able to assimilate. Black people were assimilable not because of any affirmative virtues of their own, then, but because of what they were not, because of their blank plasticity, because they had no prior or competing national allegiance. The Chinese had to be excluded *not despite their superiority to Black people, but because of it*.

According to this view, European immigrants could become freedom-loving Americans regardless of their prior political allegiances, but the Chinese, burdened with inflexible and servile minds, were incapable of such a shift. Their maniacal loyalty to the Emperor in China and to the Chinese Six Companies within San Francisco proved their despotic

[137] Quoted in Wenzer 2003, 169.

tendencies. Since they could not assimilate into American civilization, they were almost certainly conspiring to destroy it. Everything about the comportment of the Chinese suggested a parasitical and subversive posture—from their obvious venality to their predilection for dominating certain occupational niches to the fact that they sent their bones back to China for burial.

In the debate over the Civil Rights Bill of 1866, Senator Edgar Cowan of Pennsylvania warned that granting citizenship to the Chinese would lead to the Mongolianization of the U.S.:

> [T]hat population [the Chinese] is now becoming very heavy upon the Pacific coast; and when we consider that it is in proximity to an empire containing four hundred million people, very much given to emigrating, very rapacious in their character, and very astute in their dealings, if they are to be made citizens and to enjoy political power in California, then, sir, the day may not be very far distant when California, instead of belonging to the Indo-European race, may belong to the Mongolian, may belong to the Chinese; because it certainly would not be difficult for that empire, with her resources, and with the means she has, to throw a population upon California and the mining districts of that country that would overwhelm our race and wrest from them the dominion of that country.[138]

Four years later, Senator Reverdy Johnson of Maryland, introducing a joint resolution authorizing states to legislate on Chinese immigration, echoed Cowan's concern:

> The ideas these people [the Chinese] have of government, their hatred of our race and institutions, make them a thousand times more dangerous than would be so many wild beasts. The wild beast would vote at random, like the Hottentot and the cannibal; but the Chinaman, if he could, would always vote against the interest of the white man.[139]

The African, rendered as "Hottentot" and "cannibal," could inflict only limited harm in the political arena because he was as lacking in political purpose as a "wild beast." The Chinese, on the other hand, were dangerous precisely because they had "ideas of government" and were agents of Chinese imperial designs. Thus the Black voter could be tolerated as a regrettable necessity, but never the Chinese. Again, the Chinese had to be excluded *because* of their superiority to Black people.[140]

---

[138] Quoted in Avins 1967, 126.

[139] *Congressional Globe*, 41st Congress, 2d Session, U.S. Senate, 1870, 754.

[140] Senator Oliver Morton declared during the debate over the Fifteenth Amendment that the words "citizen of the United States" had been "put in [to the amendment draft] to protect us against Chinamen" voting (quoted in Avins 1967, 382). Chinese foreignness was thus used to ensure that the Chinese would not get the vote. Charles Sumner's

Incorrigible Chinese foreignness was one of two main exclusionist rhetorics circulating in the late nineteenth-century U.S. The other rhetoric tagged the Chinese as "coolies" who represented the resurrection of the Slave Power out of the ruins of the Civil War. Calling Chinese laborers "coolies," or unfree colored labor, likened them to slaves, tainted them with Blackness, and dramatized the threat they posed to (white) "free labor." Distinguishability, of course, is a prerequisite for comparison: we do not compare identical things (x and x); we compare nonidentical things (x and y). It was precisely because the Chinese were universally understood to be not-Black, because they had not-Blackness to save, that their enemies associated them with Blackness *as a way of bringing them down.* Putting these two exclusionist logics together, the Chinese had to be excluded both because they were unenslaveable (and therefore permanently unassimilable) and because they were like slaves.[141] Anti-Blackness, in other words, defined the terms in which Chinese exclusion played out.

Chinese laborer = coolie = slave. During Senate debate over the Naturalization Act of 1870, Senator William Stewart of Nevada proffered this chain of equivalents as an argument for why Chinese immigrants should not be allowed to naturalize:

These people are brought here under these infamous coolie contracts, the same contracts that have disgraced humanity in the taking of these poor people to the West India islands and various portions of South America as slaves .... The system is very similar to the system by which African slaves were brought here .... We are a free people. America must be the asylum of all who choose to come here; but it shall not again be a refuge for slave-masters to bring labor here to speculate in it.[142]

Writer M. B. Starr made a similar point a few years later in a pamphlet entitled "The Coming Struggle, or, What the People on the Pacific Coast Think of the Coolie Invasion" (1873):

Can you change the *nature* of an institution with a new name affixed? Is it not the same old coon? .... Are the results of chattel slaves any more pleasing to the people, or safe to the country, because it is dubbed with the specious name of coolie? .... [B]efore the manacles, cutlasses and whipping-posts are out of sight the same old monster, ever ready for an opportunity to doom the liberty and

---

failed attempt to remove "white" from the naturalization law in 1870 was resisted on the grounds that it would open the door to Chinese citizenship and voting.
[141] See also Yang 2020.
[142] *Congressional Record*, 41st Congress, 2d Session, U.S. Senate, July 4, 1870, 5151.

living of the common people, is seen slowly rising out of the western waters, with a long, Black tail instead of a kinkey head.[143]

Having defeated the Slave Power once, the "common people" would not be fooled by its attempted reincarnation: *the Chinese had to go.*[144] After the California legislature amended the state constitution in 1879, Article XIX stated in part: "Asiatic coolieism is a form of human slavery, and is forever prohibited in this State; and all contracts for coolie labor shall be void."[145]

The Workingmen's Party, which spearheaded the Chinese exclusion movement in California, saw the growth of corporate power—the new "Money Power," akin to the old "Slave Power"—as a threat to their dream of an egalitarian society of white independent producers. They decried the proletarianization of the workforce that resulted from capital-intensive corporate mining (hydraulic and deep shaft) and corporate agriculture, and they advanced a comprehensive free-labor agenda, including higher wages, universal public education, and regulations to prevent land monopolies and control speculation.[146] Believing that Chinese "coolies" were instruments of economic warfare deployed by the Money Power against free labor, the Workingmen's Party took up the cry of Chinese exclusion in the name of antislavery. Rudi Batzell writes:

Drawing on the ideas and language of the anti-slavery tradition, the Workingmen saw their struggle as a sequel to the Civil War. They claimed the anti-slavery mantle as the new abolitionists, fighting against a corrupt combination of exploited Chinese labour and aristocratic corporations that was threatening to revive a social order akin to Southern slavery, thereby obliterating political democracy, the dignity of labour and freedom of speech.[147]

The Workingmen also claimed the mantle of John Brown, the famed white abolitionist who was executed, along with a number of Black abolitionists, for leading a raid on the federal armory at Harper's Ferry in 1859.

For all the talk of coolies, Chinese laborers who came to the U.S. in the nineteenth century were in fact voluntary migrants and laborers.

---

[143] Starr 1873, 41–42, 105. Italics in original.
[144] The Chinese laborer was also compared to, and thus helped to define, the white immigrant worker. See M. Jung 2008; Saxton 1995 [1971]. Fortunately for the white economic elite, white workers focused more on the threat of degraded, unfree labor from below than they did on economic exploitation from above. In their minds, Moon-Ho Jung writes, "[s]lavery, not capital, was the enemy of free labor" (2008, 55).
[145] See at: http://archives.cdn.sos.ca.gov/collections/1879/archive/1879-constitution.pdf.
[146] Batzell 2014.
[147] Batzell 2014, 181.

Their free migration was recognized in official U.S. government documents—directly in the text of the Anti-Coolie Trade Act of 1862, which barred U.S. ships from participating in the global coolie trade, and indirectly in the Burlingame Treaty, which prohibited "any other than an entirely voluntary emigration" between the two nations.[148] Chinese laborers arrived in California via the credit-ticket system, whereby they pledged to pay back the price of their ocean transport, plus interest, to a labor brokerage company. Upon disembarking in San Francisco, they were met by representatives of the Chinese Six Companies, who enrolled them as members based upon village/clan affiliations and charged them an annual fee in return for help with housing, medical care, employment, and dispute mediation.[149] Although certain aspects of this system were exploitative—interest rates on the travel loans were typically high, for example—Chinese workers enjoyed a number of qualified freedoms as wage laborers, including personal mobility and occupational mobility.[150] Those who wished to make the voyage back to China had to obtain a certificate from the Chinese Six Companies attesting that all of their debts had been repaid, but how and where and how fast they earned wages was left to them to work out.

Coolies, on the other hand, were Chinese and Indian indentured laborers transported by British, European, and American ships to the Caribbean and Latin America to meet the enormous demand for labor unleashed by the cessation of the British slave trade. As Evelyn Hu-Dehart points out, Asian coolies were hailed as marking the progressive transition from slave labor to free wage labor in the global economic system.[151] The coolie system revolved around the labor contract, and was thus "voluntary," but brutal force and coercion marked every aspect of its operation. Coolies bound for Cuba were often "recruited" in China through deception, fraud, and kidnapping, and then transported to Cuba in retrofitted slave ships, where they often died and sometimes mutinied. On Cuban plantations, multi-year indentures constrained the coolies' mobility even as they were subjected to harsh violence by plantation owners and labor bosses—a situation that produced high mortality and suicide

---

[148] See at: http://academic.udayton.edu/race/02rights/treaty1868.htm. Also, an 1885 law banned the immigration of aliens under labor contracts.

[149] Batzell 2014.

[150] This freedom of movement was not unlimited. Those who did not pay back their debts according to the terms of the credit-ticket system were prevented by the Chinese Six Companies from returning to China.

[151] Hu-Dehart 1993. See also Lowe 2015; M. Jung 2008.

rates. Coolies who sought to move on after finishing a labor contract became entangled in a legal nightmare where "recontracting" rules, "renewal clauses," and other legal loopholes permitted some employers to extend indentures indefinitely.[152]

Chinese laborer = coolie = slave contained a double elision: between the Chinese laborer and the coolie, and between the coolie and the slave. Chinese laborers in California were clearly not slaves but the mediating term of "coolie" brought the two terms into plausible relation with each other. In this sense, the term "coolie" enabled the imaginative transference of Blackness onto the Chinese immigrant, for the specific purposes of promoting exclusion. During public testimony organized by the California State Senate's Special Committee on Chinese Immigration in 1878, officials repeatedly asked witnesses whether they believed Chinese laborers in California were "coolies."[153] Some demurred, others expressed opinions, but the answers were beside the point. It was the insistent, leading manner in which the question was posed and its ritualistic repetition throughout the hearings that sutured the Chinese laborer with the "coolie" (and, transitively, the slave) in the public mind. John Chinaman, already weighted down by immutable cultural difference, found himself befouled by Blackness as well.

IX COOLIES AND SLAVES

The role of Chinese coolies in the nineteenth-century Caribbean plantation system hinged on their not-Blackness. Coolies were brought in not only to supplement slave labor as the availability of slaves diminished, but also to discipline slaves and hinder slave rebellion through the introduction of another not-Black group. Colonial powers like Britain and Spain developed plantation management strategies that self-consciously exploited the structural gap between Asians and Africans. In *The Intimacies of Four Continents* (2015), Lisa Lowe documents British ruminations on this practice. In 1803, colonial administrator John

---

[152] Yun 2008.

[153] See the report produced by this committee, *Chinese Immigration: Its Social, Moral, and Political Effect* (1878). Both this report and *The Chinese Question* (1870)—which stipulated that "fully nine-tenths" of the Chinese in California were coolies, "i.e., persons who are to all intents and purposes practically as complete slaves to their masters as ever were the Negroes of the Carolinas and Georgia" (4)—conflated Chinese laborers with coolies and slaves. Both also reprised the common characterization of Chinese female prostitutes as slaves.

Sullivan wrote a "Secret Memorandum from the British Colonial Office to the Chairman of the Court of Directors of the East India Company," in which he suggested that introducing Chinese coolies into Trinidad would help to insulate the British colony from the kind of Black insurrection going on in Saint Domingue:

> [N]o measure would so effectually tend to provide a security against this danger, as that of introducing a free race of cultivators into our islands, who, from habits and feelings could be kept distinct from the Negroes, and who from interest would be inseparably attached to the European proprietors .... The Chinese people ... unite the qualities which constitute this double recommendation.[154]

The Chinese would provide a natural firewall against Black revolt. They already believed themselves superior to Black people and shared with whites a material investment in Black subjugation. They were ready-made allies in the defense of structural anti-Blackness.[155]

Archibald Gloster, Attorney-General for Trinidad, expounded on the point:

> [The Chinese] will be a barrier between us and the Negroes, with whom they do not associate; & consequently to whom they will always offer formidable opposition. The substituting of their labour instead of Negro labour is out of the question, as to the common business of the plantation. They are not habituated to it, nor will they take to it in the same way, not can we force them by the same methods; but their industrious habits, and constitutional strength, will I think greatly aid the planters. They will cut and weed cane. They will attend about our mills. They will act as mechanics.[156]

The Chinese, being ineligible for enslavement, could not be forced to do "the common business of the plantation," and could therefore not substitute for Black slaves tout court, but their not-Blackness made them well suited to act as a buffer between Black slaves and whites. Lisa Lowe writes: "The introduction of the Chinese into the slave plantation economy was in this way described in terms of a need for a nominally 'free' labor force, one that would not substitute for the slaves, but would perform different labors and would be distinguished racially and socially from both the white European colonial planters and the Black slaves."[157] Bringing Chinese women to Trinidad and growing the Chinese population there reflected "[the white] fantasy of Chinese family civility [a]s

[154] Quoted in Lowe 2015, 22–23.
[155] Similar issues arose with Chinese immigrants in Jamaica. See Johnson 1983.
[156] Lowe 2015, 31.
[157] Lowe 2015, 31.

a way of marking a racial difference between 'Chinese free labor' and 'Negro slaves,' through imagining the Chinese as closer to liberal ideas of human person, family, and society."[158]

Despite being favored over slaves, Chinese coolies in the Caribbean were grievously mistreated and dramatic stories of their mutinies became more frequent. By 1860, with the nation on the verge of civil war over slavery, the U.S. Congress commissioned Representative Thomas Eliot of Massachusetts to prepare a report on the participation of American ships in the global coolie trade. Eliot, a Republican who would later serve as Chairman of the Committee on Freedmen's Affairs, attempted to whip up moral outrage against the trade by cataloging its atrocities. His principal rhetorical strategy was likening coolieism to African slavery, which he opposed. As we read the report, however, we cannot help but notice that analogizing coolieism to slavery tends to increase our sympathy for the coolie while diminishing our concern for the slave. Frank Wilderson calls this "the ruse of analogy," whereby the political use of the slave analogy tends to make other causes more visible and Black abjection *less* visible.[159]

The report states: "From the moment of his capture the coolie is a slave. He is the subject, first, of the meanest deception, and then of a servitude in no respect practically different from that which the confessed African slave trade binds upon its victim."[160] But Eliot quickly amends this claim: the coolie trade, he contends, *surpasses* the slave trade in its inhumanity. It is "as bad, if not worse, than … the African slave trade," "exceeding the horrors of the 'Middle Passage,'" "one degree worse than the slave trade," and "a state of slavery more horrible than any yet recorded."[161] Eliot continues:

In one respect it [the coolie trade] is more abhorrent to an honorable mind than that trade which the civilized world condemns as piracy. The captured African is not made to believe that he is changing his condition for the better; but the Asiatic coolie is entrapped and deceived by false pretences of promised gain into the power of men who, having cheated him of his freedom, enslave him for gain.[162]

[158] Lowe 2015, 33.
[159] Wilderson 2010.
[160] *Congressional Record*, 36th Congress, 1st Session, U.S. House of Representatives, April 16, 1860, Report No. 443, 3.
[161] *Congressional Record*, 36th Congress, 1st Session, U.S. House of Representatives, April 16, 1860, Report No. 443, 5, 6, 7, 15.
[162] *Congressional Record*, 36th Congress, 1st Session, U.S. House of Representatives, April 16, 1860, Report No. 443, 5.

The capture of the African is a violent but straightforward event. However, the capture of the coolie, possessor of a meaningful freedom, cruelly engages his heart, mind, and imagination. The coolie is made to dream a false dream, and in this respect, he is worse off than the slave. The reader is left to wonder if coolieism is worse than slavery not because the objective conditions are harsher but because of the nature of the being who is victimized. *The Chinese were not meant for slavery.*

Eliot's report cites a letter sent by the Honorable William Reed, U.S. Minister to China, to U.S. government officials, wherein Reed wrote of Chinese coolies: "Think of it for a moment ... *human beings*, having parents, wives, children, brothers and sisters, and all the human sensibilities and sympathies like ourselves."[163] Reed continued:

[T]he Asiatic coolie is more helpless than the African slave. The slave is claimed by someone as his property. It may be for the interest of an owner to support the health and promote the physical strength of his bondman. He is obliged by law to maintain him in sickness and in old age. The interest of the planter who buys the services of a coolie for a specified time is to get from him, during that time, the maximum amount of labor.[164]

In an effort to free the coolie, Reed, writing on the cusp of the Civil War, risked tightening the bonds of the slave. His assessment of slavery was, to say the least, unduly rosy, echoing the southern slaveholder's defense of the institution and northern white labor's claim that "wage slavery" was even worse.[165]

Does contracting one's labor, even under exploitative and coercive conditions, make one more helpless than a person reduced to chattel, or movable property? Does not being property, an "object made available for any subject," mark the outer limit of helplessness? Did slaveholders, as a matter of historical record, actually "support the health and promote the physical strength" of slaves? Was their treatment of slaves guided exclusively, or even principally, by rational thought and behavior? Or did the "bloodstained gate" of slavery described by Frederick Douglass rather reveal something else? How do we account for the slaveholders who committed acts of torture, rape, mutilation, dismemberment, and murder against slaves?[166] What do we make of Reed's

---

[163] *Congressional Record*, 36th Congress, 1st Session, U.S. House of Representatives, April 16, 1860, Report No. 443, 18. Italics in original.

[164] *Congressional Record*, 36th Congress, 1st Session, U.S. House of Representatives, April 16, 1860, Report No. 443, 29.

[165] See Fredrickson 1971; Ignatiev 2009 [1995].

[166] Marriott 2000.

interpretation of slavery as a health insurance and social welfare program for Black people?

Eliot's report achieved its goal: two years after its release, Congress passed the Anti-Coolie Trade Act (1862) banning the participation of American ships in the global coolie trade. (This did not affect the immigration of Chinese laborers to California, as they were voluntary migrants and laborers.) What accounts for this expression of official solicitude for the coolie? Many Republicans doubtless supported the law as an extension of their antislavery posture. But a contradictory motive may have been at work as well. In 1853, Humphrey Marshall, the U.S. Commissioner to China, had written to inform the U.S. secretary of state of the growing interest British Caribbean colonies had in importing Chinese coolies as plantation labor. That Marshall worried this development would favor British colonial planters in their economic competition with U.S. southern planters raises the possibility that some in Congress may have moved against the coolie trade to protect U.S. slaveholders.[167]

Lisa Yun's *The Coolie Speaks: Chinese Indentured Laborers and African Slaves in Cuba* (2008) argues that Chinese coolies in Cuba were effectively slaves. She writes: "[Coolies were] enslaved by the very structures of 'free' society and 'contractual' society based upon concepts of self-ownership."[168] Emphasizing that coolies were decoyed or kidnapped, forced to sign "papers" (labor contracts), physically abused and cruelly mistreated, and tricked into successive terms of servitude, Yun asserts that their "papers" were mere fictions disguising their slave status. Indeed, she sees "papers" serving as "the main tool for creating and maintaining [coolies'] enslavement."[169] Granting the point that Chinese coolies in Cuba were unfree and suffered greatly, does it follow from this that they were slaves?

Coolies were far fewer in number than Black slaves in Cuba: the 1862 Census showed 368,550 slaves and 34,050 coolies, or 27.1 and 2.5 percent of the overall population, respectively.[170] Spanish colonial law in Cuba distinguished between African slaves (*esclavos*) and Chinese coolies, who were described as *hombres libres* (free men) and *colonos*

---

[167] Cohen 1984.
[168] Yun 2008, xxi.
[169] Yun 2008, 111.
[170] Scott 1985, 7. Between 1847 and 1874, 125,000 Chinese laborers came to Cuba as coolies (Scott 1985, 29).

Asiaticos (Asian colonists/settlers)—terms that emphasized their voluntary migration and "free" labor (i.e., not-slave) status. Spanish Cuba,
like British Trinidad, was a Caribbean node in global circuits of anti-
Blackness. One finds other traces of the Asian–Black gap in Spanish
colonial law in Cuba. One government regulation forbade the beating of
coolies by overseers in "sight of the Blacks."[171] Reproducing the racial
hierarchy meant preserving *both* white supremacy over the Chinese *and*
Chinese supremacy over Blacks. Additionally, slaves were sold from one
master to another, but with coolies, it was their contracts that were
sold from one employer to another—a legal difference that expressed the
distinction between property and person. In 1864, the Administrative
Council in Cuba ruled that a coolie contract could not be sold to a free
Black person:

Although today there is no special provision that prohibits the Black race from
having superior races in its service, the political and social order, in harmony with
nature itself ... repudiates the disciplinary dependence of superior races under the
power of the inferior ones .... It has been constantly observed on the Island that
if the immigration of Asian colonists has not yet produced all of the advantages
that one could have hoped for, one of the most notable obstacles has been the
constant concurrence of Black bondage, looked at with repugnance by the Asians,
who naturally resist the idea of equality.[172]

It would be a violation of nature for a coolie's contract to be owned
by a Black. The Chinese coolie considered himself above any Black person, slave or free, because as an Asian, he was constitutively not-Black.
Chinese coolies in Cuba asserted this prerogative and were often met, as
in this administrative ruling, with white agreement.

   Plantation housing reflected principles of racial hierarchy and separation, so coolies were housed separately from slaves, the better to encourage their supposedly natural phobic aversion to Blackness. On Cuban
sugar plantations, work was often allocated according to an ethnological
hierarchy of aptitude and worth, by which the coolie was better suited to
working with machinery and to the skilled work of processing and refin-
ing sugar, while the slave was suited for "the dreary, mindless, bloody
work of cane harvesting."[173] Eliza McHatton Ripley, owner of a Cuban
plantation, summarized the consensus on Chinese–Black difference:
"Long before a Chinese understands enough of a foreign tongue to make

[171] Young 2014, 77.
[172] Quoted in Young 2014, 77.
[173] Guterl 2003, 219.

his simplest wants known, he understands and fulfills the duties faithfully that a negro grows gray trying to perform."[174]

During a visit to Cuba in 1874, British army captain Frederick Townshend observed that Chinese coolies were elevated above slaves in some ways and treated the same as slaves in other ways. In this situation, Townshend, echoing Representative Thomas Eliot, found the coolies especially deserving of sympathy:

Though the fate of the poor African slave in Cuba is horrible, that of the unfortunate Asiatic, who is serving under contract, struck me as even more pitiable. The wan face, feeble frame, and dejected looks of the wretched Chinamen were absolutely painful to see. *Having enjoyed the blessings of freedom up to the hour when his evil fate led him to quit his native country*, the poor Chinaman is ill-treated on board ship in a fearful manner, and on reaching Cuba, is bought, sold, subjected to the lash, and compelled to work like the negro slaves. *Against such treatment his natural intelligence, and inborn sense of freedom rebel*, and he either runs away and engages himself in some trade in the large towns, or goes about a miserable and heart-broken wretch.[175]

What kind of being was the Chinese coolie to produce this affective response in the white observer? Compared to a white man, the Chinese coolie was a lowly, unmanly wretch, but compared to the "negro slave," he was a proud, intelligent man born to the entitlement of natural freedom. Contra Yun, Townshend does not read the coolie's proximity to the slave in the sugar cane fields as an indication that the coolie *was* a slave. To the contrary, he observes that this association was an *affront* to coolies, who knew themselves to be free men, not slaves. What made plantation work "more pitiable" for the Chinese coolie was that his "natural intelligence" and "inborn sense of freedom" made working in proximity to slaves intolerable. The coolie was broken not by arduous labor but by the dishonor of being treated like a slave.

Yun argues that the legal and procedural distinctions made between coolie and slave in Cuba were empty technicalities and part of an ideological ploy to "divide and conquer" the plantation labor force. The classification of the Chinese coolie as *un hombre libre*, she argues, like the system of "papers," was a masterful fiction designed to facilitate his enslavement. The "divide and conquer" argument, however, implies

---

[174] From Ripley's 1889 autobiography *From Flag to Flag: A Woman's Adventures and Experiences in the South During the War, in Mexico, and in Cuba*, quoted in E. Wong 2015, 42.
[175] Young 2014, 55–56. Italics added.

some earlier stage of nondividedness or organic unity between the Chinese and Africans in Cuba. Such a stage never existed. In fact, ethnological differentiation between the two groups—as evidenced in Spanish colonial law and the structuring of work and life on the plantation—had been baked into the anti-Black global imaginary for centuries by the time they met on the Cuban plantation. The coolie–slave distinction was not an eleventh-hour invention of scheming Cuban planters but an artifact of the ontological scaffolding of modernity itself.

Even though the labor contract was often fraudulently secured and inadequately enforced, it nevertheless provided a regulatory structure that shaped the coolie's relations with the plantation owner in important ways. The contract specified wages and terms of service, and both the coolie and the plantation owner routinely invoked its language in their negotiations with the other. Plantation owner Eliza McHatton Ripley recalled: "The poorest, lowest coolie carried his contract on his person, and never hesitated to assert his rights."[176] Coolies knew they were not slaves and demanded recognition of this. The fact that the coolie's "papers" did not mean all that they were purported to mean does not indicate that they were therefore meaningless. "Papers" did not make the coolie a free laborer, a liberal subject, or an autonomous, rights-bearing individual. But they did function as an ontological marker of sorts, tagging the coolie as not-property, as not-slave, as a being who *had to consent to be coerced.* This is why coolie-traders held Chinese men in barracoons in Chinese port cities for weeks and even months, beating them and starving them until they agreed to sign contracts committing them to labor on Cuban plantations. (If they were illiterate, they could simply write an "X.") The coolie was different from the slave not because he was at all times treated better than the slave but because he was considered a custodian of his own freedom, and so he had to consent to its surrender, even if the consent was obtained through force. The opposite of free choice was not coerced choice; it was being thought, like the slave, to have no relation to choice at all. What Elliott Young noted about coolies in Peru was also true of Cuba: "The contracts were tiny fig leaves covering the shame of the conditions of coolie labor, but these were extremely important fig leaves."[177]

In 1874, responding to reports of the horrors of the coolie trade, the Chinese government sent a commission to investigate the plight of

---

[176] Ripley, *From Flag to Flag* (1889), quoted in E. Wong 2015, 45.
[177] Young 2014, 65.

coolies in Cuba.[178] Emerging out of China's consultation with the five great Western powers (Russia, the U.S., the U.K., France, and Germany), the commission contained representatives of Britain and France, as well as China. Momentously, China was asserting its sovereign power on the global stage, insisting upon its prerogative to protect its subjects against Western (in this case, Spanish) imperialist depredations and placating domestic critics clamoring for action against the coolie trade.[179] The symbolism was unmistakable: China was joining with two leading European powers to police a third. China was taking its place in the Family of Nations.

The commission traveled throughout the island, conducting 1,176 in-person depositions with Chinese coolies and collecting 85 petitions with a total of 1,665 signatures. Its final report juxtaposed the formal rights and protections provided to coolies (according to international conventions, Chinese law, Spanish colonial law, and labor contracts) with their actual experiences. With regard to the latter, the report allowed coolies to speak for themselves, and the result was a torrential record of physical suffering and grief, of suicide and murder, of anger and hopelessness. Almost all coolies (eight or nine out of ten) were taken against their will initially—decoyed, tricked, or kidnapped. They were then detained and beaten until they signed contracts. One recalled: "[T]he Portuguese official then forcibly seized my hand and when it had marked the paper took the latter away."[180] Once in Cuba, they were underfed, overworked, whipped, chained, and abused by overseers and planters. After the indenture terms were over, employers withheld certificates of completion to force coolies into renewing their contracts; if the coolies refused, they were arrested and taken to depots where they were forced to labor on public works projects with no wages until they agreed to sign a new labor contract.

The severity of the coolies' experience inevitably raised the question of slavery.[181] Section XXX of the report is entitled "The contract coolie is a man who has pledged himself to work according to contract for a term

---

[178] The lead commissioner was Chen Lanpin, who was also the first Chinese minister plenipotentiary to arrive in San Francisco after the Burlingame Treaty of 1868 established a Chinese consular office in the U.S. Chen Lanpin lobbied Congress to stop the Exclusion Act of 1882, which prompted President Hayes to send James Angell to negotiate a new treaty with China (H. Liu 2003).

[179] Metzger 2008; H. Liu 2003.

[180] *Report of the Commission Sent by China to Ascertain the Condition of Chinese Coolies in Cuba* (1970 [1876]), 10.

[181] African slavery in Cuba dated back to the 1500s and was not formally abolished until 1886.

of years: he is not a slave. Is he treated as a man who has consented to be bound by a contract, or as a slave? Are there slaves in Cuba—or were there, and what is or was their treatment?"[182] What is asserted here is the legal distinction between the slave, bound by nature and for life, and the coolie, "who has consented to be bound by a contract." The treatment of the coolies, the report asserts, was objectionable precisely because it collapsed this distinction, reducing them to slaves. Despite the promise of the section title, the report does not discuss the presence and treatment of African slaves themselves; rather, it cites one coolie after another saying that they are treated exactly like slaves. Slaves, in absentia, serve as the index of the abject, the marker of the boundary of the human.

Rather than reading this testimony as evidence that coolies *were* slaves, Rebecca Scott, in *Slave Emancipation in Cuba: The Transition to Free Labor, 1860–1899* (1985), writes:

An examination of the *treatment* of Chinese contract laborers by planters, however, does not tell the whole story of their situation. Equally striking as the reports of abuses are the accounts of protests and complaints by the Chinese workers themselves. It is clear from the commission report that these indentured laborers were aware of a distinction between slave labor and free, one which they felt was not being observed. Many believed that they were being treated as slaves by an incomparably barbarous group of foreigners who refused to recognize them as free men.[183]

The coolies' testimony shows that they jealously guarded their superior status to slaves. In bemoaning the collapse of the coolie–slave distinction, the coolies affirmed its continued relevance. "We are treated like slaves" contained the assertion "We are not slaves." It was the lament of those who knew they deserved better. To be treated "like a slave" was to be deprived of the freedom, dignity, and honor one naturally and rightfully possessed as someone who was not a slave. For not-Blacks, to be treated "like a slave" was to be the casualty of a potentially fatal misreading. A few years after the commission issued its damning report, China moved to halt the coolie trade to Cuba. In the end, the *colonos Asiaticos* in Cuba found their bearings against the abject figure of the African slave.

In 1879, a half-decade after the Chinese commission in Cuba wrapped up its work, President Rutherford Hayes vetoed a Chinese exclusion bill that he thought violated the Burlingame Treaty. He then pressed China

---

[182] *Report of the Commission Sent by China to Ascertain the Condition of Chinese Coolies in Cuba* (1970 [1876]), 58.
[183] Scott 1985, 33. Italics in original.

into hurriedly negotiating a new treaty with the U.S. In the Angell Treaty of 1880, China agreed that the U.S. could regulate, limit, or suspend but "not absolutely prohibit" Chinese immigration, and that it could restrict the entry of only laborers and not "other classes." For its part, the U.S. government promised to "exert all its power to devise measures for their [Chinese migrants'] protection and to secure them the same rights, privileges, immunities, and exemptions as may be enjoyed by the citizens or subjects of the most favored nation, and to which they are entitled by treaty."[184] Eager for U.S. support in its struggle with Japan over the Okinawa Islands, China agreed to a dramatic restriction in Chinese migration to the U.S.[185]

Congress enacted Chinese exclusion in 1882. The final legislation was called An Act to Inaugurate Certain Treaty Stipulations Relating to Chinese, a benign title that helped the Chinese save face by suggesting more bilateralism than actually pertained. But the language of mutual cooperation was not entirely disingenuous. The urgent negotiation of the Angell Treaty, like the Portuguese official grabbing the Chinese prisoner's hand and forcing him to sign, like the system of "papers" ensnaring the coolie, expressed *the necessity of procuring, even if through coercion, the Asiatic's consent to their own subjugation.* U.S. officials were intent upon restricting Chinese migration, and they asked for and received China's permission to do so.

Over a decade later, the San Francisco-based satirical magazine *The Wasp* published a drawing entitled "The Question of the Hour," featuring a monstrous creature who is both a species hybrid (human and animal) and a racial hybrid (Chinese and Black).[186] The creature has a tag labelled "The Geary Act" hanging around its neck and is tied to a pole labelled "Constitutional Law." Lying on its stomach with its chin resting on its hands, it grins broadly as a flustered Uncle Sam stands over it, muttering: "Gosh! I've got this critter lassoed right enough but how in thunder am I going to git him over thar to China?" The "question of the hour" was the unfinished business of Chinese exclusion: how to get hold of the Chinese laborers still living in the U.S., remove them from the aegis

---

[184] See at: https://china.usc.edu/sites/default/files/forums/ANGELL%20TREATY.doc.

[185] H. Liu 2003.

[186] *The Wasp*, January–June 1893, 10–11; www.latinamericanstudies.org/chinese-immigrants-2.htm. Although this drawing is undated, it mentions the Geary Act, so it is safe to assume that it was published after 1892. In *The Wasp*, the Chinese were most frequently depicted as pestilential animals (wild pigs, grasshoppers) or dragon-like monsters, but not as apes, suggesting that they were viewed as an ominous threat but not as actual transitional figures between humans and beasts. See C. Kim 2015.

of constitutional law, and expel them from the nation. The Geary Act of 1892, which extended the 1882 Exclusion Act's provisions and instituted a resident permit system for all Chinese living in the U.S., disciplined and controlled their movement, but stopped short of effecting their expulsion.

Dan Caldwell reads this image as demonstrating the "Negroization" of the Chinese in late nineteenth-century California.[187] We know that the figure of the coolie enabled the transference of Blackness to the Chinese, bolstering the case for their exclusion. But the references to China, the Geary Act, and constitutional law in *The Wasp* drawing indicate that there is more going on in this scene. This is a scene structured by law and right, a scene premised on relations between sovereign powers. It depicts not "an object available for any subject" but, to the contrary, a figure whose immunities from violation are driving Uncle Sam to distraction. Even when contingently Blackened in the struggle over exclusion, the Chinese laborer is (at least partially) protected by his constitutive not-Blackness. The creature is tied by a rope to the pole labelled "Constitutional Law," and it is clear that the rope secures it against those who would fling it out of the nation. Hence the satisfied smile.

Chinese foreignness, then, was not an analogue of anti-Blackness, an equivalent form of racism that developed on a track parallel to it, but rather a phenomenon that was birthed and contoured *in relation to anti-Blackness*. The foreignness of the Chinese indexed, simultaneously, their exclusion from the American nation and their belonging in human relationality and considerablity. In this sense, Chinese foreignness was a space of persecution and dispossession that was also, more fundamentally, a space of standing and recognition. Harassed, despised, persecuted, and expelled, the Chinese still retained property of inestimable value—their not-Blackness.[188] They still had "something to save." Barred from entry into the nation, John Chinaman was rescued by the slave from an even more terrible fate.

X *THE SLAUGHTER-HOUSE CASES*

Meanwhile, as the "Chinese problem" was getting sorted, the reconsolidation of structural anti-Blackness proceeded apace in the postbellum period. We have seen that southern states passed Black Codes to restrict freedpeople's mobility, force them to remain on the plantation, and

---

[187] Caldwell 1971.
[188] See Cheryl Harris (1993) on "whiteness as property." See also the discussion of *Plessy v. Ferguson* (1896) below.

reproduce as nearly as possible the economic and social relations of slavery. Congressional Republicans called out the Black Codes for imposing "badges of servitude" on freedpeople, and in an attempt to override these laws, Senator Lyman Trumbull of Illinois introduced the bill that would become the Civil Rights Act of 1866. In addition to establishing Black (birthright) citizenship for the first time, it attempted to secure Black people's rights of contract, property, and person:

[C]itizens, of every race and color, without regard to any previous condition of slavery or involuntary servitude, except as a punishment for crime whereof the party shall have been duly convicted, shall have the same right, in every State and Territory in the United States, to make and enforce contracts, to sue, be parties, and give evidence, to inherit, purchase, lease, sell, hold, and convey real and personal property, and to full and equal benefit of all laws and proceedings for the security of person and property, as is enjoyed by white citizens, and shall be subject to like punishment, pains, and penalties, and to none other, any law, statute, ordinance, regulation, or custom, to the contrary notwithstanding.[189]

Opponents accused the bill of overreach, insisting that the Thirteenth Amendment meant only to strike down the formal institution of slavery and nothing more. The bill exceeded this mandate, they argued, by going beyond civil equality to *social equality*—a fateful move that augured the end of white civilization. Would the bill in question prohibit his state's practice of segregating school children by race, Senator Edgar Cowan of Pennsylvania wanted to know?[190] Would it, asked Senator Reverdy Johnson of Maryland, force the repeal of anti-miscegenation laws?[191] The go-to tactic of those who opposed racial reform, whether in the South or North, was to warn of the slippery slope between the proposed reform and interracial sex. Reform would lead to miscegenation and Black rape, which in turn would lead to the destruction of the white race. (Selectively) maintaining the sexual and reproductive barrier between whites and Blacks was imperative.

The bill's proponents offered assurances that this firewall would be left intact. Trumbull explained that anti-miscegenation laws would not be affected insofar as these applied equally to whites and Blacks and were therefore not "discriminatory" under the proposed law. Representative James Wilson of Iowa introduced the bill into the House of Representatives with these words:

[189] The Civil Rights Act of 1866. See at: https://en.wikisource.org/wiki/Civil_Rights_ Act_of_1866.
[190] Avins 1967, 127.
[191] Avins 1967, 128.

[The bill] provides for the equality of citizens of the United States in the enjoyment of "civil rights and immunities." What do these terms mean? Do they mean that in all things civil, social, political, all citizens, without distinction of race or color, shall be equal? By no means can they be so construed. Do they mean that all citizens shall vote in the several States? No; for suffrage is a political right which has been left under the control of the several States, subject to the action of Congress only when it becomes necessary to enforce the guarantee of a republican form of government (protection against a monarchy). Nor do they mean that all citizens shall sit on the juries, or that their children shall attend the same schools. The definition given to the term "civil rights" in Bouvier's Law Dictionary is very concise, and is supported by the best authority. It is this: "Civil rights are those which have no relation to the establishment, support, or management of government."[192]

Wilson anxiously assured his colleagues of all that the bill *would not do*, of how many areas of life it would *not disturb*. The bill would *not* provide for political rights, it would *not* offer social equality, it would *not* mean that "in all things civil" Blacks would receive equal treatment. Rather, it would secure for Blacks the minimum entitlements associated with non-slave status. Reassured about its limited scope, Congress passed the bill.

Despite its limitations, the Civil Rights Act of 1866 did "effectively nationalize" civil rights, making them a matter of federal concern for the first time.[193] Less than a decade later, in its first official interpretation of the Thirteenth and Fourteenth Amendments, the U.S. Supreme Court rendered a decision that effectively denationalized civil rights again, returning them to the exclusive jurisdiction of the states. *The Slaughter-House Cases* (1873) concerned a 1869 Louisiana law that vested a single New Orleans corporation with the exclusive privilege of building and operating stock-landings and slaughterhouse facilities in New Orleans and surrounding parishes, forcing butchers to use only these facilities (and for a fee). The ostensible purpose of the legislation was to protect public welfare by regulating the slaughtering of animals. The plaintiffs, a group of white butchers, contended that the law violated the Thirteenth Amendment's prohibition on involuntary servitude, as well as the Fourteenth Amendment's privileges and immunities, equal protection, and due process clauses.

The plaintiffs' attorney was John Campbell, who had resigned from the U.S. Supreme Court to join the Confederacy during the Civil War

---

[192] *Congressional Globe*, 39th Congress, 1st Session, U.S. House of Representatives, March 1, 1866, 1117.
[193] Gressman 1952, 1326. The Civil Rights Act of 1866 covered both state action and private/individual action.

and later served as assistant secretary of war to Jefferson Davis. The lawsuit was but one prong of Campbell's multifarious campaign to continue waging the Civil War by nonmilitary means.[194] Having set his sights on the Republican-controlled Reconstruction legislature in Louisiana, Campbell carefully "portray[ed] the slaughterhouse corporation as the corrupt venture of carpetbaggers and their Black lackeys."[195] After persuading the federal district court that the slaughterhouse law created "a corrupt monopoly that unconstitutionally denied the butchers their 'right to exercise their trade,'" Campbell argued in front of the U.S. Supreme Court that the Louisiana legislature was oppressing the white butchers and "went so far as to assert that the Fourteenth Amendment had been framed not to protect African Americans but to shield whites from governments in which uneducated Blacks and immigrants participated."[196]

Justice Samuel Miller, writing for the majority, rejected Campbell's arguments and upheld the Louisiana state law as a legitimate exercise of police power for the general welfare. "The obvious purpose [of the Thirteenth Amendment]," he wrote, "was to forbid all shades and conditions of African slavery."[197] Indeed the "one pervading purpose" of the Reconstruction amendments was "the freedom of the slave race, the security and firm establishment of that freedom, and the protection of the newly made freeman and citizen from the oppressions of those who had formerly exercised unlimited dominion over him."[198] So while the amendments were not restricted to Black people, Miller insisted that "the language and spirit" of the amendments should "have their fair and just weight in any question of construction,"[199] thus discouraging a "microscopic search" for other applications.[200] The Louisiana law, Miller declared, did not deprive the butcher of "the right to labor,"[201] "destroy the business of the butcher, or seriously interfere with its pursuit,"[202] let alone subject him to involuntary servitude.

There were no Black rights directly at stake in this case. Miller's forceful statements had less to do with his commitment to advancing Black

---

[194] Ross 2003.
[195] Ross 2003, 245.
[196] Ross 2003, 250.
[197] *The Slaughter-House Cases* (1873), 69.
[198] *The Slaughter-House Cases* (1873), 72.
[199] *The Slaughter-House Cases* (1873), 72.
[200] *The Slaughter-House Cases* (1873), 69.
[201] *The Slaughter-House Cases* (1873), 61.
[202] *The Slaughter-House Cases* (1873), 62.

rights and more to do with his desire to narrow the application of the amendments so that they would not offer other groups an opening for making claims against the state. Indeed, his reading of the Fourteenth Amendment in particular delivered a staggering blow to civil rights. According to Miller, the first section of the Fourteenth Amendment specified that citizenship of the United States and citizenship of a state were two distinct things.[203] Further, the amendment's privileges and immunities clause—"No State shall make or enforce any law which shall abridge the privileges or immunities of *citizens of the United States*"[204]—applied only to the former, not to the latter. In Miller's view, this meant that safeguarding the rights and privileges that attached to state citizenship (which included the "fundamental rights" specified in the Civil Rights Act of 1866) was left to the states and was beyond the domain of federal action.[205] No one, including Black people, could look to the federal government to enforce civil rights. With this ruling, Miller undercut the purpose of the Civil Rights Act, which was precisely to bring federal power to bear in thwarting the racially discriminatory actions of the states. Congressional debates indicate that the framers of the Fourteenth Amendment actually meant for the privileges and immunities clause to apply to "fundamental rights," but Miller refused to countenance this expanded congressional power over the states.[206]

Justice Stephen Field, dissenting, challenged Miller's interpretation of both the Thirteenth and Fourteenth Amendments, arguing that both protected the butchers against deprivation of their rights by state legislation. Drawing on the Civil Rights Act of 1866, whose sponsors said that denial of civil rights constituted involuntary servitude, Field argued

---

[203] Section I of the Fourteenth Amendment states: "All persons born or naturalized in the United States, and subject to the jurisdiction thereof, are citizens of the United States and of the state wherein they reside. No state shall make or enforce any law which shall abridge the privileges or immunities of citizens of the United States; nor shall any state deprive any person of life, liberty, or property, without due process of law; nor deny to any person within its jurisdiction the equal protection of the laws."

[204] Italics in the decision but not in the original.

[205] Democrats used the distinction made in *The Slaughter-House* Cases (that the Fourteenth Amendment protects the privileges of national citizenship but not the privileges of state citizenship) to argue against the Civil Rights Act of 1875, insisting that public accommodations were a privilege of state citizenship only and that Congress therefore had no power to regulate them. See Avins 1967.

[206] Was Miller trying to strip the privileges and immunities clause of meaning, affirm the biracial government of Louisiana, or preserve federalism? See Lurie (2005) and Gressman (1952) for discussion of this issue. Miller also dismissed the butchers' due-process and equal-protection claims.

that the Louisiana law, by impinging on the butchers' "right to pursue a lawful and necessary calling,"[207] was the "essence of slavery."[208] Field also argued that the Fourteenth Amendment had made citizenship of the United States dependent upon place of birth and not upon state laws, so that "[t]he fundamental rights, privileges, and immunities which belong to him as a free man and a free citizen now belong to him as a citizen of the United States, and are not dependent upon his citizenship of any State."[209] As such, these rights could not be abridged by state legislation: "The fourteenth amendment places them under the guardianship of the National Authority."[210]

Field's arguments grew out of a long tradition of white Americans describing their political and economic hardships as "slavery." During the War of Independence, colonists condemned British tyrants for "enslaving" them politically. White workers suffering the ravages of industrialization in the nineteenth century argued that their situation was one of "wage slavery."[211] The overriding question for these white workers, Amy Dru Stanley notes, was "whether the buying and selling of their labor as a market commodity rendered them like or unlike chattel slaves."[212] White workers often claimed that they were *worse off* than slaves because slaves supposedly received the basic necessities of life from slaveholders.[213] As David Roediger observes, the "very structure of the argument against white slavery typically carried proslavery implications."[214] Why did southern whites call a law compelling butchers to use a particular slaughterhouse "the essence of slavery" while denying that the term applied to the convict lease system in the postbellum South? Any restriction upon white male (economic) freedom was an abomination,

---

[207] Justice Stephen Field's dissent in *The Slaughter-House Cases* (1873), 88.
[208] Justice Stephen Field's dissent in *The Slaughter-House Cases* (1873), 90.
[209] Justice Stephen Field's dissent in *The Slaughter-House Cases* (1873), 95.
[210] Justice Stephen Field's dissent in *The Slaughter-House Cases* (1873), 101.
[211] Ignatiev 2009 [1995]; Roediger 2007 [1991].
[212] Stanley 1998, 82.
[213] Sinha 2017.
[214] Roediger 2007 [1991], 76. See Roediger (2007 [1991]) for a discussion of how white laborers compared themselves to Black slaves during the Jacksonian period and then turned to a "free labor" cry by the 1850s. When they alluded to their own situation as "white slavery," this was "not an act of solidarity with the slave but rather a call to arms to end the inappropriate oppression of whites" (Roediger 2007 [1991], 68). See Eric Foner (1988) as well for white labor's claims that white workers were worse off than Black slaves—that they worked longer hours, had less value returned to them, and were not assured of the protection of a master.

while the most egregious violations of Black male freedom did not register as violations in the first place.

In *The Slaughter-House Cases*, therefore, the majority ruled that civil rights were not a federal concern, and the dissenting justice insisted that they were and that white men's civil rights were being violated. Ironically, the champions of federal power in this case were Field, a Democrat who was no friend to Black people; the white butchers, who along with other Louisiana whites opposed the state's biracial Reconstruction government; and their lead attorney, former assistant secretary of war for the Confederacy, John Campbell. While racial slavery was reconstituting itself in a new form in the South, and the limits of Black "freedom" were everywhere making themselves clear, these men tried to commandeer the constitutional machinery of antislavery in defense of their white male prerogatives. Although they lost this small battle, they would soon taste victory when Reconstruction and its historic experiment in biracial governance collapsed.

XI *THE CIVIL RIGHTS CASES*

In 1870, Senator Charles Sumner, a Radical Republican, introduced a new civil rights bill providing that "all persons within the jurisdiction of the United States" would be entitled the "the full and equal enjoyment" of public accommodations such as inns, public conveyances, and theaters, subject only to laws applied without regard to race. During congressional debate, Democratic and Republican critics alike argued that public accommodations were not a "civil" matter but a "social" matter and condemned the bill for forcing together two races whom nature had clearly set apart. Sumner and Black Republicans in Congress offered assurances that the bill would leave social inequality intact. After they deleted language prohibiting school segregation by race in furtherance of this point, the bill was enacted as the Civil Rights Act of 1875.[215] Civil

---

[215] Avins 1967. The first section of the act read: "Be it enacted by the Senate and House of Representatives of the United States of America in Congress assembled, That all persons within the jurisdiction of the United States shall be entitled to the full and equal enjoyment of the accommodations, advantages, facilities, and privileges of inns, public conveyances on land or water, theaters, and other places of public amusement; subject only to the conditions and limitations established by law, and applicable alike to citizens of every race and color, regardless of any previous condition of servitude." (The legislative record demonstrates that the bill meant "all persons" to include the Chinese.) See at: https://sharetngov.tnsosfiles.com/tsla/exhibits/aale/pdfs2/1875CivilRightsAct.pdf.

rights for Black people could only be granted once Black abjection had been ritualistically affirmed, after which the rights were soon nullified on paper and/or in practice.

A decade after the U.S. Supreme Court decided *The Slaughter-House Cases*, it struck down the Civil Rights Act of 1875 in *The Civil Rights Cases* (1883). John Hope Franklin argues that the statute was a dead letter from the start, referring to whites' broad determination to resist it, especially but not only in the South.[216] Consolidating five cases involving anti-Black discrimination in public accommodations, *The Civil Rights Cases* finalized the denationalization (i.e., evisceration) of civil rights enforcement.[217] Justice Joseph Bradley, who wrote for the majority, had been the tiebreaker on the special electoral commission set up to adjudicate the contested presidential election of 1876 and had thus been party to the Compromise of 1877, by which Republican Rutherford Hayes secured the U.S. presidency with the promise to dismantle Reconstruction and grant southern states "home rule." Bradley's imperative in *The Civil Rights Cases*, according to John Anthony Scott, was to reconcile the actuality of federal power created by the Reconstruction amendments (and recognized in previous jurisprudence by Bradley himself) with the political necessity of restricting it in the arena of Black rights.[218]

At a time when "private" actors such as the Ku Klux Klan were launching murderous campaigns against Black people with impunity, Justice Bradley wrote in *The Civil Rights Cases* that the prohibitory aspect of the Fourteenth Amendment's first section—"No state shall make or enforce any law which shall abridge the privileges or immunities of citizens of the United States; nor shall any state deprive any person of life, liberty, or property, without due process of law; nor deny to any person within its jurisdiction the equal protection of the laws"— addressed only state action and not individual action on the part of private actors. The innkeepers and theater operators charged with discrimination in the cases at hand were private actors, "[a]nd so, in the present case, until some State law has been passed, or some State action through its officers or agents has been taken, adverse to the rights of citizens sought to be protected by the Fourteenth Amendment, no legislation of the United States ... can be called into activity."[219] When

---

[216] Franklin 1974.
[217] The cases were from Kansas, California, Missouri, Tennessee, and New York.
[218] Scott 1970–1971.
[219] *The Civil Rights Cases* (1883), 11, 13.

individuals interfered with the civil rights of others, this constituted an "ordinary civil injury" to be redressed in state court.[220] Thus, Bradley concluded, the Civil Rights Act of 1875, which prohibited discriminatory actions on the part of these private actors, was not authorized by the Fourteenth Amendment.[221]

Nor was it authorized by the Thirteenth Amendment. While this amendment did sanction "primary and direct" legislation to realize the goal of abolishing slavery and involuntary servitude, Bradley wrote, the discriminations involved in the cases at hand had nothing to do with this goal. The framers of the Civil Rights Act of 1866 had clarified that eliminating the "burdens and disabilities, the necessary incidents of slavery" required only the guaranteeing of fundamental rights (rights of property and person), "the enjoyment or deprivation of which constitutes the essential distinction between freedom and slavery." Equal access to public accommodations, on the other hand, related to "what may be called the social rights of men and races" and had no connection to slavery and involuntary servitude.[222] Foreshadowing the court's ruling in *Plessy v. Ferguson* thirteen years later, Bradley declared that enforcing social separation did not perpetuate slavery and was thus not actionable under the Thirteenth Amendment.

Admonishing would-be plaintiffs of the future, he intoned: "It would be running the slavery argument into the ground to make it apply to every act of discrimination."[223] Society had done enough for Black people, he wrote, and was in danger of doing too much:

When a man has emerged from slavery, and, by the aid of beneficent legislation, has shaken off the inseparable concomitants of that state, there must be some stage in the progress of his elevation when he takes the rank of a mere citizen and ceases to be the special favorite of the laws, and when his rights as a citizen or a man are to be protected by the ordinary modes by which other men's rights are protected.[224]

Only a handful of years after Reconstruction's collapse, as the anti-Black order was reconsolidated throughout the nation, Bradley opined that Black people had become the law's "special favorite." *It was time for them to do for themselves.*

---

[220] *The Civil Rights Cases* (1883), 24.
[221] *The Civil Rights Cases* (1883), 19.
[222] *The Civil Rights Cases* (1883), 22.
[223] *The Civil Rights Cases* (1883), 24.
[224] *The Civil Rights Cases* (1883), 25.

In his dissent, Justice John Marshall Harlan argued that inns, public conveyances, and theaters, which were licensed by the state government and had certain duties and responsibilities to the public, were different from other private actors. Because they were "clothed with a public interest" and exercised "quasi-public" functions, their discriminatory acts in fact constituted "badges of servitude" that Congress could directly legislate against, based upon enforcement power expressly granted by the Thirteenth Amendment.[225] Moreover, Harlan continued, the Fourteenth Amendment empowered Congress to enforce all of the rights and provisions it laid out, affirmative as well as prohibitive. The citizenship clause of the amendment granted Black people both state citizenship and citizenship of the United States, which meant (contra *The Slaughter-House Cases*) that they were protected by the amendment's privilege and immunities clause. One of these immunities was the exemption from racial discrimination in civil rights, which Harlan described as "a new constitutional right, secured by the grant of State citizenship to colored citizens of the United States."[226] Having conferred the right, the federal government could legitimately use primary and direct legislation to enforce it. Thus the Civil Rights Act of 1875 was a constitutional exercise of congressional power.

It was "scarcely just to say that the colored race has been the special favorite of the laws," Harlan continued. The Civil Rights Act of 1875 did not privilege Black people but only "enable[d] the Black race to take the rank of mere citizens"[227] in the face of white resistance and hostility. Moreover, Harlan argued, the Civil Rights Act of 1875 did not promote social equality:

I agree that government has nothing to do with social, as distinguished from technically legal, rights of individuals. No government ever has brought, or ever can bring, its people into social intercourse against their wishes. Whether one person will permit or maintain social relations with another is a matter with which government has no concern .... The rights which Congress, by the act of 1875, endeavored to secure and protect are legal, not social, rights.[228]

Again, it was what an act did not do, what it left intact, that spoke in its favor. It was a measure of Harlan's commitment to the social separation of the races that he abandoned his characteristic concern about power and caste here, depicting the "social" sphere as private, voluntaristic, and

[225] Justice John Marshall Harlan's dissent in *The Civil Rights Cases* (1883), 42, 41.
[226] Justice John Marshall Harlan's dissent in *The Civil Rights Cases* (1883), 50.
[227] Justice John Marshall Harlan's dissent in *The Civil Rights Cases* (1883), 61.
[228] Justice John Marshall Harlan's dissent in *The Civil Rights Cases* (1883), 59.

dissociable from legal and political dynamics. In his famous dissent in *Plessy* v. *Ferguson* (1896), as we shall see, Harlan would again insist that social inequality and separation were natural and impervious to legal intervention.

Michael Horan argues that *The Civil Rights Cases* sealed the Compromise of 1877, delivered a death blow to Reconstruction, and sacrificed Black people on the altar of sectional "reconciliation."[229] After the collapse of Reconstruction, the federal government indeed left freed-persons to the mercy of their former masters. It might be more precise, though, to say that Black people had been sacrificed long before they reached this altar. *The Civil Rights Cases* did not mark the moment of their abandonment. They were always already abandoned.

XII LYNCHING AND RELATIONALITY

When anti-lynching activist Ida B. Wells published *The Red Record* in 1895, she estimated that more than 10,000 Black people had already been lynched in the U.S. She arrived at this figure by counting the lynchings reported in white newspapers and then factoring in the many lynchings that had been done surreptitiously and were never reported. In addition to the underreporting problem, there was the challenge of drawing a line between so-called legal executions and lynchings. Legal executions often involved accelerated show trials with myriad irregularities, wherein white juries were determined to convict and execute Black defendants, irrespective of the evidence. Lynchings, meanwhile, did not occur outside the scope of the law, or without the sanction of the law: local sheriffs allowed mobs to take prisoners and/or directly participated in the murders themselves; state and local officials declined to prosecute members of lynch mobs; coroner's juries ruled that the murders happened "at the hands of persons unknown"; and federal officials declined again and again to pass anti-lynching legislation. As Barbara Holden-Smith writes, lynchings were "uninvestigated, unprosecuted, unpunished, and undeterred by the agents of law at every level of government."[230] Though most lynchings occurred in the South, and the staunchest defenders of lynching hailed from the South, lynchings of Black people occurred throughout the country.

More than 100 anti-lynching bills were introduced in Congress between 1882 and 1951; of these, only three passed the House and

---

[229] Horan 1972.
[230] Holden-Smith 1996, 39.

not one survived the southern filibuster (or threat of the filibuster) in the Senate.[231] Southern congressmen blasted all of these bills as federal interference that violated states' rights. Lynching was nothing more or less than regular murder, they insisted, which made it a state concern, not a federal concern. When anti-lynching advocates argued that states' failure to protect Black victims counted as "state action" that violated the Equal Protection Clause of the Fourteenth Amendment, southern congressmen retorted that state officials who allowed or participated in lynching were acting not as part of the state but as individuals, and that they were therefore beyond the corrective reach of the Fourteenth Amendment.[232]

Lynching was justified as the noble defense of white womanhood and white civilization against the Black rapist. Criminalizing Black victims went hand in hand with exonerating white lynch mobs. Consider an article entitled "More Rapes, More Lynchings," published in *The Daily Commercial*, a Memphis newspaper:

No man can leave his family at night without the dread that some roving Negro ruffian is watching and waiting for this opportunity. The swift punishment which invariably follows these horrible crimes doubtless acts as a deterring effect upon the Negroes in that immediate neighborhood for a short time. But the lesson is not widely learned nor long remembered .... There is small reason to hope for any change for the better. The commission of this crime grows more frequent every year. The generation of Negroes which have grown up since the war have lost in large measure the traditional and wholesome awe of the white race which kept Negroes in subjection, even when their masters were in the army, and their families left unprotected except by the slaves themselves. There is no longer a restraint upon the brute passion of the Negro.[233]

Slavery had kept everything in its natural place, and emancipation destroyed this organic social hierarchy, loosening the Negro beast. Lynching sought to correct the problem by restoring the "traditional and wholesome awe of the white race" that had obtained under slavery. As an institution, it was nostalgic for the plantation.

In a 1922 debate over one of the anti-lynching bills, Representative Hatton Sumners of Texas began with the standard southern take on slavery:

Away back yonder our ancestors, the men from New England, many of them, brought their shiploads of slaves from the jungles of Africa and sold them to my

---

[231] Holden-Smith 1996.
[232] Rable 1985.
[233] Wells-Barnett 2021 [1892], 43.

people. It was a tragedy, in so far as the white people were concerned. I do not know how you think about it, but it was not a tragedy in so far as the Black man was concerned. Sometimes I think God Almighty had a hand in that, because slavery was the only door that swung open to give the Black man a chance to get away from savagery of the jungle.[234]

God made the African into a slave to save him, but the civilizing burden this placed on whites was heavy indeed. Slavery was a boon for Black people and a "tragedy" for whites. Sumners continued:

[O]f course they [Blacks] are more inclined to commit crimes than white men are. It would be a most unreasonable thing not to expect it. Only a short time ago their ancestors roamed the jungles of Africa, in absolute savagery .... [Y]ou do not know where the beast is among them. Somewhere in that Black mass of people is the man who would outrage your wife or your child, and every man who lives out in the country knows it.[235]

Thus the necessity (and, in Sumner's eyes, the terrible beauty) of lynching:

God Almighty drew them ["lines of racial distinction"] in the councils of His infinite wisdom, and put the instinct of racial preservation there to protect them. You ask me what we will do to protect it. We will do whatever is necessary, that is all. Men who do not live in the presence of the danger do not hear the call. Nature does not waste her energies. When men respond to that call, they respond to a law that is higher than the law of self-preservation. It is the call to the preservation of the race .... It is the call of the blood.[236]

Whites who opposed lynching were denounced as hypocrites who had more compassion for Black rapists than for their victims. Representative James Buchanan of Texas, echoing Justice Bradley in *The Civil Rights Cases*, commented that the Black race had too "long enjoyed its distinction as the most favored race protégé ever coddled and petted by the sentimental sacrifice of an indulgent people."[237] And to the sponsors of a later (equally unsuccessful) anti-lynching bill in 1938, Senator Theodore Bilbo of Mississippi warned: "[U]pon your garments and the garments of those who are responsible for the passage of this measure will be the blood of the raped and outraged daughters of Dixie."[238]

[234] *Congressional Record*, 67th Congress, 2d session, U.S. House of Representatives, January 4, 1922, 797–798.
[235] *Congressional Record*, 67th Congress, 2d session, U.S. House of Representatives, January 4, 1922, 798–799.
[236] *Congressional Record*, 67th Congress, 2d session, U.S. House of Representatives, January 4, 1922, 799.
[237] Holden-Smith 1996, 55.
[238] Quoted in Rable 1985, 217.

Lynching ritually affirmed the slaveness of the Black. It reasserted white control in uncertain times. Black Codes, convict leasing, segregation laws, and Ku Klux Klan attacks worked together to suppress Black physical, economic, and political mobility in the post-Reconstruction South, but these practices were not perfectly efficient: there was still room for a modest number of Black people to prosper economically, own land, open businesses, or register and vote. For these and other exigencies, there was lynching. Ida B. Wells's *Red Record* contains a list of "reasons" given for lynching, and it included, among other things, disputing a contract, not moving out of the way for a white person on the road or sidewalk, looking at a white person the wrong way, and "incendiarism" or saying incendiary things. "No reason" is also on the list. (Wells's research demonstrated that only a quarter of lynchings involved even the accusation of rape, which did not stop southern congressmen from making Black rape the centerpiece of their defense of lynching.)[239] In *Dred Scott*, Justice Daniel said the Black would always be a slave, that this was an indelible status impervious to legal-political developments like emancipation. Lynching, similarly, declared: No matter what their age, place of residence, occupation, gender, income, or behavior, the Black was always, simply by virtue of being Black, only one step away from the noose.

Amy Louise Wood notes the haunting similarity of lynching photos to hunting photos.[240] In both, the killers have strung up the bodies of their victims and pose proudly beside them, the ecstasy of killing still visible on their faces. In both, the killers use photography to preserve the killing for all time, far past the point at which the victims' bodies, as organic matter, would have disappeared. Lynchings were sometimes called "Negro barbecues," where, "[a]s at a cookout, human victims were also butchered and roasted, often with members of the crowd offering suggestions on technique."[241] Lynching, like hunting and barbecuing, was an ontologizing ritual that located the victim outside the realm of human being and mattering. Anything could be done to the animal or the Black; nothing counted as a violation.[242]

Spectacle lynchings, with crowds in the many thousands, involved a kind of sadistic, orgiastic excess that was largely absent when whites killed

---

[239] See also Holden-Smith 1996.
[240] Wood 2011.
[241] Dray 2002, 81. See also Woodard 2014.
[242] See C. Kim 2017.

animals for sport and/or food. The animal qua animal failed to generate this much heat. The passion roused by the Black qua Black, on the other hand, was boundless. Crowds of up to 10,000 white men, women, and children roared as the Black victim was dragged into view and the torture began. White men gouged out the victim's eyes, broke their bones, cut off their fingers and ears and toes, chopped off their sex organs and shoved them in their mouths, bored holes into their flesh with metal tools, disemboweled them, hung them, shot them hundreds of times, and burned them at the stake.[243] Then white children scavenged in the ashes for what David Marriott calls *"memento mori*: toes, fingers, or—most highly prized—a Black penis, a Black scrotum."[244] They could not make the victim suffer enough. Drawing on Frantz Fanon's discussion of negrophobia, David Marriott observes that "the violated body of the Black man [came] to be used as a defence against the anxiety, or hatred, that body appear[ed] to generate."[245]

Lynch law, like slave law, denied Black relationality. The violence of lynching was inflicted on the victim's loved ones as well—those who saw them dragged away and had no recourse when they did not come home. Koritha Mitchell observes that lynching photos reflected the white vantage point on events, depicting Black victims as "isolated brutes with no connection to a family or community, or to institutions like marriage."[246] Whether shown just before or after death, the victim stood amid a sea of white people, mute, powerless, and fatally alone. We see the brutalized individual Black body, Mitchell writes, but not the ripple effects on the victim's kin and community.[247] Lynching reproduced the Black as an isolate, reenacting the victim's social death as a condition that exceeded the photographic frame and the temporal moment.

White relationality, on the other hand, was greatly enlivened by lynching. When spectacle lynchings were advertised in the newspaper in

[243] Dray 2002.

[244] Marriott 2000, 9. The frequency of sexual mutilation and rape as aspects of lynching suggest the need for a Fanonian psychoanalytic reading of the role of fantasy, envy, projection, and castrating rage in these events. Castration was "often the centerpiece of the entire lynching ritual, and was accompanied by extensive comment, laughter, and debate about the size of the victim's organ, as well as appreciative touching, even stroking of the member. Afterward, it was the ultimate souvenir" (Dray 2002, 82).

[245] Marriott 2000, 12.

[246] Mitchell 2011, 7.

[247] By contrast, Black playwrights "direct the gaze away from the brutalized body, finding its representational capacity to be insufficient .... [They] insis[t] that truth cannot be gleaned from bones and charred flesh, mutilated corpses, or pictures of them." (Mitchell 2011, 194).

advance, parents took time off work and wrote their children notes to excuse them from school. They came from all over by the thousands, by train, bus, and car, for a family and community outing like no other. They bought snacks and photographs from vendors who set out their wares, hoping for brisk sales. The pleasure of murdering Black people together was so keen for whites that they compulsively tried to extend it, not only through the preservation of the victim's body parts—the keeping of Sam Hose's knuckles in a jar in a store windowsill—but through the circulation of postcards featuring lynching photos to family and friends long after the event. "Wish you were here."[248] When the mailing of lynching postcards was prohibited by law in 1908, the practice of sharing lynching photos went underground.[249]

In lynching photos, David Marriott writes, "the camera lens is a means to fashion the [white] self through the image of a dead Black man."[250] Lynching was a rite of initiation through which the white father passed white manhood as an "inheritance" to his white male child, the "gift" of being "the man holding the knife instead of the man being cut."[251] It was also an institution that defined white womanhood and motherhood in the afterlife of slavery. This is the point of Kerry Marshall's unforgettable triptych "Heirlooms and Accessories" (2002).[252] A faded inkjet print of a well-known photograph of the lynching of Thomas Shipp and Abram Smith in Marion, Indiana, in 1930 is the backdrop for each part of the triptych. The image is faded, or whitewashed, so that it is barely perceptible. The faces of three white women of three different generations in the lynch mob are foregrounded, with each face enclosed in a shiny locket hanging from a free-floating chain. The wood frames of the triptych are covered in rhinestones.

By fading out the lynching photo, Marshall refuses the spectacularization of Black suffering and aborts the voyeuristic pleasure of seeing the brutalized, bleeding Black corpse. Instead, he asks us to focus on the white women in the mob, agents of violence who are normally overlooked in favor of their male counterparts. Here, too, horror lies. By joining the lynch mob and acting as *accessories* to murder, these white women produce the *heirlooms and accessories* they will pass on from generation to generation—white identity, white prerogative,

---

[248] Marriott 2000, 9.
[249] Apel 2004.
[250] Marriott 2000, 6.
[251] Marriott 2000, 19.
[252] See at: https://studiomuseum.org/collection-item/heirlooms-accessories.

white violence. The lockets, chains, and rhinestones prettify, reminding us that white aesthetics are an aesthetics of Black death. Jewelry carries a double meaning here, as Thomas Shipp and Abram Smith were lynched on the pretext that they had raped a white woman, Mary Ball—even though Mary Ball was seen wearing Abram Smith's jewelry and watch prior to that day, suggesting that she knew him well.[253] Lynching, then, is the disavowed backdrop against which whites secure property rights, intergenerational ties, community, gender, and reproductivity. By contrast, under the legal principle of *partus sequitur ventrem* ("that which is brought forth follows the belly"), children born to a slave mother followed her into slavery. Saidiya Hartman writes: "The [slave] mother's only claim [was]—to transfer her dispossession to the child."[254]

When coroner's juries habitually returned the verdict "at the hands of persons unknown," even though the identities of many of the lynchers were known, they not only refused to hold individual members of lynch mobs legally accountable, they also collectivized moral responsibility among all whites. Killing was rendered anonymous ("persons unknown") because it was done on behalf of the white race, by whites qua whites. All whites authored each lynching, so no particular individuals did. As with the Fugitive Slave Act of 1850, the point was that it could be *any Black* (lynch mobs often treated Black victims as fungible; if they couldn't find the intended victim, they lynched their friend or mother or son), and it could be *any whites*, because the issue was not just a runaway slave here or an alleged rape there, but rather maintaining the prerogatives of whiteness in an anti-Black order.

Millions of Black people left the South and went North between 1910 and 1970, in part because of lynching. There they found only partial relief. In the North, the code of racial etiquette was more flexible, but collusion between governmental and private actors produced systematic racial segregation that accomplished many of the same purposes as Jim Crow in the South. Lynchings in the North, while not as numerous as those in the South, were similarly tied to the enforcement of segregation's boundaries. Despite the sectional flag-waving of Senator Bilbo and others who imagined themselves resisting the War of Northern Aggression, maintaining Black abjection was still a *national* priority. And Blackness continued to be, as Bryan Wagner writes, "a condition

[253] Apel 2004.
[254] Hartman 2016, 166.

of statelessness."[255] When, on occasion, a European or Asian immigrant was lynched, the U.S. government sometimes paid monetary restitution to the alien's home country.[256] But restitution was not made for the more than 10,000 Black people who were lynched. There was nowhere to send the payment to.

XIII THE NOT-BLACKNESS OF YICK WO

Once Chinese exclusion had been achieved, the "Question of the Hour" was how to get rid of the Chinese who were already here or, more vexing still, were being born here. This was addressed in part by tinkering with the exclusion regime to make it more difficult for Chinese residents to reenter the U.S. after traveling to China, and in part by generating state and local laws aimed at making life intolerably difficult for them.[257] While the courts deferred to the federal government's plenary power on immigration matters, the Ninth Circuit often struck down state and local laws aimed at the Chinese, on the grounds that they violated the Equal Protection Clause of the Fourteenth Amendment.[258] Lawmakers responded by passing facially neutral laws that they hoped would pass constitutional muster despite their discriminatory intent. San Francisco, home to the largest concentration of Chinese in the U.S., issued a spate of facially neutral ordinances that, among other things, ordered the cutting of prisoners' hair (to humiliate Chinese prisoners whose queues were a mark of fealty to the Emperor), mandated a certain amount of "cubic air" per person in a dwelling (to prevent the Chinese from living cheaply in crowded quarters), and prohibited the use of poles to carry objects on sidewalks (to harass Chinese vendors who carried vegetables and other goods this way).[259]

Many of the city's ordinances targeted the Chinese operators who dominated the local laundry business. In *Yick Wo* v. *Hopkins* (1886), the U.S. Supreme Court considered a San Francisco ordinance that was facially neutral but applied in a discriminatory way against Chinese laundrymen.[260] The ordinance, passed in 1880, directed all laundry operators,

---

[255] Wagner 2009.

[256] Goldsby 2006.

[257] The 1882 statute was revised in 1884 and again in 1888 before being amended and extended by the Geary Act in 1892.

[258] McClain 1994.

[259] McClain 1994.

[260] This was a compound case. Wo Lee filed a petition in the U.S. Circuit Court of California; Yick Wo filed a petition in the California Supreme Court. The cases presented substantially the same facts and legal questions, so the court decided to combine them.

except those whose facilities were in brick or stone buildings, to apply to the Board of Supervisors for a license to continue operating their businesses.[261] Justified as a legitimate exercise of police power to promote public safety, the ordinance's purported aim was closer regulation of the laundries located in wood "frame" buildings, which were deemed a potential fire hazard. Uncoincidentally, however, the majority of the laundries operating in San Francisco at the time were Chinese-owned, and most of these were in wood "frame" buildings. More than 200 Chinese (including Yick Wo, who had been in business for twenty-two years) applied to the Board for licenses and all were denied; more than eighty whites applied and all but one were approved.[262] What caught the court's attention was not the substance of the ordinance but the manner in which it was administered.

Counsel for Yick Wo argued that the right to labor, or to pursue a "necessary and harmless" occupation like running a laundry, was a fundamental and natural right that should not be subject to the "absolute and capricious will of any small number of men" on the Board of Supervisors. "[A]ll persons" and not just citizens were protected in this fundamental right.[263] The 1880 ordinance deprived Yick Wo of property and property rights without due process and was, in addition, discriminatory against the Chinese in violation of the Fourteenth Amendment, Sections 1977 and 1979 of the Revised Statutes, and the Burlingame and Angell Treaties. Yick Wo was protected in his fundamental right to operate a laundry *despite* the fact he was an alien ("all persons") and *because* he was an alien (treaty protections).[264] Here plaintiff's counsel cited the district court case *In re Tiburcio Parrott* (1880) (where the court struck down Article XIX of the California Constitution, which denied employment to Chinese immigrants, on the grounds that the Burlingame Treaty guaranteed the Chinese the "absolute, fundamental and natural right" to labor),[265] as well as the circuit court case *In re Quong Woo* (1882) (where the court struck down a San Francisco laundry ordinance on the grounds that treaty relations guaranteed that the Chinese person "has,

---

[261] In San Francisco, the city and county boundaries exactly coincide. The Board of Supervisors is thus also the legislative body for the city.

[262] *Yick Wo v. Hopkins* (1886).

[263] Argument of Hall McAllister, L. H. Van Shaick and D. L. Smoot, for Appellant and Plaintiff in Error (1886), 3, 6.

[264] See Chin 2008; Bernstein 2008; Joo 2008 for a revisiting of *Yick Wo* and debate over the role of treaties in this case.

[265] *In re Tiburcio Parrott* (1880), 507.

under the pledge of the nation, the right to remain and follow any of the lawful, ordinary trades and pursuits of life, without let or hindrance from the State, or any of its subordinate municipal bodies, except such as may arise from the enforcement of equal and impartial laws").[266]

The "right to labor" argument can be traced back to Justice Stephen Field's dissent in *The Slaughter-House Cases*, where he argued that that the (white) butchers of New Orleans possessed the "right to pursue a lawful and necessary calling," and that the infringement of this right constituted "the essence of slavery." "[E]quality of right" in the "lawful pursuits of life" meant the state could only regulate such activities if the burdens were equally imposed on all those similarly situated.[267] Field, who had authored the opinion in *In re Quong Woo* and other circuit court cases extending Fourteenth-Amendment protection to the Chinese, was in fact a sitting member of the U.S. Supreme Court in *Yick Wo*.[268] Thus it is not surprising that Yick Wo's counsel decided to represent his client, in part, as *homo economicus* like the white butchers—that is, as a universal, generic, de-raced man dedicated to property accumulation through private economic activity. It was of no import that the Chinese were not citizens, he pointed out, because "all persons" had the right to engage in the "ordinary avocations of life" unmolested by a discriminatory state. Echoing the indignant tone of Field's *Slaughter-House* dissent, he expressed outrage at the 1880 ordinance, which brought about "the destruction of business and property rights, the forfeiture of money and the sacrifice of liberty for no higher reason than that these subordinate lawmakers have seen fit to declare unlawful a thing which hurts no one, which benefits many and which *for the purposes of oppression*, rather than good government, they have placed on the plane of nuisance."[269]

---

[266] Argument of Hall McAllister, L. H. Van Shaick and D. L. Smoot, for Appellant and Plaintiff in Error (1886), 8, citing *In re Quong Woo* (1882), 819. Italics in this brief but not in original. This case struck down a San Francisco ordinance that required laundry operators to receive permission to operate their businesses from the Board of Supervisors, who required the recommendation of no fewer than twelve citizens and taxpayers (i.e., whites) living on that block.

[267] Justice Stephen Field's dissent in *The Slaughter-House Cases* (1872), 109.

[268] However, Field was also the author of three U.S. Supreme Court decisions adverse to the Chinese: *Barbier* v. *Connolly* (1885) and *Soon Hing* v. *Crowley* (1885)—two cases where the court left standing discriminatory laundry ordinances—and the Chinese exclusion case, *Chae Chan Ping* v. *United States* (1889). In this last case, he authored the unanimous opinion upholding the Scott Act banning almost all Chinese immigration to the U.S. See Joo 1995.

[269] Argument of Hall McAllister, L. H. Van Shaik and D. L. Smoot, for Appellant and Plaintiff in Error (1886), 4. Italics added.

Presenting Yick Wo as *homo economicus* emphasized his common ground with whites seeking to protect their economic rights. Gabriel Chin writes: "[O]nce the decision is understood to be based on protecting property, the race of the person arbitrarily deprived of his property becomes irrelevant."[270] In this sense, Chin argues, Yick Wo could have been white. It might be more on point to say, following Thomas Joo, that what was critical in the case was Yick Wo's not-Blackness.[271] At this historical moment, with Jim Crow being nailed down all across the South, it was Yick Wo's not-Blackness that allowed him to imaginatively stand in for, or stand beside, the white butcher. One did not have to be white to be *homo economicus*, but one did have to be not-Black. The corollary discussion of Yick Wo as an alien protected by treaty guarantees, by emphasizing his foreignness, again differentiated him from Blackness as a condition of statelessness.

Counsel for defendant Peter Hopkins, Sheriff of San Francisco, countered that the Board of Supervisors was properly concerned with preventing fires and that the 1880 laundry ordinance was a valid exercise of police power toward this end.[272] Yick Wo, he claimed, was part of an evil Chinese plot to take over the laundry business and the city at large. The Chinese laundry association, the Tung Hing Tong, was a renegade "syndicate" that had set itself up as an alternative municipal power structure, flagrantly challenging the Board of Supervisors's authority:

Do we know that there are in San Francisco a large number, to wit, 3,000 foreigners, who have created a *Tung Hing Tong* association, which exercises legislative, executive and judicial power in this city and county in opposition to the lawful authorities .... That it does not admit American citizens to membership, and that it owes no allegiance to the laws of the land .... The industry of its members so untiring that they "are willing to work as many hours a day as nature will permit," *** by relays of help the whole twenty-four hours of each day continuously, Sundays

---

[270] Chin 2008, 1363.

[271] In "*Yick Wo* Re-Revisited: NonBlack Nonwhites and Fourteenth Amendment History" (2008), Thomas Joo argues that the importance of Yick Wo's "nonBlackness" has been overlooked by legal historians. During Reconstruction, Joo argues, the court declined to apply the Fourteenth Amendment to economic rights or the rights of "nonBlacks" in *The Slaughter-House Cases*. However, "[a]fter the federal government abandoned Reconstruction in the 1870s, the court undertook to redefine the Fourteenth Amendment away from the protection of Black political rights and toward the protection of economic rights" (p. 1428). In this context, Joo argues, Yick Wo's "nonBlackness as distinct from Blackness" (p. 1427) allowed him to serve as a transitional figure, enabling the court to "make the transition gradually, expanding the Amendment's coverage from one despised minority to another despised, but nonBlack, minority, rather than applying it directly to the dominant white race" (p. 1435).

[272] Points and Authorities for Defendant and Respondent (1886).

included. Interjection: We have read of the slave trade, the man sellers of Africa and the man dealers of California, but where is the emancipation proclamation and the xiiith amendment? Have not the man dealers got a bonanza? That the concentrated power wielded by the *Tung Hing Tong*, springing from the united purpose, the united action, and the united contributions of its numerous constituents, renders it a formidable opponent to the municipal government of San Francisco.[273]

Though Yick Wo was self-employed, the coolie–slave slander was invoked to dramatize the threat he posed to white laundrymen. Defendant's counsel continued:

[T]he *Tung Hing Tong* came down on our municipality before the pains of parturition under the new [California] constitution had ceased, and with its pruning knife, held by judicial hands, emasculated the municipality .... The *Tung Hing Tong*, exulting in its success, mocks the weakness of which it was the cause, and taunts the municipality because, when dazed and crippled, its legislation was abortive .... Emasculated as the city has been by the *Tung Hing Tong*, we retain sufficient energy to raise a cry of alarm before the *Tung Hing Tong* drives us from our homes into the ocean .... [A]lthough the *Tung Hing Tong* with profane and polluted feet has trampled on our laws, the day of restoration is coming and the darkness of the night of subjugation will be forgotten in the effulgence of the day of deliverance .... It is not the fault of the respondent that the petitioner has hung the dragon flag of the Chinese empire over his door, and dared the municipality of San Francisco to touch it.[274]

Chinese laundries were not innocent economic concerns but a beachhead for Chinese imperial forces determined to castrate the city and, eventually, the nation. Yick Wo's laundry work was cover for this nefarious politico-military scheme. *Homo economicus?* More like *homo bellicosus*.

Justice Stanley Matthews, writing for the court, was unconvinced. He struck down the 1880 ordinance and declared that the Fourteenth Amendment protects "all persons" within the territorial jurisdiction of the U.S. "without regard to differences of race, of color, or of nationality," including "subjects of the Emperor of China."[275] The enforcement of the ordinance, Matthews observed, showed "arbitrary and unjust discriminations, founded on differences of race between persons otherwise in similar circumstances"[276] and thus violated the constitutional rights of Yick Wo and other Chinese laundry operators:

[273] Points and Authorities for Defendant and Respondent (1886), 17–18.
[274] Points and Authorities for Defendant and Respondent (1886), 100, 101, 103. These quotations are from the excerpt included in this brief of a brief filed previously with the California Supreme Court.
[275] *Yick Wo v. Hopkins* (1886), 356.
[276] *Yick Wo v. Hopkins* (1886), 356.

[T]he facts shown establish an administration directed so exclusively against a particular class of persons as to warrant and require the conclusion that, whatever may have been the intent of the ordinances as adopted, they are applied by the public authorities charged with their administration, and thus representing the State itself, with a mind so unequal and oppressive as to amount to a practical denial by the State of that equal protection of the laws which is secured to the petitioners, as to all other persons, by the broad and benign provisions of the Fourteenth Amendment to the Constitution of the United States. Though the law itself be fair on its face and impartial in appearance, yet, if it is applied and administered by public authority with an evil eye and an unequal hand, so as practically to make unjust and illegal discriminations between persons in similar circumstances, material to their rights, the denial of equal justice is still within the prohibition of the Constitution.[277]

What made the discrimination "unjust and illegal" was that it was grounded in racial-national hostility:

The fact of this discrimination is admitted. No reason for it is shown, and the conclusion cannot be resisted that no reason for it exists except hostility to the race and nationality to which the petitioners belong, and which, in the eye of the law, is not justified. The discrimination is therefore, illegal, and the public administration which enforces it is a denial of the equal protection of the laws and a violation of the Fourteenth Amendment of the Constitution.[278]

Locating Yick Wo's rights in the Fourteenth Amendment, the Angell Treaty, and Section 1977 of the Revised Statutes, Justice Matthews quoted directly from the last:[279]

[A]ll persons within the jurisdiction of the United States shall have the same right in every State and Territory to make and enforce contracts, to sue, be parties, give evidence, and to the full and equal benefit of all laws and proceedings for the security of persons and property *as is enjoyed by white citizens* and shall be subject to like punishment, pains, penalties, taxes, licenses, and exactions of every kind, and to no other.[280]

Justice Matthews continued: "The questions we have to consider and decide in these cases, therefore, are to be treated as invoking the rights of every citizen of the United States equally with those of the strangers and aliens who now invoke the jurisdiction of the court."[281] The question, in other words, was not whether it was acceptable to treat "strangers and

---

[277] *Yick Wo v. Hopkins* (1886), 373–374.
[278] *Yick Wo v. Hopkins* (1886), 374.
[279] Section 1977 was enacted in 1870, right after the signing of the Burlingame Treaty, and was "in essence a statute implementing the treaty" (Chin 2008, 1382).
[280] *Yick Wo v. Hopkins* (1886), 369. Italics added.
[281] *Yick Wo v. Hopkins* (1886), 369.

aliens" this way, but whether it was acceptable to treat "every citizen" (i.e., a white citizen) this way. Forget Yick Wo for a moment, Justice Matthew seemed to be saying, and imagine an everyman, a white butcher, *homo economicus* in his place. Then the question had but one answer:

[T]he fundamental rights to life, liberty, and the pursuit of happiness, considered as individual possessions, are secured by those maxims of constitutional law which are the monuments showing the victorious progress of the race in securing to men the blessings of civilization under the reign of just and equal laws, so that, in the famous language of the Massachusetts Bill of Rights, the government of the commonwealth "may be a government of laws, and not of men." For the very idea that one man may be compelled to hold his life, or the means of living, or any material right essential to the enjoyment of life at the mere will of another seems to be intolerable in any country where freedom prevails, *as being the essence of slavery itself.*[282]

Thus the same Court that had struck down the Civil Rights Act of 1875 in *The Civil Rights Cases* three years earlier, and had impatiently accused Black people of "running the slavery argument into the ground to make it apply to every act of discrimination," now declared that restrictions on the economic activity of the *homo economicus* were the "essence of slavery" and thus intolerable. It was Yick Wo's not-Blackness that allowed him to merge momentarily with the white working man (and enjoy some of his privileges) in the imagination of the court.

Yick Wo was, all told, an important if unsung character in the post-Reconstruction devastation of Black freedom dreams and the consolidation of the postbellum racial order. As the constitutional amendment passed to aid Black people was deployed to shore up the prerogatives of whites (and the Chinese) in a reconfigured anti-Black order, the transitive, substitutional capacities of the Chinese proved important. Affective commitments to white economic rights were mobilized on behalf of the Chinese, and they, in turn, were used to establish a legal framework protective of white economic rights. Each served the other in stabilizing a property regime and social order built upon the phobic avoidance of Blackness.

XIV *YICK WO* IN *PLESSY*, OR JIM CROW'S ALIBI

The full historical import of *Yick Wo* v. *Hopkins* would not become clear until a decade later. In 1896, in *Plessy* v. *Ferguson*, the U.S. Supreme Court gave its imprimatur to the system of racial segregation that had

---

[282] *Yick Wo* v. *Hopkins* (1886), 370.

been constructed by southern whites since the Civil War, authorizing its violence and terror for another half-century. At issue in the case was the constitutionality of an 1890 Louisiana statute, informally known as the Separate Car Law, that required railway companies "to provide equal but separate accommodations for the white and colored races." During Reconstruction, the Louisiana state convention had written a new constitution which guaranteed all citizens "the same civil, political, and public rights" and explicitly prohibited segregation in public accommodations, including "any conveyance of a public character."[283] But Democrats who took over the state legislature and governorship after Reconstruction wrote a new state constitution aimed at consolidating Jim Crow. The Separate Car Law of 1890 was part of this effort.

A New Orleans Creole organization called the *Comité des Citoyens* (Citizens' Committee) challenged the segregation statute in court.[284] Composed of persons of "mixed descent," the Creole community in New Orleans had a long, distinctive history as an intermediate caste between slaves and whites in the informal "three-caste system" inherited from French and Spanish colonial rule.[285] French and Spanish colonial administrators in Louisiana had shown tolerance for interracial relationships, and those of "mixed descent" had enjoyed certain freedoms and opportunities denied to slaves. Creoles in New Orleans identified as *gens de couleur libres* (free persons of color) rather than as Negroes or Black people and indeed "saw themselves as of a particular class higher than the low status ascribed to the Blacks of the fields who formed the mass of ex-slaves."[286] The *Comité des Citoyens* was so named to emphasize their status as citizens, which they traced not to the Civil Rights Act of 1866 or the Fourteenth Amendment, but rather to the 1803 Louisiana Purchase Treaty, which stipulated that residents of the formerly French territory were to receive all the rights and privileges of citizens of the United States.[287]

The Separate Car Law diminished the social distance between Creoles and Black people while expanding the distance between whites and these two groups. Organizing to challenge the law, the Creole community chose as a test subject Homer Plessy, a shoemaker of "mixed descent,

---

[283] Scott 2008; Davis 2004, 8.
[284] Davis 2004.
[285] Berlin 1974.
[286] Davis 2004, 15.
[287] Scott 2008.

in the proportion of seven eighths Caucasian and one eighth African blood," and in whom "the mixture of colored blood was not discernible."[288] By prearrangement with the railway company, which resented the additional financial burden imposed by the segregation law, Plessy attempted to ride in a railway car reserved for whites and was arrested and jailed. As planned, the case made its way to the U.S. Supreme Court, with renowned civil rights attorney Albion Tourgée at the helm.

Plessy was recruited precisely because of his ability to pass as white, as part of the legal strategy was to show the difficulty and arbitrariness of classifying people by race. Reflecting ongoing distrust between the Creole and Black communities in New Orleans, some Black organizations objected to the choice and charged the *Comité des Citoyens* with advocating only for those of "mixed descent" and leaving Black people behind.[289] Thomas Davis lends some credence to this charge when he argues that the *Comité des Citoyens* was defending its group identity by trying to "conserv[e] or preserv[e] the complex subtlety of a mixed blood racial system that slavery generated."[290] According to Mark Golub, however, attorney Albion Tourgée's purpose was to make a radical assault upon the idea of racial caste and the system of white supremacy.[291] These tensions were evident in Tourgée's Brief for Plaintiff in Error.

The brief poses the following question: "Is not the question of race, scientifically considered, very often impossible of determination?"[292] If Plessy, in whom "the mixture of colored blood was not discernible," was not "white," then who was "white?" "Will the court," Tourgée asked, "hold that a single drop of African blood is sufficient to color a whole ocean of Caucasian whiteness?"[293] Racial indeterminacy had revolutionary implications because it meant there was no objective basis for a system of racial segregation. Without a foundation in nature, Jim Crow would be revealed as unacceptably arbitrary. In practice, Tourgée pointed out, it was left to the railway conductor to determine who was "white" and who was "colored"—a call he was neither authorized nor qualified to make.

---

[288] *Plessy v. Ferguson* (1896), 538. See Davis (2004) for the argument that *Plessy* is mistaken for an equal accommodations case, when it was actually primarily a case about the New Orleans Creole elite's anxieties about their particular racial identity and status as persons of "mixed descent."

[289] Golub 2005.

[290] Davis 2004, 2.

[291] Golub 2005.

[292] Brief for Plaintiff in Error (1896), 6.

[293] Brief for Plaintiff in Error (1896), 31.

Sorting people by race on a public conveyance, Tourgée continued, violated the Thirteenth and Fourteenth Amendments. "Slavery," he wrote, "was a caste, a legal condition of subjection to the dominant class, a bondage quite separable from the incident of ownership."[294] Ownership of Black people (what he called "chattelism") ceased after the Civil War, but slavery as a Black–white caste system did not. Against those who read the Thirteenth Amendment narrowly as dismantling the formal institution of slavery and nothing more, Tourgée proposed an expansive reading of the Thirteenth Amendment as a live instrument for fighting ongoing Black subordination: "[T]he purpose of this Amendment was not merely to destroy chattelism and involuntary servitude but the estate and condition of subjection and inferiority of personal right and privilege, which was the result and essential concomitant of slavery."[295] The Separate Car Law ran afoul of the Amendment: "The effect of a law distinguishing between citizens as to race, in the enjoyment of a public franchise, is to legalize caste and restore, in part at least, the inequality of right which was an essential incident of slavery."[296]

In addition, Tourgée argued, the railway conductor had deprived Plessy of his liberty and property without due process of the law, a violation of the Fourteenth Amendment. Plessy had lost not only the value of his ticket but another form of property as well:

The man who rides in a car set apart for the colored race will inevitably be regarded as a colored man or at least be suspected of being one. And the officer has undoubtedly the power to entail upon him such suspicion. To do so, is to deprive him of "property" if such reputation *is* "property." Whether it is or not, is for the court to determine from its knowledge of existing conditions. Perhaps it might not be inappropriate to suggest some questions which may aid in deciding this inquiry. How much would it be *worth* to a young man entering upon the practice of law, to be regarded as a *white* man rather than a colored one? Nineteen-twentieths of the property of the country is owned by white people. Ninety-nine hundredths of the business opportunities are in the control of white people .... Probably most white persons if given a choice, would prefer death to life in the United States *as colored persons*. Under these conditions is it possible to conclude that the *reputation of being white* is not property? Indeed, is it not the most valuable sort of property, being the master-key that unlocks the golden door of opportunity?[297]

[294] Brief for Plaintiff in Error (1896), 32.
[295] Brief for Plaintiff in Error (1896), 33.
[296] Brief for Plaintiff in Error (1896), 14.
[297] Brief for Plaintiff in Error (1896), 9. Italics in original.

How much was it worth to be seen as white?

That the mixture of colored blood is not discernable in him [Plessy], that he is entitled to every right, privilege and immunity secured to citizens of the United States of the white race by the constitution of the United States, and that such right, privilege, recognition and immunity are worth to him the sum of Ten Thousand Dollars if the same be at all susceptible of being estimated by the standard value of money.[298]

Tourgée names a large sum here, while also intimating that the value of the reputation of being white is not necessarily "susceptible of being estimated" in dollars.[299] How does one measure the value of property that is the condition of possibility for all other property?

The Fourteenth Amendment, Tourgée continued, "*create[d] a new* citizenship of the United States embracing new rights, privileges, and immunities, derivable in a *new* manner, controlled by *new* authority, having a *new* scope and extent, dependent on national authority for its existence and looking to national power for its preservation."[300] Challenging the court's ruling in *The Slaughter-House Cases*, which had identified the rights that attach to state citizenship as beyond the reach of federal authority, he argued that the national government "ha[d] the right, through its Courts, to inquire into and decide upon the force, tenor and justice of all provisions of State laws affecting the rights of the citizen."[301] It was thus appropriate and necessary for the court to find that the Separate Car Law created "such an interference with the personal liberty of the individual as is impossible to be made consistently with his rights as an equal citizen of the United States and of the State in which he resides."[302]

According to Tourgée, states developed the idea of "police regulations"—regulations that necessarily infringed upon individual rights and privileges in the name of protecting public health, morals, and welfare—in response to this sudden increase in federal power, and thus their motives for invoking it always had to be examined. He wrote: "The question is whether this is an unrestricted right: whether the State has the right under the claim of protecting public health or regulating public morals, to restrict the rights of the individual to *any extent* it may see fit?"[303]

---

[298] Brief for Plaintiff in Error (1896), 30.
[299] There were cases in which Louisiana district courts had recognized whiteness as a reputation and matter of property. See Davis 2004.
[300] Brief for Plaintiff in Error (1896), 12. Italics in original.
[301] Brief for Plaintiff in Error (1896), 15.
[302] Brief for Plaintiff in Error (1896), 11.
[303] Brief for Plaintiff in Error (1896), 17.

The court in *The Slaughter-House Cases* gave Louisiana leeway in this regard, he conceded, but it had intimated it would have been less forgiving had the rights of Black citizens been at stake.

What was the motive of the legislators who justified the Separate Car Law as a "police regulation?" Tourgée queried:

[I]s [sitting next to each other] dangerous to the public health? Does this contaminate public morals? If it does from whence comes the contamination? Why does it contaminate any more than in the house or on the street? Is it the white who spreads the contagion or the Black? And if color breeds contagion in a railway coach, why exempt [Black] nurses [working for white families] from the operation of the Act?[304]

It was hard to escape the conclusion that the Separate Car Law was "not a matter of public health or morals, but simply a matter intended ... for the gratification and recognition of the sentiment of white superiority and white supremacy of right and power."[305] There was, Tourgée warned, the potential for virtually limitless abuse of the police power for racially oppressive purposes:

Why may it [the state] not require all red-headed people to ride in a separate car? Why not require all colored people to walk on one side of the street and whites on the other? Why may it not require every white man's house to be painted white and every colored man's Black? Why may it not require every white man's vehicle to be of one color and compel the colored citizen to use one of different color on the highway? Why not require every white business man to use a white sign and every colored man who solicits custom a Black one?[306]

It was the court's responsibility to use its newly expanded powers to protect Black citizens from such arbitrary acts of discrimination.

The Brief on Behalf of the Defendant, Criminal District Court Judge John Howard Ferguson, countered Tourgée's arguments in a cursory way. It dismissed the argument about the Thirteenth Amendment by observing that the court had ruled in *The Civil Rights Cases* that denial of access in public accommodations, theaters, and "public conveyances" "d[id] not subject that person to any form of servitude, or tend to fasten upon him any badge of slavery, even though the denial be founded on the race or color of that person."[307] (This was a motivated misreading, however, since the Court in *The Civil Rights Cases* addressed

---

304 Brief for Plaintiff in Error (1896), 18–19.
305 Brief for Plaintiff in Error (1896), 26.
306 Brief for Plaintiff in Error (1896), 29.
307 Brief on Behalf of Defendant in Error (1895), 35.

discriminatory actions on the part of individuals and distinguished these from discriminatory actions on the part of the state.)[308] The brief then declared: "Equality of accommodation does not mean *identity* of accommodation." The Fourteenth Amendment was violated "only when the States attempt by legislation to establish an *inequality* in respect to the enjoyment of any rights or privileges," which the Separate Car Law did not do. As for racial indeterminacy, the brief cited two separate dictionaries as defining "colored" as "wholly or partly" of the African race and insisted there was no ambiguity in making racial assignments: "[A]s a rule, there is no question as to which race a man belongs."[309]

Claiming that they had lacked time to adequately prepare the case, the defendant's attorneys then reproduced in full the ruling of the Louisiana Supreme Court in *Ex parte Plessy* (1893), authored by Justice Charles Fenner. In this ruling, Fenner dismissed Plessy's Thirteenth Amendment claim, based on the same misreading of *The Civil Rights Cases*, and arrived at what he saw as the heart of the case: whether "separate but equal" violated the Fourteenth Amendment. Here Fenner cited numerous state and federal court decisions that held that "separate but equal" as applied to public conveyances or schools did not "abridge any privilege or immunity of citizens or otherwise contravene the XIV amendment."[310] He wrote: "To hold that the requirement of separate though equal accommodations in public conveyances violated the XIVth Amendment would on the same principles necessarily entail the nullity of statutes establishing separate schools and of others, existing in many States, prohibiting inter-marriage between the races."[311] *First, integrated railway cars, next, interracial sex.* And then:

We have been at pains to expound this [Separate Car Law] statute, because the dissatisfaction felt with it by a portion of the people seems to us so unreasonable that we can account for it only on the ground of some misconception. Even if it were true that the statute is prompted by prejudice on the part of one race to be thrown in such contact with the other, one would suppose that to be a sufficient reason why the pride and self-respect of the other race should equally prompt it to avoid such contact, if it could be done without the sacrifice of equal accommodations. It is very certain that such unreasonable insistence upon thrusting the company of one race upon the other, with no adequate motive, is calculated ... to foster and intensify repulsion between them rather than to extinguish it.[312]

[308] Lofgren 1987.
[309] Brief on Behalf of Defendant in Error (1895), 36, 37, 40. Italics in original.
[310] Brief on Behalf of Defendant in Error (1895), 46.
[311] Brief on Behalf of Defendant in Error (1895), 50.
[312] Brief on Behalf of Defendant in Error (1895), 50.

How could Black people have so little "pride and self-respect" that they would insist upon "thrusting th[eir] company" upon whites who did not welcome it? Writing at a historical juncture when lynching was surging in the U.S., Fenner understood all too well the efficacy of invoking, even indirectly, the rapacious Black brute.

Writing for the majority of the U.S. Supreme Court, Justice Henry Billings Brown dismissed Tourgée's argument that the Separate Car Law ran afoul of the Thirteenth Amendment:

We consider the underlying fallacy of the plaintiff's argument to consist in the assumption that the enforced separation of the two races stamps the colored race with a badge of inferiority. If this be so, it is not by reason of anything found in the act, but solely because the colored race chooses to put that construction on it.[313]

The danger, Brown argued, quoting Justice Bradley in *The Civil Rights Cases*, was rather "running the slavery argument into the ground." He then turned to the Fourteenth Amendment claim:

The object of the [Fourteenth] amendment was undoubtedly to enforce the absolute equality of the two races before the law, but, *in the nature of things*, it could not have been intended to abolish distinctions based upon color, or to enforce social, as distinguished from political, equality, or a commingling of the two races upon terms unsatisfactory to either. Laws permitting, and even requiring, their separation in places where they are liable to be brought into contact do not necessarily imply the inferiority of either race to the other, and have been generally, if not universally, recognized as within the competency of the state legislatures in the exercise of their police power.[314]

"Absolute equality" as a goal had to be understood in light of "the nature of things." It had to be tempered by the fact that nature had made the white race superior to the Black race, which made "commingling" intolerable for both. The role of law was to respect nature's dictates, not countermand them:

[The plaintiff's argument] assumes that social prejudices may be overcome by legislation, and that equal rights cannot be secured to the negro except by an enforced commingling of the two races .... Legislation is powerless to eradicate racial instincts or to abolish distinctions based upon physical differences, and the attempt to do so can only result in accentuating the difficulties of the present situation.[315]

---

[313] *Plessy v. Ferguson* (1896), 551.
[314] *Plessy v. Ferguson* (1896), 544. Italics added.
[315] *Plessy v. Ferguson* (1896), 551.

By bringing the law into conformity with the irresistible commands of nature, Brown suggested, the Separate Car Law enhanced public safety and welfare. Hence the official title of the statute: "An act promoting the comfort of passengers on railroad trains." Nature was a mighty force the law could not resist and, at the same time, a fragile equilibrium requiring the law's vigilant protection.[316]

Finally, Brown turned to Tourgée's charge that the police power could be used to justify any arbitrary measure, including "requir[ing] all colored people to walk on one side of the street and whites on the other." Brown responded: "[E]very exercise of the police power must be reasonable, and extend only to such laws as are enacted in good faith for the promotion of the public good, and not for the annoyance or oppression of a particular class."[317] It all came down, then, to the question of what counted as "promotion of the public good" and what counted as "oppression of a particular class." Brown stated: "[T]he case reduces itself to the question whether the statute of Louisiana is a reasonable regulation."[318] But could the court be relied upon to call out a discriminatory police regulation as unreasonable? Brown's answer was affirmative. Here, at the crux of the *Plessy* case, Brown turned to *Yick Wo* for support:

[I]n *Yick Wo v. Hopkins*, 118 U.S. 356, it was held by this court that a municipal ordinance of the city of San Francisco to regulate the carrying on of public laundries within the limits of the municipality violated the provisions of the Constitution of the United States if it conferred upon the municipal

---

[316] This is all the court said about property rights in this case, ignoring what could be reasonably construed as the statute's violation of the property rights of both passengers and railway companies (Bernstein 2008). Bernstein (1990) argues that after *Yick Wo* (where the court upheld both equal rights and economic freedom), the court only protected occupational liberty for whites and not for Black people. It upheld state economic regulations that explicitly discriminated against Black people and women and struck down state economic regulations that had an adverse impact on whites. Given the role that claims about natural difference played in subtending Jim Crow, it is not surprising that Brown chose not to take up Tourgée's argument about racial indeterminacy in any meaningful way (Golub 2005). Brown mentions the issue of determining racial classification only to dismiss it: "The power to assign to a particular coach obviously implies the power to determine to which race the passenger belongs, as well as the power to determine who, under the laws of the particular state, is to be deemed a white who a colored person. This question, though indicated in the brief of the plaintiff in error, does not properly arise upon the record in this case, since the only issue made is as to the unconstitutionality of the act so far as it requires the railway to provide separate accommodations and the conductor to assign passengers according to their race" *Plessy v. Ferguson* (1896), 549.
[317] *Plessy v. Ferguson* (1896), 550.
[318] *Plessy v. Ferguson* (1896), 550.

authorities arbitrary power .... It was held to be a covert attempt on the part of the municipality to make an arbitrary and unjust discrimination against the Chinese race.[319]

Brown invoked the court's ruling in *Yick Wo as proof that the court was willing and able to recognize a racially discriminatory law and strike it down.* At a moment of crisis generated by Plessy's dramatic challenge to Jim Crow, with the legitimacy of the court (and the broader U.S. state) at stake, *Yick Wo* testified to the court's fairness and neutrality. Which is to say, *Yick Wo* alibied the Plessy Court, and thereby Jim Crow.

Brown suggested that a court that would strike down an anti-Chinese ordinance would be equally prepared to strike down an anti-Black one. In *Yick Wo*, the court found the laundry ordinance to be an "arbitrary and unjust discrimination" because "[n]o reason for it is shown, and the conclusion cannot be resisted that no reason for it exists except hostility to [Yick Wo's] race and nationality."[320] In *Plessy*, however, the court ruled that the railway statute was undertaken for the "promotion of the public good" and thus reasonable. The difference was plain: distancing from the contamination of Blackness was the very definition of "the public good," whereas no such phobic avoidance governed relations with the Chinese. Hostility toward the Chinese laundryman was irrational, while hostility toward the Black railway passenger was rational and necessary. The Chinese migrant was *homo economicus*, the Black man an inveterate rapist.[321] *Yick Wo* did not in fact offer proof that the court would call out anti-Black discrimination in the future—in fact, Yick Wo's favorable ruling had depended upon his not-Blackness. By denying the Asian–Black gap and implying a false equivalence between the two not-white groups, Brown was able to pretend that the court's actions toward the Chinese were perfectly predictive of how it would act toward Black people. Through this fateful bait and switch, Brown used *Yick Wo* to give the court cover as it nailed down Jim Crow for another half-century.

Legal scholars have noted that *Yick Wo* was reproductively challenged, that it was an aberration of sorts with no clear progeny.[322] But

---

[319] *Plessy* v. *Ferguson* (1896), 550.
[320] *Yick Wo* v. *Hopkins* (1886), 356, 374.
[321] This is not to suggest that the members of the court were pro-Chinese, but only that they operated as if there were an ontological distinction between the Chinese and Black people.
[322] Chin 2008; Herbert 2008.

if we look beyond the realm of formal jurisprudence, at ideological and political discourses writ large, *Yick Wo*'s fecundity is not in question. What the discussion of *Yick Wo* in *Plessy* inaugurated, momentously and irretrievably, was the historical practice of invoking Asians—viewed as the lesser of two evils and structurally advantaged relative to Black people—as hedges against Black critique and witnesses for the U.S. state. *Yick Wo* in *Plessy* accomplished nothing less than entering "Asian. *n*. 1: false alibi" into the American grammar book.[323]

XV JUSTICE HARLAN AND THE CHINESE

In his *Plessy* dissent, Justice John Harlan argued that the three Reconstruction amendments accomplished nothing less than "remov[ing] the race line from our governmental systems."[324] Citing *Strauder* v. *West Virginia* (1880), in which the court struck down a state law that excluded "colored" citizens from juries as a violation of the Equal Protection Clause of the Fourteenth Amendment, Harlan wrote that the court said the Fourteenth Amendment bestowed upon Black people the "right to exemption from unfriendly legislation against them distinctively as colored" that "impl[ied] inferiority in civil society" and tended "towards reducing them to the condition of a subject race."[325] The Louisiana Separate Car Law was, in Harlan's view, exactly the type of unfriendly legislation the amendment meant to prohibit. Behind the "guise of giving equal accommodation," it illegitimately "interfere[d] with the personal freedom of citizens" on the basis of race and imposed a "badge of servitude wholly inconsistent with the civil freedom and the equality before the law established by the Constitution."[326] By upholding this law, the court was encouraging states to pass laws that thwarted the purpose of the Reconstruction amendments.

Harlan took up and expanded on Tourgée's observations about the potential abuse of the police power:

If a State can prescribe, as a rule of civil conduct, that whites and Blacks shall not travel as passengers in the same railroad coach, why may it not so regulate the use of the streets of its cities and towns as to compel white citizens to keep on one side of a street and Black citizens to keep on the other? Why may it not, upon like ground, punish whites and Blacks who ride together in streetcars or

---

[323] On the American grammar book, see Spillers 2003.
[324] Justice John Marshall Harlan's dissent in *Plessy* v. *Ferguson* (1896), 555.
[325] Justice John Marshall Harlan's dissent in *Plessy* v. *Ferguson* (1896), 556.
[326] Justice John Marshall Harlan's dissent in *Plessy* v. *Ferguson* (1896), 557, 562.

in open vehicles on a public road or street? Why may it not require sheriffs to assign whites to one side of a courtroom and Blacks to the other? And why may it not also prohibit the commingling of the two races in the galleries of legislative halls or in public assemblages convened for the consideration of the political questions of the day?[327]

To Tourgée's original list of venues where the police power could be misused, Harlan added courtrooms, legislative halls, and public assemblages. An uncurtailed police power, he suggested, would threaten Black participation in political life and undermine the political equality guaranteed by the Reconstruction amendments. Since political equality was the least controversial of the three kinds of equality (political, civil, and social), Harlan was playing to his strongest suit.

However, in his *Plessy* dissent, as in his dissent in *The Civil Rights Cases*, Harlan's vision of racial equality was circumscribed by his belief in white superiority and the enduring necessity of social inequality between Black people and whites. His declaration that "Our Constitution is color-blind" must be read together with the lines that preceded it:

The white race deems itself to be the dominant race in this country. And so it is in prestige, in achievements, in education, in wealth and in power. So, I doubt not, it will continue to be for all time if it remains true to its great heritage and holds fast to the principles of constitutional liberty. But in view of the Constitution, in the eye of the law, there is in this country no superior, dominant, ruling class of citizens. There is no caste here. Our Constitution is color-blind, and neither knows nor tolerates classes among citizens. In respect of civil rights, all citizens are equal before the law.[328]

In this passage, Harlan not only affirmed the principle of color-blindness but also offered assurance that it meant nothing more than race neutrality and the repudiation of caste in the limited sphere of civil rights. In his view, color-blind law neither threatened white dominance nor promoted social equality:

[S]ocial equality no more exists between two races when traveling in a passenger coach or a public highway than when members of the same races sit by each other in a street car or in the jury box, or stand or sit with each other in a political assembly, or when they use in common the street of a city of town, or when they are in the same room for the purpose of having their names placed on the registry of voters, or when they approach the ballot box in order to exercise the high privilege of voting.[329]

[327] Justice John Marshall Harlan's dissent in *Plessy v. Ferguson* (1896), 557–558.
[328] Justice John Marshall Harlan's dissent in *Plessy v. Ferguson* (1896), 558.
[329] Justice John Marshall Harlan's dissent in *Plessy v. Ferguson* (1896), 561.

As in his dissent in *The Civil Rights Cases*, Harlan defended integrated public accommodations on the grounds that they left social inequality intact.

Immediately thereafter, Harlan mentioned the Chinese:

> There is a race so different from our own that we do not permit those belonging to it to become citizens of the United States. Persons belonging to it are, with few exceptions, absolutely excluded from our country. I allude to the Chinese race. But, by the statute in question, a Chinaman can ride in the same passenger coach with white citizens of the United States, while citizens of the Black race in Louisiana, many of whom, perhaps, risked their lives for the preservation of the Union, who are entitled, by law, to participate in the political control of the State and nation, who are not excluded, by law or by reason of their race, from public stations of any kind, and who have all the legal rights that belong to white citizens, are yet declared to be criminals, liable to imprisonment, if they ride in a public coach occupied by citizens of the white race.[330]

By what logic could the Chinese ride in the white railway car, while Black people, who had fought for the nation and possessed all of the formal rights of citizenship, could not?[331]

Gabriel Chin points to this passage, as well as Harlan's writing in other cases, as evidence of Harlan's "animosity" toward the Chinese. Chin writes: "Harlan merely wanted to reform America's nineteenth century racial hierarchy, expanding the number of favored races by one rather than attacking race distinction root and branch."[332] In his view, Harlan tried to elevate Black people at the expense of the Chinese, in an "early example of the comparative evaluation of non-white racial groups to determine their entitlement to legal protection or recognition." Due to his "pernicious use of one minority group as a proxy to attack another," Chin concludes, Harlan does not deserve his current reputation as a champion of civil rights.[333]

Chin assumes that Black people and the Chinese were equally situated as unfavored races in the nineteenth-century racial hierarchy. From there he reads Harlan's comparative comments as an effort to elevate Black people over the Chinese. But the Chinese were from the start advantaged by their not-Blackness, which is precisely why they were, despite their alienage, allowed to ride in white railway cars when Black people were not. The Louisiana House of Representatives had in fact explicitly considered segregating the Chinese as well under the

---

[330] Justice John Marshall Harlan's dissent in *Plessy* v. *Ferguson* (1896), 561.
[331] See J. Lee 2011.
[332] Chin 1996–1997, 182.
[333] Chin 1996–1997, 171.

Separate Car Law.[334] Representative Borland had offered and then with-drawn an amendment stipulating that "the words 'colored races' used in this bill shall be held to mean and include negroe's [sic], mongolians and malays."[335] Representative Allain had then offered an amendment "[t]hat the Mongolian, or races other than colored, shall ride in white passenger cars, and shall be subject to all of the provisions of this act."[336] Which would prevail: the principle of white supremacy or the principle of anti-Blackness? The lawmakers could not reach agreement on either amendment, so in the end they neither mandated the segregation of the Chinese nor explicitly affirmed their right to ride in white railway cars. When railway conductors subsequently allowed the Chinese to ride with whites, they reflected the racial common sense of the era.

To be clear, Harlan did not argue that the Chinese should *not* be allowed to ride in white railway cars; his focus was not on the Chinese per se, but rather on drawing a contrast between the privileges enjoyed by Chinese aliens and Black citizens, respectively. His point was "if y, why not x?" His purpose in mentioning the Chinese, then, was to highlight both the struc-tural advantage they enjoyed relative to Black people and, relatedly, the sin-gularity and extremity of Black abjection. So while Gabriel Chin denounces Harlan for trying to elevate Blacks at the expense of the Chinese, it might be more accurate to say that Harlan was asking why the Chinese were being elevated at the expense of Blacks. Ironically, what Chin charges Harlan with—aiming only to "expan[d] the number of favored races by one rather than attacking race distinction root and branch"—applies rather to the racial advancement strategies adopted by some Chinese immigrant leaders in the U.S., for example, in response to the ruling in *People* v. *George Hall.*

Harlan's overall record on the Chinese is decidedly mixed. Although he joined the unanimous opinion in *Yick Wo*, as well as other lower court decisions protecting the rights of Chinese aliens, he also dissented in the Chinese birthright citizenship case, *United States* v. *Wong Kim Ark* (1898) and strongly defended the federal government's plenary power to restrict Chinese immigration in any way it chose.[337] It all depends on

---

[334] Hoffer 2012.

[335] *Official Journal of the Proceedings of the House of Representatives of the State of Loui-siana* (May 12, 1890), 181.

[336] *Official Journal of the Proceedings of the House of Representatives of the State of Loui-siana* (May 12, 1890), 181.

[337] Gordon (2014) argues that Harlan was a nativist but not anti-Chinese, citing Harlan's record of protecting the constitutional rights of resident aliens (as opposed to immi-grants) and pointing out that his decisions were explainable by factors other than anti-Chinese animus.

what parts of his record we choose to emphasize, as well as which bench-
mark of anti-Chinese animus we employ.

XVI *GONG LUM V. RICE*

During Reconstruction, southern planters developed an experimen-
tal plan to replace Black labor with Chinese labor. Powell Clayton, the
Reconstruction Governor of Arkansas, commented: "Undoubtedly the
underlying motive for this effort to bring in Chinese laborers was to punish the negro for having abandoned the control of his old master, and to
regulate the conditions of his employment and the scale of wages to be
paid him."[338] The Chinese, heralded as more intelligent, hardworking, and
capable than Black people, were also, to the delight of the planters, aliens
who could not vote. Echoing Governor Clayton, James Loewen observes:

> The apolitical noncitizen coolie, it was thought, would be a step back toward the
> more docile labor conditions of slavery times .... [T]he "Chinaman" would not
> only himself supply a cheaper and less troublesome work force but in addition his
> presence as a threatening alternative would intimidate the Negro into resuming
> his former docile behavior.[339]

As under British colonialism in Trinidad, the Chinese were introduced
into the U.S. South as a third group that would help whites keep Black
people in their place. For planters outraged by Black people's new personal and economic mobility during Reconstruction, and intimidated
by the threat of Black political power, Chinese labor offered hope. In
July 1869, the Memphis Chinese Labor Convention drew 500 delegates
(planters, railroad executives, industrialists) from Alabama, Georgia,
Kentucky, Mississippi, South Carolina, Louisiana, Arkansas, Tennessee,
Missouri, and California, all of whom came to explore the possibility of
importing Chinese indentured labor into the South. Not long after, small
numbers of Chinese contract laborers arrived from China, California,
and Cuba to work on southern plantations.[340]

The southern experiment with Chinese labor was short-lived and
unsuccessful. Planters discovered that Chinese labor was not superior
to Black labor, nor as cheap or docile as they had hoped. Chinese laborers complained, rebelled, and abandoned their indentures or long-term
contracts. Most left the plantations within a year or two, discontent with

---

[338] Loewen 1988 [1971], 23.
[339] Loewen 1988 [1971], 23.
[340] Cohen 1984.

the planters' duplicity and the overseers' brutality.[341] Like Italian immigrant laborers before them, the Chinese quickly came to view plantation labor as "nigger work" to be escaped at the first opportunity.[342] When Reconstruction collapsed, eclipsing Black freedom dreams and shifting power back into the hands of planters, the main rationale for hiring Chinese labor disappeared.

Some of the Chinese workers who left the plantations moved to small southern towns and opened up grocery stores. The small Chinese population that settled in the Mississippi Delta after Reconstruction, made up of male laborers who had left the plantations or railroads, concentrated almost exclusively in this occupation.[343] By the 1920 Census, "the grocery store had essentially become the sole occupation of the Delta Chinese."[344] Even decades later, while doing fieldwork for his 1971 book *The Mississippi Chinese: Between Black and White*, James Loewen found that 97 percent of the Chinese in the Delta were involved in, or retired from, the grocery trade.[345]

The Chinese grocery store in the Mississippi Delta served a mostly Black clientele and was an artifact of Jim Crow. Black sharecroppers were instructed to buy goods at the plantation commissary, but many exerted their economic independence by choosing to shop elsewhere— often at Chinese groceries, since most white storeowners would not serve them.[346] When white grocers served a Black clientele, they found that "operating close to the caste line wrecks one's position in the white class structure and brings down upon one status threats so severe that, as with Negro status itself, one's very identity as an acceptable member of the human species is endangered."[347] White grocers serving Black customers faced a fatal loss of white status, in other words. Chinese grocers did not have this to lose, and they benefited from the willingness of white wholesalers to extend them credit and the willingness of white elites to tolerate their success in this niche. With Black customers as a captive market, and Black store ownership rates depressed through discrimination in

---

[341] Cohen 1984; Loewen 1988 [1971].

[342] Berard 2016, 32.

[343] There were 174 Chinese people in Mississippi in 1910; 211 in 1920. The Chinese population in the Mississippi Delta reached 1,200 or so by 1960, at which point they constituted less than 5 percent of the population there (J. Jung 2008, 19, 31).

[344] J. Jung 2008, 7.

[345] Loewen 1988 [1971], 36.

[346] Berard 2016; J. Jung 2008.

[347] Loewen 1988 [1971], 50.

education, employment, and lending, the Chinese stepped in where Black people could not and whites would not.[348] It was the property of not-Blackness that enabled them to rise to this position of moderately elevated economic and social status.

Some of the Chinese who became grocers in the Delta worked in California or Cuba or other parts of the U.S. South first; others came directly from China, entering the U.S. surreptitiously via Canada.[349] All traveled the global circuits of anti-Blackness, absorbing lessons about "nigger work" and not-Blackness along the way. By the early twentieth century, Chinese ideas about Blackness had much in common with Western ideas, in part because they were influenced by the latter. When the Qing dynasty was overthrown by the Republican revolution of 1911, the revolutionaries, who were influenced by social Darwinism and eugenics, proclaimed the racial superiority of the Han people (the Qing rulers were Manchu not Han) and valorized yellow and white over brown, black, and red. Philosopher Kang Youwei's influential text *One World* (1913) argued that the Chinese and whites were the fittest groups in terms of evolutionary survival and would eventually become indistinguishable, while inferior races, especially Blacks, would disappear through natural selection.[350] A typical Chinese primary school curriculum in the Republican era taught: "Mankind is divided into five races. The yellow and white races are relatively strong and intelligent. Because the other races are feeble and stupid, they are being exterminated by the white race. Only the yellow race competes with the white race. This is so-called evolution."[351] Coming from this cultural and intellectual milieu, Chinese arriving in the Delta already understood the rules of the game.

The operating practices of Chinese grocers bolstered the racial caste system. White customers were treated with greater respect than Black customers:

Obeying the unwritten rules of social etiquette embedded in the racial structure of the Delta, they [Chinese grocers] respectfully greeted white, but not Black, customers as Mister "Smith" or Missus "Jones," for example. Chinese did not address most white customers by their first names, but tolerated white customers

---

[348] See Johnson (1983) for a discussion of the Chinese moving from plantation laborers to food merchants in post-emancipation Jamaica.

[349] Gong Lum belonged to the second group. He was drawn to the Mississippi Delta because a relative operated a store there (Berard 2016).

[350] Shih 2013.

[351] Dikötter 1994, 408.

greeting them by their first names. This arrangement created a sense of familiarity that made white customers feel at ease or even superior during conversations with Chinese who exhibited politeness bordering on the excessive.[352]

The Chinese were deferential to whites and withheld full respect from Black people. One Chinese man who came to the Mississippi Delta as a boy to work in his uncle's store recalled: "We [Chinese] don't mix with nobody, we keep our mouth shut, no talk, just work .... We don't want to become *Bok Guey* [whites] and we sure don't want to become 'colored' like the *Hok Guey* [Blacks], no sir, those people were treated worse than dogs. We don't want that to happen to us anyhow, anywhere, anyway."[353] *Blackness is a point from which the greatest distance must be forged.*[354] James Loewen notes: "In the presence of whites, the [Chinese] grocer would joke about Blacks, telling whites of the Cantonese derogatory term for 'nigger' and relating amusing requests of illiterate sharecroppers."[355] Ridiculing Blackness created a brotherhood between Asians and whites, a fraternity of not-Blackness.

In the rigidly binary geography of Jim Crow, the Chinese were often permitted to use the facilities and public accommodations reserved for whites. Adrienne Berard writes: "Despite their status as outsiders, the Mississippi Chinese were able to achieve a higher social standing than their Black neighbors and customers. In fact, it was their outsider status itself that mitigated against their being classed as Black in America."[356] If foreignness was an escape hatch from being race-d, however, it was an imperfect one, and the Chinese had only uneven access to white accommodations. They were clearly not-Black, but they were also not-white. When a Chinese American community leader in Greenville needed an appendectomy, he was denied admission to a white hospital and sent to a Black hospital. There "he was assigned a private room so that he would not have to share quarters with a Negro. And there a white surgeon attended him."[357] He was sent to a Black hospital because he was not-white, and then given special treatment there by a white surgeon because he was not-Black. The Chinese cemetery in Greenville emerged in response to such dilemmas of racial location. One elderly Chinese man recalled: "The Chinese ran into difficulties with whites who wouldn't let

---

[352] J. Jung 2008, 99.
[353] Quan 1982, 44.
[354] Gordon 1997, 53.
[355] Loewen 1988 [1971], 79.
[356] Berard 2016, 28.
[357] Cohn 1967 [1935], 234–235.

them use the *Bok Guey fun cheng* [white graveyard]. And the Chinese didn't want to be buried with the *Lo Mok* [Blacks] 'cause we was a different people, so we all got the Chinese cemetery started."[358]

Be white, but above all don't be Black. In pursuing these principles, the Chinese community in the Delta had to face two inconvenient facts: first, Chinese grocers and their families served a mostly Black clientele in Black neighborhoods (and they lived in the back of their stores); second, a small minority of Chinese men married, lived with, and/or had children with Black women. (Prior to 1920, there were very few Chinese women in the Mississippi Delta, and state law prohibited intermarriage between whites and "Mongolians," and between whites and "Negroes or Mulattos," but not between "Mongolians" and "Negroes or Mulattos.") Both of these circumstances, and especially the latter, threatened to taint the Chinese with Blackness in the eyes of whites.

Intent upon gaining white acceptance and favor, Chinese grocers strategically embraced Christianity, gave their children white names, and cultivated white social contacts through church and business.[359] Gong Lum, who ran a thriving grocery store in Rosedale in the 1920s, named his two daughters Berda and Martha after two prominent white women in Bolivar County. He asked a white couple whom he met through the First Presbyterian Church to be their godparents.[360] Berda and Martha attended church and school with white children. However, on September 15, 1924, nine-year-old Martha Lum was turned away from the Rosedale Consolidated High School where she had been attending.[361] The principal informed her that the Board of Trustees was enforcing the state constitution, which barred Chinese students from attending white schools. He was referring to Mississippi's 1890 constitution, written to "Redeem" the state after Reconstruction, in which Article 8 (Education), Section 207 stated simply: "Separate schools shall be maintained for children of the white and colored races." The question was: why were the Chinese suddenly being classified as "colored" and barred from white schools they had been attending for years without incident?

Writing about the children of Chinese–Black unions in the Delta, David Cohn observed: "To the casual eye these children are often indistinguishable from full-blooded Chinese. The fear arose in the white

[358] Quan 1982, 38.
[359] Loewen 1988 [1971].
[360] Rhee 1994; Berard 2016.
[361] Martha's older sister Berda was also turned away from the school, but the lawsuit focused on Martha.

community that if Chinese children were permitted to attend the public schools these Chinese-Negro half-breeds would go along."[362] "The issue, therefore," Vivian Wong writes, "was not whether Chinese children should be allowed to attend white schools, but rather how can Chinese-Black children and, consequently, Black children be denied access to white schools."[363] In Greenville, school officials admitted Chinese students into a white school only after Chinese community leaders testified that the children were "pure" Chinese, and with the stipulation that "if there was one drop of Black blood in a Chinese student, he was excluded."[364] By the one-drop rule, the children of Chinese–Black unions were not Chinese; they were simply Black. Thus it was not anti-Chinese sentiment per se but rather negrophobia, the phobic hatred and avoidance of Blackness, that led to Martha Lum's expulsion from the white school. Martha had been accepted in the white school until the possibility arose that she was in fact Black, a Trojan horse who looked not-Black on the outside but carried Blackness within. The Chinese body had to be interdicted to prevent it from smuggling the contamination of Blackness into white spaces. What looks like a story about anti-Chinese discrimination is, more fundamentally, a story about anti-Blackness.

The Chinese community in the Delta felt betrayed by the school's decision. They had left the plantations, opened businesses, observed the anti-Black etiquette of Jim Crow, and curried the favor of prominent whites—in sum, they had followed the rules of the game and distanced from Blackness. To be sent to the "colored" schools in this way was a shocking derogation in status. Martha Lum's mother, Katherine, declared: "I did not want my children to attend the 'colored' schools. If they had, the community would have classified us as negroes."[365] At issue was not just Martha's schooling but the entire community's status as not-Black, their having "something to save."

Rosa Lee Black, a white woman who lived in Rosedale at the time, recalls that her father, a school trustee, along with most white residents, actually opposed the expulsion of Martha Lum. Jeannie Rhee writes: "While the Rosedale residents themselves would have purged the school

[362] Cohn 1967 [1935], 156. In the film *Mississippi Triangle* (1983), Rosa Lee Black, a white woman whose father was on the school board in Rosedale, recalls that the "key to the lawsuit" was that someone claimed that Martha Lum was "part Black," which prompted Martha to respond that she was "pure Chinese" with "no Black blood."

[363] V. Wong 1993, 21.

[364] Quan 1982, 49.

[365] Berard 2016, 72.

of any Chinese if they evidenced even a trace of African-American lineage, the pure Chinese were entirely another matter to them at this point."[366] Many whites offered the Lums support, and Gong Lum retained a prominent white firm that offered to take the case almost entirely pro bono. The Lums sued, and the case traveled from the circuit court (where the Lums prevailed) to the Mississippi Supreme Court (where the school district prevailed) to the U.S. Supreme Court (where the Mississippi Supreme Court ruling was affirmed).[367]

In the appellee's brief to the Mississippi Supreme Court, Gong Lum's attorney, Earl Brewer, declared:

[I]t is clearly shown by the authorities cited herein that the Chinaman is not a "colored person" within the meaning of our laws. He would therefore not go to the negro school as a negro. The court will take judicial notice of the fact that members of the Mongolian race under our Jim Crow statute are treated as not belonging to the negro race. The Japanese are classified with the Chinese. These two races furnish some of the most intelligent and enterprising people. They certainly stand nearer to the white race than they do to the negro race. If the Caucasian is not ready to admit that the representative Mongolian is his equal, he is willing to concede that the Mongolian is on the hither side of the half-way line between the Caucasian and the African.[368]

Martha Lum was a "Mongolian" and thus not a "negro" or "colored." Brewer might have stopped there, since the crux of the case was that the language of Section 207 of Article 8 of the 1890 state constitution did not apply to Martha. However, he thought it important to emphasize further that the Chinese were not located halfway between whites and "the negro race," but rather "on the hither side of the half-way line" between the two. If Martha was not-white, she was even more definitively not-Black. The Chinese belonged with whites in a category defined by the exclusion of Black people. Brewer understood that if the courts foregrounded Martha's not-whiteness, she would lose, but if they foregrounded her not-Blackness, she would win.

The Mississippi Supreme Court's unanimous ruling in *Rice* v. *Lum* (1925) dismissed Brewer's "Martha is not Black" argument with a "Martha is not white" argument of its own. Justice Ethridge, writing

---

[366] Rhee 1994, 122.

[367] Judge William Aristide Alcorn of the 11th Circuit Court of Mississippi ordered the school to readmit Martha Lum, implying that the Chinese, even though they were not white, had rights that Black people did not have (Rhee 1994).

[368] Appellee's Brief to the Mississippi Supreme Court in *Rice* v. *Gong Lum* (1925), 774. Note the similarity of this language to Reverend Speer's objections to the California Supreme Court's *People* v. *George Hall* decision in 1854, discussed above.

for the court, characterized Section 207 as reflecting the "broad, dominant purpose of preserving the purity and integrity of the white race."[369] With this legislative intent in mind, Ethridge cited various cases (*In re Ah Yup, Ozawa* v. *United States, Yamashita* v. *Hinkle*) as having adjudicated Asian not-whiteness, as well as Section 2859 of the Mississippi code of 1892, which prohibited whites from marrying "negroes," "mulattos," those having "1/8 or more negro blood," "Mongolians," and those having "1/8 or more Mongolian blood." Then, citing Chief Justice Murray's decision in *People* v. *George Hall* ("The word 'Black' may include all negroes, but the term 'negro' does not include all Black persons"), Ethridge concluded: "[T]he word 'white,' when used in describing the race, is limited strictly to the Caucasian race, while the word 'colored' is not strictly limited to negroes or persons having negro blood."[370] "White" was a restrictive term, "colored" an expansive one. The relevant boundary was between whites and all those who posed a threat to white racial purity.

In the Brief of the Plaintiff in Error to the U.S. Supreme Court, Lum's new attorney James Flowers again emphasized Martha Lum's not-Blackness.[371] Martha was "not a member of the colored race nor of mixed blood but [was] of pure Chinese origin or descent." As a native-born citizen of the United States and the state of Mississippi, she had a right to attend public school, and the Rosedale Board of Trustees and other educational officials were denying her the "privileges and immunities incident to her citizenship" by barring her from Rosedale solely because she was of Chinese descent. This was deprivation of right "without process of law" and a clear denial of "equal protection of the law."[372] Flowers then elaborated on the equal protection claim:

The classification [of "white" and "colored" students with regard to schooling] is made for the exclusive benefit of the law-making race. The basic assumption is that if the children of two races associate daily in the school room the two races will at last intermix; that the purity of each is jeopardized by the mingling of the children in the school room; that such association among children means social intercourse and social equality. This danger, the white race, by its laws seeks to divert from itself. It levies the taxes on all alike to support a public school system but in the organization of the system it creates its own exclusive schools for its children and other schools for the children of all other races to attend together. *If*

---

[369] *Rice* v. *Lum* (1925), 786.
[370] *Rice* v. *Lum* (1925), 780.
[371] Flowers took over the case when Brewer left to prosecute a lynching case (Berard 2016).
[372] Brief and Argument for Plaintiff in Error (1925), 4, 5, 5.

there is a danger in the association it is a danger from which one race is entitled to protection just the same as another. The White race may not legally expose the Yellow race to a danger that the dominant race recognizes and, by the same laws, guards itself against. The White race creates for itself a privilege that it denies to other races; exposes the children of other races to risks and dangers to which it would not expose its own children. This is discrimination.[373]

Flowers strongly affirmed Jim Crow's anti-Black logic—it was not the principle of racial separation he questioned, only the placement of the Chinese in the "colored" category. It was a constitutional violation to exclude Martha from the white school, he argued, because doing so would expose her to the grievous "danger" of associating with Black people and thus deny her the equal protection of the law. *The Chinese deserved to be protected from Blackness, too.*

Flowers continued:

That the negroes were once slaves and, as a race, had to begin as children, is judicially known, even adjudicated. Laws are upheld that recognize this well-known fact. Because of their racial peculiarities, physical as well as moral, the white race avoids social relations with the members of that race. Such intercourse is objectionable; in many instances would be repulsive and impossible. The White race protects itself against conditions that would require social contact—this, as the Mississippi court says, to preserve the integrity of the Caucasian race, But has not the Chinese citizen the same right to protection that the Caucasian citizen has? Are they not all equal before the law? Can we say to the Chinese child "you must associate with children of the negro race but we will not allow the same association to our own children?" Can we arrogate to ourselves the superior right to so organize the public school system as to protect our racial integrity without regard to the interests or welfare of citizens of other races?[374]

"Equal before the law," then, meant being able to achieve comparable distance with whites from Black people. The point was not equal protection *for* Black people, as the Fourteenth Amendment intended, but rather equal protection *from* Black people. Flowers's gambit was that whites' hatred of Black people was strong enough to arouse their sympathy for the Chinese, who, after all, were only trying to avoid Black people, too. The problem for Flowers was that the Chinese were being rejected in this historic instance not because of their Chineseness, but because they were potential conduits of Blackness. Negrophobia, in other words, was *also working against him.*

---

[373] Brief and Argument for Plaintiff in Error (1925), 9–10. Italics added.
[374] Brief and Argument for Plaintiff in Error (1925), 13–14.

The Brief for the Defendant in Error reprised the Mississippi Supreme Court's argument that the Chinese were not white under the law. It also emphasized that the constitutionality of racially segregated schools had been decisively affirmed. In *Plessy*, the brief pointed out, the Court stated that the Louisiana Separate Car Law was no more obnoxious to the Fourteenth Amendment than congressional action to segregate public schools in Washington, D.C., clearly assuming the constitutional soundness of the latter. Then, citing the Mississippi 1892 anti-miscegenation statute, the brief concluded:

Were the school authorities within their rights in adopting the course which they did with reference to her [Martha Lum's] education and association? Under the laws of the state of Mississippi plaintiff in error could never lawfully marry a member of the white race. On the other hand there is no law in the state prohibiting intermarriage between members of the Chinese and negro races. Is it not better to confine her association, so far as is possible, to those with whom she may associate on more intimate terms in the future years?[375]

By invoking a law structured by white supremacy, which subordinated all not-white groups to whites, counsel for the defendant sought to emphasize Martha's not-whiteness and proximity to Blackness. His mention of Chinese–Black unions then reminded the court indirectly of the threat such unions could pose to the system of Jim Crow.

Chief Justice William Howard Taft wrote the brief and unanimous decision for the court:

The question here is whether a Chinese citizen of the United States is denied equal protection of the laws when he is classed among the colored races and furnished facilities for education equal to that offered to all, whether white, brown, yellow, or Black. Were this a new question, it would call for very full argument and consideration; but we think that it is the same question which has been many times decided to be within the constitutional power of the state legislature to settle, without intervention of the federal courts under the federal Constitution.[376]

The case came down to whether "separate but equal" schools could be squared with the Equal Protection Clause, and this matter had been adjudicated repeatedly, with the same affirmative result. It did not make a difference that the students in this case were Chinese and not Black:

Most of the cases cited arose, it is true, over the establishment of separate schools as between white pupils and Black pupils, but we cannot think that the question is any different, or that any different result can be reached, assuming the cases

---

[375] Brief for Defendants in Error (1926), 36.
[376] *Gong Lum* v. *Rice* (1927), 85–86.

above cited to be rightly decided, where the issue is as between white pupils and the pupils of the yellow races. The decision is within the discretion of the state in regulating its public schools, and does not conflict with the Fourteenth Amendment.[377]

Rather than reflecting on the differential positioning of the Chinese and Black people, the court dodged the issue and lumped the two groups together. With the ruling of the Mississippi Supreme Court affirmed, Martha Lum was barred from attending her school or any other white school in the state.

XVII THE NOT-BLACKNESS OF THE MISSISSIPPI CHINESE

But that was not the end of the story. *Gong Lum* provisionally classified the Chinese as "colored" in order to contain the contamination of Blackness, but the ruling went against racial common sense and thus invited resistance on the ground. The Delta Chinese community promptly devised a collective strategy in response to the ruling. If the U.S. Supreme Court was going to focus on the not-whiteness of the Chinese, to the point of categorizing them with Black people, then the Chinese would step up their efforts to prove their not-Blackness.

Chinese families began by refusing to send their children to "colored" schools. The Lums moved to Elaine, Arkansas, where a white school was willing to admit Martha and Berda. Other Chinese families, too, opted for white schools in other areas, or for private tutors, religious schools, or returning to China. Church officials helped the Chinese community to persuade the Bolivar County School Board to open an all-Chinese public school in 1933. Other clergy opened religious schools to instruct Chinese students. Then, with pro-Chinese feeling running high after the Second World War, most white public schools in the Delta opened their doors to the Chinese, and separate Chinese schools shut down.[378] During the postwar period, as the social and economic standing of the Chinese in the Delta rose, one town after another permitted Chinese children to enroll in white schools, while maintaining the bar on Black children.[379] Though *Gong Lum* remained on the books, then, within a few decades "it was as if the decision had never been handed down."[380]

[377] *Gong Lum* v. *Rice* (1927), 87.
[378] Rhee 1994; Koshy 2001.
[379] Greenwood admitted Chinese students to white schools in the 1930s, Clarksdale in 1941, Greenville in 1945. The latest held out until the early 1950s (Loewen 1988 [1971], 93.)
[380] Rhee 1994, 129.

As indicated above, the Chinese, for their part, had to do their best to discourage Chinese–Black unions. James Loewen writes: "In several towns, school officials stated explicitly to Chinese leaders that no consideration regarding the overriding issue of school exclusion would be shown them unless social associations between Chinese and Negroes in the community were ended."[381] The Greenville School Board made Chinese admission conditional on the promise that "the Chinese themselves must see to it that no children of Chinese-Negro blood apply through their community."[382] It wasn't enough for the Chinese to police Chinese-Black children, they had to excise the taint of Blackness entirely from within their ranks. The result was the systematic excommunication of Chinese-Black families from the Delta Chinese community. Chinese community leaders "set out to eradicate the Chinese-Negro minority, by influencing Chinese males to end Negro relationships and throw out their Chinese-Negro kin, or by forcing the families to leave the community."[383] Tactics for driving these families out of town included but were not limited to social ostracism, telling whites that they had "questionable racial ancestry," and pressuring white wholesalers to stop extending credit to them. Some targets capitulated to these tactics; others closed their stores and left town with their families, rather than abandoning them. Social ostracism achieved its purpose, and, as a result, the Chinese were granted significant social and economic mobility in the Delta by the 1950s. Decades later, when filmmakers made a documentary about the Delta Chinese, entitled *Mississippi Triangle* (1983), Chinese community leaders tried unsuccessfully to stop them from talking to Chinese-Black families. They had hoped to erase the latter altogether from history and memory. But Arlee Hen, who had a Black mother and Chinese father, spoke at length in the film. She died during filming and was denied burial in the Chinese cemetery because of her "mixed blood."

The emergence of the civil rights movement in the 1950s, in tandem with the heating up of the Cold War, created a domestic and international legitimacy crisis for the U.S. state. In this context, southern whites' commitment to Black subordination gave a boost to Chinese American mobility in the region. James Loewen writes: "[T]he Chinese played a symbolic role for whites: when the Civil Rights Movement made whites feel guilty about their racism, they accepted Chinese, as if to say 'I'm not

---

[381] Loewen 1988 [1971], 76.
[382] Cohn 1967 [1935], 235.
[383] Loewen 1988 [1971], 76.

a racist, it's just Blacks who are the problem.'"[384] The Chinese continued to be welcomed into white churches, schools, and neighborhoods
during this period and were even recruited by Citizens Councils, white
supremacist organizations that actively opposed civil rights. "Upper-
class Mississippians," Loewen wrote, "could now reassure themselves that
they were good Americans and good Christians and that their oppression of Negroes was called forth by that race's particular and peculiar
lack of capacity."[385] *White is best, but the most important thing is not-
Blackness. Better Asians than Blacks.* As with the invocation of *Yick Wo*
in *Plessy* a half-century before, whites responded to Black critique by
elevating Asian Americans instead—as the lesser of two evils—and then
invoking them as an alibi for themselves and the U.S. state.

John Jung notes that the Delta Chinese had to walk a fine line during
the civil rights movement:

> During the battle over school desegregation that arose in the 1960s, some Chi-
> nese hedged their bets, making private contributions to both the National Asso-
> ciation for the Advancement of Colored People and the white segregationist
> Citizens' Councils. To be acceptable to whites, they had to distance themselves
> from Blacks. But being economically dependent on Blacks, as well as living in
> Black neighborhoods, they had to treat Blacks better than whites did.[386]

Chinese grocers could not afford to be seen as supporting the civil rights
movement or opposing it. Some were forced to alter their treatment of
Black customers, however, as this Chinese grocer notes regretfully:

> Today things ain't like what they used to be in the past. The *Lo Mok* [Blacks]
> were easier to get along with back then …. I remember one time I caught these
> two *Hok Guey Doy* [Black male children]. One was trying to steal a can of tuna
> fish. The other was opening up boxes of cereal trying to get the toys out. You
> know, usually I'd have one of my children follow the *Lo Mok* around the store
> so this kind of thing wouldn't happen …. But anyway, I caught them two boys,
> took them out back and whupped their butts. They were so scared they wouldn't
> tell no one. Then I called their mother and told her what happened. She appreci-
> ated it and told me to teach them a lesson. You know, I was giving them credit
> in those days and they didn't want to be dropped. Now it's different—you touch
> one of them, and they raise all kind of hell, call the NAACP, take you to court,
> boycott your store …. It ain't worth it …. The times have changed, ain't what
> it used to be.[387]

---

[384] Loewen 1988 [1971], 196.
[385] Loewen 1988 [1971], 99.
[386] J. Jung 2008, 135.
[387] Quan 1982, 90–91.

Gone were the days when the grocer could, with impunity, surveil Black children, take them out back and beat them, and then intimidate their parents with the threat of withdrawing credit. The civil rights movement indirectly enhanced Chinese mobility, but it also deprived Chinese grocers of some of the anti-Black prerogatives they had enjoyed.

Gong Lum is typically remembered as a moment when white supremacy came for Asian Americans and they joined Black people in the struggle against educational segregation. It is only by bringing structural anti-Blackness back into the picture from which it has been redacted that we can recognize this as a distortion of historical truth. On the surface, the case appears to indicate that the Chinese were seen and treated as Black, and that the principle of white supremacy, or the domination of whites over not-whites, was determinative in their lives. But excavating the history of the case corrects this impression. It was not the Chineseness of the Chinese that triggered their expulsion from white schools, nor their not-whiteness in some generic sense, but rather the specific concern that they might, because of the history of Chinese–Black unions in the Delta, serve as a Trojan horse for smuggling the contamination of Blackness into white spaces. Thus the court's derogation of the Chinese must be understood in relation to foundational anti-Blackness and the prime directive to reproduce this structure of power above all else.

For the Chinese, capitalizing on their not-Blackness was the key to their survival and mobility. In *Gong Lum* and elsewhere, they did not challenge the principle of "separate but equal" but rather objected to being classified as "colored." Martha Lum's attorney took great pains to signal that the Chinese looked upon Black people with as much distaste as whites did. When the one-drop rule threw their status into doubt, the Chinese decided to set the record straight by erasing their Black kin. In addition, fortuitously, the Black civil rights struggle helped to fuel Chinese Americans' upward mobility by incentivizing southern whites to perform anti-racism by showing greater acceptance toward them instead of Black people.

The Mississippi Chinese were subordinated by white supremacy, trying to survive in a foreign land, and faced with a social structure that punished association with Blackness. They were caught in circumstances not of their own making, like all historical subjects. Still, there is a difference between them and Yick Wo, who was just trying to keep his laundry open in San Francisco and never assented to being invoked in *Plessy* in defense of Jim Crow. Yick Wo had no say in whether or how he was weaponized against the Black struggle. But the Delta

Chinese, who participated in their own weaponization, are a more complicated story. Did they have a meaningful choice about how to act in an anti-Black world? Some Chinese grocers in the Delta endured ostracism and economic hardship, or sold their stores and moved, rather than abandon their Black wives and children. The others made a bargain with whites to get ahead on the backs of Black people (including their own kin). The question of Asian American implicatedness in structural anti-Blackness is raised by the Chinese American experience, and the question is not resolved by the Japanese immigrants who gained a foothold in California during the era of Chinese exclusion. This is the topic of Part Two.

Part Two

Ostracism/Initiation

I INTRODUCTION

The story of the Japanese immigrants who came to the U.S in the late nineteenth and early twentieth centuries is conventionally narrated as a second Asian exclusion drama. White Californians, driven by material self-interest and anti-Asian animus, set their sights on Japanese immigrants and their descendants and colluded over many decades in attempting to drive them out of the nation. Once again, incorrigible Asian foreignness was the crux of the argument. This exclusionary drive culminated during the Second World War with the internment of roughly

120,000 Japanese Americans, two-thirds of whom were native-born U.S. citizens, on the grounds that their loyalty to the nation during wartime could not be reliably ascertained. If internment was the low point, however, it was not the end of the story. Changing racial dynamics during the war and Cold War created the conditions for Japanese Americans to rise from this nadir and achieve a meaningful degree of assimilation into society and the polity during the postwar period.

Like the conventional story of nineteenth-century Chinese immigration, this narrative depends upon an unacknowledged redaction of structural anti-Blackness. What whites did to Asian immigrants is centered in the plot, as if white supremacy were the whole story. Japanese Americans' racial victimhood is highlighted, while their advantageous not-Blackness and the Asian–Black gap are overlooked.[1] In Part Two, I bring structural anti-Blackness back into the picture as a national and global phenomenon and reinterpret the Japanese American story in relation to it. During the early twentieth century, Asian nations disparaged Africa while declaring their determination to catch up with the West. This was true in Japan, whose rapid modernization and industrialization during the Meiji era enabled it to win the Russo-Japanese War in 1905 and become the first Asian world power. Traveling global circuits of anti-Blackness, Japanese immigrants arriving in the U.S. understood and to some significant degree accepted the structural invitation to dissociate from Blackness. Intent first and foremost upon differentiating themselves from the Chinese (from whom they had inherited the Asiatic/ Mongolian label), they imagined the latter as a buffer between themselves and Blackness, a means of dramatizing their own distance from the bottom.

As not-whites, Japanese immigrants and their descendants were targeted by immigration restrictions, alien land laws, and internment, all of which aimed to thwart their economic success in the agricultural sector on the West Coast. Ideas about the treacherous Asiatic were once again invoked by white working people in the context of capitalist competition. However, if Japanese immigrants were cast out of the nation, literally by exclusion legislation and symbolically by internment, they were still seen as the lesser of two evils. Constituted as not-Black, they have been (at least partially) exempted from the various forms of state and private violence—from convict leasing, to lynching, to hypersegregation,

---

[1] Although Ellen Wu (2014) does not discuss structural anti-Blackness per se, her excellent analysis of "not-blackness" is a valuable exception to the trend.

to race riots, to police murder, to mass incarceration—that have afflicted Black people during the "afterlife" of slavery. The obvious exception was wartime internment. However, even during internment, a collective experience marked by loss, trauma, and suffering, the not-Blackness of Japanese Americans mitigated their treatment in the camps, hastened their release, and enabled their recovery and assimilation afterward. In-camp blackface performances by Japanese internees themselves represent their ongoing dissociation from Blackness in that context. Not-Blackness did not spare them from the serious harm of internment, but it did spare them from being reduced to the zero mattering of Blackness. Even in the very worst of times, Blackness provided a floor beneath which Japanese Americans could not fall.

From the early twentieth century onward, radical Black internationalists took to the world stage to oppose the Western colonization of Africa and the oppression of Black people throughout the diaspora. Challenging the legitimacy of the U.S. racial-capitalist state, thinkers like W. E. B. Du Bois and Paul Robeson advanced a global analysis of how racism, colonialism, and capitalism worked in tandem to facilitate the subjugation and exploitation of the majority of the world's population living in Africa, Asia, Latin America, and the Caribbean. Faced with this concerning pivot in the Black struggle, the U.S. state also had to confront the onslaught of Japanese race propaganda during the Second World War. Japanese commentators shot arrow after arrow at the United States' "Achilles heel," continually reminding the global community of Jim Crow, lynching, and other "Southern Horrors."

To deflect criticism and bolster its legitimacy, the U.S. state devised a strategy of performative anti-racism. Japanese Americans were recruited to star in this production before the war's end and then called back for repeat performances during the Cold War, as the U.S. and Soviet Union settled into a long fight for the hearts and minds of Third World peoples. Thus Japanese American political functionality, like that of the Chinese before them, consisted of being invoked as (false) witnesses to the fundamental openness and fairness of the U.S. political and economic system. By staging the "rehabilitation" of Japanese Americans after the camps and facilitating their assimilation into American society, the U.S. government was not only able to demonstrate anti-racism on the cheap but also depict Japanese Americans' progress as a rebuke to the Black struggle. *If the Japanese can make it here, surely anyone can.*

This is the context in which the "model minority myth" first emerged in public discourse. Presuming minority equivalency, or the comparable positioning of all not-white groups under white supremacy, the myth implicitly narrated the rise of Japanese Americans as proof of their evolutionary fitness as compared with Black people. Structural anti-Blackness and the Asian–Black gap drop out of sight, and Japanese Americans' mobility is (mis)attributed solely to their cultural endowments. It is worth noting that at that very historical moment, blackface minstrelsy, the nation's preeminent cultural form, was being driven off stage by new anti-racist norms generated by civil rights activism and the war. Did the model minority myth, which staged Japanese American mobility as a spectacle of transcending Blackness, signal the return of the repressed? Does this explain in part the myth's resonance and tenacity?

Some observers cite Japanese Americans' rapid assimilation during the postwar period as proof that racial positions in the U.S. vary over time. While Japanese Americans undoubtedly gained in socioeconomic status and cultural capital during this period, I argue that they nevertheless retained their basic racial position in relation to whites and Black people. In other words, they remained not-white but above all not-Black. They were invited to stand in the vestibule of whiteness, but never actually enter whiteness, and their not-Blackness remained a self-renewing resource of the highest value. This is not to say that racial positionality is impervious to history, but only that the overall structure of an anti-Black order has shown itself to have enough give and take built in to absorb many contingent developments without fundamentally changing. Racial formation processes are dynamic and fluid *and* structured by the articulation of white supremacy and anti-Blackness.

II JAPANESE SCHOOLCHILDREN IN SAN FRANCISCO

Japanese and Western racial ideologies in the early twentieth century concurred on a tripartite schema of white over Asian over Black—with one crucial point of contention. Pointing to Japan's rapid modernization during the Meiji era and its victory in the Russo-Japanese War of 1905, the Japanese insisted that they were superior to all other Asian peoples and nearly on par with whites. Whites, however, were not so sure. They tended to think that the Japanese still belonged in the Asiatic/Mongolian category, even if they were demonstrably superior to other Asians in certain ways. One thing was too obvious to require elaboration: the not-Blackness of the Japanese, their categorical superiority to Black people. If even the Chinese were not-Black, it went without saying that the Japanese were as well. The Japanese focused on proving themselves superior to the

Chinese, their nearest Asian competitors, with the implicit understanding that even the Chinese were superior to Blacks. A, elevating itself over B, did not need to argue its superiority over C.

Once again, San Francisco was a key site of struggle. At the start of the twentieth century, as the California legislature passed repeated resolutions calling for Congress to restrict Japanese immigration, the *San Francisco Chronicle* ran a series of articles warning that Japanese immigration posed as great a danger as Chinese immigration and therefore warranted the same solution. At the same time, white labor unions and fraternal and civic associations came together to form the Asiatic Exclusion League (also known as the Japanese and Korean Exclusion League), whose goal was to locate the Japanese and Koreans in the Asiatic/Mongolian category more definitively, so as to bring them under the purview of Chinese exclusion.[2]

San Francisco had already decided to segregate Chinese schoolchildren by this time, having opted in 1885 to create a Chinese primary school in Chinatown rather than allow Chinese students to attend white schools.[3] Japanese students, though, lived in white neighborhoods and attended white neighborhood schools all over the city. In 1906, 93 out of 25,000 San Francisco school-age children were of Japanese descent, and they attended twenty-three different elementary schools.[4] The newly formed Asiatic Exclusion League objected to this situation, and on April 18, 1906, Mother Nature provided an assist in the form of an earthquake. The quake caused a fire that almost destroyed Chinatown and drove many families out of the area, leaving the Chinese school half empty. Pressured by the League, the Board of Education renamed it the Oriental School and passed a resolution compelling all Japanese and Korean students living in the city to leave their schools and matriculate in this one.[5] This was a blow to the Japanese immigrants who insisted on their superiority to the Chinese.

Reactions from the Japanese immigrant community and the Japanese public in the homeland were heated. Japanese community leaders filed a lawsuit against the city, arguing that the directive violated the U.S.–Japan Treaty of 1894, which guaranteed Japanese people living in the U.S. treatment on par with citizens of the "most favored

[2] Ferguson 1947.
[3] See *Tape* v. *Hurley* (1885).
[4] Eng 2006, 3. See Wollenberg (1976) for the history of how California dealt with race and public schooling in the second half of the nineteenth century.
[5] Wollenberg 1976.

nation."[6] Since the "most favored nation" was understood to mean a close Western ally such as Britain, the treaty in effect guaranteed that Japanese immigrants would be treated like white British immigrants. Japanese immigrant leaders also filed complaints with the Japanese consul, appealed to the Japanese ambassador to the U.S., Viscount Aoki Shuzo, and solicited help directly from the Japanese government. The Japanese Association, the leading Japanese immigrant organization in the U.S., wired newspapers in Japan and asked them to mobilize Japanese public opinion for their cause. One Japanese newspaper wrote obligingly:

Japan has been wounded in her tenderest spot—her national pride. The Japanese regard themselves as the equals of any other people on earth. They believe themselves to be superior, intellectually, morally, and in every other way, to the Chinese. Anything which tends to place them on a level with the Chinese before the world is degrading and humiliating to them, and they will resent it.[7]

Ambassador Aoki denounced the segregation of Japanese schoolchildren as "an act of discrimination carrying with it a stigma and odium which it is impossible to overlook."[8] A U.S.-based Japanese immigrant newspaper, meanwhile, exclaimed: "Our national dignity besmeared—to arms, our countrymen!"[9]

Japanese immigrant parents vowed to keep their children home rather than send them to school with Chinese (and Korean) children. The situation anticipated the *Gong Lum* (1927) case, still twenty-one years in the future. In both cases, Asian immigrant parents took for granted the rightness of educational segregation as a reflection of the natural hierarchy of greater and lesser races. They raised their voices in objection only when their children came to be classified as one of the lesser races. For Chinese parents in Jim Crow Mississippi, having their children placed with Black schoolchildren was a stigma that could not be borne. For Japanese parents in San Francisco, having their children placed with Chinese (and Korean) schoolchildren was nearly as bad.

---

[6] This treaty stated, in part: "In whatever relates to rights of residence and travel; to the possession of goods and effects of any kind; to the succession to personal estate, by will or otherwise, and the disposal of property of any sort an in any manner whatsoever which they may lawfully acquire, the citizens or subjects of each Contracting Party shall enjoy in the territories of the other the same privileges, liberties, and rights, and shall be subject to no higher imposts or charges in these respects than native citizens or subjects or citizens or subjects of the most favored nation." Quoted in Burke 1907, 4.

[7] Eng 2006, 8, quoting from Herbert Johnson, *Discrimination against the Japanese in California* (Berkeley: Courier, 1971).

[8] Esthus 1966, 138.

[9] Quoted in Metcalf 1971, 20–21.

The lawsuit *Aoki* v. *Deane* (1907) was filed by a Japanese American family after a white school in San Francisco turned away their ten year-old Japanese-born son on the grounds that he was "Mongolian" and thus ineligible to enroll per the Board of Education resolution.[10] (Because of the long-standing presence of the Chinese in California, "Mongolian" was by this time an established legal category there. The 1890 Mississippi constitution, by contrast, knew only "colored" and "white," which is why the *Gong Lum* case arose in the first place.) Appearing before the California Supreme Court, the U.S. attorney argued that the Japanese should be admitted to white schools because they were not "Mongolian" but rather a separate race, and that they were vested with specific rights by the U.S.–Japan Treaty of 1894.[11]

City Attorney William Burke responded that the Treaty of 1894 pertained only to commerce and navigation and did not speak to educational rights—and that if it did, it was unconstitutional because the power to regulate public schools was a police power reserved to the states and immune from federal interference.[12] Then, turning to the matter of racial classification, he swerved. After affirming that the Japanese "certainly belong to the class designated 'Mongolian' by ethnologists and historians in classifying the distinct families or races of the earth"— which argument alone could have been dispositive in the case—he raised the issue of segregated Black schoolchildren.[13] Since there were very few Black schoolchildren in the city, and they were not mentioned in the Board of Education resolution, why did Burke bring them up?

Burke began by discussing the appropriateness of segregated schools for "the colored race" and cited *Plessy* as an authority for the claim that school segregation laws are within the police power. By invoking Black people as the paradigmatic segregated group, he naturalized segregation as a sound policy for keeping races in their proper place. Then, noting

---

[10] Because the Gentlemen's Agreement was signed at this point, this case was never adjudicated.

[11] Wollenberg 1976.

[12] Burke writes: "THE POWER, THEREFORE, TO REGULATE AND CONDUCT OUR PUBLIC SCHOOLS IS AMONG THE POLICE POWERS OF THE STATE RESERVED BY THEM. IT IS THE MOST SACRED OF THEM .... THE PARENT AND THE STATE HAVE A RIGHT TO BE SOLICITOUS ABOUT THE ENVIRONMENTS OF THE CHILD. AND THEY HAVE A RIGHT TO KNOW THAT NO CONTAMINATING INFLUENCES SURROUND IT" (1907, 9). Capitalization and bold face in original.

[13] Burke 1907, 15.

that "colored" schoolchildren were demanding desegregation as citizens of the U.S. and individual states, Burke wrote:

IF NO SUCH RIGHTS ARE GUARANTEED TO THEM UNDER THE CONSTITUTION AS CITIZENS OF THE UNITED STATES AND OF THE STATES, CAN IT BE SAID THAT GREATER RIGHTS ARE ACCORDED SUBJECTS OF A FOREIGN COUNTRY UNDER A TREATY THAN CAN BE ACCORDED TO CITIZENS OF THE UNITED STATES UNDER THE SHELTERING FOLDS OF THEIR OWN FLAG AND THE CONSTITUTION OF THEIR OWN COUNTRY?[14]

Like Justice Harlan in his *Plessy* dissent, Burke suggested that (Asian) foreigners should not be treated better than (Black) citizens—but here the intent was to secure Asian segregation, not Black desegregation. The implication was that if Japanese schoolchildren were to be desegregated, Black schoolchildren would have to be, too. Note that Burke did not argue from the intrinsic inferiority or unworthiness of Japanese schoolchildren (who had been peacefully attending school with white schoolchildren for many years). Instead he adopted the fail-safe strategy of arguing that they had to be segregated *to ensure the continued segregation of Black school-children*. The choice was between segregating Japanese schoolchildren and desegregating Black ones.

An article published in the *Harvard Law Review* that same year, entitled "Rights of the Japanese in California Schools," similarly argued that the U.S.–Japan Treaty of 1894 could not be read as prohibiting the segregation of Japanese schoolchildren because giving aliens more privileges than citizens was beyond the treaty-making power.[15] It also contended that the treaty only regulated the treatment of Japanese migrants *as subjects of Japan and not as a race*. In other words, discriminatory actions targeting the Japanese qua Japanese nationals were prohibited by the treaty, but school segregation, which instead targeted the Japanese as a race, was beyond the purview of the treaty. While this distinction was legally dubious, it spoke an ethnological

---

[14] Burke 1907, 14. Capitalization and bold face in original.

[15] "Rights of the Japanese in California Schools" in *Harvard Law Review* 20:4 (February 1907), 337–340. No author is named in this article. It also argues that Section 1662 of the political code of California (1903) says the state can establish separate schools for Indians and Mongolians or Chinese—and "'Mongolian' is used here in its broadest sense and includes Japanese" (338). This article responds to Edwin Maxey, "Exclusion of Japanese Children from the Public Schools of San Francisco," *Yale Law Journal* 16:2 (December 1906), 90–93. Maxey argues that in light of the U.S.–Japan Treaty of 1894, San Francisco discriminates against Japanese subjects when it denies them the privileges that the British and Germans, for example, enjoy.

truth: Japan was owed respect as a world power, but its subjects were still Mongolians.

Again, the discussion found its way to Black schoolchildren, who were invoked as proof that school segregation was about race and not nationality:

A colored British subject would have to attend the schools for negro children, and a white British child the schools for white children, wherever there is segregation of negroes and whites. It is merely incidental that Japanese subjects are very generally of the Japanese race; German subjects are generally white, and would have to attend the schools for whites. The whites are segregated as much as the negroes or the Japanese. It must be clear that it is the Japanese as a race, not as subjects of the emperor of Japan, who are segregated, since American citizens of Japanese descent are included as Japanese. To interpret the treaty to stipulate against school segregation of the Japanese as a race, as contrasted with Japanese subjects, would be to adopt a very strained construction which would raise grave questions as to the extent of the treaty-making power.[16]

Nor did the treaty's "most favored nation" clause protect Japanese schoolchildren from segregation:

If Japan and her friends are correct in their claim [about this clause], the colored subjects of Great Britain from Jamaica or the Bermudas [sic] could come to Washington and insist upon attending the white schools here in spite of the school authorities of the District, or even of the Congress.[17]

Reductio ad absurdum: desegregating the Japanese would lead to desegregating Black people, an obviously intolerable outcome. Once again, the choice was between segregating Japanese children and desegregating Black children. Once again, the *summum malum* of Black integration was invoked to quiet white misgivings about derogating the Japanese. If whites were hesitant to segregate Japanese schoolchildren, their phobic hatred of Blackness would help get them over the hump.

At the dawn of the twentieth century, Akira Iriye notes, the U.S. and Japan were eyeing each other warily, anticipating a clash of their imperial ambitions in the Pacific theater.[18] President Theodore Roosevelt was concerned to restrain Japan after its spectacular victory in the Russo-Japanese War of 1905, but he also relied on Japan to contain Russian advances in Asia.[19] In this context, he received news of San Francisco's school segregation resolution with dismay and denounced it as a "wicked

[16] "Rights of the Japanese in California Schools," February 1907, 338–339.
[17] Hayes 1907.
[18] Iriye 1994.
[19] Neu 1966.

absurdity" in his annual message to Congress, while also calling for legislation to allow Japanese migrants to naturalize.[20] Mindful of what
Secretary of State Elihu Root had conveyed in a confidential memo—that
the Japanese were a proud and sensitive people, and that one tenth of
the insults the U.S. had visited upon China would result in automatic
war with Japan—Roosevelt reassured the Japanese government that the
U.S. wanted friendly relations, while trying to persuade San Francisco to
retract the resolution.[21] When San Francisco resisted, he sent Secretary
of Commerce and Labor Victor Metcalf to pressure them, but Metcalf
came back empty-handed. Roosevelt then invited the mayor and the
entire Board of Education of San Francisco to the White House to discuss the matter further, and there, at last, an agreement was reached:
San Francisco would rescind its segregation resolution, and Congress, in
return, would halt Japanese immigration into the U.S.

Per the informal Gentlemen's Agreement (1907–1908) between the
U.S. and Japan, Japan agreed to restrict emigration to the continental U.S.
by giving passports only to nonlaborers or laborers who were resuming
a formerly acquired domicile, joining a parent, wife, or child, or assuming control of an already acquired farming interest.[22] The name of the
accord was meant to convey bilateral cooperation among equals and thus
to "safeguar[d] [Japan] … from open humiliation among the civilized
nations."[23] Japanese Ambassador Hanihara was therefore able to describe
the agreement as "an understanding with the United States Government
by which the Japanese Government voluntarily undertook to adopt and
enforce certain administrative measures designed to check the emigration
to the United States of Japanese laborers."[24] Japan reluctantly went along
in order to avoid a worse outcome—namely, having its diasporic subjects
classified with inferior races like the Chinese and Koreans (literally) and
Blacks (symbolically). Like the 1882 Act to Inaugurate Certain Treaty
Stipulations Relating to Chinese, the Gentlemen's Agreement emphasized
that Asian immigrants had international standing in the Family of Man,
that they had to consent to being coerced.[25]

---

[20] Ichioka 1977.
[21] Esthus 1966, 138.
[22] Buell 1922.
[23] Inui 1925, 197.
[24] Tupper and McReynolds 1937, 38.
[25] The unusual informality of the agreement—it was never formally recorded or ratified
by Congress—would become an issue in later immigration debates. David Hellwig
(1977) notes that some Black newspapers questioned Roosevelt's involvement in the

White supremacy, with an assist from anti-Blackness, scored a victory in the San Francisco affair. The drive to segregate Japanese (and Korean) students failed because of Japan's strength on the world stage, but a larger prize was secured: the halting of most Japanese immigration to the U.S. San Francisco officials had successfully forced President Roosevelt's hand on the matter, which increased the Japanese public's resentment against the U.S. and moved the two nations one step closer to a Pacific war.[26]

III THE JAPANESE "RACIAL MIND"

Anti-Blackness had historical roots in Japanese culture and was watered by Western racial science. For centuries, Japanese proverbs valorized white skin as beautiful and associated Blackness with negative symbolic meanings, albeit unevenly. Japanese commentators referred to Africans as subhumans and animals as early as the 1500s, when Portuguese and Dutch traders brought African servants to Japan and Western racial ideologies first began to permeate Japanese society.[27] John Russell writes: "As Western influence grew, Western conventions for representing blacks also took root."[28] During the early 1800s, Dutch scholars and missionaries introduced Johann Blumenbach's fivefold racial classification system (Caucasian, Ethiopian, Mongolian, Malay, American) to Japan, and after Japan's "opening" to the West in the 1850s, the island nation leaned into a racial ideology that emphasized "the lowly blacks and the lofty whites."[29]

When Commodore Perry's ships arrived in Tokyo Harbor in 1853, they forcibly ended Japan's 200 years of self-imposed isolation and "opened" the nation to the West. Perry and his ships returned to Japan

---

San Francisco affair. *The Indianapolis Freeman*, for example, asked why the president worked so hard to prevent the segregation of Japanese schoolchildren while showing indifference to generations of Black schoolchildren who had endured the same fate. Though they opposed the white supremacist treatment of Japanese Americans, Black commentators could not help but note that they were invested with mattering in the U.S. racial imaginary in a way that Black people were not, and that this was about race *and* nationality.

[26] In 1921, California passed a law adding Japanese Americans to the list of children that school districts could segregate in elementary schools. Some schools in Sacramento County did this, but "legal segregation for *Nisei* was sporadic and short-lived, lasting only from 1921 until 1947" (Lyon 2012, 15).

[27] Russell, February 1991.

[28] Russell, October 1991, 418.

[29] Russell, February 1991, 6.

the following year to negotiate a trade treaty, and on this second trip the crew of the USS Powhatan treated Japanese negotiators to an "Ethiopian" minstrel show onboard the ship.[30] Perry had brought with him weaponry, the telegraph, and the steam engine as symbols of Western technological might, but nothing impressed the Japanese more than that other distinctly American product: blackface minstrelsy. According to the playbill, the show consisted of the songs and dances of "the plantation 'niggas' of the South."[31] Japanese officials expressed delight with the performance. One laughed so hard that he leaned on Commodore Perry and, to the latter's annoyance, "crushed [his] new epaulettes."[32] Another embraced Perry after the performance, declaring "Nippon [Japan] and America, all the same heart." According to one American observer, "the two countries became closer to one another in shared mirth over the denigration of African peoples."[33] Or, as Brian Rouleau puts it: "Literal diplomatic breakthrough became a function of the comic skewering of blackness."[34]

Blackface minstrelsy, like lynching, promoted relationality among not-Black people. At a moment of U.S. aggression against Japan, with Commodore Perry and his ships "opening" Japan through a show of force, blackface minstrelsy soothed tensions between the two nations. As the U.S. coerced Japan into negotiating a trade treaty under threat of military conflict, shared not-Blackness served as a basis for rapprochement, connection, and even mutual pleasure. Nor was Perry's "Ethiopian" minstrel show an anomaly. U.S. sailors put on blackface minstrelsy performances in other parts of Japan, Shanghai, and Hong Kong, among other places. What Brian Rouleau calls "maritime minstrelsy" was a portable political salve offered to Asian audiences who were feeling the sting of Western imperialist intrusion.[35] Even as they were forced to submit to U.S. power, it meant something to have their not-Blackness affirmed.

[30] See Rouleau (2012) or this link for paintings of the performance: https://visualizingcul tures.mit.edu/black_ships_and_samurai/bss_essay05.html.
[31] Rouleau 2014, 49.
[32] Rouleau 2012.
[33] Rouleau 2012.
[34] Rouleau 2014, 50.
[35] "Maritime minstrelsy" served as a vehicle for building not-Black community wherever the U.S. Navy ventured. The USS Powhatan's crew performed the "Ethiopian" show in Hong Kong and Shanghai as well, and U.S. sailors did minstrel shows along Mexico's coast and as far south as Antarctica (Rouleau 2014; Johnson 2019). In addition to establishing diplomatic relations, the Perry expedition sought to facilitate trade and open safe ports for American trading ships and whaling ships. The Treaty of Kanagawa (1853) established diplomatic relations between the two nations and gave American ships access to two Japanese ports.

Commodore Perry deployed the spectacle of Blackness to consolidate his power in other ways as well. When he first arrived in Japan in July 1853, after extensive negotiations, he went on shore in Oragawa to present a letter from President Millard Fillmore. "On either side of the Commodore marched a tall, well-formed negro, who, armed to the teeth, acted as his personal guard. These blacks, selected for the occasion, were two of the best looking fellows of their color that the squadron could furnish. All of this, of course, was but for effect."[36] The following year, when Perry landed in Edo Bay, he had six armed Black guards escorting him. John Russell notes "[Perry's] use of their bodies as a twofold projection of American power: The blacks are imposing, yet not so powerful that they have escaped domestication, for they serve—and protect—a white master."[37]

Japanese visitors to the U.S. during this period noted and endorsed American negrophobia. In the summer of 1860, several Japanese delegates visited the U.S. to ratify the 1858 Treaty of Amity and Commerce, in which Japan opened its markets and ports to the U.S. in the hope of avoiding China's experience with Western imperialist aggression. As they toured the East Coast, the Japanese delegates were paraded and fêted by business interests eager to conclude trade deals with Japan, prompting resentful white workers to deride the delegates as "niggers." In response, the *New York Herald* declared that the Japanese were comparable to the French and Spanish, and that they could be distinguished from "Negroes" both by the shape of their nose (long and curved instead of "broad, flat, and weak") and their larger foreheads.[38] Middle-class Black observers, meanwhile, admired the Japanese visitors as "colored gentlemen" and asked that the respect shown to them be extended to Black Americans. As Ikuko Asaka notes, however, the feeling was "anything but mutual."[39] The Japanese delegates wrote in their diaries: "The blacks are inferior as human beings and extremely stupid," and "It seems that the whites are beautiful and shrewd and intelligent; and the blacks are ugly and stupid. So the whites always despise the blacks."[40]

Less than a decade later, the Meiji era (1868–1912) began, and Japan launched an intensive economic modernization project to catch

---

[36] Observation by Frances Hawkes, the biographer who wrote an official account of Perry's mission, based in part on Perry's own journals, quoted in Johnson 2019, 55.

[37] Russell 1997, 93.

[38] Asaka 2014, 981–982.

[39] Asaka 2014, 973.

[40] Leupp 1995, 7–8.

up to the West. During this period, Japanese commentators imagined a global racial hierarchy in which Asians were located midway between Europeans and Africans, echoing the tripartite imaginings of nineteenth-century European race scientists such as Arthur de Gobineau (white over yellow over black) and George Cuvier (Caucasian over Mongol over Negro). Fukuzawa Yukichi's *Outline of Civilization* (1875), for instance, argued that the West was "civilized," while Asians were "semicivilized" and Africans were "savages."[41] Similarly, an anonymous journalist wrote in a Japanese newspaper in 1876: "The highest race is that of the whites (Europeans and Americans). In the middle is the yellow race (Chinese, Japanese, Koreans, Ryukyuans and other Asians), and lowest are the black and red races (aboriginal peoples of Africa, Australia, and South America)."[42] The influx of U.S. cultural products into Japan at the turn of the century—including Sambo dolls, *Uncle Tom's Cabin*, *Gone with the Wind*, *Tarzan*, and Stephen Foster's minstrel songs—reinforced an already established anti-Blackness.[43]

The Japanese believed themselves to be superior to other Asian peoples and destined to rule over them. In the late 1800s, Japan inaugurated its imperial expansion into Asia, claiming that it was bringing culture, progress, and civilization to stagnant, backward Asian peoples.[44] In rapid succession, Japan defeated China in the Sino-Japanese War of 1894, annexed Korea and Formosa, and defeated Russia in the Russo-Japanese War of 1905, "confirm[ing] its sense of superiority in Asia and equality with the West."[45] Meanwhile, the U.S. was building its own Pacific empire by fighting the Spanish–American War in 1898 and annexing Hawai'i and the Philippines that same year. The Taft-Katsura Agreement signed by the U.S. and Japan in 1905 specified that the U.S. would recognize Japan's interests in Korea and Manchuria, while Japan would recognize U.S. sovereignty over the Philippines. The agreement admitted Japan "into the ranks of the world powers" and forestalled, temporarily, the clash of emergent empires.[46]

According to Naoko Shimazu, Japanese foreign policy makers were divided in the early twentieth century, with one faction calling for pan-Asian solidarity (under Japanese leadership) against the West, and the

[41] Russell, February 1991, 6.
[42] Leupp 1995, 9.
[43] Tajima and Thornton 2012.
[44] Kushner 2006.
[45] Iriye 1994, 98.
[46] Yamashita and Park 1985, 145.

other calling for Japan to escape Asia and become part of the West. Those associated with the latter view advised Japan to dissociate from backward China and Korea and embark on a linear "'graduation' from an Asian to a western nation."[47] Japanese leaders incorporated both perspectives, in a sense, by constructing an official narrative about Japan proving its equality with the West by establishing its leadership over Asia. Glossing Japan's imperialist agenda, the narrative convinced some not-white leaders around the world that Japan was their best hope for pushing back against (Western) imperialism. Shimazu notes that when nationalist movements in Asia celebrated Japan's victory over Russia as proof that white nations were vincible, "[t]his was ironic because whilst the colonized peoples saw the victory as an advancement of eastern civilisation, the Japanese themselves tended to perceive their victory as a proof of their achieving the 'civilised' status of the West."[48]

Through the 1870s and 1880s, as Japan sought to revise its "unequal treaties" with Western powers, the government "looked with disfavor on labor emigration, for fear that uneducated laborers would make it harder to obtain such revisions by reinforcing the western image of Japan as an uncivilized nation."[49] By the 1890s, though, with modernization proceeding apace in the heavily populated island nation, overseas expansion through migration came to be seen as the nation's salvation. Citing the example of the West, the government resolved that "Japan must follow suit; it must develop as an expansive, powerful race; scatter its people all over the earth, and concentrate on the extension of overseas settlement and trade. Only then could the Japanese be the white race of Asia, the superior race in the world."[50] By creating far-off markets for Japanese goods and sending remittances back home, migrants would help to finance continued industrialization within Japan, securing the strength of the economy, military, and the state. As Akira Iriye notes, however, "the line between emigration and colonization was rather tenuous."[51] Japanese writers called for "the establishment by the Japanese people of new Japans everywhere in the world."[52] The Japanese government explicitly viewed migrants as agents of its imperial designs and actively encouraged migration to the U.S., South America, Hawai'i, and Southeast Asia.

[47] Shimazu 1995, 22.
[48] Shimazu 1995, 35.
[49] Ichioka 1988, 4.
[50] Iriye 1994, 40.
[51] Iriye 1994, 131.
[52] Tokutomi Soto, quoted in Iriye 1994, 44.

Japanese officials screened emigrants to the U.S. because they did not want them to be treated like the lowly Chinese, as that would reflect badly on Japan. They continued surveillance of Japanese immigrants after their settlement in the U.S., fretting aloud about migrants' lower-class habits and behaviors.[53] Through the Japanese Association of America, which was described as "a virtual arm of the Japanese government,"[54] officials pushed moral reform upon Japanese immigrants in an effort to prevent their "Sinification" and "construct a respectable community of Japanese citizen-subjects in the American West."[55] These efforts were accompanied by educational campaigns aimed at reducing anti-Japanese prejudice among whites. Japanese officials were optimistic that this combination of tactics would convince white Americans that the Japanese were in fact their equals.

Their optimism was misplaced, however, and before long a spiral of anti-Japanese persecution had taken hold. The Gentlemen's Agreement had restricted Japanese immigration but not stopped it altogether, and in 1909, a restive California legislature debated seventeen bills directed against Japanese immigrants, including a school segregation bill.[56] The Japanese public reacted with outrage. When California lawmakers debated an alien land law in April 1913, 20,000 people gathered in Tokyo to demand war with the U.S. In a reprise of the San Francisco school controversy, President Woodrow Wilson dispatched Secretary of State William Jennings Bryan to California "for the purpose of persuading the legislature to avoid giving offense to Japan."[57] Bryan asked the lawmakers to delay action until a new bilateral treaty had been completed, or, alternatively, to make the proposed alien land law apply to all aliens and not just the Japanese. Disregarding these requests, the state legislature passed the California Alien Land Law of 1913, which stated that "aliens ineligible to citizenship" could not acquire, possess, enjoy, use, cultivate,

---

[53] Yamashita and Park 1985.
[54] Azuma 2005, 43. See Ichioka (1988) for discussion of the Japanese Association of America, founded in 1908, and its position between the local Japanese consulates and the local immigrant associations.
[55] Azuma 2005, 47.
[56] Japanese immigration to the U.S. peaked in 1907 at 10,000, then dropped to 2,700 by 1910 (Lake and Reynolds 2008, 263). By 1920, only 1.2 percent of California's agricultural land was owned by Japanese Americans (Ferguson 1947, 77). Japanese immigrant farmers specialized in supplementing rather than competing with white farmers; they focused on opening up new lands with labor-intensive, high-yield agricultural practices (Daniels 1972).
[57] Bailey 1932, 42.

occupy, or transfer real property in agricultural land.[58] Aliens eligible to citizenship—for example, white immigrants—would continue to be able to own land. Although the law did not mention the Japanese by name, it was clearly aimed at undercutting their standing in agriculture. In 1920, California voters approved a ballot initiative that closed loopholes in the earlier law, making it harder still for Japanese immigrants to own agricultural land.[59] As a result, Japanese land ownership in California dropped significantly.[60]

In an article entitled "Japan Among the Nations" (1913), published during the debate over the alien land law, Admiral Alfred Thayer Mahan wrote:

> While recognizing what I clearly see to be the great superiority of the Japanese as of the white over the negro, it appears to me as reasonable that a great number of my fellow-citizens, knowing the problem we have in the colored race among us, should dread the introduction of what they believe will constitute another race problem, and one much more difficult because the virile qualities of the Japanese will still more successfully withstand assimilation, creating a homogenous foreign mass, naturally acting together, irrespective of national welfare.[61]

The Japanese were more likely than Black people to act in a concerted way against the U.S. public interest. Like the Chinese before them, the Japanese had to be kept out not despite their superiority to Black people but *because of it*.

The Alien Land Law of 1913 was "a painful and humiliating experience for the Japanese government." As Naoko Shimazu writes, the law "pointed up the gap between the way Japan saw itself and the way the West saw it."[62] Foreign Minister Kato gave a speech on the subject, in which he stated:

> What we regard very unpleasant about the Californian question … is the discrimination made against our people in distinction from other nations. We would not mind disabilities if they were equally applicable to all nations. We are not vain enough to consider ourselves at the very forefront of enlightenment; we

---

[58] In English law, the practice of limiting aliens' property rights on the basis of suspect loyalties went back to the 1600s (Kettner 1978).

[59] Japanese Americans had evaded the 1913 law by taking advantage of various loopholes such as forming agricultural landholding corporations and putting land in the name of children or other relatives. The 1920 law effectively shut down these practices.

[60] In a series of cases in 1923, the U.S. Supreme Court ruled that California and Washington alien land laws did not violate the U.S. Constitution or the U.S.–Japan Treaty of Commerce and Navigation of 1911.

[61] Quoted in Robinson 2001, 21–22.

[62] Shimazu 1995, 30, 31.

know that we still have much to learn from the West. But … we thought our-selves ahead of any other Asiatic people and as good as some of the European nations.[63]

It was not the deprivation of privilege (land ownership) per se, but rather the symbolics of selective dispossession that caused shock and offense. By targeting the Japanese (even if not by name), California punctured their collective fantasy. They thought they had broken out of the Asiatic/Mongolian category and pulled even with some Western nations, but the alien land law showed them that for all of their accomplishments, they would never be considered the equal of whites.

IV THE "RACIAL EQUALITY CLAUSE"

The Japanese government never forgot that Russia, Germany, and France had intervened to prevent it from taking control of the Liaotung Peninsula after its defeat of China in the Sino-Japanese war of 1894. Twenty years later, during the First World War, to the dismay of its American and British allies, the Japanese government acted on the premise that "the temporary power vacuum created in East Asia due to the preoccupation of the other powers with the war in Europe … presented an excellent opportunity for Japan to pursue unchecked its interests in China."[64] In the land grab that attended the close of the war, Japan focused on obtain-ing German territories and rights in China and the Pacific. By the time the victorious nations gathered at the Paris Peace Conference in Versailles in 1919 to form a new international organization, the League of Nations, with the stated aim of preventing another world war, Japan's standing relative to its American and European allies was a matter of significant concern to all parties.

Mindful of its status as the only not-white major power at the confer-ence, Japan proposed the inclusion of what came to be known as the "racial equality clause" in the League of Nations charter:

The equality of nations being a basic principle of the League of Nations, the High Contracting Parties agree to accord as soon as possible to all alien nation-als of states, members of the League, equal and just treatment in every respect making no distinction, either in law or in fact, on account of their race or nationality.[65]

[63] Shimazu 1995, 36.
[64] Shimazu 1995, 38.
[65] Quoted in Shimazu 1995, 71.

Symbolically, this was an attempt to affirm Japan's status as an equal to the other major powers. Concretely, it was a bid to protect Japanese nationals living in the U.S., the British Commonwealth, and elsewhere from ongoing discrimination. According to Naoko Shimazu, the proposal was a "highly particularistic and nationalistic" move that was "never intended to have any universal implications."[66] Shimazu writes: "[W]hat Japan defined as racial equality was equality for herself in relation to the West, and not equality in the absolute sense of the term. Quite clearly, then, 'racial equality' was a misnomer because the Japanese sought to gain the status of honorary whites and nothing more."[67]

The Japanese themselves did not call the proposed clause the "racial equality clause." Their initial title was "Abolition of Racial Discrimination," which they changed to "Principle of Equality of Nations and Just Treatment of Their Nationals" in order to eliminate the controversial mention of race and clarify the measure's limited scope.[68] Still, the misnomer stuck and sparked an enthusiastic reaction from African and Asian nations, "allow[ing] the Japanese to enlist Afro-Asian sympathies without actually having to practice racial equality towards those nations themselves."[69] Baron Makino Nobuaki, leader of the Japanese delegation, recounted a meeting with a Liberian official:

In Paris, a nigger named Lewis ... from Liberia Africa came to me .... He appealed to me about how they were oppressed by telling me "We greatly appreciate your striving for racial issues [at the conference]." He said "Our circumstance is like the following" and told me how they were oppressed .... He asked us to strive harder [on their behalf]. But I replied to him, "I sympathize with you. But I cannot represent your country."[70]

Demanding recognition of its own parity with the West, Japan was given unearned credit for championing the cause of the racially oppressed peoples of the world. It was the screen upon which these groups projected their political longings. Nor did Japan consistently discourage such projections. As Atsushi Tajima and Michael Thornton write, "The notion that Japan had a special rapport with other 'colored' people was part of a strategy to claim a status as 'honorary Whites' and a special place for Japan in the international racial hierarchy."[71]

---

[66] Shimazu 1995, 80, 79.
[67] Shimazu 1989, 94.
[68] Tajima and Thornton 2012, 355.
[69] Shimazu 1989, 94.
[70] Tajima and Thornton 2012, 355.
[71] Tajima and Thornton 2012, 346.

Even though the "racial equality clause" was not intended to promote equality for Black people, the imperative of maintaining structural anti-Blackness on a global scale contributed to its defeat. Speaking on the topic of racial equality, a British official at the conference said that "he believed that it was true in a certain sense that all men of a particular nation were created equal but not that a man in Central Africa was created equal to a European."[72] The Japanese were not pleading on behalf of the Central African, of course, but *reductio ad absurdum*—disproving the argument (for racial equality) by showing the absurdity of its ultimate implications—was an effective rhetorical strategy, especially when it triggered the phobic hatred of Blackness. During a meeting with Makino Nobuaki, U.S. diplomat Colonel Edward Mandell House scribbled a handwritten note to President Wilson: "The trouble is that if this Commission should pass it [a racial equality clause], it would surely raise the race issue throughout the world."[73] House grasped that the clause's potential impact far exceeded its framers' intentions. The last thing the U.S. government wanted to do was hand ammunition to the critics of Jim Crow and Western imperialism. The Japanese had to be rebuffed lest they inadvertently open a door through which Black people and others could walk. President Woodrow Wilson, who had initially supported the Japanese proposal, reversed himself. House's warning was likely a contributing factor, as was pressure from California legislators, who saw the clause as antithetical to their dreams of Japanese exclusion.

After the conference rejected the "racial equality clause," the U.S. embassy in Tokyo issued a statement to the Japanese press wherein "regret was expressed that the claims of Japan for race equality were not admitted and it was explained this was due to the fears of the British and American delegates that it had a bearing, not only on the immigration question, but on the treatment of subject races such as Indians and Negroes in their dominions."[74] This was an extraordinary announcement. Not only did U.S. officials publicly admit their shared commitment with the British in maintaining global domination over Black and other subject peoples, but they expected this news to soften the blow for the Japanese. *This isn't about you, it's about Negroes. We know you agree that they must be kept in their place.* As with the "Ethiopian" minstrel show on the USS Powhatan, negrophobia was used to smooth

[72] Quoted in Horne 2004, 37.
[73] Allerfeldt 2004, 553.
[74] Horne 2004, 36–37.

white–Asian tensions. Once again, the Japanese were invited to forgive white aggression in the name of a shared hatred for Blackness.

In the wake of the Paris Peace Conference, the *Issei* (first-generation Japanese immigrants) in California reaffirmed the greatness of the Japanese race and its superiority to other not-white races. The *"Issei* pioneer thesis," based on Shiro Fujioka's *Pioneers of Japanese Development* (1927) and the 1940 work of an anonymous Japanese immigrant, *The History of Japanese in America*, clarified that *Issei* saw themselves as part of the Japanese diaspora, and not as a racial minority group within the U.S.[75] As Japanese subjects abroad, they celebrated the expansionist tendencies found in Japanese "racial blood" and embraced Japan's destiny of becoming a great colonial power. As Eiichiro Azuma argues, they wrote themselves into the history of the American West not as an oppressed group but as co-conquerors and co-pioneers with whites: "Elements of the racial ideologies from Anglo-American manifest destiny and imperial Japanese expansionism were joined to form the *Issei*'s vision of the past, which placed them on a par with white frontier settlers and above the rest in their expropriation of the wilderness."[76] Thus the *Issei* claimed an exalted place in American imperial history, Japanese imperial history, and world history. Akira Iriye observes: "[T]hey [the *Issei*] were far more in touch with currents of thought in the mother country than historians have assumed; they were much more part of the phenomenon of Japanese expansion than mere victims of American persecution."[77]

The *"Issei* pioneer thesis" was "a Japanese version of the Horatio Alger story," in which the Japanese traced their progress "from migrant laborers to sharecroppers and from tenant farmers to idealized landowning farmers."[78] One *Issei* historian wrote: "We, the Japanese in America, all crossed the Pacific [and] entered North America with such a heroic determination. Unfamiliar with the language and customs, we still managed to build today's foundations with many tears and much sweat."[79] Glorifying themselves, however, meant denigrating others, as Eiichiro Azuma observes:

Many [Japanese] immigrants condescendingly argued that the *Nisei* could avoid the "pitiful" circumstances of other racial minorities, such as Native Americans, blacks, or Mexicans in the United States, as long as they preserved a "superior

[75] Azuma 2005.
[76] Azuma 2005, 92.
[77] Iriye 1994, 138.
[78] Azuma 2005, 94.
[79] Quoted in Azuma 2005, 93.

national spirit" and "racial consciousness." The converse was also implied: but for their unique traits, the American-born Japanese could lose their distinction from other minorities, who had surrendered to a tragic fate as a result of their defeat in the racial competition.[80]

Decades before the "model minority myth" was ginned up by U.S. government propaganda agencies and the mainstream media, the *Issei* were presenting themselves as a naturally superior race that was leaving other not-white groups in their dust.

The *Issei* assigned the *Nisei* (second-generation Japanese Americans) a crucial role in the Japanese nationalistic project. They were to be inculcated with the *Issei* pioneer thesis through various means, including English-language essay contests sponsored by Japanese immigrant dailies, instruction in Japanese language schools, and oratorical contests run by regional chapters of the Japanese American Citizens League (JACL). Starting in the 1920s, the *Nisei* were also given special instruction in *Nippon seishin* or "Japanese spirit" in order to increase their race pride and consciousness.[81] Some *Nisei* were sent to Japan for additional instruction. In the words of one Japanese professor:

[T]he main purpose of educating *Nisei* in Japan was to "activate" patriotic sentiments that had been dormant in the bosom of their racial mind due to their American upbringing. The acquisition of proper knowledge ... would infallibly drive the *Nisei* to collaborate with their racial homeland of their own volition in "achieving the grand national mission" .... To the Japanese elite, racial ties were innate and immutable, while citizenship was contingent and expedient .... [Thus there was a] baseline expectation that *Nisei* allegiance to the United States could be compromised, trivialized, or overridden when the call of blood became ... too difficult to resist.[82]

Once "activated" for "the grand national mission," the *Nisei* would cast off their loyalty to the U.S. and join the Japanese imperial project. Less than a generation later, when U.S. Army officials claimed the necessity of interning all Japanese Americans on the West Coast, their arguments echoed this one, almost word for word.

[80] Azuma 2005, 128.

[81] Azuma 2005. The expansion of Japanese military activities in China and Mongolia in the 1930s stirred *Issei* nationalism. When Japan set up the puppet regime of Manchukuo in China and Mongolia, the League of Nations condemned Tokyo, but Japanese immigrants in the U.S. cooperated with local Japanese consulates to promote pro-Japan publicity that justified Japan's actions as self-defense, alleged Chinese atrocities against the Japanese, and emphasized the inability of the Chinese to govern themselves.

[82] Azuma 2005, 147.

V *TAKAO OZAWA* V. *UNITED STATES*

California's alien land laws persuaded *Issei* leaders to focus on achieving U.S. citizenship. After the first alien land law passed in 1913, the San Francisco-based paper *Nichibei Shimbun* urged Japanese immigrants to pursue naturalization rights on their own, rather than looking to the Japanese government, whose performance in this area had been disappointing.[83] Gaining U.S. citizenship was not seen as being disloyal to Japan.[84] Indeed, the Japanese government and the Japanese Association of America urged *Issei* to Americanize and assimilate in the U.S. as demonstrations of their love for the home country.[85] Meanwhile, their children, the *Nisei*, would serve as a "bridge of understanding" between the U.S. and Japan, maintaining peace between the two emergent empires. The pro-assimilation JACL, a *Nisei* organization that played a vital role in articulating Japanese Americanness during and after internment, was born of this idea.

In 1914, a number of *Issei* organizations came together to form a coordinating body, the Pacific Coast Japanese Association Deliberative Council, for the purpose of finding a test case for naturalization rights.[86] As it happened, Takao Ozawa, a Japanese immigrant living in Hawai'i, had already initiated such a lawsuit on his own. Born in Japan in 1875, Ozawa had moved to San Francisco in 1894 and then settled in the territory of Hawai'i in 1906, where he filed for naturalized citizenship in 1914. Section 2169 of Title XXX of the Revised Federal Statutes of 1875, which governed naturalization, stated: "The provisions of this title shall apply to aliens being free white persons and to aliens of African nativity and to persons of African descent."[87] Although this was usually interpreted by the courts as disqualifying Japanese immigrants, hundreds of them had managed to be naturalized over the years.[88] Amidst this uncertainty, Ozawa pressed his claim to become a U.S. citizen on the grounds that the Japanese were "white" and thus eligible to naturalize.

The Ozawa case is usually depicted as a struggle between whites and Asians in the context of white supremacy. Once again, bringing structural anti-Blackness back into the picture from which it has been redacted

---

[83] Ichioka 1988.
[84] *Issei* could obtain dual citizenship at this time.
[85] Carbado 2009.
[86] Ichioka 1977.
[87] A 1906 act standardized naturalization procedures but left Section 2169 intact.
[88] Ichioka 1977.

illuminates the whole scene. What Ozawa actually tried to do was elevate himself into whiteness by harnessing the power of negrophobia. In a self-authored brief submitted to the District Court in the territory of Hawaiʻi, Ozawa reflected on the meaning of the phrase "free white person." It had something to do with character: here Ozawa claimed he did not drink, smoke, play cards, or gamble and emphasized his "honesty" and "industriousness."[89] It had something to do with attachment: here he stated "at heart I am a true American" and cited his longtime residence in the U.S. and detachment from Japanese language and culture.[90] And, crucially, it had a lot to do with not-Blackness:

The term "white" was not used to exclude any race at all. It was used simply to distinguish black people from others, as it was used in Arkansas Statute V8TV, which provide that All Person Not Vividly African shall be deemed to belong to "white race." And again, the Constitution of Oklahoma Act of 1891 read as follow: "Whenever in this Constitution and laws of this state, the words colored or colored persons, negro or negro race are used, the same shall be construed to mean to apply to all persons of African descent. The term *'white' shall include all other persons.*" Under Michigan Constitution a person having less than one fourth African blood is white person .... In Kentucky, a person having one fourth of African blood is white person .... In Louisiana, if the proportion of African blood did not exceed one eighth, the person was deemed white .... In Ohio, all persons in which white blood predominates or where it amounts to over one half are white persons .... In Maine, a person having but one sixteenth or one eighth of colored blood is a white person .... Circuit Judge J. H. Rogers said "white" as used in legislation of the slave period meant *person without mixture of colored blood (negro) whatever actual complexion might be.* Thus the above ... will sufficiently prove that the term "White person" were used to include all persons other than black people.[91]

Instead of Black being a catchall category for whoever was not-white, as in *People* v. *George Hall*, white was a catchall category for whoever was not-Black. Citing slave law and Jim Crow state constitutions, Ozawa insisted that "white" was defined solely through the exclusion of "colored blood."[92] Whoever was not-Black was white, including those of Japanese descent. Given the language of Section 2169, Ozawa could just as well have argued that he was "of African descent" and thus eligible

---

[89] Ozawa printed his brief for private circulation: "Naturalization of a Japanese Subject in the United States of America," October 1922.

[90] Ozawa 1922, 4. Ozawa had not attended Japanese language schools or Japanese immigrant churches. He had refused to register his information with the Japanese consulate in Honolulu. His wife was educated in the U.S., and his children spoke English only.

[91] Ozawa 1922, 14–15. Italics in original. Errors are in original text.

[92] Ozawa quoted several authorities as saying that the Japanese were white or partly white.

to naturalize, but claiming whiteness was more palatable (because it did not involve identifying with the most phobogenic group) and more plausible (because if the whiteness of the Japanese was in question, their not-Blackness was not). The point was to leverage his not-Blackness, not erase it. The question was: just how much was his not-Blackness worth?

Not as much as Ozawa had hoped, said District Court Judge Charles Clemons. Clemons wrote in his ruling that "yellow/oriental" was a distinct legal category encompassing both the Chinese and Japanese, and that "white" had a specific, exclusionary meaning, rather than being a catchall category for what was left after removing Blackness.[93] Ozawa was not-Black, but he was not therefore white. Thus he was ineligible to naturalize under Section 2169. Ozawa appealed the ruling, and when the Ninth Circuit Court of Appeals referred the case to the U.S. Supreme Court without a decision, the Pacific Coast Japanese Association Deliberative Council got on board, retaining eminent New York lawyer and former U.S. attorney general George Wickersham as Ozawa's counsel. At the same time, Japanese consul Moroi Rokuro and a group of Japanese diplomats and businessmen tried to dissuade Ozawa from pursuing the case, arguing that it was premature and would arouse too much white resistance. Japanese American newspapers fiercely debated the matter.[94] When Ozawa decided to press forward, the U.S. government requested that the Supreme Court delay its ruling in order to avoid angering Japan—first, until after the end of the First World War, and then until after the Washington Conference on Arms Limitation concluded in 1921.[95] Thus the Supreme Court did not hear the case until 1922, six years after the District Court issued its ruling.

The Brief for Petitioner (Ozawa) reprised and elaborated on many aspects of Ozawa's original brief, including the focus on his not-Blackness.[96] Congress had repeatedly praised Japan as a world power during the debate over the Asiatic Barred Zone Act of 1917, the brief pointed out, and had chosen to exempt Japan from the immigration restrictions that it imposed on other Asian nations at that time. John Sharp Williams, senator from Mississippi, had given an impassioned defense of the Japanese on the Senate floor, which the brief quoted in part:

[93] Carbado 2009.
[94] Ichioka 1977; 1988.
[95] This conference was organized by the U.S. and Britain to persuade Japan to limit its growing naval forces (Ichioka 1988).
[96] Brief for Petitioner, *Takao Ozawa* v. *United States* (1918).

There are some 14,000,000 negroes in the South. They are spreading themselves all over the United States. Everybody admits that they are an inferior race to the Japanese …. The Senate has today and yesterday voted down half a dozen amendments to this bill to exclude negroes from immigration into the United States. Neither the Independent Senator from the State of California nor the Democratic Senator will dare to say that the Japanese are inferior to negroes …. You stand around and smile and risk international complications with Japan on a race issue about the Japanese, who are as highly civilized as you are …. The Japanese are not a race of barbarians … they are a race of people who have proven their ability to stand in the front ranks of civilization.[97]

Like the Chinese, the Japanese were constitutively not-Black. Which is to say, Asian mattering was constructed against the zero mattering of Blackness. In the case of the Japanese, their national accomplishments enhanced their not-Blackness, placing them "in the front ranks of civilization."

The Brief for Petitioner then repeated Ozawa's initial argument that "'free white persons' means one not black, not a negro, which does not exclude Japanese."[98] It stated:

White is defined in the Standard Dictionary as "1.***poposed [sic] to *black.*** 2. Having a light complexion. (1) Of the color of the Eurafrican or Caucasian race: opposed especially to *negro*, but often to the yellow, brown, or red races of men." The Century defines white as "1.***The opposite of *black* or *dark.* ***" …. Webster defines it as "1. The opposite of *black* or *dark***" and defines a white person as "a person of the Caucasian race (6 Fed. 256). In the times of slavery in the United States, *white person* is construed in effect as a person without admixture of colored blood." "White person" is defined in the new Standard Dictionary as "1. Any person of the Eurafrican race. 2. (U.S.) Any person without admixture of negro or Indian blood. Since 1865 various legal constructions of this term have been made in different States, as in Arkansas, where a white person is one having no negro blood, or in Ohio, where one is a white person who has just less than half negro blood in his veins." Webster's New International Dictionary: "In various statutes and decisions in different States since 1865 *white person* is construed in effect as a person not having any negro blood (Arkansas and Oklahoma). A white person is one having less than one-eighth of negro blood (Alabama, Florida, Georgia, Indiana, Kentucky, Maryland, Minnesota, Montana, Tennessee, Texas, Maine, North Carolina and South Carolina). A white person is one having less than one-fourth of negro blood (Michigan, Nebraska, Oregon and Virginia). A white person is one having less than one-half of negro blood (Ohio)."[99]

[97] Brief for Petitioner, *Takao Ozawa v. United States* (1918), 29–30.
[98] Brief for Petitioner, *Takao Ozawa v. United States* (1918), 40.
[99] Brief for Petitioner, *Takao Ozawa v. United States* (1918), 50–51. Italics in original.

Once again, the argument for Ozawa's right to naturalize was grounded upon the phobic hatred of Blackness sedimented into U.S. law. *The Chicago Defender*, a leading Black newspaper, denounced the Ozawa case as a "great blunder." Black Americans who had strongly supported Japan as a leader of the "colored races" were disappointed to see the Japanese "begging to be classed not as a yellow people, but as a branch of the Aryan tree."[100]

The Brief for Respondent (the U.S. government) had the comparatively easy task of demonstrating that U.S. lawmakers had never seen Asiatics/Mongolians as "white." It pointed to the congressional debate over the 1870 Naturalization Act, wherein legislators had explicitly considered and then rejected the idea of allowing the Chinese to naturalize, as well as to subsequent court decisions affirming the prohibition on Asian naturalization. It cited *In re Saito*, a case involving a Japanese man who was denied the right to naturalize because, according to the court, "[t]he Japanese, like the Chinese, belong to the Mongolian race."[101] Finally, the brief argued that Section 2169 of the Revised Statutes was binding, and that exceptions had been carved out in 1918 for Filipinos and Puerto Ricans who served in the U.S. military, but not for the Japanese. "White persons," it concluded, was not a catchall phrase intended to mean all who are not Black. "White" meant something beyond not-Blackness, and it was something Mongolians lacked.

Justice Sutherland, writing for the majority of the U.S. Supreme Court, agreed that Section 2169 was binding in this case, and that the Japanese were not "white" and were thus ineligible for naturalization. The 1790 Naturalization Act's mention of "free white persons" meant "not that Negroes and Indians shall be excluded, but ... in effect, that only free white persons shall be included." According to Sutherland, "[t]he intention was to confer the privilege of citizenship upon that class of persons whom the fathers knew as white, and to deny it to all who could not be so classified." Whiteness was a positive property, not just the absence of Blackness. It is true that the law did not have in mind "the brown or yellow races of Asia," but Ozawa's counsel failed to show that if they had had them in mind, they would have decided to confer the naturalization right upon them. Citing a long string of cases showing "white" means "Caucasian," Sutherland concluded that Ozawa "is clearly of a race which is not Caucasian."[102]

---

[100] Kearney 1994, 127.
[101] Brief for the United States, *Takao Ozawa v. United States* (1922), 12.
[102] *Takao Ozawa v. United States* (1922), 195, 195, 198.

As an Asian immigrant, Ozawa was poised at the turbulent juncture of white supremacy and anti-Blackness. Recognizing the boon of his not-Blackness, his gambit was to ride it as far upward as he could, seeking the limit of its value. What he discovered was that anti-Blackness could fuel his mobility, but only to a point. It was powerful enough to carry him to the doorstep of the citadel of whiteness, but not powerful enough to get him inside. In the gap between not-Blackness and whiteness, in that space of longing, Asian immigrant dreams continued to grow.

VI JAPANESE EXCLUSION

As the Ozawa case was making its way through the courts, California lawmakers demanded that the federal government go beyond the Gentlemen's Agreement and halt Japanese immigration completely. To preserve the purity of the white race and the supremacy of white civilization, they argued, all Japanese had to be barred from the nation. Although there were echoes of pro-lynching discourse here, the Japanese threat was conceived of differently than the Black threat. It is not that the Japanese threat was never sexualized—nativists raised doubts about Japanese schoolboys during the San Francisco school segregation crisis, for example, and anti-miscegenation laws in California and elsewhere forbade white–Asian unions—but rather that it was figured as primarily civilizational rather than sexual. The danger posed by the Japanese was not rape and miscegenation but the destruction of white society and culture through demographic inundation and economic competition. The Japanese were shrewd, worthy adversaries to be kept at bay, not fiendish beasts to be hunted down and killed in an orgy of violence.

The matter of Japanese exclusion arose during the U.S. Senate debate over the bill that would become the Asiatic Barred Zone Act of 1917. According to Senator Ellison Smith of South Carolina, the aim of the bill was to enact the exclusion of Asiatics without giving offense to Japan. This was to be accomplished by drawing a geographic "barred zone" around certain Asian countries rather than relying on the category "aliens ineligible to citizenship," which had been used to target the Japanese in the California alien land laws.[103] Some lawmakers, however, wanted to include Japan in the barred zone as well, arguing that the Gentlemen's Agreement was allowing too many Japanese to enter. Before long, the debate turned to Black immigrants from Africa and the Caribbean.

---

[103] *Congressional Record*, 64th Congress, 2d Session, U.S. Senate, December 13, 1916, 262.

Senator James Reed of Missouri asked why the barred zone had not been drawn to include Africa:

I can see no common sense in a proposition which denies to the inhabitants of Asia the right to land in America and opens the door to all of the inhabitants of Africa. There is only one reason that can be assigned, which is that there are some of the former inhabitants of Africa who now live in this country and who vote. There is not a man on the floor of the Senate who dares make the public assertion that from the standpoint of citizenship the people of Asia are not fully equal to the inhabitants of Africa.[104]

As in Thomas Nast's drawing "The Civilization of Blaine," Reed posed the question "why x and not y, when y is at least equal to x?" Like Nast, Reed pointed to the political self-interest of his Republican colleagues. He continued:

[I]t seems to me that every effort ought to be made to keep out of this country all people who are not capable of thorough amalgamation into the life of our people and who are not capable of being brought into thorough sympathy with our laws and our institutions ... but if we are to exclude the Asiatic, which is the proposition brought forward by the committee, then by what line of reasoning are we to admit the African? Every Asiatic nation has had its civilization, some of them older than ours, and from some of those countries, the inhabitants of which will be excluded by the terms of this amendment, we have gained many of the great precepts of our civilization. In many of these countries the inhabitants of which are to be excluded wonderful architecture still stands to manifest the genius of the past. In many of the countries, whose inhabitants we propose to exclude, there have existed wonderful governments and wonderful men. But if you turn to Africa, the country you do not propose to include in the exclusion, you can not find a single civilization except at the northern extremities; and those civilizations have died centuries ago, and the races that created them have disappeared. The great body of the African race has never developed a civilization of any kind. There is no civilization there now, and never has been. I do not know upon what theory men proceed who say "We will go into Asia and exclude the Asiatics, and then we will hold our arms open to the Africans." Is there any good faith back of this measure?[105]

This paean to Asiatic civilizational accomplishment looks at first glance like an argument in favor of Asian immigration, but it was not. Reed fastened on Asians' putative superiority to Black people not as an argument *for* the former but rather as an argument *against* the latter. Senator Ellison Smith of South Carolina responded that there was no need to bar African immigrants because they were few in number, and the literacy

---

[104] *Congressional Record*, 64th Congress, 2d Session, U.S. Senate, December 11, 1916, 157.
[105] *Congressional Record*, 64th Congress, 2d Session, U.S. Senate, December 11, 1916, 158.

clause of the bill under consideration would prevent them from entering in any case. Also, it would complicate the drawing of the barred zone considerably to stretch it to include Africa. Since Smith argued neither the African's intrinsic worthiness nor their equality or superiority to the Asian, he tacitly affirmed Reed's comparative valuation.

Like Reed, another senator from a Jim Crow state, Senator John Sharp Williams of Mississippi, also valorized the Japanese in an effort to close the gate to Black immigrants, while at the same time opposing Japanese immigration. He rebuked his colleagues from California for devaluing the Japanese, needlessly antagonizing the Japanese government, and overlooking the Black threat. (Ozawa's counsel included the first part of Williams's statement in the Brief for Petitioner to the U.S. Supreme Court, but he omitted the second part, which is italicized here.) Williams intoned:

There are some 14,000,000 negroes in the South. They are spreading themselves all over the United States. Everybody admits that they are an inferior race to the Japanese .... The Senate has today and yesterday voted down half a dozen amendments to this bill to exclude negroes from immigration into the United States. Neither the Independent Senator from the State of California nor the Democratic Senator will dare to say that the Japanese are inferior to negroes .... You stand around and smile and risk international complications with Japan on a race issue about the Japanese, who are as highly civilized as you are, and you dare not, because of congressional situations here and there, declare as to the negro that this is a white man's country, because the negro has a vote .... The Japanese are not a race of barbarians; they are not a race of veneered men; they are a race of people who have proven their ability to stand in the front ranks of civilization. *I do not want them here, not because they are inferior, but because they are different. I want a homogeneous population here; I want a population in the United States which shall be entirely and altogether white, as far as we can make it so, with our past history behind us; not because I assert that I as a white man am necessarily superior to the other man, but because he is different from me, and he is unassimilable by me and I am unassimilable by him.*[106]

Williams's disclaimer about not asserting superiority was probably made in bad faith—like most white lawmakers at the time, he almost certainly viewed the Japanese as different *and* inferior—but the fact that he made it on the U.S. Senate floor indicates the general regard with which the Japanese were viewed.

[106] *Congressional Record*, 64th Congress, 2d Session, U.S. Senate, December 12, 1916, 214. Italics added.

Responding to Williams's rebuke, Senator John Works of California hastened to remind his southern colleagues that he had in fact voted to extend the immigration ban to Africans:

I have always believed, and I have never hesitated to say so, that it is a great mistake that negroes were granted the franchise. I have said so in public addresses delivered before the negroes themselves. I think it has resulted in great injury to the colored race and has been of practically no benefit to them; but we have the negro here; we have granted him the franchise; and what can we do upon this side of the Chamber, or we who are representing States on the Pacific coast, to relieve the South from the presence of the negro?[107]

I am as dedicated a negrophobe as you. But Black rights had already been decided, Works pleaded, and Japanese immigration was the issue at hand.

Congress ultimately decided not to include Japan in the Asiatic Barred Zone Act of 1917, but it revisited Japanese exclusion several years later, with a different outcome. In 1924, a bill was introduced that curtailed southern and eastern European immigration via a restrictive quota system and barred "aliens ineligible to citizenship" altogether. Since all other Asian groups had been banned by prior legislation, it was clear that "aliens ineligible to citizenship" meant the Japanese. Secretary of State Charles Hughes sent a letter to Representative Albert Johnson of Washington, the bill's sponsor, objecting that the bill violated the 1911 U.S.–Japan Treaty of Commerce and Navigation and suggesting that the U.S. could avoid offending Japan by placing it under the quota system along with other nations. Since the quota would be calculated based upon how many Japanese were in the U.S. in 1890, the annual quota would be less than 250, Hughes argued, and the quota system in combination with the Gentlemen's Agreement would provide a "double control" on Japanese immigration.[108]

Proponents of Japanese exclusion were undeterred. They responded that the bill did not violate the 1911 U.S.–Japan Treaty, that Japan's sensitivity should not be allowed to dictate U.S. policy, and that the Gentlemen's Agreement was both ineffective (many Japanese immigrants were still entering the nation, including so-called "picture brides," who then procreated) and possibly illegitimate (it was an informal agreement and never ratified by Congress). It was not enough to drastically reduce

[107] *Congressional Record*, 64th Congress, 2d Session, U.S. Senate, December 12, 1916, 215.
[108] *Congressional Record*, 68th Congress, 1st Session, U.S. House of Representatives, April 4, 1924, 5586.

the number of Japanese immigrants; they had to be barred altogether, as a matter of principle and as an acknowledgment of the racial war underway. A March 13 statement by James Phelan, former senator from California, responding to Secretary Hughes's letter, captured the emotional tenor of the exclusion campaign: "The fact is that Japan is laying the foundation of a permanent colonization on the Pacific slope which will spready quickly to other parts of the West. It is apparent that the only way to check Japanese immigration is to impose an exclusion law such as we have against all other Asiatics. At present, we have surrendered our sovereignty to Japan."[109]

The following month, on April 11, 1924, the Senate discussed a letter received from Japanese Ambassador Hanihara the day before. The letter said in part:

In return [for faithfully enforcing the Gentlemen's Agreement] the Japanese Government confidently trusts that the United States Government will recommend, if necessary, to the Congress to refrain from resorting to a measure that would seriously wound the proper susceptibilities of the Japanese nation .... To Japan the question is not one of expediency but of principle. To her the mere fact that a few hundreds or thousands of her nationals will or will not be admitted into the domains of other countries is immaterial, so long as no question of national susceptibilities is involved. The important question is whether Japan as a nation is or is not entitled to the proper respect and consideration of other nations.[110]

As with the alien land laws, Japan's concern was less with the bill's material effects than with its symbolic import on the world stage. Being lumped with other Asians through immigration exclusion was an insupportable humiliation. Hanihara warned of "the grave consequences which the enactment of the measure ... would inevitably bring upon the otherwise happy and mutually advantageous relations between our two countries."[111] Attempting to stave off passage of the bill, Japanese Foreign Minister Kijuro Shidehara hastily drafted a new treaty whereby the U.S. and Japan would mutually prohibit immigration and Japanese immigrants would be guaranteed the same rights as the citizens of other nations.[112]

Hanihara's letter backfired. The mention of "grave consequences" was read as a threat, which reenergized calls for the assertion of U.S.

---

[109] *Congressional Record*, 68th Congress, 1st Session, U.S. Senate, March 13, 1924, 4073.
[110] *Congressional Record*, 68th Congress, 1st Session, U.S. Senate, April 11, 1924, 6073–6074.
[111] *Congressional Record*, 68th Congress, 1st Session, U.S. Senate, April 11, 1924, 6074.
[112] Hirobe 2001.

sovereignty. Senator David Reed of Pennsylvania declared: "I, for one, feel compelled, on account of that veiled threat, to vote in favor of the exclusion."[113] Former Senator James Phelan called for the Gentlemen's Agreement to be revoked on the grounds that it delegated sovereign authority over U.S. affairs to Japan.[114] When Secretary of State Hughes requested a grace period (until March 1, 1925) during which the U.S. and Japan could negotiate a mutually agreeable immigration treaty, the Senate refused to grant it. The Immigration Act of 1924 went into effect on July 1, 1924, barring "aliens ineligible to citizenship" from entering the U.S.

Although Japanese exclusion was put into effect, it is striking that the debates were rife with stipulations about the fundamental worthiness of the Japanese. Indeed some of the most ardent exclusionists went so far as to argue Japanese *superiority* to whites as grounds for keeping them out. (We can look in vain for comparable statements about Black people in the *Congressional Record* or any other official archive.) In 1921, in a brief prepared for the State Department (and subsequently read into the Senate record), V. S. McClatchy, head of the Japanese Exclusion League in California, charged Japanese immigrants with trying to colonize the U.S. on behalf of Japan and called for their total exclusion. Yet he also clarified:

There is no claim or belief as to racial inferiority involved in this issue. There is, on the contrary, a frank admission that because of conditions fully explained herein, the white race may not hope to survive in this country if compelled to meet the Japanese in competition for economic advantage and racial existence. Our own people may be lacking in thrift, and unwilling to work long hours without recreation; they may not be defended for an apparent tendency to race suicide; but the less their ability to compete with an alien unassimilable race if permitted to invade our land, the greater the necessity for affording them necessary protection.[115]

Japanese exclusion would act as a racial tariff of sorts, protecting underdeveloped domestic residents from more capable foreign competitors. Representative Theodore Burton of Ohio echoed this view on the House floor on May 9, 1924:

---

[113] *Congressional Record*, 68th Congress, 1st Session, U.S. Senate, April 14, 1924, 6305.
[114] James Phelan, former U.S. senator and mayor of San Francisco, along with V. S. McClatchy and California Attorney General U. S. Webb, went as a delegation to Washington, D.C., to discuss the Japanese question. Also active on the matter were the American Legion, the National Grange, the American Federation of Labor, and the Native Sons of the Golden West.
[115] McClatchy 1921.

What are the virtues of the Japanese? Untiring industry; economy; thrift; loyalty to their country, to their ruler; and readiness to imitate and adopt the best to be found in other portions of the world .... It is no disparagement to them or their civilization that we desire to adopt such a law as this. The plain truth is, in the first place, that in competition in many lines of endeavor they surpass us, because they are more industrious, more constant in their labor, and more economical in their habits of living.[116]

White Americans could not hope to prevail against the Japanese without a strong assist from the U.S. government. And this from the detractors of the Japanese!

Even if we grant that these arguments may not have been entirely sincere, and that many lawmakers likely believed in white superiority, the fact that Japanese superiority to whites could be credibly discussed in congressional debates is itself testimony to the unusual respect accorded them. This respect was due in no small measure to Japan's emergence as a world power, but it also depended upon the not-Blackness of the Japanese as a condition of possibility. For Japanese immigrants and their descendants, as for the Chinese before them, foreignness was the basis for exclusion, but it was also, and more fundamentally, an index of their standing and belonging in the Family of Man.

Despite the backhanded compliments, the Japanese immigrant community saw the Immigration Act of 1924 as "the culminating act of rejection by the United States."[117] Yuji Ichioka explains that "Japanese immigrant leaders felt doubly affronted ... because [the act] ranked the Japanese, not as the equal of Europeans, but on the same low level as previously excluded Asian people, the very people whom they themselves judged to be inferior."[118] The Seattle-based paper *Taihoku Nippo* insisted that the U.S. be forced to pay due respect to Japan and the Japanese people. The reaction in Japan was even more intense, where an outraged press sparked mass rallies and conventions denouncing the U.S. and calling for war. *Tokyo Asahi*, a leading paper, declared July 1 a day of national humiliation and "American peril," and *The Japan Times* called the immigration statute a virtual declaration of war and demanded a military buildup in preparation for conflict.[119] Two decades later, in the preamble to his piece "The Background Causes to the Greater East Asia

---

[116] *Congressional Record*, 68th Congress, 1st Session, U.S. House of Representatives, May 9, 1924, 8229.
[117] Ichioka 1988, 244.
[118] Ichioka 1988, 250.
[119] Hirobe 2001; Lake and Reynolds 2008.

War" (1946), the Japanese emperor wrote: "If we ask the reason for this war [the Second World War] ... [t]he racial equality proposal demanded by Japan [in 1919] was not accepted by the powers. The discriminatory sentiment between the white and yellow remains as always. And the rejections of immigrants in California. These were enough to anger the Japanese people."[120]

VII BLACK INTERNATIONALISM

Issei who fought to gain citizenship hoped it would bring them under the "sheltering folds" of flag and constitution and secure them the full protection of the state. What they found instead was that *race*, which ran orthogonally to citizenship, determined who mattered and who did not. It was not citizenship but whiteness that invested one with full value. It was not the lack of citizenship but Blackness that deprived one of all value. This was a lesson that had been continuously driven home for Black people since the period of racial slavery. As they endured lynching, convict leasing, debt peonage, Jim Crow laws, de facto segregation, disenfranchisement, criminalization, police violence, race riots, employment discrimination, and more, Black people understood what it meant to hold citizenship as an evacuated status.

How were Black politics to be conceived at the start of the twentieth century, when citizenship and voting rights were secured on paper and denied in reality? When the recognition of Black rights was openly discussed in congressional debates as a fateful mistake? What kind of politics were called forth by the status of zero mattering? By the "condition of statelessness?" Was allegiance owed to a government that not only failed to provide protection to Black citizens but colluded with private interests to maintain and deepen their subordination? What kind of politics was possible outside allegiance to the nation-state? Was the goal of Black politics to make Black citizenship meaningful for the first time or to dismantle the structures of power that had always made it impossible? How did Black politics in the U.S. articulate with Black struggles abroad? With the struggles of other "colored races?" How did the Black struggle at home and abroad articulate with global anti-capitalism?

The emergence of a Black liberal-left anti-colonialist front in the early twentieth century marked the definitive internationalization of the U.S. Black freedom struggle, as activists rethought segregation and

---

[120] Lake and Reynolds 2008, 308.

discrimination at home in relation to Western colonialism and imperialism abroad.[121] Lines of political affiliation and conflict were reimagined and redrawn, and Black internationalists in the U.S. developed a sense of political kinship with Africans and Asians laboring under the yoke of colonial and imperial oppression half a world away. Out of what W. E. B. Du Bois called "that dark and vast sea of human labor in China and India, the South Seas and all of Africa … that great majority of mankind, on whose bent and broken backs rest today the founding stones of modern history," new political formations and subjectivities and visions were taking hold.[122] The "colored" races of the world were rising up together against Western domination, and as a global majority, they believed it was their destiny to prevail.[123] By the time the Second World War emerged, Walter White of the NAACP observed: "[The war] has given to the Negro a sense of kinship with other colored—and also oppressed—peoples of the world …. [T]he struggle of the Negro in the United States is part and parcel of the struggle against imperialism and exploitation in India, China, Burma, Africa, the Philippines, Malaya, the West Indies, and South America."[124]

Black internationalism, especially its more radical iterations, threatened the legitimacy of the U.S. racial-capitalist state by calling out the injuries of segregation, discrimination, and capitalist exploitation; explicating their connection to historical patterns of Western colonialism and imperialism; and advancing alternative visions of what Robin Kelley calls "freedom dreams." It sparked fierce debates at the start of the First World War about whether Black people should serve in the U.S. military at all. How should Black people relate to a war among Western colonial and imperial powers jockeying for control over the "colored races" of the world? How much allegiance, if any, did Black people owe to the U.S. government?

---

[121] See Gallichio 2000 and Von Eschen 1997.

[122] Du Bois 1998 [1935], 15–16. There were important political divergences and tensions within the Black internationalist front. While Walter White of the NAACP carefully refrained from attacking the legitimacy of the U.S. state or capitalism per se, for instance, Black leftists like W. E. B. Du Bois and Paul Robeson kept both in their sights (Anderson 2003). For Black leftists, the U.S. state was neither a neutral arbiter of justice nor the protector of American citizens against internal and external enemies, but rather a purveyor of racial violence and capitalist exploitation at home and around the world (Gallichio 2000; Von Eschen 1997). Walter White, on the other hand, saw Black citizenship as a precious promise waiting to be redeemed through positive state action. He did not question the basic legitimacy of political and economic institutions.

[123] See Meriwether (2002) on the rethinking of Africa that accompanied this new Black internationalism.

[124] Von Eschen 1997, 7–8.

In July 1917, with the war well underway, W. E. B. Du Bois published a controversial editorial entitled "Close Ranks" in *The Crisis*, wherein he urged Black people to gain self-respect and political standing by fighting on behalf of the nation: "Let us, while this war lasts, forget our special grievances and close our ranks shoulder to shoulder with our own white fellow citizens and the allied nations that are fighting for democracy."[125] Months later, he elaborated on this call to arms, writing "first your Country, then your Rights!"[126] Harlem-based author and critic Hubert Harrison accused Du Bois of trying to gain favor with military intelligence officials in his bid for a U.S. Army captaincy.[127] Chandler Owen and A. Philip Randolph, socialist editors of *The Messenger*, also criticized Du Bois's position, arguing that Black people owed no allegiance to the U.S. state and should not sacrifice their lives for it. When Owen and Randolph were arrested and charged with treason the following year due to their anti-war organizing, the judge released them on the assumption that, as Black men, they were not capable of self-directed political action and must have been led astray by white socialists.

The violence inflicted upon Black troops during and after the First World War impacted these debates. It was the U.S. Army's policy to segregate Black soldiers and use them primarily as manual laborers, denying them the power and prestige of bearing arms and appeasing southern white civilians who objected to the notion of Black soldiers altogether. Black labor battalions in the South were described as "more closely resembl[ing] convict-lease labor gangs as opposed to military units."[128] Still, this derogation in status did not satisfy white officers, white soldiers, white military police, white civilian police, and white civilians, who showed unremitting hostility toward Black soldiers and devised myriad ways to debase and harm them. White aggression led to continuous racial conflict, so that "training camps became literal battlefields" where Black soldiers defended their dignity and often their lives against their "fellow Americans."[129] This dynamic led to the Houston Rebellion of August 1917, where Black soldiers with the Third Battalion of the Twenty-fourth Infantry at Camp Logan were court-martialed for defending themselves against white violence. Thirteen Black soldiers were hanged. After the war, Black veterans returning home were

[125] Williams 2010, 75.
[126] Washburn 1986, 19.
[127] Williams 2010.
[128] Williams 2010, 109.
[129] Williams 2010, 93.

"met by a wave of racial violence unmatched since the aftermath of the Civil War," including white pogroms and lynchings.[130] James Weldon Johnson of the NAACP referred to the demobilization of 1919 as "the Red Summer."

None of this escaped the notice of Caribbean-born journalist Cyril Briggs, who founded the African Blood Brotherhood for African Liberation and Redemption in Harlem, New York, at the close of the war. Theorizing the articulation of global racism and global capitalism, the African Blood Brotherhood "[f]us[ed] revolutionary Marxism, black nationalism, and diasporic race consciousness."[131] With several chapters in the U.S. and the Caribbean, its aim was to lead "an international, anti-colonial struggle of all oppressed races for socialism in Africa and Asia."[132] African Blood Brotherhood members maintained a specific focus on Black oppression even as they envisioned a global field of social-ist political action encompassing the African continent, the African dias-pora, Asia (especially China, India, and Japan), and the West. As Minkah Makalani explains, they emphasized "the centrality of the international black working class to a pan-African liberation movement" and called for the establishment of "a worldwide Negro federation" that would protect Black interests everywhere.[133] It would be the laborers in the African (and Asian) diaspora, not the European proletariat, who would usher in global socialism.

In December 1920, referencing U.S. tensions with Japan and Mexico, Cyril Briggs wrote in *The Crusader* that Black people had a duty

NOT TO FIGHT AGAINST JAPAN OR MEXICO, BUT RATHER TO FILL THE PRISONS AND DUNGEONS OF THE WHITE MAN (OR TO FACE HIS FIRING SQUADS) THAN TO SHOULDER ARMS AGAINST OTHER MEM-BERS OF THE DARKER RACES. The Negro who fights against either Japan or Mexico is fighting for the *white man* against himself, for the *white race* against the darker races and for the perpetuation of *white domination of the colored races*, with its vicious practices of *lynching, jim-crowism, segregation and other forms of oppression.*[134]

In the context of a worldwide race war, Black people could not afford to be fooled by the ruse of nationality. Race, not nation, was the key axis organizing affiliation and conflict on a global scale. Only an alliance of

---

[130] Williams 2010, 224.
[131] Williams 2010, 262.
[132] Makalani 2011b, 151.
[133] Makalani 2011a, 59. See also Robinson 1983.
[134] Kornweibel 1998, 139. Capitalization and italics in original.

the "darker races" could end white domination and global capitalism and usher in a period of lasting socialist peace.

Briggs distinguished the African Blood Brotherhood from two other prominent Black internationalist projects underway at the time. He denounced Marcus Garvey's call for Westernized Black people to uplift and civilize Africa, as well as the United Negro Improvement Association's embrace of capitalism and empire, as evidence of a reactionary sensibility. In addition, he criticized W. E. B Du Bois's Pan-African Congress movement for trying to reform rather than dismantle Western colonial governance in Africa and Asia.[135] The African Blood Brotherhood looked instead to international communism as an infrastructure upon which to build a global Black working-class movement.[136] In 1919, the Communist International (Comintern) Congress called for the end to colonial exploitation of Africa and Asia and declared its support for national liberation movements in those areas. The following year, Lenin released his "Preliminary Draft Theses on the National and Colonial Questions" urging national communist parties "to support revolutionary movements among the dependent nations and those without equal rights," including the Black freedom struggle.[137] These policy shifts were the result of "constant efforts [by Black internationalists] to have international communism address race and anticolonial liberation, to situate Africa and Asia at the center of proletarian struggle, and to help build a world Negro movement."[138]

Alarmed by the rise of Black internationalism, in particular its communist variants, U.S. government agencies raised doubts about the political loyalty of Black organizations and newspapers. A dense network of federal agencies dedicated to surveilling, investigating, harassing, and prosecuting domestic "enemies" of the state was created during the First World War and its aftermath—including J. Edgar Hoover's Bureau of Investigation, the forerunner of the FBI—and this state machinery was quickly bent to the task of ferreting out Black subversion.[139] During the

---

[135] The African Blood Brotherhood and the UNIA briefly collaborated but then stopped, with Garvey accusing the ABB of being run by white communists (Solomon 1998).

[136] Makalani 2011a.

[137] Solomon 1998, 40.

[138] Makalani 2011a, 229. As the Comintern Congresses developed their position on the Black struggle over the next several years, culminating in their declaration that Black people in the U.S. South were an oppressed nation with a right to self-determination, national communist parties in the U.S., U.K., France, and South Africa refused to make this adjustment (Makalani 2011a).

[139] Kornweibel 1998.

Red Scare (1917–1920), the U.S. government developed the strategy of delegitimating the Black struggle by painting it red. Black critique of governmental policies, as expressed in newspaper editorials or civil rights campaigns, was dismissed as the handiwork of the Bolsheviks, thus reinforcing the trope of Black political incapacity. Rather than acknowledge that stateless Black internationalists were turning to communism for assistance against a hostile and oppressive state, U.S. officials insisted that communists were manipulating child-like Blacks against their own country. An Office of Naval Intelligence report in 1919 declared that Blacks were emotional and lacking in self-control and thus easily incited by motivated whites. As Theodore Kornweibel observed, "the widespread perception [existed] among worried whites that black militancy could be inspired only by renegade whites—particularly communists and anarchists—not by domestic social, economic, or political conditions."[140]

U.S. officials accused Black editors and journalists of obeying communist directives to magnify racial incidents and stir up "race hatred" among the Black masses. J. Edgar Hoover produced two separate reports linking Black publications to communism, in 1919 and 1920, with the first stating ominously: "The Negro is 'seeing red.'"[141] The accusation was levelled not just at A. Philip Randolph and Chandler Owen's *Messenger*, a socialist-oriented newspaper, or at Cyril Brigg's *Crusader*, a communist-oriented newspaper, but at most if not all major Black publications, including Marcus Garvey's *Negro World*, the NAACP's *Crisis*, *The Chicago Defender*, and *The New York Amsterdam News*. Robert Vann of *The Pittsburgh Courier*, a leading Black paper, commented: "The only conclusion therefore is: As long as the Negro submits to lynchings, burnings and oppressions, and says nothing, he is a loyal American citizen. But when he decides that lynchings and burnings shall cease even at the cost of some human bloodshed in America, then he is a Bolshevist."[142] Foreshadowing the Cold War dynamics that would emerge a half-century later, the U.S. government used the Bolshevist libel to discourage and deflect Black critique.

Some Black internationalists viewed Japan as the "champion of the darker races" in the interwar period.[143] After its victory in the Russo-Japanese War of 1905, Japan was hailed by *Chicago Defender* columnist

---

[140] Kornweibel 1998, 60.
[141] Washburn 1986, 27.
[142] Washburn 1986, 27–28.
[143] Gallichio 2000, 3.

A. L. Jackson as the "living refutation of the white man's theory of white supremacy" and by the NAACP's James Weldon Johnson as "perhaps the greatest hope for the colored race of the world."[144] W. E. B. Du Bois, Marcus Garvey, and the Nation of Islam's Elijah Muhammad all believed Japan was leading a global insurgency of colored peoples against white racism and imperialism. This was the context in which a group of prominent Black leaders, including A. Philip Randolph, Ida B. Wells, and William Monroe Trotter, went to the Paris Peace Conference in 1919 to ask Japanese officials to support their protest against the proposed League of Nations. Japanese delegates offered assurances that they would raise the issue of racial equality at the conference. What they did not say was that they were only concerned with racial equality for the Japanese.

With their working-class and anti-fascist sensibilities, Black leftists tended to be more skeptical about the Japanese. A. Philip Randolph was ambivalent about meeting with the Japanese delegation in Paris, and together with fellow socialist Chandler Owen voiced pointed criticism of Japanese colonialism in Asia. In the May–June 1919 issue of *The Messenger*, they admonished their Japanophile colleagues:

A word of warning, however, to the unsuspecting and to those not thoroughly versed in social science. The Japanese statesmen are not in the least concerned about race or color prejudice. The smug and oily Japanese diplomats ... do not suffer from race prejudice. They teach in the Rockefeller Institute, wine and dine at the Waldorf Astoria, Manhattan or Poinciana, divide financial melons in Wall Street, ride on railways and cars free from discrimination. They are nothing even for the Japanese people and at this very same moment are suppressing and oppressing mercilessly the people of Korea and forcing hard bargains upon unfortunate China.[145]

Japanese diplomats enjoyed class privileges and not-Blackness while in the U.S., and all the privileges of colonial rule in Asia. Since the Japanese benefited from the global racial and capitalist order, why would they lead a revolution against it?

But the dream of Japanese leadership did not die easily. Du Bois persisted in defending Japan after its invasion of China in 1937, arguing that Japan was imposing order until China could progress to the point where it could be free of the threat of European imperialism. *The Philadelphia Tribune*, too, said Japan was helping its Asian "cousin" throw off the yoke of white imperialism, while *The Chicago Defender* said it was

[144] Kearney 1994, 123, 119.
[145] Onishi 2007, 202.

China's weakness before the West that made it Japan's "manifest destiny" to rescue Asia for the Asians.[146] The fantasy was that Japan's Asian Monroe Doctrine would deal a death blow to Western imperialism in Asia and initiate its total collapse on a global scale, culminating in the liberation of Africa. Deeply invested in imagining Japan as an antidote to Western imperial power, some Black internationalists balked at acknowledging that Japan was less concerned with leading a global charge against imperialism than it was with establishing an empire of its own.

VIII "YOU DO NOT HAVE A COUNTRY"

The advent of the Second World War brought debates about Black citizenship, allegiance, and internationalism to the fore once again in Black communities, and this time, the tone was more pessimistic. There had been little racial progress in the U.S. armed forces since the last world war. At the start of the war in 1941, the U.S. Marines and U.S. Coast Guard would not accept Black men, the U.S. Navy enlisted them only as messboys, and the U.S. Army had a limited quota for Black soldiers, whom they placed in segregated, noncombatant units. The Red Cross rejected "black blood" donations as contaminating, and although they later reversed this decision, they continued to keep Black donations segregated from other donations. Shortly after the bombing of Pearl Harbor, at a Black leadership conference organized by the NAACP and National Urban League in New York City, Judge William Hastie (civilian aide to the secretary of war) introduced a resolution declaring that "colored people are not wholeheartedly and unreservedly all out in support of the present war effort."[147]

Reluctantly, due to the exigencies of war, the U.S. government permitted Black men to enlist and fight. But they were placed in segregated units under the command of white officers and trained at segregated military camps, where they were subjected to ongoing psychological and physical violence by white officers, white soldiers, white military police, white civilian police, and white civilians. The War Department's official position was that "[t]he Army would not be used as a sociological laboratory for effecting social change within the military establishment," and indeed, wherever they went, army officials sought to preserve the racial status quo and mollify whites who were offended by the sight of Black

---

[146] Gallichio 2000, 65.
[147] McGuire 1993, xxxiv–xxxv.

soldiers.[148] Making Black men soldiers appeared to invest them with manhood, honor, nationality, agency, and power, challenging the anti-Black order in a way that many whites felt compelled to respond to. In this sense, the army became a site where the white compulsion to maintain Black abjection was acted out over and over again.

Black soldiers were assigned to service and supply roles and were denied entry into specialized training schools. They dug ditches, cleaned latrines, cooked, worked on docks, drove military vehicles, and buried the dead. Letters from Black troops to their loved ones painted a dismal picture of how they were "humiliated, despised, denied regular Army privileges, insulted by post commanders, subjected to military and civilian police brutality, accused of crimes they did not commit, constrained by traditional mores, unfairly discharged from military service, denied adequate medical services, [and] court martialled excessively."[149] Being treated like dogs was a recurrent theme of these letters. Black soldiers were forced to work in bad weather without proper clothing or sufficient food and were punished when they were too ill to work. They were subjected to electric shock treatments, beatings, and killings. They were falsely accused of rape and unfairly punished by white military police, white civilian police, and white civilians. When Black soldiers defended themselves against white aggression, some officers on southern military bases ordered the removal of the firing pins from their rifles.[150] Black soldiers and veterans were also lynched, sometimes while in uniform, because they were in uniform. The relentlessness and ferocity of white violence against Black soldiers bespoke a phobic hatred that is distinctive in the modern world.

Black leaders protested these abuses in different ways. A. Philip Randolph's March on Washington Movement threatened mass mobilization on the Mall, prompting President Franklin D. Roosevelt to issue Executive Order 8802 (1941) banning discrimination in the defense industry. (Black people protesting racial discrimination in the nation's capital during a war that was supposedly being fought for freedom and democracy—this was a public relations nightmare to be avoided.) Executive Order 8802 did not cover the military itself, so Roy Wilkins, Walter White, and Mary McLeod Bethune launched a public campaign calling for the desegregation of the armed forces and the end to racial

[148] McGuire 1983, 152.
[149] McGuire 1993, xxxv.
[150] Sitkoff 1971.

abuses therein. Prominent groups like the NAACP, the National Urban League, and the March on Washington Movement got on board. It was not until 1948 that President Harry S. Truman issued Executive Order 9981 banning discrimination in the armed services.

Those with a more radical bent were not satisfied with demanding integration and improved conditions. Their critique went beyond the abuse of Black soldiers to the role that the U.S. and its allies played as purveyors of racist, imperialist, capitalist violence around the world. Echoing Cyril Briggs, they rejected the ruse of nationality, insisted on recognizing the war as a global race war, and opposed Black participation in the U.S. military. The National Negro Congress, a leftist organization, passed a resolution in 1940 urging Black people to refuse to fight for democracy abroad as long as they faced segregation at home.[151] This sensibility was also captured in a popular saying of Black draftees about the Pacific War: "Here lies a black man killed fighting a yellow man for the glory of a white man."[152] A few decades later, in his critique of the Vietnam War, Black Power advocate Stokely Carmichael would repeat this aphorism almost verbatim.[153]

In Philadelphia in February 1942, Harry Carpenter, a Black truck driver, was overheard yelling at a Black soldier: "You're a crazy nigger wearing that uniform .... This is a white man's Government and war .... When the war is over, the white folks will be kicking you niggers around just like they did before .... [W]hat the hell are you fighting for, you have no flag, *you do not have a Country*."[154] Carpenter expressed a radical Black internationalist perspective: Blackness in the afterlife of slavery continued to be a "condition of statelessness," which meant the Black soldier's military service was a self-deceiving absurdity.[155] U.S. officials, concerned that Carpenter's words would undermine morale among Black troops, arrested him and charged him with treason, or betraying his country—an ironic charge, given the substance of Carpenter's argument. Thurgood Marshall, who had just founded the NAACP Legal Defense and Educational Fund, got the charge reduced and then dismissed.

---

[151] McGuire 1993.

[152] Sitkoff 1971, 666–667.

[153] Carmichael added a nod to the emerging American Indian Movement: "The war is the white man sending the black man to make war on the yellow man to defend the land he stole from the red man" (quoted in Montgomery 2014). Muhammad Ali sounded a similar note when asked why he refused to enlist: "No Vietcong ever called me a nigger."

[154] Anderson 2003, 15. Italics added.

[155] Wagner 2009, 2.

Those Black soldiers who did don an American uniform faced an unbearable contradiction. This was the point of Langston Hughes's "Beaumont to Detroit: 1943":

> Looky here, America
> What you done done—
> Let things drift
> Until the riots come
>
> Now your policemen
> Let the mobs run free.
> I reckon you don't care
> Nothing about me.
>
> You tell me that hitler
> Is a mighty bad man.
> I guess he took lessons
> From the ku klux klan.
>
> You tell me mussolini's
> Got an evil heart.
> Well, it mus-a been in Beaumont
> That he had his start—
>
> Cause everything that hitler
> And mussolini do
> Negroes get the same
> Treatment from you
>
> You jim crowed me
> Before hitler rose to power—
> And you're STILL jim crowing me
> Right now, this very hour.
>
> Yet you say we're fighting
> For democracy.
> Then why don't democracy
> Include me?
>
> I ask you this question
> Cause I want to know
> How long I got to fight
> BOTH HITLER—AND JIM CROW.[156]

Hughes's suggestion that Nazism was genealogically linked to American racism rested on solid empirical ground. Adolf Hitler was an avid fan

---

[156] Hughes and Rampersad 1995, 281. Capitalization in original.

of American eugenicist Madison Grant's *The Passing of the Great Race* (1916), which he referred to as his "bible."[157] As James Whitman writes in *Hitler's American Model: The United States and the Making of Nazi Race Law* (2017), "[W]hen the leading Nazi jurists assembled in early June 1934 to debate how to institutionalize racism in the new Third Reich, they began by asking how the Americans did it."[158] In many cases, the Nazis thought American racial practices were too extreme. When U.S. officials prosecuted the defeated Nazis in the postwar Nuremburg trials, German racial hygienists claimed that they had drawn inspiration from race policy and discourse in the U.S.[159]

In the last stanza of the poem, the narrator asks how long he has to fight both Hitler and Jim Crow. Readers would have recognized the reference to the "Double V" campaign that had begun a year earlier when James Thompson, a twenty-six-year-old black cafeteria worker at a Kansas aircraft company, wrote a letter to the *Pittsburgh Courier*, the largest black newspaper in the nation, asking:

Should I sacrifice my life to live half American? .... Would it be demanding too much to demand full citizenship rights in exchange for the sacrificing of my life? Is the kind of America I know worth defending? .... The V for victory sign is being displayed prominently ... then let we colored Americans adopt the double VV for a double victory. The first V for victory over our enemies from without, the second V for victory over our enemies from within. For surely those who perpetuate these ugly prejudices here are seeking to destroy our democratic form of government just as surely as the Axis forces.[160]

A month after receiving Thompson's letter, the *Pittsburgh Courier* ran an editorial stating:

We, as colored Americans, are determined to protect our country, our form of government, and the freedoms which we cherish for ourselves and for the rest of the world, therefore we adopted the Double "V" War Cry—victory over our enemies at home and victory over our enemies on the battlefields abroad. Thus, in our fight for freedom, we wage a two-pronged attack against our enslavers at home and those abroad who would enslave us. WE HAVE A STAKE IN THIS FIGHT ... WE ARE AMERICANS, TOO![161]

The *Courier* took up Thompson's language but changed its valence for its own purposes. Thompson, writing in a sober tone reminiscent of

---

[157] Kühl 1994, 85.
[158] Whitman 2017, 113.
[159] Kühl 1994.
[160] Washburn 1981, 1.
[161] Washburn 1981, 3. Capitalization in original.

Hughes's poem, had signaled his reluctance to fight for a racist state and proposed the Double V idea as a way of managing this contradiction. The *Courier* editorial repressed Thompson's skepticism and turned the Double V "War Cry" into an affirmation of Black political belonging and the stakes Black people had in the war.

Although the Double V campaign retained an aspect of political critique, it also boosted the legitimacy of the U.S. state, which was under fire from radical Black internationalists, Japanese race propagandists, and other foreign critics. The *Courier* urged Black people to embrace "our country, our form of government" and join the war effort in order to realize the promise of full citizenship. In Lee Finkle's view, the Double V campaign was used by politically moderate Black editors to temper the radical mood of the Black masses and mobilize them in support of the war.[162] In other words, it pretended militancy while in fact moderating it. E. Washington Rhodes of the *Philadelphia Tribune* wrote at the time: "It was the Negro Press which changed this attitude [that it was a white man's war in which Black people had no stake] by insisting that Negroes are American citizens and as such had the duty to fight."[163]

Black editors were responding in part to intense pressure by the U.S. government to drum up support for the war. U.S. government agencies approached Black public opinion as a national security issue during the war, investigating Black publications, accusing them of turning their readers against the war, and even charging them with sedition when they expressed pro-Japanese views. In the spring of 1942, the newly formed Office of War Information (OWI) conducted a survey in Harlem, New York, to take the pulse of the Black community. In response to the question "Would you be better off if America or the Axis won the war?" a large majority of Harlem residents, as expected, said they would be worse off under German rule. But a surprising 49 percent said they would be treated *the same or better* under Japanese rule as under American rule, and only 28 percent said they would be worse off under Japanese rule.[164] The results startled OWI pollsters. Harlemites were not thinking of the Allies versus the Axis, the nation versus its enemies, but rather of whites versus the darker races. Alarmed OWI officials set about designing a propaganda campaign to

---

[162] Finkle 1973.
[163] Finkle 1973, 708.
[164] Koppes and Black 1986, 386. Twenty-three percent said they did not know.

nurture feelings of national unity and discourage color consciousness among Black people, and the FBI launched a formal investigation of "Foreign-Inspired Agitation among the American Negroes," hoping to thwart the impact of Japanese race propaganda upon susceptible Black minds.[165]

In 1938, three years before the U.S. entered the war, Representative Martin Dies of Texas had formed the House Committee Investigating Un-American Activities, which demonstrated a special interest in the threat of Black subversion. Dies's book *The Trojan Horse in America* (1940) warned of Joseph Stalin's tactical innovation of using domestic organizations in other countries as "Trojan Horses" to undermine their governments. In chapter IX, entitled "A Trojan Horse for Negroes," Dies accused Stalin of stoking race hatred among Black Americans in order to provoke a civil war in the U.S. Communists lured "negroes" to meetings in the U.S. and in Moscow by "giv[ing them] a taste of 'social equality,'" including dancing with white women, and by promising "negro rule," or "absolute dominion over the white race in the South."[166] In Dies's reading, then, Black people were discontent not because of racial injustice but because they were drunk with Soviet-induced fantasies of interracial sex and Black supremacy. Dies wrote:

It is certain that the Negroes in the United States enjoy more liberties and a higher standard of living than the Negroes in any other country, and that communist success in this country would plunge the Negro race into slavery .... Under our free institutions, the Negro has made great progress in the United States. Despite propaganda and misrepresentation, he lives in peace with the white people of the South. Lynching has practically disappeared. The white and the Negro understand each other through long years of association. There are, of course, some in both races who are exceptions to this rule, but upon the whole there is no other country on the face of the earth where two distinct races enjoy such friendly relationships. This can only be broken by the success of misguided reformists and foreign agents.[167]

The supertext in this discussion was one of "great progress" and "friendly relationships"; the subtext was that Jim Crow kept Black people in their place so that lynching was scarcely necessary anymore. Communism would unravel this achievement and disorder the natural hierarchy between whites and "Negroes." The overall effect of Dies's arguments was to deepen the association of Blackness and communism

[165] Gallichio 2000, 137.
[166] Dies 1940, 119, 122.
[167] Dies 1940, 118.

in the American imaginary, tarring each with the stain of the other. In this sense, his work presaged the powerful convergence of anti-Blackness and anti-communism that would emerge later during the Cold War.

The political critique developed by radical Black internationalists during the interwar years continued to influence Black public opinion throughout the Second World War, efforts to thwart it notwithstanding. Luminaries such as Paul Robeson, Alphaeus Hunton, and W. E. B. Du Bois worked through the Council on African Affairs (CAA), founded in 1942, to keep African and Asian decolonization and independence front and center in public affairs. When Indian leaders sought an immediate guarantee of independence in exchange for supporting the British war effort, the CAA sponsored a Rally for the Cause of a Free India in Manhattan in September 1942, declaring "[a] Free India will strengthen democracy everywhere and speed the liberation of all colonial peoples."[168] Penny Von Eschen writes: "Embracing an antiimperialist and anticapitalist politics, the CAA insisted that 'our fight for Negro rights here is linked inseparably with the liberation movements of the people of the Caribbean and Africa and the colonial world in general.'"[169] In the same spirit, Paul Robeson's Crusade to End Lynching linked lynching to colonialism and indicted President Truman's failure to act against lynching as inconsistent with the Nuremberg Principles. Some critics took Robeson to task for introducing "extraneous issues" into the fight against lynching, but for radical Black internationalists, the linkages between lynching at home and colonialism and fascism abroad were the very heart of the matter.[170]

In the interwar period, radical Black internationalist critique generated a chronic, slow-burning legitimacy problem for the U.S. state. This became a full-blown legitimacy crisis during the Second World War, when heightened global scrutiny of racial segregation and discrimination put the U.S. state increasingly on the defensive. The U.S. state's use of violence, repression, and red-baiting to stymie the Black struggle led, dialectically, to intensified Black critique, which the state then responded to with self-exculpatory performances of anti-racism. These were the fraught circumstances in which Japanese American political functionality emerged and took shape.

---

[168] Von Eschen 1997, 29.
[169] Von Eschen 1997, 20.
[170] Von Eschen 1997, 111.

IX THE DOUBLED NATURE OF INTERNMENT

The historiography on internment and its aftermath suggests a hockey-stick graph: Japanese American fortunes spiraled downward due to decades of discriminatory legislation, reached a nadir with internment, and then ticked upward with the advent of the Cold War. We might call this narrative "from persecution, to incarceration, to acceptance." It emphasizes that internment was neither an exception nor a mistake, but rather the end point of a long historical arc of exclusionary actions against the Japanese. At the same time, it ends on a sanguine note: the Cold War's reorganization of affiliations and animosities around the communist/anti-communist fault line sparked the rehabilitation of Japanese Americans as loyal and assimilable Americans. The tragedy of internment notwithstanding, racial meanings proved to be historically contingent and surprisingly fluid.

Bringing structural anti-Blackness back into the picture reminds us that shifting racial constructions can and do conceal enduring racial positionalities. Pushed down by white supremacy and lifted up by anti-Blackness, Japanese Americans have always been not-white but above all not-Black, both excluded from the privileges of full membership in society and partly immunized against the phobic hatred and gratuitous violence inflicted upon Black people. The descent into internment did not divest Japanese Americans of their not-Blackness; nor did their facilitated "rehabilitation" afterward invest them with whiteness.

What was worked out during the course of the war was Japanese Americans' relation to the nation—whether they would be considered bona fide U.S. citizens or treated as immutably foreign. In *Wong Kim Ark* (1898), the U.S. Supreme Court ruled that birthright citizenship applied to the Chinese, but the matter was far from settled in the U.S. racial imagination, which continued to associate even native-born Asian Americans with incorrigible foreignness. Given their putatively fanatical devotion to foreign despots, were Asiatics really capable of U.S. citizenship? Borrowing from the imagery of the U.S. government's brief in *Wong Kim Ark*, could an Asiatic, having suckled at the breast of an Asiatic mother, ever be loyal to the U.S. state? Japan's bombing of Pearl Harbor on December 7, 1941, gave these questions new urgency. The *Nisei* were native-born U.S. citizens in the eyes of the law, but where did their allegiance actually lie? Were they Japanese or American?[171]

---

[171] Prior to 1924, Japanese law said children born to Japanese citizens living abroad were automatically subjects of Japan (following the principle of *jus sanguinis*, by which

The dubiousness of *Nisei* citizenship was a central theme in the hearings organized by Congressman John Tolan in February and March 1942.[172] Tolan, a liberal Democrat from California, originally planned fact-finding hearings in the hope of averting mass evacuation, but President Roosevelt surprised him by issuing Executive Order 9066 authorizing the evacuation of Japanese Americans from the West Coast. Thus the Tolan hearings became a forum on *how* evacuation should be conducted. Many of those who testified argued the propriety of treating German and Italian aliens on an individual basis and evacuating the Japanese (aliens and citizens) as a group, insisting that *Nisei* citizenship was no guarantee of *Nisei* loyalty.[173] Japanese Americans, they declared, should be grateful for the chance to prove their loyalty by submitting to internment.

During the hearings, Representative Laurence Arnold of Illinois questioned California Attorney General (and future Chief Justice of the U.S. Supreme Court) Earl Warren about the *Nisei*:

MR. ARNOLD: Do you have any way of knowing whether any one of this group that you mention [*Nisei*] is loyal to this country or loyal to Japan? ....

ATTORNEY GENERAL WARREN: Congressman, there is no way that we can establish that fact. We believe that when we are dealing with the Caucasian race we have methods that will test the loyalty of them, and we believe that we can, in dealing with the Germans and the Italians, arrive at some fairly sound conclusions because of our knowledge of the way they live in the community and have lived for many years. But when we deal with the Japanese we are in an entirely different field and we cannot form any opinion that we believe to be sound. Their method of living, their language, make for this difficulty. Many of them who show

the nationality of the child is the same as that of their parent(s), regardless of place of birth). Since U.S. law followed the principle of *jus soli*, by which the nationality of the child was determined by place of birth, *Nisei* born before 1924 had dual citizenship in the U.S. and Japan. When dual citizenship became a liability for *Nisei* in the eyes of suspicious whites, Japanese Americans petitioned the Japanese government to amend the Japanese Nationality Act (Ichioka 1988). In 1924, Japan amended the Act, requiring parents to register their children at the Japanese consulate if they wanted dual citizenship, and also allowing *Nisei* to renounce Japanese citizenship retroactively (Tamura 2012).

[172] The House Select Committee Investigating National Defense Migration sponsored hearings known as the Tolan Hearings. Afterwards, the committee produced the *Preliminary Report and Recommendations on Problems of Evacuation of Citizens and Aliens from Military Areas*, March 19, 1942.

[173] Murray 2008. German Americans and Italian Americans were not subjected to mass exclusion or incarceration. Instead, the U.S. government provided loyalty hearings for individuals who were arrested because of suspect activities.

you a birth certificate stating that they were born in this State, perhaps, or born in Honolulu, can hardly speak the English language because, although they were born here, when they were 4 or 5 years of age they were sent over to Japan to be educated and stayed over there through their adolescent period at least, and then they came back here thoroughly Japanese.[174]

Unlike U.S. Army General John DeWitt, who insisted that "a viper was a viper" no matter where it was born, Warren did not declare that the *Nisei* were disloyal to the U.S. Rather, he emphasized the impossibility of knowing one way or the other because of the inscrutability of the Japanese body and mind. The Japanese American was an *epistemological problem*. Since there was no room for uncertainty in the context of war, in any case, DeWitt's vulgar racism and Warren's genteel racism converged on the same conclusion: *Better safe than sorry*.

In this way, a historic act of racial aggression was presented as a prudent decision to err on the side of caution. Government officials opined about the difficulty of separating "the sheep from the goats," or loyal from disloyal Japanese Americans.[175] This was a reference to Matthew 25:31–46, the "Judgment of Nations," where Jesus separates the righteous nations from the wicked ones, granting eternal life to the former and inflicting eternal punishment on the latter. Ironically, the allusion highlighted the contrast between Jesus, who justly discerned between the good and the wicked based upon their actions, and the U.S. government, which was using Japanese descent as a proxy for wickedness. Decades later, it was revealed that U.S. government officials had allowed internment to proceed despite being aware of numerous reports, including one conducted by the FBI and another by the Office of Naval Intelligence, that cleared Japanese Americans of charges of disloyalty.[176]

The halting formulation of the mass internment policy reflected ambivalence, hesitation, and doubt. The initial plan, according to the U.S. Department of the Interior, was to remove Japanese Americans from the West Coast in order to distance them from sensitive military installations and thwart their potential cooperation with Japanese

---

[174] House Select Committee Investigating National Defense Migration, *Preliminary Report and Recommendations on Problems of Evacuation of Citizens and Aliens from Military Areas*, March 19, 1942, 11015.
[175] Fujitani 2011.
[176] Irons 1983.

invaders. This was to be done through evacuation and relocation measures that were entirely voluntary. The removal plan drawn up by the
Director of the War Relocation Authority (WRA) offered financial assistance for Japanese Americans to move out of areas of military significance, called for small work camps to be set up throughout the Western
interior states as temporary relocation sites, and sought to facilitate the
resettlement of Japanese Americans from these sites to urban centers
or agricultural enterprises where they could find work.[177] Hoping to
secure their approval of relocation, California Governor Culbert Olson,
a liberal Democrat, called *Nisei* leaders to a meeting in Sacramento on
February 6, 1942.[178]

The federal government's plan quickly hit a snag. Japanese American
residents of the Western coastal states lacked the desire and/or where-
withal to resettle. As importantly, they had nowhere to go, as residents
of Western interior states refused to accept them.[179] White Westerners
flooded their elected officials with phone calls, and these officials, in
turn, accused California, Oregon, and Washington of "dumping unde-
sirables" on them.[180] Milton Eisenhower, the head of the WRA, was
shaken by a meeting with Western governors and state attorneys general
in Salt Lake City in April 1942, where he requested "the cooperation
of the people and officials in facilitating their [Japanese Americans']
resumption of normal living," and found that almost all attendees
refused to cooperate. Declaring their violent opposition to Japanese
American resettlement in their states, they pushed for detention camps
instead.[181] Dorothy Swaine Thomas and Richard Nishimoto wrote:
"The original evacuation had not been intended to limit the free movement of evacuees in any way once they were outside the narrow coastal
strip of the Prohibited Zone. The reaction of the inland areas, however,
resulted in evacuation becoming detention; and in the plan of domicile at temporary refuges becoming a plan for confinement in centers
designed to last for the duration of the war."[182] Secretary of War Henry
Stimson informed President Franklin D. Roosevelt that the plan for
voluntary evacuation and relocation had been abandoned because of

---

[177] *The Relocation Program*, n.d.
[178] Kurashige 2008.
[179] Robinson 2001.
[180] *The Relocation Program*, n.d., 5.
[181] *The Relocation Program*, n.d., 6.
[182] Thomas and Nishimoto 1969, 26.

logistical challenges, and that Japanese Americans would remain under army control until popular prejudice had died down enough for them to be resettled.[183] Meanwhile, Milton Eisenhower of the WRA "reluctantly established plans for the indefinite wartime incarceration of Japanese Americans."[184]

Internment, then, was an ad hoc policy that the U.S. government backed into as a result of its own white supremacist beliefs and its failure to anticipate the racial hostility of white officials and civilians in Western states.[185] Even before it conceived of mass internment as a response to unfolding developments, the WRA was already looking ahead and concerned to facilitate Japanese Americans' "resumption of normal living." Once internment was underway, the WRA continued to foreground plans for Japanese Americans' release and reentry into society. When Commissioner of Indian Affairs John Collier proposed that internment camps be built on Native American reservations, he calibrated his appeal accordingly: "[T]he Interior Department is better equipped than any other Agency of the Federal Government to provide for the Japanese aliens the type of treatment and care which will make them more acceptable as members of American populations and is better equipped to provide the rehabilitation of this group subsequent to the war and its reintegration into the stream of American life."[186]

The U.S. government dealt with German and Italian aliens on an individual basis, while 120,000 Japanese Americans, two-thirds of whom were native-born U.S. citizens, were forcibly evacuated from their homes, placed in assembly centers, and eventually incarcerated in internment camps in the swamps, deserts, and mountainous areas of the west and south. There they lived for up to three years behind barbed wire and under armed guard. Tar paper barracks provided inadequate protection from the heat and cold, food and medical care were substandard,

---

[183] Robinson 2001.

[184] Robison 2001, 131.

[185] Some organized groups attempted (unsuccessfully) to strip *Nisei* of birthright citizenship and/or deport them. In 1942, Native Sons of the Golden West and the American Legion filed a lawsuit to compel the San Francisco Registrar of Voters to strike *Nisei* from the voting rolls. Their ultimate goal was to undermine the right of birthright citizenship as guaranteed in *Wong Kim Ark*. See *Regan* v. *King* (1942). In January 1943, the American Legion passed a resolution calling for the deportation of all Japanese living in the U.S. During the Second World War, many Southern and West Coast congressmen proposed resolutions for deporting disloyal Japanese Americans (Collins 1985).

[186] Leong and Carpio 2016, 106.

and wages paid for various forms of work within the camp were paltry. Dissenters were beaten or placed in the stockades or sent to Tule Lake camp, which became a holding pen for those perceived to be the most recalcitrant. Financial losses to Japanese Americans—in the form of homes, bank accounts, equities, property leases, and crops—were estimated at $400 million.[187] No dollar figure could measure the psychic trauma inflicted on people who knew they were being punished collectively for a crime they had not committed. All of the internees' lives were interrupted and damaged; some were destroyed.

Despite the blatant violations of civil and constitutional rights, internment was carried out in a way that showed a baseline recognition of the prisoners' mattering. The internees' not-Blackness protected them from the worst possible outcomes. Here it is important to note not only what the U.S. state did to Japanese Americans but also what it *did not do to them*. Lynching serves as one point of contrast. Another is the convict leasing system, which had been operating in the South for decades by this time. As discussed in Part One, this system, which Douglas Blackmon called "slavery by another name," involved arresting and convicting tens of thousands of Black youth and adult men on trumped-up charges and then selling their labor to local agricultural and industrial interests. Convict laborers were chained to their beds at night, whipped, abused, starved, denied medical care, and forced to work to the point of collapse. They were utterly expendable labor factors in the capitalist machine, and indeed mortality rates sometimes approached 45 percent.[188] Since arrests and leasing arrangements were not always recorded, many prisoners entered the system and perished, with their families never knowing what had happened to them. Convict leasing was fueled by greed, but the debasement of Blackness was its condition of possibility.

By contrast, internment was seen by its architects and administrators as a form of imprisonment that should be managed humanely and ended as soon as possible.[189] Efforts were made to make things liveable

---

[187] Chuman 1976.

[188] Blackmon 2008, 57.

[189] The treatment of the internees was overdetermined by diplomatic considerations as well. The State Department was trying to persuade Japan to exchange nationals, which meant "that any adverse report about the treatment of Japanese nationals in WRA centers that reached the eyes and ears of authorities in Tokyo from any source might destroy the results of months of patient and extremely vital diplomatic negotiations by the State Department" (WRA, *A Story of Human Conservation* 1946, 18). Some Japanese Americans felt abandoned by the Japanese state during internment, having appealed to it for help to no avail (Weglyn 1976).

in the meantime, to mitigate the harshness of incarceration, to allow for community and social life, and, crucially, to prepare internees for reintegration into American society after the war. In general, families lived together in the barracks of the internment camps. Some internees found scrap lumber and materials and made furniture and curtains for their personal living areas. Most worked in various capacities in the camp, earning a minimal wage. They tended collective gardens and raised livestock to supplement the limited food provisions. Social and organizational life flourished in the spaces provided: there were softball leagues, school dances, boy scout meetings, religious services, and charity drives, and internees from different camps came together for sports and socializing.[190] Camp newspapers run by internees offered high-quality reporting on events inside and outside camp, sometimes provoking censorship from government officials. Internees were also given day leaves (to go into neighboring towns for religious services or shopping or visiting), short-term leaves for medical or business reasons, seasonal leaves to accept agricultural jobs in other states, and indefinite leaves to move to other cities to accept jobs or matriculate in college. Despite the barbed wire and armed guards, internment was provisional and porous.[191]

Community councils in the camps promoted self-governance and created a bridge between internees and camp officials, again with the aim of preparing internees for assimilation after the war. Secondary schools were established, where white teachers with Japanese American aides taught elementary and high school curricula that met state guidelines, as well as a "program of patriotism and national allegiance."[192] *Issei* attended Americanization classes. Internment, then, "presented unparalleled promise for refashioning ethnic Japanese into model Americans," Ellen Wu writes, and "[i]nternee life was designed with this goal in mind."[193] What began as a voluntary evacuation and relocation plan became a grand (coercive) experiment in Americanizing the Asiatic.

Curtains and charity drives notwithstanding, forced relocation and incarceration under armed guard were by their very nature acts of violent

---

[190] Howard 2008.
[191] Takashi Fujitani notes the doubleness, writing that World War II was "not simply a time when racism against Japanese Americans led solely to their incarceration and exclusion from white America [but] ... also ironically the period during which plans were laid, and in some ways put into practice, for the incorporation of Japan, its emperor, and Japanese Americans into a new U.S. global hegemony, with America now cast as inclusive of Asians" (Fujitani 2011, 119).
[192] Howard 2008, 152.
[193] Wu 2014, 12.

domination that inflicted deep and enduring harm. It is not gainsaying or minimizing Japanese Americans' suffering in the camps to approach it from a different direction and ask how it was shaped and delimited by their not-Blackness.[194] Even during the ordeal of internment, even at the height of wartime hysteria, Japanese Americans' not-Blackness made certain options for dealing with them unthinkable. My point is not that internment was not as bad as slavery—though it was not, by any conceivable measure—but rather that internment must be understood *in relation to* slavery, as contoured a priori by the racial positionalities slavery produced.[195]

X THE NOT-BLACKNESS OF INTERNEES

Most of the internment camps were located in the West, but two, Jerome and Rohwer, were located in Arkansas. The U.S. government also built three prisoner-of-war facilities (two for Germans and one for Italians) in Arkansas, a Jim Crow state committed to the prevention of Black mobility (physical, economic, political, social) through a wide variety of legal and extralegal means.[196] Thus the war brought differentially positioned groups—white European prisoners of war, Japanese American internees, and Black soldiers and residents—into proximity in the carceral systems of the segregated South. Bracketing race for a moment, it would be reasonable to assume that U.S. soldiers and ordinary Arkansans would have the highest status among these, then internees, then enemy soldiers. In

---

[194] But what about the atomic bombs dropped on Japan? What do these acts say about the moral considerability of the Japanese in the eyes of white Americans? The racial aspect of the decision to drop the bombs seems clear. Years of animalizing and dehumanizing the Japanese paved the way for nuclear attacks that were unthinkable against European targets. At the same time, within a few years of postwar occupation by the U.S., the Japanese were again seen as civilized, progressive, and worthy pupils of the West. The exterminationist impulse toward the Japanese was contingent upon wartime conditions and reversible as well.

[195] The heated debate over what to call the internment camps and internees continues. WRA head Dillon Myer instructed his staff to say "relocation center" and "evacuees" (which suggest a protective motive) instead of "camp," "internment center," "internees," or "prisoners" (which indicate domination and coercion). Some scholars and activists, for example, Edison Uno, prefer the phrase "concentration camps." See Okamura (1982), where the author compares the "linguistic deception" of the U.S. government to Nazi techniques. I follow Alice Murray (2008) in using "internment camp" rather than "concentration camp" because the latter is inextricably linked to the extermination that took place in Nazi death camps.

[196] In June 1944, the Jerome internment camp was emptied and reconstructed as a German prisoner-of-war camp. Jerome internees were transferred to the Rohwer camp.

fact, this hierarchy was *precisely inverted* in Arkansas because of race: white European prisoners of war had higher standing than Japanese American internees, who in turn, had higher standing than Black soldiers and residents. Even in the heat of wartime, race trumped citizenship, nationality, and allegiance.

German and Italian prisoners of war were treated with consideration and respect. As whites, they were allowed to attend local colleges and universities, which Arkansas Governor Homer Adkins refused to allow *Nisei* to do, on the grounds that admitting the Japanese might open the door for Black students.[197] In the prisoner-of-war camps, German and Italian officers had separate quarters that provided extra privacy and comfort. Entertainment included performances by brass bands, symphony orchestras, and theater groups, as well as screenings of American films. Tennis courts were open for use, and Italians could play *bocci* to get a taste of home. White residents of neighboring areas who objected to Japanese American internees working in town offered no resistance to German and Italian POWs taking up various jobs. C. Calvin Smith writes: "[M]any white Arkansans shared the Germans' views on racial supremacy and saw them as racial equals who had been forced into an unfortunate confrontation with the United States."[198] As after the Civil War, the fraternity of whiteness overrode other distinctions. Germans and Italians had taken up arms against the U.S., it was true, but in the eyes of white Arkansans and officials operating the prisoner-of-war camps, they were all part of the same racial brotherhood.

If Japanese American internees were not-white, they were above all not-Black. When internees left camp for shopping, school outings, and intercamp sports games, they came into contact with local Black and white residents. At these moments, they were read by the binary symbolic order of Jim Crow as not-Black. *White is best but the most important thing is not-Blackness. Better the Jap than the Negro.* The need to keep Black people isolated and abjected overrode the need to keep certain areas all white. (Here we see anti-Blackness determining the parameters of white supremacy's operation.) The bus, like the railway car, was a paradigmatic site of racial segregation, and internees were allowed (indeed

---

[197] On July 8, 1942, Governor Homer Adkins of Arkansas sent a telegram to Assistant Secretary of War John McCloy explaining that he would not permit *Nisei* students to attend college in his state partly because "it would provide an entering wedge for Negroes to make application to our state colleges which would further complicate matters" (Bearden 1986, 111).

[198] C. Smith 1994, 360.

required) to sit in the white section on the bus.[199] Also, they "almost exclusively patronized white stores, visited white churches, participated in white conferences, and stayed in white hotels."[200] John Howard notes the incongruity: "[E]ven as federal prisoners, many Japanese Americans showed a significant ability to move in and across a number of spaces segregated as white."[201] Neither Black soldiers nor Black civilians enjoyed this kind of mobility. At the same time, White Arkansans did not accept Japanese Americans as white, as evidenced by their resistance to having internees work in town or attend state colleges. Rather than saying that the internees were granted provisional whiteness, therefore, it makes more sense to say they were granted recognition as not-Black.

When a Jerome internee offered his seat on the bus to a Black woman, the white driver pushed her to the back of the bus and instructed him to sit in the white section up front.[202] The Japanese American was given a reprieve from the full weight of white supremacy not for his own sake but in order to better nail down structural anti-Blackness. Similarly, the state declined to charge local whites who were suspected of shooting Jerome internees in separate incidents, but chose to prosecute a Black man accused of propositioning and exposing himself to two Japanese American female internees. The man was tried and convicted of indecent exposure and aggravated assault and sentenced to two years in prison with no possibility of parole.[203] In relation to whites, Japanese Americans were target practice, but in relation to Black people, they were human beings deserving the state's protection. Japanese Americans were assigned worth to the precise extent that it reinforced structural anti-Blackness to do so.

Some Japanese Americans were quite deliberate about curating their not-Blackness. John Howard writes: "*Nisei* and *Issei* throughout the war years fretted over modes of segregation and marginalization that cast them as similar to, as similarly positioned with, blacks on American racial scales."[204] Managers at the Wilson Plantation in Arkansas had this in mind when they sought to attract Japanese American workers after the war by promising: "School buses are provided by The Plantation

---

[199] On occasion, internees intervened on behalf of Black passengers or joined them at the back of the bus.
[200] Howard 2008, 130.
[201] Howard 2008, 130.
[202] Howard 2008.
[203] Howard 2008.
[204] Howard 2008, 233.

to carry all children to and from schools. Your children will attend the white schools."[205] This, then, was the lure: the not-Blackness of Japanese Americans would continue to be recognized after the war, with all the benefits this entailed. There would be no more Martha Lums.

The same lure was extended to *Nisei* who moved to the Midwest during and after the war. From 1943 to 1944, Chicago was the leading resettlement site for *Nisei* leaving the camps.[206] *Nisei* who applied for leave from internment camps and resettled in Chicago reported that white workers told them they accepted the Japanese but not Black people in the workplace. One *Nisei* worker remarked: "The white people here received us with open arms and yet hated the Negroes with venom."[207] In industrial plants, white management and white workers accorded the *Nisei* higher status in the workplace, endowed them with better job classifications, paid them better wages, and treated them more respectfully than they did Black workers—even though the latter had seniority over the *Nisei*. *Nisei* workers were invited to use white locker rooms, while Black workers were forced to use segregated locker rooms.[208] Like the Cuban sugar planters of the 1800s, white managers and workers in mid-century Chicago industrial plants saw Black workers as dirty, lazy, undependable, and unintelligent, and Asian workers as capable, smart, adaptive, and productive.

Dave Okada points out that the *Nisei* were not only elevated over Black people, they were elevated *because there were Black people*:

The *Nisei* workers were placed in a situation in which their status was relatively undefined. Within that social situation another racial group was assigned an inferior role and position based on the prevalent cultural norms regarding their status. The fact that the characteristics of the *Nisei* workers could be invidiously compared with those of the Negro workers made it possible for the *Nisei* to enjoy higher status than the Negroes.[209]

Charlotte Brooks, too, observes that white employers "liked to compare the resettlers favorably to other nonwhite laborers—almost always African Americans."[210] Structural anti-Blackness, or the foundational abjection of Blackness, elevated the *Nisei* wherever they went.

[205] Howard 2008, 233.
[206] Sixty thousand *Nisei* left the camps before the end of the war; nearly 20,000 of these went to Chicago (Fujino 2018, 179).
[207] Uyeki 1953, 114.
[208] Okada 1947.
[209] Okada 1947, 51.
[210] Brooks 2000, 1668.

Nisei in Chicago, for their part, distanced from Black people. They "quickly gravitated toward the white world ... [and] worked to separate themselves from black Chicagoans, their neighborhoods, and the sectors of the economy in which they had traditionally predominated." They sought housing away from Black people and joined whites in fleeing neighborhoods that Black people were moving into. When white co-workers made anti-Black comments, *Nisei* workers remained silent, implicitly exchanging compliance for structural advantage. One *Nisei* worker complained that a "*hakujin* [white] foreman [who] tried to treat us like Negroes didn't realize that we weren't used to being pushed around like the Negro workers." Similarly, Japanese Americans working as domestics "chafed at employer attempts to treat them as inferiors and equate them with blacks."[211] Like Chinese coolies in Cuba, these *Nisei* laborers were intent upon protecting that which they still had to save— namely, the public and psychological wage of not-Blackness.

Dave Okada notes that Black workers in wartime Chicago identified with the *Nisei*, reached out to them, and showed no resentment toward them, but the *Nisei* had no interest in an alliance of the darker races. To the contrary, they jealously guarded their not-Blackness. When white workers at a union meeting complained that the company might bring in Black workers, a Congress of Industrial Organizations representative reminded them the union had a nondiscrimination policy and pointed out there were "people of different color already working with you right here," meaning the *Nisei*. A white worker came up to a *Nisei* worker after the meeting and said: "Why you fellows, you're not colored— you're white. That's why we like you." Despite this gesture, a number of *Nisei* workers refused to go to union meetings from that point on. One explained: "I haven't felt like going since. I don't feel comfortable when people talk about how we're like other colored groups."[212] *We are not Black.* Clearly, elevating *Nisei* workers over Black workers discouraged cross-racial labor organizing in the industrial workplace.

At a social level, too, *Nisei* in wartime Chicago obeyed the dictate "above all don't be black." Eugene Uyeki writes:

The *Nisei* in their behavior identify themselves with the Caucasians and not with the Negroes. The *Nisei* regard their own social status as being somewhere between the Caucasians and the Negroes. In refusing to identify themselves with the Negroes, the *Nisei* realize that to do so would entail a lowering of their social

---

[211] Brooks 2000, 1657, 1669, 1665.
[212] Okada 1947, 81, 81, 82.

status. This, they refuse to do .... The *Nisei* are quite aware that if there should be any great number of marriages with Negroes, their own status as a group would go down in the regard of the white majority groups. This the *Nisei* have refused to allow, and there is collective effort manifested toward the ostracization of marriages of *Nisei* with Negroes.[213]

One *Nisei* told his daughter she could marry anyone, "just as long as it's not a kulombo [Negro]."[214] Marrying "anyone" else might dilute her Japaneseness, but at least it would not dilute her not-Blackness. Only one group threatened to do that. Like the Chinese immigrants in the Mississippi Delta, *Nisei* settlers in Chicago used social ostracism to discourage Japanese–Black unions and keep the not-Blackness of Japanese Americans intact.

XI BLACKFACE MINSTRELSY IN THE CAMPS

In her book, *The Spectacle of Japanese American Trauma: Racial Performativity and World War II* (2008), Emily Roxworthy discusses the staging of blackface minstrelsy performances by Japanese Americans in the internment camps. In the fall of 1942, she recounts, a *Nisei* vaudeville troupe called the Nuthouse Gang performed at the Tule Lake camp in California. An article in the camp newspaper the *Tulean Dispatch*, dated September 16, 1942, features a hand-drawn illustration of one of the Nuthouse actors in blackface.[215] An official WRA photograph shows Nuthouse Gang members performing in blackface at the October 1942 Harvest Festival at the Tule Lake camp: the Japanese American man and woman had blacked up to play, respectively, a "zip coon" character and a "mammy" character. The following spring, when the Tule Lake camp held a "hidden talent" competition officiated by white judges, a *Nisei* man won the top prize for "acting black."[216]

Several years after the publication of her book, Roxworthy revisited this topic in "Blackface Behind Barbed Wire: Gender and Racial Triangulation in the Japanese American Internment Camps" (2013). Here she recounts the staging of a blackface minstrelsy production at the Santa Anita Assembly Center in California, a racetrack where forcibly evacuated Japanese Americans were held before being transported to

---

[213] Uyeki 1953, 117, 140–141.
[214] Uyeki 1953, 146.
[215] "Hilarious Antics of 'Nuthouse Gang' Keep Tuleans Screaming for More" *The Daily Tulean Dispatch*, September 16, 1942, 2.
[216] Roxworthy 2008, 156, 171.

internment camps. There, living in converted horse stalls still smelling of manure, *Nisei* girls who were members of the Girls' Club sponsored an event called "Jamboree Jingles" in August 1942. They made and distributed 350 "mammy" pins to advertise the event, and their printed flyer included lyrics of several minstrel songs as well as sketches of "mammies" and a pickaninny child eating watermelon. During the event itself, *Nisei* girls blacked up and sang minstrel songs full of plantation nostalgia.[217]

Roxworthy appears uncertain about how to interpret the archival material she has unearthed. Relying on the concept of white supremacy (and my theory of racial triangulation), but not the concept of anti-Blackness, she cannot fully make sense of the events. So, in "Blackface Behind Barbed Wire," she argues that "the oppressive and insular conditions of incarceration and a political climate that was attacking the performers' own racial status rendered these blackface performances somehow exceptional and even resistant."[218] Committed to seeing Japanese American internees as victims of white supremacy alongside Black people, Roxworthy cannot account for their use of blackface, except by saying that it was somehow rendered "resistant" by the context.

Wendy Kozol, too, wrestles with these issues in her study of the photography of camp life. When the War Relocation Authority hired photographers to record the lives of Japanese American internees and resettlers for propaganda purposes, Kozol recounts, the images produced showed the subjects as wholesome and relatable Americans—smiling, sitting with their family members in living rooms, playing sports, and engaging in war-related work. Living their lives, in other words, as if they were not incarcerated.[219] The dark underside of camp life—coercion, family deterioration, illness, suicide, suffering, and trauma—was carefully concealed. Among other things, the WRA photographers recorded *Nisei* blackface performances in camp. What was more American than blackface minstrelsy? One photograph, taken at the Thanksgiving Harvest Festival at the Gila River camp in Arizona in 1942, shows laughing Japanese American teenage girls who are blacked up and dressed in rags.[220] Another photograph, taken at the same festival, shows Japanese American boys and girls, also blacked up and dressed in rags, enacting a slave auction.

[217] Roxworthy 2013.
[218] Roxworthy 2013, 123.
[219] National Archives at College Park, Central Photographic File of the War Relocation Authority, 1942–1944, Record Group 210.
[220] See at: www.discovernikkei.org/en/nikkeialbum/albums/103/slide/?page=5.

Like Roxworthy, Kozol seems unsure of what to make of this. At first, she reflects: "Perhaps this slave reenactment narrativizes Japanese American claims for citizenship and freedom through a blackface performance that invokes the history of slavery and African Americans' struggle for freedom ... associating their experiences with other American histories of racial oppression."[221] Then, dissatisfied with this take, she wonders if *Nisei* blackface actually "reproduce[s] hierarchies of color" and asks: "[I]s this another example of asserting the privilege of not being black?" "[N]o matter how subversive the intent," she concludes, "blackface depends on subordinating African Americans through caricature. Thus even resistant moments that use this particular strategy cannot escape the hegemonic structures embedded in this historically racist practice."[222]

In his commentary on the closing of the Jerome camp in Arkansas in late 1944, John Howard makes a similar point. Jerome was the first of the ten internment camps to close, and internees marked the moment with extended festivities: "As incarcerated Japanese Americans prepared for transfer to Rohwer or elsewhere, they threw a series of campwide farewell parties and performances. At one, white camp officials and Japanese Americans shared the stage—and they even shared a dance .... There onstage in Arkansas, the last dance was an 'All-American Minstrel Show.'"[223] This event was advertised in advance in an article entitled "Minstrel Show Slated For Thursday" in Jerome's camp newspaper, *The Denson Tribune*: "Participated in by Caucasians and non-Caucasians, islanders and mainlanders, an All-American Minstrel Show will be presented this Thursday at 8pm .... Musical numbers by the Inkspot quartet composed of Amy Sasaki, Edith Shintaku, Tom Sugimoto and Shiro Takemoto. Vocal solos, accordion solos, tap dancing directed by Ginger Ikeguchi, baton drills, skit by the Yoshida sisters, and other events."[224] Howard observes: "Inmates and keepers, prisoners and guards, together donned special makeup, blackface, to show themselves, to convince each other, what they collectively were not: black."[225]

Why does blackface minstrelsy show up again and again in Japanese American history as a rite marking momentous occasions? Blackface was and is ubiquitous in U.S. society because it ritualistically reinforces Black

[221] Kozol 2001, 243.
[222] Kozol 2001, 243–244.
[223] Howard 2008, 149.
[224] *The Denson Tribune*, May 2, 1944, vol. II, no. 35, 1. ddr.densho.org/ddr-densho-144-1661.
[225] Howard 2008, 238.

abjection, promotes not-Black relationality, and stabilizes the anti-Black order. In this sense, it has much in common with lynching. Like lynching, blackface minstrelsy is made possible by what Frank Wilderson describes as the Black's "infinite and indeterminately horrifying and open vulnerability" to violence.[226] Blackface minstrelsy invades, violates, displaces, and takes over those who cannot resist. Frantz Fanon: "The black man has no ontological resistance in the eyes of the white man."[227]

But not only the white man. The Black man has no ontological resistance in the eyes of not-Black people more broadly, including Japanese Americans. In blacking up, Japanese Americans demonstrated that they too possessed the power to violate Black flesh, that they, like whites, were the one holding the knife and not the one being cut. Thus blackface minstrelsy performs crucial symbolic work at pivotal moments in white–Japanese relations. Like the "Ethiopian" minstrel show held upon the USS *Powhatan* at the "opening" of Japan in 1854, blackface performances in camp restored and recognized white–Asian relationality after a spectacular act of white aggression threatened to destroy it. The unequal encounter—between the U.S. naval ships and the Asian nation forced to submit, between the white camp administrators and the Japanese American internees they imprisoned—was glossed by the parties' equal participation in the riotous joys of anti-Blackness.

XII OSTRACISM AS INITIATION

Black internationalist critique kept the U.S. racial state on the defensive during the interwar period, and the international scrutiny occasioned by the war dialed up the pressure further. Emulating a well-worn Soviet strategy, Japanese propagandists mocked U.S. claims of racial democracy by pointing to Jim Crow. A week after the bombing of Pearl Harbor, a Japanese radio broadcast mentioned Jim Crow laws and asked: "If these limited rights exist in America, how can Mr. Roosevelt promise them sincerely in the whole world? How can America be fighting for them?"[228] Another Japanese broadcaster stated: "[Roosevelt] says the United States is for racial equality, while the United States is where the Negro cannot be a high officer or ride in Pullman cars. The equality slogan is hypocrisy."[229] High-profile lynchings of Black people in the U.S. were cited

[226] Wilderson 2010, 38.
[227] Fanon 1952, n.p.
[228] Padover 1943, 197.
[229] Padover 1943, 197.

by Japan as a cautionary tale of what the darker races could expect if the U.S. won the war.[230] Some of these messages were aimed in particular at Black audiences in the U.S.: shortwave radio broadcasts known as "Negro Propaganda Operations" warned that "unless the Imperial Japanese forces were victorious, Blacks would continue to be mired in petty slavery and subjugated as second class citizens."[231]

Japan saw itself as leading the colored races of the world to victory against the West. The concept of a Greater East Asia Co-Prosperity Sphere was announced as a counterweight to the Western alliance, to the dismay of U.S. diplomats in areas like Burma, Indonesia, and India. Promising an equal and mutually beneficial partnership among Asian nations— "Asia for the Asiatics"—the concept served as cover for Japan's imperial designs and its "belief that the Japanese were destined to preside over a fixed hierarchy of peoples and races."[232] Thus Japan cloaked its racial supremacist beliefs and will to empire in the language of racial equality, while accusing the U.S. of doing the same. Japanese pilots dropped leaflets over China that said in Chinese: "To liberate Asia from the white man's prison is the natural duty of every Asiatic. All of you Asiatics who have groaned under the yoke of the white man, unite!"[233] What the leaflets neglected to mention was that a liberated Asia would be governed by the pure, divinely descended Yamato race.[234]

U.S. propagandists met their Japanese counterparts halfway. Their goals were manifold: to distinguish U.S. segregation policies from Nazism, answer the worldwide denunciations of Jim Crow, counter Japan's claims that the war was a race war, advance the United States' self-styled image as the beacon of democracy, and boost the Allied war effort. As Takashi Fujitani writes, the U.S. and Japan both undertook "vigorous campaigns in which each presented itself as the authentic

---

[230] Capeci 1998.
[231] Masaharu and Kushner 1999, 11.
[232] Dower 1986, 8.
[233] Dower 1986, 207.
[234] In 1943, the Japanese Ministry of Health and Welfare produced a multivolume project, "An Investigation of Global Policy with the Yamato Race as Nucleus." John Dower writes that the "dominant theme in these pages was that the peoples or races of the world form a natural hierarchy based on inherent qualities and capabilities ... and true morality and justice entailed treating peoples in according with their varying characteristics and abilities" (1986, 264). The project proposed a new cartography of the world, with Japan and Asia at the center of the map. One aspect was the expansion of the Japanese nation through permanent settlers creating "Japan-towns" (*Nippon-machi*) throughout Asia.

defender of freedom, equality, and anti-imperialism while pointing to the other as not only the true racist power and oppressor but also as duplicitous in its denunciations of racism."[235] It was a contest to *appear* less racist than their opponent, and the stakes could not have been higher.[236]

American anti-Blackness needed an alibi, again. A half-century before, with Jim Crow under legal challenge in *Plessy*, the U.S. Supreme Court had invoked Yick Wo, the Chinese immigrant laundry operator, to alibi the U.S. racial state. This is how "Asian. *n.* 1: false alibi" was first written into the American racial grammar book. The crisis of the Second World War resurrected this strategy, as U.S. government officials conceived, planned, and facilitated the phoenix-like rise of Japanese Americans from internment to success as a spectacle of U.S. racial democracy aimed at a global audience. The critique of Jim Crow, in other words, was answered with the (facilitated) assimilation of Japanese Americans. Japanese Americans were lifted up, the better to nail down structural anti-Blackness. *White is best but the most important thing is not-Blackness. Better Asians than Blacks.*

But how to recast internment in real time as something other than a racial persecution campaign of historic proportions? By representing it not as the end point in a long series of discriminatory attacks, but as the starting point of a progressive rehabilitation narrative.[237] Having backed into internment, U.S. officials figured out how to refigure it in a way that maximized its dramatic value. One complication was persuading the

---

[235] Fujitani 2011, 9.

[236] In Congressional debate over repealing Chinese exclusion and granting some Chinese the right to naturalize, supporters of repeal argued it was the key to thwarting Japan's insistence that the war was a race war and its "Asia for the Asiatics" slogan. Representative Walter Judd: "There cannot be a great war between the white and colored races in the next 10 years, or the next 100 years, or the next 300 years, if we keep ourselves—the white people—and the Chinese, the largest and strongest of the colored peoples, on the same side—the side of freedom and democracy" (Dower 1986, 168–169). Also see Fujitani 2011.

[237] Fujitani writes of this doubled aspect of internment: "Our images of Japanese rule over Korea as well as of Japanese American internment are dominated by signs of the negative operations of power: sex and labor under direct coercion, barbed wire, segregation, physical violence, policing, surveillance, expulsion from the national community, unfreedom, and death. These images are not unwarranted, because such practices and displays of power were part of the Japanese and American systems of racialized population management. Yet they reveal only one cluster in the arsenal of technologies available for managing these people during wartime .... I want to insist that such spaces or explosions of brutality and repression existed alongside and in fact supplemented another project: one of welcoming newly constituted national subjects such as Japanese Americans and Korean Japanese into the nation" (Fujitani 2011, 21).

U.S. public that Japanese Americans were in fact loyal to the nation. A similar issue arose on the military front. In response to the bombing of Pearl Harbor, the War Department had declared all Japanese Americans, regardless of citizenship, ineligible for induction into the armed forces. Selective Service reclassified all Japanese American registrants as "4-C," or "non-acceptable aliens," which excluded them from regular military service (with the exception of those serving in military intelligence as interpreters and translators). In January 1943, however, the War Department decided to admit eligible *Nisei* into the army with an eye to creating segregated, all-*Nisei* special combat units. (A year later, in January 1944, *Nisei* were made subject to the draft.) This policy shift was overdetermined by various factors—tireless lobbying by Mike Masaoka of the JACL, who saw military service as the key to *Nisei* assimilation; the need to mobilize all available manpower for the war effort;[238] and, perhaps most crucially, the key contribution that all-*Nisei* fighting units could make to the spectacle of Japanese American assimilation and success.

In September 1942, in his "Memorandum on Policy towards Japan," U.S. foreign policy advisor Edwin Reischauer called upon the U.S. government to induct and deploy Japanese American soldiers as a way of neutralizing Japanese race propaganda and countering Japanese attempts to cast the war as a race war. He wrote: "Up to the present the Americans of Japanese ancestry have been a sheer liability to our cause, on the one hand presenting a major problem of population relocation and military surveillance in this country and on the other hand affording the Japanese in Asia with a trump propaganda card. We should reverse this situation and make of these American citizens a major asset in our ideological war in Asia."[239] At a meeting held to persuade the president of the need for all-*Nisei* combat units, U.S. officials pressed this argument, and WRA head Dillon Myer recalls that "the propaganda angle was the main ground on which Roosevelt could be reached."[240]

The WRA needed to prove the loyalty of internees being released from camp, and the War Department needed to prove the loyalty of internees being inducted into the army. The two worked together to produce a double-duty questionnaire that was administered in a process known as "registration" to adult internees in all camps during February and March of 1943. Male citizens of draftable age (seventeen and older) were

---

[238] Fujitani 2011.
[239] Fujitani 2011, 104–105.
[240] Robinson 2001, 167.

required to fill out Selective Service Form 304A, "Statement of United States Citizen of Japanese Ancestry," wherein questions 27 and 28 cut to the heart of the matter. Question 27 asked: "Are you willing to serve in the armed forces of the United States on combat duty, whenever ordered?" Question 28 asked: "Will you swear unqualified allegiance to the United States of America and faithfully defend the United States from any or all attack by foreign or domestic forces, and forswear any form of allegiance or obedience to the Japanese emperor, or any other foreign government, power, or organization?"[241]

As a fact-finding mission, registration was a failure. Rather than revealing the inner thoughts of internees, it triggered their anxious attempts to game the system. Expressing consternation and dismay, some internees gave answers to protest their incarceration or to minimize their vulnerability to the coercive power of the state. In this context, some *Nisei* answered "no" to questions 27 and 28, not because they were disloyal to the U.S., but because they wanted to protest the ongoing violation of their civil and constitutional rights. Others answered "no" to these questions because they did not want to be drafted and separated from their ageing parents, who had no one else to care for them.[242] Fifteen to twenty percent of all internees were labelled "disloyal" on the basis of the questionnaire and moved to Tule Lake camp, which became a holding pen for those judged to be "spoilage" for the duration of the war.[243]

---

[241] Cited in Fujitani 2011, 132. All other adults over seventeen (noncitizen male adults and all adult women, citizen and not) were given the WRA form "War Relocation Authority Application for Leave Clearance," which was a slightly modified version of the original form. For example, question 28 was changed to: "Will you swear unqualified allegiance to the United States of America and forswear any form of allegiance or obedience to the Japanese emperor, or any other foreign government, power, or organization?" (Fujitani 2011, 153). As Takashi Fujitani notes, "The form's authors had not considered that aliens ineligible by U.S. law from naturalizing as citizens would become stateless if they forswore allegiance to all other foreign governments." After *Issei* complained, the WRA issued a revised form for aliens that asked instead: "Will you swear to abide by the laws of the United States and to take no action which would in any way interfere with the war effort of the United States?" (Fujitani 2011, 133).

[242] Thomas and Nishimoto 1969.

[243] Howard 2008, 207. "Spoilage" is the term Thomas and Nishimoto use as the title of their 1969 study. When labor disputes and complaints over living conditions arose at Tule Lake, the Japanese government requested that the Spanish consul visit there and ascertain what was going on. The visit took place, but nothing came of it. An editorial written by an internee in the camp newspaper, the *Tulean Dispatch* (November 11, 1943), entitled "Mother Country Has Not Forsaken Us," stated: "Remembering that our mother country will not forsake us to the end, we should be patient, avoid rash acts, and endeavor to promote peace and public welfare. We should show greatness worthy

As political spectacle, however, registration worked quite well. Purporting to separate the sheep from the goats, it produced a justification for reversing the internment process, resettling Japanese Americans across the land, and inducting Japanese Americans into the U.S. armed forces. In the crucible of registration, Japanese Americans were tested, found innocent (for the most part), cleansed of taint, and set on the path toward rehabilitation. Registration was the initiation rite that symbolically marked Japanese American (re)entry into the national community. Consider what one army captain said to a group of *Nisei* men who were about to register:

The fundamental purpose (of registration) is to put your situation on a plane which is consistent with the dignity of American citizenship. You may object that ... your life here is not freedom .... Many millions of Americans agree with your point of view [or] we would not be here .... The [registration] is ... an acknowledgement that the best solution has not been found for you ... in your relation to the United States .... Your government would not take these steps unless it intended to go further in restoring you to a normal place in the life of the country, with the privileges and obligations of other American citizens.[244]

Registration was an act of restoration to a status that had not yet been achieved. General John DeWitt, head of the Western Defense Command of the U.S. Army, objected that registration contradicted the original rationale for internment: if Japanese Americans' loyalty was discernible through a questionnaire, why had it been necessary to incarcerate them?[245]

Typically, in hazing rituals, the initiate gives consent and voluntarily submits to the will of the group in order to become a member. Camp registration, Takashi Fujitani notes, "required the active participation of internees as free subjects making rational decisions, not as slaves or nonhuman objects displaying passive obedience."[246] The scene of coercion

---

of Japanese" (quoted in Thomas and Nishimoto 1969, 152). However, the appeals of the Tuleans to the Japanese government were ineffective. A small minority at Tule Lake embraced the "disloyal" label and were actively pro-Japan, planning to renounce U.S. citizenship and move to Japan. Once Congress passed the Denationalization Act in 1944, this minority encouraged *Nisei* and *Kibei* (second-generation Japanese Americans largely educated in Japan) to give up their U.S. citizenship and come under the protection of the Japanese government. After the war, the U.S. government would not allow renunciants to recant so they fought a legal battle for almost twenty years to regain U.S. citizenship (Robinson 2001).

[244] Collins 1985, 24–25.
[245] Fujitani 2011.
[246] Fujitani 2011, 127. Fred Lee (2007) also characterizes the registration process as a ritual of extracting consent.

had to be represented as a scene of free will. By pressuring internees into declarations of "unqualified allegiance" to the U.S., officials made them implicitly affirm that the political contract between the U.S. state and Japanese American citizens was *intact*, that it had not been destroyed by internment. This meant, by extension, that internment had constituted a legitimate exercise of political authority. In this sense, registration secured the internees' *retroactive consent to being interned*. Consent went back in time and erased the crime. For the same reason, Elmer Davis, Director of the Office of War Information, insisted that for propaganda purposes, the all-*Nisei* combat units had to be composed of volunteers not draftees.[247] It was the act of obedience, the choice to affirm the state's uninterrupted authority, that mattered most of all.[248]

After registration, in the spring of 1943, the WRA began implementing its leave clearance program, allowing those deemed loyal to apply for a leave permit to resettle east of the Rocky Mountains, contingent upon an educational opportunity or offer of employment. Tens of thousands of mostly young *Nisei* were released from the camps through this program. The federal government, with the help of civic groups and clergy, launched a massive public relations project to ease their resettlement. Having cast Japanese Americans as a suspect people who had to be interned for the security of the nation, it fell to the government to reconstruct them as good neighbors, dependable employees, and loyal citizens. The spectacle of Japanese American mobility depended on the success of this propaganda campaign.

The WRA public information campaign included a pamphlet called "Myths and Facts About the Japanese Americans: Answering Common Misconceptions Regarding Americans of Japanese Ancestry," which offered assurances that Japanese Americans were not spies and could in fact assimilate into U.S. society. According to the pamphlet, internment was an "opportunity" given to Japanese Americans to show their loyalty to the nation, as well as a blessing in disguise that had broken up the feudal control of the *Issei* in Little Tokyos and freed the *Nisei* to assimilate fully into U.S. society. WRA officials depicted themselves not as wardens of the innocent but as defenders of minority rights, heroic foils to racist Nazi officials. Chastising whites who rejected Japanese American

---

[247] Lyon 2012.

[248] Rhetorically, the registration questionnaire set it up so that *Nisei* men who answered "no"/"no" to questions 27 and 28 appeared as active deciders and determined abrogators of the political contract, rather than relatively powerless victims responding to an already abrogated contract.

resettlers, the pamphlet insisted that public tolerance on this issue was "the true test of American democracy."[249]

Nisei journalist Larry Tajiri echoed the WRA's reinterpretation of internment in his article "Farewell to Little Tokyo," published in the winter of 1944:

> This is the great paradox, the amazing contradiction which marks the wartime treatment of Americans of Japanese descent—the fact that the evacuees in losing a part of America are having opened to them the whole of it; that as the full force of the war effort is beginning to be expended against the Pacific enemy, circumstances should be auspicious for the integration of Japanese Americans into the mainstream of American life. The WRA today has more than fifty local offices engaged in the single task of promoting their resettlement. Local committees of citizens and interested organizations have been formed in most of the key relocation areas to hasten their integration. Never before has a "minority" group had as distinct an opportunity to trumpet down the walls of racial isolation.[250]

What Tajiri did not mention was that the not-Blackness of Japanese Americans was the condition of possibility for these developments. Japanese Americans were buffeted about by the racial suspicions of elected officials, policy makers, military commanders, and the public—right up until the point when it seemed there was more to be gained from their rehabilitation than from their persecution. From that point forward, called on to vouch for the fairness of an anti-Black order, their fortunes took a turn for the better.

XIII THE NOT-BLACKNESS OF THE *NISEI* SOLDIER

Prior to the Second World War, the few soldiers of Japanese descent in the U.S. armed forces had been folded into white units. However, the *Nisei* who volunteered in camp after registration were placed into all-*Nisei* fighting units in the army. The army's decision to segregate *Nisei* soldiers from both white and Black soldiers served several purposes: subordinating *Nisei* as not-whites, elevating them as not-Black in order to maintain the singular abjection of Blackness, and making the achievements of *Nisei* soldiers hypervisible for propaganda purposes. *Nisei*, however, took issue with the decision because they were concerned about the stigma of being treated like Black people.[251] The written questions submitted by internees to the WRA and War Department "often invoked

---

[249] Murray 2008, 89, 85.
[250] Robinson 2012b, 76.
[251] Lyon 2012.

the term 'Jim Crow' and, reflecting their understanding of African Americans as the most abjected group within the military, worried about themselves falling into the category of 'Negroes.'"[252] Even in the midst of internment, at the nadir of their experience, Japanese Americans knew they had "something to save." *We are not Black.*

Contemplating the segregation of *Nisei* soldiers, the U.S. Army, too, had Blackness on its mind. An internal and confidential memo authored by Army Provost Marshal General Allen Gullion in November 1942 advised that *Nisei* be placed into segregated units in order to protect and preserve the practice of segregating Black soldiers:

Although it is true that colored enlisted men have always in our service been segregated into colored units while the few Japanese who have served in the Army, prior to this war, were the subject of general assignment, the fact of colored segregation would be emphasized by the re-adoption of general assignment of Japanese-Americans. In view of the fact that the colored people and their friends have, since the beginning of this war, been increasingly bitter in their protests against segregation of colored people, no one short of the Commander-in-Chief should order the general assignment of Japanese-Americans with its resulting emphasis on colored segregation.[253]

As with the Japanese American schoolchildren in San Francisco, the argument for segregation had less to do with the intrinsic traits of the *Nisei* themselves—or on any notion that the *Nisei* were like Black people—than with the disruptive effect their nonsegregation could have on Black segregation. *Nisei* soldiers had to be segregated because *not* segregating them would make it harder to maintain Black segregation.

The all-*Nisei* 442nd Regimental Combat Team began training at Camp Shelby in Mississippi in May 1943, a year before their departure to the European front.[254] Even in an army structured in negrophobia, Camp Shelby was notorious. William Hastie Jr., a prominent Black jurist and civil rights advocate, mentioned Camp Shelby in a public statement in June 1943:

The environs of Camp Shelby are more than familiar to the military authorities who have surveyed and studied that very area because of the acute problems of racial relations which confront the Army there. It is only the sensational cases of

---

[252] Fujitani 2011, 170.
[253] Lyon 2012, 122.
[254] The 100th Infantry Battalion (composed of Japanese Americans from Hawai'i) trained at Camp McCoy in Wisconsin in 1942 before going to Camp Shelby. In June 1944, the 100th Infantry Battalion was attached to the 442nd Regimental Combat Team in Europe.

shootings, killings and rioting which attract public attention. But day by day the Negro soldier faces abuse and humiliation …. The Army itself is busy with booklets, lectures and various devices of indoctrination, teaching our soldiers how to treat the peoples of India, the South Sea Islanders, the Arabs, everyone but their fellow American soldiers.[255]

A few years earlier, prominent Black newspapers such as the *Baltimore Afro-American* and the *Pittsburgh Courier* had reported on Black soldiers' complaints about racial discrimination at Camp Shelby. One front-page article in the *Baltimore Afro-American* was entitled "Miss. Camp Dixie's Worst." Black soldiers were placed in service units where they did manual labor, rather than in combat units; they were refused service at entertainment establishments in nearby Hattiesburg; and they were denied access to the camp amenities provided to white soldiers, including guesthouses, a library, a movie theater, a recreation hall, and a baseball field.[256] Both white European prisoners of war and Japanese American internees enjoyed privileges denied to Black soldiers.

For *Nisei* soldiers at Camp Shelby, not-Blackness was the ticket to mobility and freedom. Jason Morgan Ward observes that local officials in the South "decided to keep them [*Nisei* servicemen] on the white side of the color line."[257] This was not an informal, unspoken arrangement but a matter of explicit policy. The Hattiesburg City Council held a special meeting where they decided that Japanese American soldiers from nearby Camp Shelby would use white public facilities in town. Arvarh Strickland writes: "This meant that they could patronize white establishments, were not to enter black sections of the city, and were discouraged from having friendly relationships with African Americans."[258] The prohibitory emphasis was revealing: the policy was more about warning *Nisei* soldiers away from Black people than it was about inviting them into the company of whites. It was more about reinforcing the isolated abjection of Blackness than it was about enlarging the *Nisei*'s freedom per se. Army officers allowed *Nisei* soldiers to play in the white sports leagues at Camp Shelby (Black soldiers were confined to the "colored" sports league) and instructed them to "put [themselves] in the white category" when they were faced with "white" and "colored" signs on everything from water fountains to public toilets in the Jim Crow South.[259]

[255] McGuire 1993, 187.
[256] Yamashita 2019.
[257] Ward 2007, 76.
[258] Strickland 1997, 156.
[259] Howard 2008, 129.

On one occasion, local whites from Little Rock, Arkansas, met with army officials in Washington, D.C., to complain about *Nisei* soldiers from Camp Robinson being treated as whites, but even here the main objection was not to the integration of the *Nisei* per se but what it might mean for the maintenance of Black segregation. In his notes on the meeting, Brigadier General F. B. Mallon wrote: "It appears that the fear on the part of the local residents of Little Rock lies in their belief that any equality shown to the Japanese by white people may result in the negroes in this vicinity increasing their demands."[260]

The position of *Nisei* soldiers training in Mississippi was complicated by *Gong Lum* v. *Rice* (1927). Journalist Larry Tajiri wrote:

Although the *Nisei* became "whites" when they crossed the Mason and Dixon line, as far as transportation facilities were concerned, a problem arose in Mississippi when the wives of some of the GIs sent their *Nisei* children to school. Why? Because Mississippi had a number of Chinese Americans [who brought suit] to the Supreme Court some decades before, and the tribunal had ruled that the Chinese children, not being of the "white" race, must attend the Jim Crow schools. In the case of the *Nisei* children, who were the sons and daughters of GIs, the authorities "solved" the problem by assigning the children to a segregated classroom in the "white" school. This expedient pleased no one and merely served to emphasize the ridiculousness of the whole idea of racial segregation.[261]

As discussed in Part One, the school board in Rosedale, Mississippi, had shut Chinese children out of white schools because some of them came from Chinese-Black families and were viewed as vectors of Black contamination. In *Gong Lum*, the high court sanctioned this policy. Did the bar apply to Japanese American schoolchildren as well? Local authorities came up with a solution that reflected the racial common sense of the era with extraordinary precision and clarity: placing Japanese American students in a separate classroom within the white school, which signaled that they were categorically superior to Black people, a head above the Chinese, and just one step below whites. They had reached the antechamber of whiteness.

Thelma Chang notes that *Nisei* soldiers sometimes challenged the norms of Jim Crow. Taking the bus from Camp Shelby into town, they watched with dismay as white bus drivers enforced segregated seating rules against Black GIs. On more than one occasion, *Nisei* soldiers beat up white drivers who were violent toward Black passengers. There were

---

[260] Duus 1987, 55.
[261] Quoted in Robinson 2012b, 109.

quieter forms of protest as well. Oscar Miyashiro, a *Nisei* soldier from Hawai'i, recounted: "Sometimes the [white] people from Hattiesburg complained that we were riding with the blacks in the back of the bus. So the colonel said, 'You sit in the white section, the colored are in the back.'"[262] The *Nisei* soldiers refused to obey. Joseph Hattori, another *Nisei* soldier, explained: "It was beyond our power to change it so when we sat in the back of the bus on purpose, we were making a statement."[263] *Nisei* who hailed from Hawai'i, where racial dynamics were different from the mainland, were especially affronted by and outspoken against Jim Crow.[264]

Other *Nisei* soldiers, though, followed orders and accepted the racial role assigned to them, even if reluctantly. As Daniel Inouye, *Nisei* soldier and future U.S. senator from Hawai'i, said about Camp Shelby: "We were ordered to observe the laws and customs of Mississippi as they related to race relations."[265] Claude, a *Nisei* soldier stationed at Camp Shelby, explained the situation to his friend in a letter that was redacted by military censors. His friend recalled:

Claude wrote about the "(censored) situation" down there. I am guessing that the censored word is "negro" because the context of the rest of the paragraph points toward a situation like that, and because while browsing through Holmes' *The Negro's Struggle for Survival* the other day, I noticed the negro population, as shown on the 1930 census map of the U.S. to be most dense in Mississippi. The letter in part read as follows: "I must tell you about the (censored) situation down here. We, who came from the islands, haven't thought about (censored) matters too seriously—at least not like down here. We have been specifically instructed to keep away from them. Have nothing to do with them what-so-ever. Don't even talk to them. Keep away from places where they congregate. I was (censored) when I heard all these things. It seems that for over a hundred years the (censored) have maintained this (censored) and if we ever did do anything that would be against this custom, they would look down upon us. It's pretty rough for us, but if that's the law around these parts we'll have to play accordingly."[266]

Nisei soldiers themselves were not immune to the lure of anti-Blackness. According to Masayo Duus, when the all-*Nisei* 442nd Regimental Combat Team got attached to the all-Black 92nd Division for a month,

---

[262] Chang 1991, 124.
[263] Chang 1991, 125.
[264] Yamashita 2019.
[265] Chang 1991, 125.
[266] Yamashita 2019, 193.

the former were less pleased than the latter.[267] The Black troops tried to be friendly with the *Nisei* troops, who in turn kept their distance.

A *Nisei* captain with the 100th Infantry Battalion stated:

I certainly wouldn't want to be placed with Negro troops. I worked with them in one of the Army camps for a while and they are bad soldiers. They are dirty and messy and the Army unit is only as strong as the weakest point. I certainly wouldn't feel confident if I were fighting side by side with the Negroes.[268]

In April 1945, in a letter to his wife, Reverend Yamada expressed the widespread belief that Black men were too cowardly and ignorant to make good soldiers: "We have been associating with the Negro troops. One of the boys asked why they were pushed back so often. The Negro soldier replied, 'We weren't pushed back, we ran back.' They are unfortunately poor fighters. They don't have the determination nor the understanding of their part in the scheme of things."[269] After the war, a *Nisei* veteran observed: "They [Black soldiers] always turned their backs to the enemy and ran. They never covered our flanks."[270]

A month before they departed for the European front, the all-*Nisei* 442nd Regimental Combat Team at Camp Shelby was entertained by an "All-American" minstrel show.[271] White performers blacked up, and Japanese American soldiers laughed at their antics as they prepared to go abroad to fight on behalf of a racial state that was incarcerating their families. Commodore Perry's sailors had put on a blackface minstrel show to mark Japan's forced "opening" to the West, internees at the Jerome camp had put on a blackface minstrel show with their captors to mark their readmission to U.S. society, and here, too, blackface minstrelsy functioned to smooth antagonisms between whites and Asian Americans by reminding them that for all their differences, they had the most important thing in common.

Nisei on the West Coast were forcibly evacuated from their homes and placed behind barbed wire in internment camps, in clear violation of their civil and constitutional rights. There, subjected to "registration," they were pressured into declaring their allegiance to the nation and, for the young men, into volunteering for combat. Entering the army straight from the internment camps, *Nisei* young men left families and loved ones

[267] Duus 1987.
[268] Briones 2012, 208.
[269] Duus 1987, 228.
[270] Duus 1987, 227–228.
[271] Howard 2008.

behind, including ageing parents who lacked protection. Placed in seg-regated units, they, along with their counterparts from Hawai'i, were sent into the most harrowing combat situations on the European front, where they sustained extremely heavy casualties and performed, by all accounts, with exceptional valor. Thinking through how *Nisei* soldiers' not-Blackness shaped their experience neither denies their suffering nor diminishes their accomplishments. It only expands and complicates the story. In a society structured in anti-Blackness, there are no simple Asian American stories.

XIV MIKE MASAOKA AND POSTCONTRACTUAL CITIZENSHIP

Formed in 1930, the Japanese American Citizens League (JACL) was a *Nisei* organization focused on the question of citizenship. Politicians from the West Coast of the U.S. had criticized the dual citizenship of the *Nisei* as proof of their divided political loyalties. In response, Japan, whose citizenship law was based on *jus sanguinis* (the right of the blood, meaning that a child of a Japanese father was Japanese regardless of birthplace), modified its law in 1925 to automatically release children born abroad to Japanese parents from Japanese citizenship (with the proviso that parents could apply within two weeks after the child's birth to retain dual citizenship). The newly formed JACL persuaded thousands of *Nisei* to relinquish dual citizenship (or not apply to retain it) as a way of signaling their unimpeachable patriotism to the U.S. In addition, it lobbied successfully to amend U.S. law to permit Japanese American veterans who had served honorably in the First World War to naturalize.[272]

The JACL came under fire for its accommodationist stance during evacuation and internment, but the organization was not an ideologi-cal anomaly. David Yoo's research on Japanese immigrant papers, including *Rafu Shimpo* in Los Angeles and *Nichibei Shimbun* in San Francisco, sheds light on how *Nisei* were thinking about the political scene and their place within it during the interwar years. Both papers depicted racism in the U.S. as aberrational rather than structural, argued that *Nisei* could lift themselves up by their own bootstraps, and urged them to prove their worth "by being model citizens whom

---

[272] Chuman 1976. In June 1935, President Roosevelt signed the Nye-Lea Act into law, granting U.S. citizenship to those of Asian (mostly Japanese) descent who had served honorably in World War I.

others could not help but admire and welcome."[273] All of these themes were central to the JACL's program.

To transform Japanese Americans from suspected traitors into bona fide Americans, it helped to emphasize their not-Blackness. Mike Masaoka, national secretary of the JACL, instinctively understood this. Representing Japanese Americans as a minority group who offered a new kind of unconditional loyalty to the U.S. racial state, he invoked Black people as a point of contrast without ever mentioning them. Unlike Black people, whose noisy protests embarrassed the nation, he seemed to say, Japanese Americans were a model minority whose quiet devotion paid homage to the nation. Japanese Americans' success "proved" that minorities could make it in the U.S. if they tried hard enough. Once again, the Asian–Black gap was denied by those invested in its reproduction, and a more convenient story of Asian virtue and Black dereliction was invoked as an alternative explanation for status differentials.

Masaoka was not shy about noting his accomplishments—he titled his autobiography *They Call Me Moses Masaoka*[274]—and yet his contributions may be underappreciated. He was in fact not only offering a Japanese American rendition of the model minority trope but also theorizing about what kind of *politics* model minorityhood implied. Here he laid out a new theory of citizenship whereby the state demanded total allegiance from citizens, and they, in exchange, forfeited the right to demand anything at all from the state. They gave everything and were entitled to nothing in return. Citizenship was not a contractual exchange, then, but a relationship of domination and submission wherein the citizen's devotion was unequivocal and not contingent on the state's actions. We might call this *a theory of postcontractual citizenship*.

Postcontractual citizenship was bound to be expressed with exaggerated affect, because it was, by definition, more than volitional, more than rational, indeed *in excess of* reason. It reflected a spirit of passionate self-abnegation. In the "Japanese American Creed," read into the U.S. Senate record in May 1941, Masaoka wrote:

I am proud that I am an American citizen of Japanese ancestry, for my very background makes me appreciate more fully the wonderful advantages of this Nation. I believe in her institutions, ideals, and traditions; I glory in her heritage; I boast of her history; I trust in her future. She has granted me liberties and opportunities such as no individual enjoys in the world today. She has given me an education

---

[273] Yoo 1993, 75.
[274] Masaoka 1987.

befitting kings. She has entrusted me with the responsibilities of the franchise. She has permitted me to build a home, to earn a livelihood, to worship, think, speak, and act as I please—as a free man equal to every other man. Although some individuals may discriminate against me, I shall never become bitter or lose faith, for I know that such persons are not representative of the majority of the American people. True, I shall do all in my power to discourage such practices, but I shall do it in the American way—above board, in the open, through courts of law, by education, *by proving myself to be worthy of equal treatment and consideration.* I am firm in my belief that American sportsmanship and attitude of fair play will judge citizenship and patriotism on the basis of action and achievement, and not on the basis of physical characteristics. Because I believe in America and I trust she believes in me, and because I have received innumerable benefits from her, I pledge myself to do honor to her at all times and in all places; to support her constitution; to obey her laws; to respect her flag; to defend her against all enemies, foreign or domestic; to actively assume my duties and obligations as a citizen, cheerfully and without any reservations whatsoever, in the hope that I may become a better American in a greater America.[275]

Rather than seeing "liberties and opportunities" as rights owed to citizens, Masaoka saw them as favors bestowed by a benevolent maternal power. Yet having rights by definition meant claiming one's freedom as an entitlement, not at the sufferance of others. Why should Japanese American native-born citizens, who possessed the same rights as all other citizens, have to prove themselves worthy of equal treatment? Why should they alone be called upon to demonstrate their loyalty to the state? Ironically, Masaoka's creed reproduced the racial logic of internment by suggesting that Japanese Americans were intrinsically different from other U.S. citizens, that they bore a unique burden of proof because of their race, and that they should be grateful for the opportunity to prove their worthiness in the eyes of the state.

Black people are the absent referent in the "Japanese American Creed."[276] Masaoka's rapturous praise for the U.S.—"I glory in her

---

[275] Masaoka 1941. Italics added. Masaoka was barely earning a living and lacked the resources to build a home when he wrote the Japanese Creed. Takashi Fujitani notes that this text reflects Masaoka's "almost fanatical desire to prove his (white) Americanness" (Fujitani 2011, 191).

[276] In Masaoka's testimony at the Tolan Hearings, he emphasized that Japanese Americans were self-sufficient and law-abiding, implicitly contrasting them with Black people: "[I]n the depression years very few Japanese, if any, went on the relief rolls .... I think that is an attitude of thrift and simple living which is characteristic of the American pioneers .... We have a wonderful record of staying out of jail .... The Japanese have a fine record, I believe, of abiding by the law. We stay off the relief rolls." House Select Committee Investigating National Defense Migration, *Preliminary Report and Recommendations on Problems of Evacuation of Citizens and Aliens from Military Areas,* March 19, 1942, 11155.

heritage; I boast of her history; I trust in her future"—represented a disavowal of the foundational abjection of Blackness in the U.S. As a growing chorus of critics at home and abroad condemned the nation for Jim Crow and lynching, Masaoka posited an alternative reality where the American dream was available to anyone willing to put in the work. Point by point, without mentioning it by name, he countered the Black freedom struggle's premises and arguments and vouched for the U.S. state in unequivocal terms. *Discrimination was an aberration, and there were ample avenues of redress. The best response was to try harder to prove oneself worthy. U.S. citizenship was a gift of inestimable value.* To the delight of U.S. officials, then, Masaoka's new kind of minority politics was a politics of adoration that tended to counteract Black critique.[277]

Masaoka pursued this new kind of minority politics with admirable consistency. After the bombing of Pearl Harbor, JACL officials assisted the government in identifying over 1,000 *Issei* to be rounded up, detained, and interrogated as potential Japanese spies on the West Coast. With internment looming in early 1942, Masaoka offered an eleventh-hour proposal to avert it. *Nisei* soldiers would form a volunteer suicide battalion to demonstrate their loyalty, and "to assure the skeptics that the members of the 'suicide battalion' would remain loyal ... the families and friends of the volunteers would place themselves in the hands of the government as 'hostages.'"[278] Again, Masaoka recapitulated the racial logic that put the *Nisei*'s loyalty into question in the first place. Why was self-immolation a prerequisite for *Nisei* belonging? Why use the term "hostages," as if the *Nisei* soldiers were in a state of siege with the U.S. government? Later that year, the Japanese Army formed the Special Attack Corps composed of suicide bomber pilots. Kamikaze pilots, as they came to be known, were viewed by the American public as fanatical, unthinking, murderous drones of the Japanese empire—as all that distinguished the Japanese

[277] See Diane Fujino (2018) for discussion of the Nisei Progressives, an organization that presented a clear alternative to Masaoka's politics. The Nisei Progressives formed in 1949 in Los Angeles, New York, and Chicago. According to Fujino, they emphasized "deep solidarity," or risking or sacrificing their direct self-interest in the name of justice for others. Among other things, they supported the Black freedom movement, including Paul Robeson's activism. Their constitution's preamble stated: "Our particular problems are the responsibility of all people. The problems of all people are our responsibility" (Fujino 2018, 184).
[278] From William Hohri's introduction to Deborah Lim's "Research Report Prepared for the Presidential Select Committee on JACL Resolution #7," 1990, 38, 13–14, quoted in Fujitani 2011, 185.

from Americans.[279] Ironically, Masaoka had proposed that *Nisei* act as kamikazes first, and in order to prove their Americanness.

In April 1942, Masaoka delivered an eighteen-page letter on behalf of the JACL to the War Relocation Authority, in which he cast the looming event of internment as an opportunity to create "Better Americans in a Greater America."[280] Once internment had begun, JACL officials encouraged Japanese Americans to cooperate fully with all aspects of the process, characterizing compliance as the highest form of patriotism. JACL president Saburo Kido elaborated:

> We are going into exile as our duty to our country, because the President and the military commanders of this area have deemed it necessary. We have pledged our full support to President Roosevelt and to the nation. This is a sacred promise which we shall keep as good patriotic citizens .... "We also serve" must be our badge of courage in these trying days, for we also serve, each in his own way, this country of which we are so fond. What greater love, what greater testimony of one's loyalty could any one ask than this, leave your homes, your business, and your friends in order that your country may better fight a war?[281]

Like Masaoka, Kido defined patriotism as unquestioning obedience to the state and a permanent readiness to provide "testimony of one's loyalty." Hence his endorsement of the government's baseless claim that internment was a "military necessity." In return for this devotion, which exceeded anything WRA officials had allowed themselves to hope for, they appointed the JACL as representatives of the *Nisei* and favored JACL members with special favors and privileges within the camps.

The JACL was also a driving force behind the induction of *Nisei* soldiers into the U.S. armed forces.[282] In November 1942, over the opposition of many *Issei* and *Nisei* within the camps, the JACL decided to press President Roosevelt to allow the *Nisei* to prove their loyalty through military service. By February 1943, the War Department announced it would form an all-*Nisei* combat unit composed of volunteers from the mainland and Hawai'i. Only 1,208 *Nisei*, or fewer than 6 percent of those eligible, enlisted from within the camps; many more *Nisei* volunteered in Hawai'i, where Japanese Americans were not interned.[283] Despite these

---

[279] Konstantopoulos 2007.

[280] Wu 2014, 79.

[281] Chuman 1976, 170.

[282] See Salyer (2004) for a history of the linkage between military service and naturalization rights for Asian Americans.

[283] Lyon 2012. In January 1944, the Selective Service restored *Nisei* eligibility for the draft (which had been cancelled at the start of the war) to fill the ranks of volunteer *Nisei* segregated combat units that had seen heavy casualties.

disappointing numbers, it was important for the units to be composed entirely of volunteers, since the spectacle of all-*Nisei* combat units was meant to emphasize their "consent."

According to documents from the Office of War Information, Takashi Fujitani writes, "the propaganda machinery of the U.S. government was already preparing to spin the story of Japanese American war heroes even before the campaign to recruit them had begun."[284] For the duration of the war and years after, pamphlets, radio broadcasts, newsreel footage, and newspaper and magazine articles celebrated the *Nisei* soldiers for their bravery and invaluable contributions to Allied victories. Government agencies, JACL officials, journalists, and Hollywood producers all had a hand in this campaign. In 1944, liberal journalist Carey McWilliams joined the chorus of praise:

The *Nisei* have met the test of their loyalty in a magnificent manner under the most trying circumstances. The fact that they have done so will, in the long run, finally remove those longstanding doubts and misgivings. In this sense, one can even say that the war has been a war of liberation for the *Nisei*—liberation from doubt, suspicion, hatred, and distrust.[285]

The war was not only an opportunity for *Nisei* to prove their patriotism, then, but the occasion of their liberation. The celebration of the soldiers' military performance displaced the question of why they should need to prove their loyalty in the first place. The splendor of their courage was used to whitewash the ugly circumstances of internment. Several years later, the MGM feature film *Go for Broke* (1951) consolidated the image of *Nisei* soldiers as icons of loyalty, military achievement, and national redemption. Mike Masaoka served as a consultant on this film.[286]

---

[284] Fujitani 2011, 211.

[285] McWilliams 1944, 281.

[286] One underside of this campaign was the suppression and delegitimation of Japanese American dissent. There was no room in the celebratory narrative of *Nisei* hyperpatriotism to acknowledge that some *Nisei* men answered "no"/"no" to questions 27 and 28, for a variety of reasons not having to do with disloyalty. Or that others answered question 28 with "Yes [I will declare unqualified allegiance], provided I am treated as a full-fledged American citizen" (Howard 2008, 201). Or that members of the Heart Mountain Fair Play Committee were convicted and imprisoned for undertaking draft resistance on the grounds that the government had violated their rights. *Nisei* draft resistance was in fact quite widespread (Lyon 2012), and it followed other forms of protest and resistance that went underreported in the camps. Yet there were no Hollywood movies or Department of Interior pamphlets lionizing *Nisei* conscientious objectors. Until quite recently, the figure of the iconic *Nisei* soldier rendered them nearly invisible.

XV "WE CHARGE GENOCIDE"

As a new global order emerged during the course of the Second World War, Western elites worried about how to sustain prevailing racial and colonial arrangements. Black internationalists, meanwhile, considered how to leverage the new order in a renewed attack on these arrangements. The Atlantic Charter signed by President Roosevelt and U.K. Prime Minister Winston Churchill in 1941 articulated the principle of national self-determination and championed the "four freedoms" (of speech, of worship, from want, from fear), but Churchill clarified that it did not apply to colonial holdings.[287] Walter White of the NAACP urged Roosevelt to assert the Charter's universal scope:

> Not only would this have its effect upon the colored peoples of the world, who constitute four-fifths of the world's population, through its demonstration that no longer will black, brown, and yellow peoples be treated as inferior or exploited by white peoples, but it would also have profoundly salutary effect upon the very serious domestic situation with respect to Negro–white relations.[288]

Rising out of the ruins of world war as a new global power, the U.S. stood to benefit from doing the right thing in relation to "four-fifths of the world's population." Anti-racism, in short, made good political sense.

U.S. officials understood that if they *gave the appearance of* championing racial democracy, they could reap some public relations benefit without having to give up the benefits accrued from racial domination. Deliberately failing to provide for enforcement of various articles was a favorite tactic in international law during this period. In 1943, a special project group of the State Department produced draft articles for the United Nations, including one that prohibited discrimination on the basis of race, nationality, language, political opinion, and religion. An internal evaluation report specified that this article was intended "to prevent the enactment of laws like the notorious Nuremberg laws," and reassured southern lawmakers that the article would "not interfere with the laws of some of our states for the segregation of races," as there was no enforcement clause which might raise "constitutional or political difficulties in various states."[289] (Despite such assurances, southern lawmakers viewed

---

[287] Harris 1991. President Roosevelt favored the decolonization of Africa and Asia and the establishment of a system of trusteeships that would avert violent liberation struggles and provide cover for U.S. military control over certain areas, but Prime Minister Churchill resisted taking steps to dismantle the British Empire.

[288] Lauren 1983, 5.

[289] Lauren 1983, 9.

the United Nations as a cloaked attempt to destroy Jim Crow and were among the strongest opponents of international organization in the post-war period.)

As Brenda Plummer observes, the State Department's Area Committee on Africa, formed that same year, was "a milieu that deeply denigrated African cultures and peoples." One committee member, *New York Times* editor Anne McCormick, stated on the record: "No black people had developed a leading civilization for Africa as China and Japan had done for the peoples of eastern and southeastern Asia." Meanwhile, Undersecretary of State Sumner Welles, responding to questions about colonialism, commented that Africans were "in the lowest rank of human beings" and did not desire autonomy.[290] Even as they condemned the racism of the Nazis and created the international legal architecture to name and sanction it, U.S. officials based their own approach to Africa on nineteenth-century race science.

In 1944, a conference was held at Dumbarton Oaks in Washington, D.C., to outline the structure of the United Nations and lay the groundwork for the U.N. Conference on International Organization (UNCIO), to be held in San Francisco the following year. The parties, all Western nations (with the exception of China, which joined only in the second round of discussions), advanced a clause specifying that the U.N. could not meddle in the internal affairs of states absent a direct threat to world peace, resolved that the U.N. would only consider human rights complaints filed by member states, not individuals, and declined to make any statement about segregation or colonialism. That is, they put safeguards in place to ensure that the new international regime, with its emergent conception of universal human rights, would not upset the racial and colonial status quo. Du Bois, watching the proceedings at Dumbarton Oaks, observed that "750 million colored and black people would have no voice in the proposed world forum."[291] When China proposed a resolution opposing racial discrimination, it was rejected by the other parties in an eerie throwback to the Paris Peace Conference of 1919.

Black internationalists from the U.S. arrived at the UNCIO in 1945 with a two-pronged agenda: advancing racial equality at home and self-determination for colonized peoples abroad. Prior to their departure for the conference, in April 1945, NAACP officials had held a conference at the New York Public Library in Manhattan—with attendees from the

---

[290] Plummer 1996, 109, 110, 110.
[291] Harris 1991, 131.

Caribbean, India, Southeast Asia, Africa, and the U.S.—to discuss how they might press the federal government to take action against colonialism.[292] At the UNCIO, the NAACP delegation sought a strong U.N. declaration on human rights and equality for all races and peoples, as well as the creation of an international body to oversee the colonies' transition to independence.[293]

As the U.S. and British delegations worried on the record about the impact of human rights and anti-discrimination proposals on racial and colonial affairs, U.S. officials contrived the solution of the "domestic jurisdiction" clause. John Foster Dulles, advisor to U.S. Senator Arthur Vandenberg, issued a statement that the U.N. Charter would "guarantee freedom from discrimination on account of race, language, religion, or sex" and then added: "Nothing contained in the present Charter shall authorize the United Nations to intervene in matters which are essentially within the domestic jurisdiction of any state or shall require the Member to submit such matters to settlement."[294] Paul Lauren writes: "Human rights and racial nondiscrimination foundered on the rock of national sovereignty."[295] Like U.S. federalism, with its deference to "states' rights," the United Nations, with its deference to "domestic jurisdiction," was deliberately structured from the start to protect extant racial and colonial structures of power.

Rising U.S.–Soviet tensions also influenced the struggle to define the U.N.'s reach and power. John Skrentny writes: "The cultural rules of human rights ... shaped a propaganda battle of Soviet attempts to prove to the world that America violated the human rights rules—that America was illegitimate—while the Americans sought to defend themselves from the charge."[296] When the Soviets moved to form a Subcommission on the Prevention of Discrimination and Protection of Minorities under the auspices of the U.N. Commission of Human Rights, U.S. officials tried and failed to block the move. A State Department report, entitled "Problems of Discrimination and Minority Status in the United States," observed

---

[292] Harris 1991.
[293] Meriwether 2002.
[294] Lauren 1983, 20.
[295] Lauren 1983, 18.
[296] Skrentny 1998, 245. The 1945 Charter of the United Nations mentions human rights seven times and treats the promotion of human rights as a major charge of the new organization. In 1946, the United Nations' Economic and Social Council established the Commission on Human Rights. In 1948, the United Nations approved the Universal Declaration of Human Rights and adopted the Convention on the Prevention and Punishment of the Crime of Genocide (Skrentny 1998).

that "[n]o other American group is so definitely subordinate in status or so frequently the victim of discriminatory practices [as Black people]" and warned that some "may be inclined to press for consideration of the Negro's case before the Human Rights Commission."[297] In August 1946, in the hope of averting this possibility, the State Department preemptively redefined "minority" as "national minority," or a group that has a distinct language and culture and wants to secede from the majority—a definition deliberately crafted to exclude Black people.[298]

As the inaugural chair of the U.N. Commission on Human Rights, Eleanor Roosevelt was a significant player in these events. She was, in Carol Anderson's words, "responsive to the public relations exigencies of the Cold War, which called for sanitizing and camouflaging the reality of America's Jim Crow democracy."[299] Thus, for example, Roosevelt thwarted India's effort in 1946 to charge South Africa with discrimination and human rights violations against Indians living there, on the grounds that it would set a precedent for attacking Jim Crow.[300] To southern Democrats who viewed the U.N. with hostility, she offered the reassurance that "the sacred troika of lynching, Southern Justice, and Jim Crow schools would remain untouched."[301] Walter White's abiding faith in Eleanor Roosevelt and the administration of Franklin Roosevelt drove a wedge between himself and his more radical Black colleagues.

It was in the context of this ongoing struggle over the promise and possibility of the United Nations that the National Negro Congress, with "profound regret," submitted a petition to the U.N., entitled "The Oppression of the American Negro: The Facts," in June 1946.[302] Written

---

[297] Anderson 2003, 74–75.

[298] Anderson 2003, 74–76.

[299] Anderson 2003, 3.

[300] In the 1950s, the U.N. General Assembly responded to India's charge that South Africa discriminated against citizens of Indian descent and violated agreements between the two nations by condemning apartheid as contrary to the principles and spirit of the U.N. Charter and its preamble, thus initiating several decades of U.N. scrutiny of South Africa. The South African government invoked the domestic jurisdiction clause in response (Dubow 2008).

[301] The phrase is Carol Anderson's. See Anderson 2003, 4. "While supporting the principle of 'eventual self-determination,' the United States implicitly claimed the right to determine when African peoples were 'mature' enough for independence" (Borstelmann 2001, 117).

[302] The National Negro Congress formed in 1936 with A. Philip Randolph as president. It was anti-capitalist and human-rights oriented. Randolph eventually left the organization because he believed it had become reflexively pro-Soviet. In 1947, the NNC merged with the Civil Rights Congress.

by historian Herbert Aptheker, the petition—which focused on lynching, economic and educational segregation, discrimination, poverty, disenfranchisement, and infant mortality—appealed to the newly constituted international legal and political authority to bring pressure on the U.S. government on behalf of Black Americans. Despite its radical internationalist orientation, the National Negro Congress made the strategic decision, perhaps because of Cold War pressures, to focus on the Black predicament in the U.S. without analyzing its connections to colonialism in Africa and elsewhere. Even thus watered down, the petition was too much. The U.N. Commission on Human Rights, chaired by Eleanor Roosevelt, deflected the petition, arguing that it provided no proof of its assertions, that the Commission could not accept petitions from NGOs, and that the Commission had no power to intervene in "domestic" affairs.[303]

The following year, W. E. B. Du Bois, on behalf of the NAACP, prepared a second, more exhaustively researched U.N. petition entitled "An Appeal to the World: A Statement on the Denial of Human Rights to Minorities in the Case of Citizens of Negro Descent in the United States of America and an Appeal to the United Nations for Redress" (1947). With the Cold War heating up, Du Bois argued that segregation and discrimination were a bigger threat to the U.S. than the Soviet Union was, and that they undermined democracy at home and the nation's standing abroad. Despite his desire to indict Western colonialism in Africa, Du Bois, too, made the strategic decision to keep his focus on Black Americans.[304] Soviet delegate Alexander Borisov requested that the Subcommission on the Prevention of Discrimination and Protection of Minorities investigate the anti-Black discrimination identified in the NAACP petition, and the Subcommission rejected his resolution.[305] U.S. delegate Jonathan Daniels opined that it would not be proper to focus only on Black people and not on other minority groups.[306] In other words, confronted by Du Bois with overwhelming documentary evidence of the singular nature and scale of anti-Black oppression, Daniels employed the tactic of despecification to deflect the charge. Eleanor Roosevelt, who served on the NAACP Board of Directors, refused to introduce "An Appeal to the World" to the U.N. General Assembly. Eventually, the petition did embarrass President

[303] Anderson 2003.
[304] Von Eschen 1997.
[305] Anderson 2003; Martin 1997.
[306] Martin 1997.

Truman into passing a number of civil rights reforms as part of his campaign against international communism.[307]

In 1948, the NAACP's Walter White, who had taken a strong internationalist and anti-colonialist line during the war, cut ties with the Black left, moved into the camp of liberal anti-communism, and embraced President Truman's Cold War argument for civil rights reforms.[308] White promised U.S. officials that he would not promote Du Bois's "An Appeal to the World." To assist the U.S. government in responding to the Soviet critique of the American race problem, he furnished a "Progress Report" on civil rights that claimed that Black people were approaching parity with whites in various spheres of life, minimized atrocities against them, and emphasized the "positive gains" in race relations.[309] At the same time, he distanced himself from the anti-capitalist agenda of Black left groups and supported the federal government's campaign to destroy them.

White's actions contributed to the deradicalization of the Black struggle in the U.S. at a pivotal historical moment. Carol Anderson argues that casting racial reform as a Cold War necessity made limited forms of "civil rights" more thinkable, but also made "human rights," or the idea of fundamental economic and social freedoms, less thinkable. When the NAACP and many other Black organizations submitted to Truman's anti-communist crusade, she concludes, they took their "eyes off the prize" of human rights.[310] The dream of a worldwide anti-colonialist alliance against the West gave way, at least in part, to the pursuit of domestic civil rights reforms via the authority of the U.S. state. As Brenda Plummer observes, the Cold War "helped weaken attachment to an internationalist ideal and reasserted the primacy of the individual nation-state as the only genuine champion and guarantor of civil rights."[311]

But radical Black internationalism was not vanquished. In 1951, William Patterson of the Civil Rights Congress, a Black left organization, submitted a third U.N. petition entitled, "We Charge Genocide: The Historic Petition to the United Nations for Relief from a Crime of the United States Government Against the Negro People." Signatories

---

[307] In 1946, Truman appointed a President's Committee on Civil Rights, which issued a report in 1947. In 1948, Truman issued executive orders desegregating the armed forces and banning discrimination in federal employment.

[308] Anderson 2003.

[309] Anderson 2003, 176.

[310] Anderson 2003, 5.

[311] Plummer 1996, 210.

included Black luminaries such as Charlotta Bass, Paul Robeson, Mary Church Terrell, W. E. B. Du Bois, Benjamin Davis Jr., Harry Haywood, Alphaeus Hunton, and Claudia Jones. Despite his radical internationalist bent, Patterson, too, kept his focus on Black people in the U.S., arguing that the petitioners were acting both "as Negroes" and "as Americans, as patriots" hoping to restore democracy at home and preserve peace abroad. What distinguished Patterson's petition from the previous two was its invocation of the concept of "genocide," which had been laid out in the U.N. Convention on the Prevention and Punishment of the Crime of Genocide, adopted in December 1948 by the U.N. General Assembly. Genocide was defined there as:

any of the following acts commited with intent to destroy, in whole or in part, a national, ethnic, racial or religious group, as such: a) Killing members of the group; b) Causing serious bodily or mental harm to members of the group; c) Deliberately inflicting on the group conditions of life calculated to bring about its physical destruction in whole or in part; d) Imposing measures intended to prevent births within the group; and e) Forcibly transferring children of the group to another group.[312]

Patterson's gambit was that a legal concept created to name the Holocaust and prevent its recurrence could make the predicament of Black people legible and actionable on the global stage.

"We Charge Genocide" argued that "a conspiracy exists in which the Government of the United States, its Supreme Court, its Congress, its Executive branch, as well as the various state, county and municipal governments, consciously effectuate policies which result in the crime of genocide."[313] Driven by the profit motive, and with full intentionality and purpose, white officials committed crimes against Black humanity: "Out of the inhuman black ghettos of American cities, out of the cotton plantations of the South, comes this record of mass slayings on the basis of race, of lives deliberately warped and distorted by the willful creation of conditions making for premature death, poverty, and disease. It is a record that calls aloud for condemnation."[314]

Page after page in the petition listed Black people who had been killed or injured in racial attacks, along with details about the circumstances:

---

[312] Quoted in Patterson 1951, xii.

[313] Patterson 1951, 6–7.

[314] Patterson 1951, xi. Carol Anderson (2003) reads Patterson as motivated by the need to raise funds for the defense of his jailed communist comrades. In her view, he used Black issues to advance the cause of communism, which was his top priority.

February 17 [1946]—TIMOTHY HOOD, veteran, was shot to death in Bessemer, Alabama, by a police chief. Previously, a street car conductor had fired five shots into Hood's body because Hood had attempted to pull down a jim crow sign. Hearing that Hood was in a nearby house, wounded, the police chief entered the home and fired into Hood's brain. The Bessemer coroner called the acts "justifiable homicide."

December [1946]—WILLIAM DANIELS, a veteran, was shot to death in Westfield, Alabama, a small mining town outside Birmingham. It was near Christmas and Daniels was doing some shopping in the Tennessee Coal, Iron and Railroad commissary store. A white woman employee complained that Daniels had jostled her. In response to her complaint, a guard called Daniels outside the store and shot him dead.

May [1947]—Sardis, Georgia. JOE NATHAN ROBERTS, 23-year-old veteran, was shot to death when he failed to say "yes sir" to a white man. A student at Temple University in Philadelphia on the G.I. Bill of Rights, Roberts was visiting relatives. No one was tried for the killing.

ISAIAH NIXON, 28-year-old war veteran, was shot and killed in the presence of his wife and children on September 6, 1948, after he had voted in that day's primary election in Montgomery County, Georgia. A jury freed M. L. Johnson, the killer.

DANNY BRYANT, 37, of Covington, Louisiana, was shot and killed in October of 1948 by Policeman Kinsie Jenkins after Bryant refused to remove his hat in the presence of whites.[315]

In the last section, "Summary and Prayer," Patterson wrote:

[I]t was easy for your petitioners to offer abundant proof of the crime. It is everywhere in American life. And yet words and statistics are but poor things to convey the long agony of the Negro people. We have proved "killing members of the group"—but case after case after case cited does nothing to assuage the helplessness of the innocent Negro trapped at this instant by police in a cell which will be the scene of his death. We have shown "mental and bodily harm" in violation of Article II of the Genocide Convention but this proof can barely indicate the life-long terror of thousands on thousands of Negroes forced to live under the menace of official violence, mob law and the Ku Klux Klan. We have tried to reveal something of the deliberate infliction "on the group of conditions which bring about its physical destruction in whole or in part"—but this cannot convey the hopeless despair of those forced by law to live in conditions of disease and poverty because of race, of birth, of color. We have shown incitements to commit genocide, shown that a conspiracy exists to commit it, and now we can only add that an entire people, not only unprotected by their government but the object of government-inspired violence, reach forth their hands to the General Assembly in appeal. Three hundred years is a long time to wait.[316]

[315] Patterson 1951, 62, 66, 66, 13, 11.
[316] Patterson 1951, 195.

Facts and figures could not convey the traumatic horrors of living while Black in the U.S. The U.S. government not only failed to protect Black citizens but was the chief participant in a conspiracy to destroy them. They had no choice but appeal to the U.N.—but would the U.N. hear their cries?

Upon learning of the petition, State Department officials sprang into action. They proffered legalistic defenses: the U.S. had not signed the Genocide Convention, not enough Black people had been lynched to qualify as a genocide, etc. They brought out Walter White to condemn the petition as Soviet propaganda that "purposely paints only the gloomiest picture of American democracy and the race question" and ignores "measureable gains [that] have been made in reducing racial bigotry"— an awkward charge, to say the least, given the petition's reliance upon NAACP source materials.[317] They arranged for Channing Tobias of the NAACP to refute the genocide charge at a U.N. meeting in Paris in 1951, where he labelled the petition a "traitorous" attempt to "discredit" the U.S. government.[318] They denied a passport to Paul Robeson, one of the signatories, who was preparing to travel to Paris to present the petition to the U.N. They attempted to seize William Patterson's passport, but he eluded them and fled to Eastern Europe. Still, for all this, the petitioners were not deterred. In December 1951, Patterson presented the petition to U.N. officials in Paris. On the same day, Robeson presented the petition to U.N. officials in New York City.[319] The U.N. never acted on the petition, but the document would forever be a matter of historical record.

Robeson was one of many Black leftists targeted by the U.S. racial state during this period. Anti-communism and anti-Blackness had been mutually imbricated ideological projects since the Red Scare of the 1920s, when Soviet critics began condemning U.S. segregation, and U.S. officials, in turn, constructed Black radicalism as a Soviet contrivance. Anti-communism amplified the threat of Blackness by attaching it to the Bolshevik menace and hobbled the struggle against anti-Blackness in important ways. Blackness, in turn, amplified the threat of communism, such that, according to Charisse Burden-Stelly, "the trifecta of foreignness, Blackness, and radicalism came to be understood as mutually constituting forms of subversion and sedition."[320]

---

[317] Janken 1998, 1088.
[318] Anderson 2003, 193.
[319] Martin 1997.
[320] Burden-Stelly 2017.

Together, the FBI and the House Un-American Activities Committee (HUAC) took the lead in persecuting Black radicals during the Cold War. Since the 1920s, the FBI's J. Edgar Hoover had waged an unremitting campaign to tie Blackness to communism and destroy them both. He was, simply put, "the most powerful, aggressive, and obsessive investigator of communist influence among African Americans in the country's history."[321] Hoover sent the results of his numerous investigations to the HUAC, which was "the nerve center of counter-subversive antiCommunism during the 1940s and 1950s."[322] When Representative John Rankin of Mississippi, an outspoken segregationist, became chair of HUAC in 1947, he set his sights on Black radicals, opining: "[The] racial disturbances you have seen in the South have been inspired by the tentacles of this great octopus, Communism, which is out to destroy everything."[323] Under Rankin's leadership, HUAC assembled information that led to charging Black federal employees with political disloyalty because of their civil rights activism. Gerald Horne writes: "With the anti-Hitler war substantially discrediting racist ideology, Rankin, Bilbo, Eastland, and others found it useful to score Black activists as being as red as their blood in their campaigns of bigotry."[324] The Cold War, in other words, provided cover for the ongoing war on Blackness.

In April 1949, radical Black internationalist Paul Robeson spoke at a Soviet-sponsored peace conference in Paris. His speech included this excerpt:

We in America do not forget that it is on the backs of the poor whites of Europe ... and on the backs of millions of black people the wealth of American has been acquired. And we are resolved that it shall be distributed in an equitable manner among all of our children and we don't want any hysterical stupidity about our participating in a war against anybody no matter whom. We are determined to fight for peace. We do not wish to fight the Soviet Union.[325]

Distorting Robeson's words, the U.S. media accused him of saying that Black people would not fight in a war against the Soviet Union. The Associated Press reported that he had said: "It is unthinkable that American Negros [sic] would go to war on behalf of those who have oppressed us for generations against the Soviet Union which in one

---

[321] Woods 2004, 86.
[322] Woods 2004, 26.
[323] Woods 2004, 28.
[324] Horne 1986, 61.
[325] King 2011, n.p.

generation has lifted our people to full human dignity."[326] Whether this
was a projection of white guilt and anxiety or a deliberate strategy to
discredit Robeson as a traitor, or both, the public reaction was explosive,
and the HUAC rushed to call for hearings on the matter.

Representatives John Rankin of Mississippi and Martin Dies of
Texas, co-chairs of HUAC, organized "Hearings Regarding Communist
Infiltration of Minority Groups" to make an example of Robeson.[327] The
most dramatic moment featured baseball star Jackie Robinson, who, at
the behest of the State Department, denounced Robeson as not speaking
for all Black Americans. (Robinson later expressed regret for this action.)
A steady parade of less famous speakers, both Black and white, ritualistically repeated that most Black people were loyal because racism was
diminishing, and that Robeson and his ilk were Soviet stooges. Thomas
Young, the Black president and general manager of Guide Publishing
Company, testified:

> The Negro in this country is as basically American as any other element of the
> population. He has been on the soil as long; he has fought to protect and preserve
> its liberties, and he has toiled to help build the Nation during all the years of our
> history. The things he yearns for and strives for are entirely compatible with the
> aims and the shibboleths of Patrick Henry and Benjamin Franklin and George
> Washington and all the others who helped found this Nation. We have got to
> acknowledge that in some respects our democratic processes have slowed down
> or failed temporarily. But any overemphasis of these circumstances obscures the
> more important fact that, despite these occasional reverses, the machinery which
> we in this country have embraced for the realization of our declared way of life
> is nevertheless accomplishing, however slowly, the most cherished aspirations of
> the Negro group. The evidences of this accomplishment are everywhere, although
> they are frequently corrupted by the miscarriages of the machinery. I think it is
> very clear that what the Negro in this country wants is simply to have our demo-
> cratic machinery functioning properly.[328]

Why was it important to affirm that Black people were contented patriots
whose aim was the perfection rather than the destruction of American
democracy? Did Black people in fact have good cause for being alienated from the U.S. and interested in communism? These questions were

[326] King 2011, n.p.
[327] Hearings Regarding Communist Infiltration of Minority Groups—Part I, Committee on
Un-American Activities, 81st Congress, 1st Session, U.S. House of Representatives, July
13, 14, 18, 1949.
[328] Hearings Regarding Communist Infiltration of Minority Groups—Part I, Committee on
Un-American Activities, 81st Congress, 1st Session, U.S. House of Representatives, July
13, 14, 18, 1949, 454.

suppressed throughout the HUAC hearings, until the moment when committee investigator Alvin Stokes asked Charles Johnson, president of Fisk University, this startling question: "[I]f the Negro is as smart as he says he is, and he is being treated unjustly in many areas, as is well known, if he is not a Communist, why isn't he?"[329] Given their status in an anti-Black society, *shouldn't* Black people be communists?

Robeson's passport was revoked, he was blacklisted, and his concert performances were cancelled. He was dubbed "Black Stalin" and "the Kremlin's voice of America," and his singing career collapsed.[330] The U.S. government's red-baiting of Black radicals, of which the takedown of Robeson was but one example, deepened the split between Black liberals and Black leftists. Walter White and the NAACP embraced Truman's anti-communist agenda and assisted his administration's efforts to destroy Black leftist groups. In September 1948, Du Bois sent a memo to the NAACP Board of Directors denouncing the Truman Doctrine and excoriating the NAACP (and White in particular) for their collusion with it. He was promptly ousted from the board. At its annual convention in 1950, the NAACP passed a resolution affirming the subordination of the Black struggle to the fight against communism, and by 1951, the NAACP's newspaper *The Crisis* was itself labelling Robeson "Moscow's No. 1 Negro" and a "Kremlin stooge."[331]

XVI BLACK GHETTOIZATION

At the start of the twentieth century, most Black people in the U.S. lived in the rural South. As they began moving into urban areas in the South and North in the early 1900s, whites responded by creating the urban ghetto.[332] Prior to this, Black people in urban areas had been only moderately segregated. In postbellum southern cities, for example, Black servants and laborers often lived on smaller alleys branching off the grand avenues occupied by wealthy whites. Jim Crow rules were put in place precisely to regulate the extensive daily contact that did occur between the two groups. In northern cities, Black people were more segregated than European ethnics, but they were still somewhat scattered residentially,

---

[329] Hearings Regarding Communist Infiltration of Minority Groups—Part I, Committee on Un-American Activities, 81st Congress, 1st Session, U.S. House of Representatives, July 13, 14, 18, 1949, 474.

[330] King 2011, n.p.

[331] Meriwether 2002, 82.

[332] Massey and Denton 1993.

and more affluent Black people often lived near whites.[333] Large-scale Black migration into urban areas in the first half of the twentieth century, though, triggered a structural adjustment across regions. Most dramatically, the two waves of the Great Migration, during the First and Second World Wars, brought millions of southern Black people into northern cities. Those leaving the South were not only fleeing the dangers of Jim Crow and lynching, but also responding to the reduced availability of southern agricultural jobs due to crop infestations and technological innovations, as well as the increased availability of industrial jobs in northern cities during wartime.

In *The Color of Law: A Forgotten History of How Our Government Segregated America* (2017), Richard Rothstein shows that deliberate, concerted policy making and discretionary decision making at every level of government (federal, state, and local), coupled with the coordinated actions of private interests, produced significant Black residential segregation in major metropolitan areas across the U.S. by the mid-twentieth century. This outcome was

not the unintended consequence of individual choices and of otherwise well-meaning law or regulation but of unhidden public policy that explicitly segregated every metropolitan area in the United States. The policy was so systematic and forceful that its effects endure to the present time. Without our government's purposeful imposition of racial segregation, the other causes—private prejudice, white flight, real estate steering, bank redlining, income differences, and self-segregation—still would have existed but with far less opportunity for expression. Segregation by intentional government action is not *de facto*. Rather, it is what courts call *de jure*: segregation by law and public policy.[334]

Here Rothstein directly contradicts the conventional wisdom that segregation outside the South grew up accidentally, haphazardly, and as the result of private actions. To the contrary, as it turns out.[335]

White municipal leaders in the South greeted Black in-migration with a flurry of exclusionary zoning ordinances defining separate living areas for whites and Black people and prohibiting white homeowners from selling to Black people. Baltimore led the way in 1910, with multiple southern cities following its lead shortly thereafter. Then, pursuant to an NAACP lawsuit, the U.S. Supreme Court, in *Buchanan* v. *Warley* (1917), ruled that racial zoning ordinances violated the "freedom of

---

[333] Massey and Denton 1993.
[334] Rothstein 2017, viii.
[335] Rothstein 2017, x.

contract" (i.e., the white homeowner's right to sell) guaranteed by the Fourteenth Amendment. Segregation as such was fine, but it could not be accomplished by state actions that infringed on (white) economic freedom. Municipal leaders continued to use nonracial zoning laws of various types to promote segregation, and they developed other means as well.[336] Racially restrictive covenants—contractual agreements among homeowners not to sell or lease to Black people (and sometimes, more broadly, to those who were not "Caucasian")—and mob violence were used in tandem to corral Black people into the least desirable parts of the city and keep them there.[337]

In the 1930s, the federal government put its authority and resources behind the drive to ghettoize Black people across the nation. The Home Owners' Loan Corporation (HOLC), established to promote homeownership, provided funds for refinancing urban mortgages and low-interest loans to owners who had lost their homes through foreclosure. In the HOLC ratings system for evaluating risks associated with loans made in different urban neighborhoods, there were four categories of neighborhood quality, with green representing the lowest risk and red representing the highest. Areas with significant numbers of black residents were marked red on agency maps—giving rise to the term "redlining"—and loans were denied to residents of those areas. As Massey and Denton observe, the federal government did not invent the association of race and neighborhood quality, but it placed its imprimatur upon it, with consequences that reverberate to this day.[338] Although HOLC's own funds were not extensive, its rating system informed the lending practices of both private banks and government agencies such as the Federal Housing Authority (FHA) and Veterans Administration (VA), all of which had a decisive hand in shaping the U.S. residential housing market during the 1940s and 1950s.

The FHA, founded in 1934 to insure bank mortgages, conducted its own property appraisals to assess risk. Borrowing from HOLC practice, it reproduced the linkage of race and risk, designating majority-Black areas, areas close to Black areas, and even integrated areas high

---

[336] Rothstein 2017.

[337] In 1926, the U.S. Supreme Court ruled in *Corrigan* v. *Buckley* that restrictive covenants were private agreements between consenting parties and that state action was not involved, which meant the Fourteenth Amendment (which pertained only to state action) could not be used to curtail them. The use of restrictive covenants increased after this.

[338] Massey and Denton 1993.

risk. Richard Rothstein writes: "Because the FHA's appraisal standards included a whites-only requirement, racial segregation now became an official requirement of the federal mortgage insurance program."[339] A 1935 FHA underwriting manual provided to appraisers warned against the "infiltration of inharmonious racial or nationality groups" and stated: "If a neighborhood is to retain stability it is necessary that properties shall continue to be occupied by the same social and racial classes. A change in social or racial occupancy generally leads to instability and a reduction in values."[340] The VA, formed after the Second World War to guarantee mortgages for returning servicemen, adopted FHA underwriting and appraisal policies. Both the FHA and VA required properties to be covered by racially restrictive covenants.[341]

The federal government's intervention was a condition of possibility for "white flight" to the suburbs. Across the nation, federal agencies guaranteed bank loans to suburban developers with the requirement that the new developments be "racially exclusive white enclaves."[342] At the same time, they financed and built a massive highway system to allow suburban whites to access jobs and services in the city. In addition, they refused to insure mortgages that would help Black people move into white neighborhoods or whites move into relatively integrated areas. In sum, federal government agencies, in cooperation with private interests, built the suburbs, facilitated the mass movement of whites from the cities into the suburbs, supported white homeownership in the suburbs, degraded integrated urban areas, corralled Black people into central city areas, and refused to support Black homeownership there.

When the U.S. Supreme Court ruled in *Shelley* v. *Kraemer* (1948) that state enforcement of racially restrictive covenants violated the Equal Protection Clause of the Fourteenth Amendment, the FHA and other federal agencies "evaded and subverted the ruling, preserving state-sponsored segregation for at least another decade."[343] Suburban developers concocted the idea of creating community associations, inserting a "whites only" clause in the bylaws, and making membership a condition of home purchase. When the FHA was involved in the financing of such developments, it recommended or insisted on the "whites only" clause. The IRS meanwhile granted tax-exempt status to churches, synagogues,

[339] Rothstein 2017, 65.
[340] Rothstein 2017, 65.
[341] Massey 2020.
[342] Rothstein 2017, 70.
[343] Rothstein 2017, 77.

hospitals, universities, and neighborhood associations that promoted residential segregation through covenants and other means. And the Federal Deposit Insurance Corporation (FDIC) implicitly sanctioned the racially discriminatory lending practices of the private banks it regulated.[344]

While many Black people were thus prevented from following whites to the suburbs, there was still the matter of protecting whites who wanted to come into the city from "the pollution of intercourse" with Black people. How could white suburbanites be expected to enter the city to work, shop, go to the theater, or enjoy a museum if they did not feel safe? The solution lay in "urban renewal" (better known as "Negro removal") schemes, which involved (1) clearing Black "slums" that were adjacent to downtown business and entertainment areas "so that white commuters, shoppers, and business elites would not be exposed to black people"; and (2) relocating Black residents into new high-density public housing projects built in or near Black areas.[345] To build these projects, existing homes in Black areas had to be razed, with many of the residents forced to move into the projects as well. Massey and Denton write: "By 1970, after two decades of urban renewal, public housing projects in most large cities had become black reservations, highly segregated from the rest of society and characterized by extreme social isolation."[346]

Discretionary power, as well as formal policy-making power, was exercised to deepen Black segregation. Rothstein emphasizes the

extraordinary creativity that government officials at all levels displayed when they were motivated to prevent the movement of African Americans into white neighborhoods. It wasn't only the large-scale federal programs of public housing and mortgage finance that created *de jure* segregation. Hundreds, if not thousands of smaller acts of government contributed. They included petty actions like denial of access to public utilities; determining, once African Americans wanted to build, that their property was, after all, needed for parkland; or discovering that a road leading to African American homes was "private." They included routing interstate highways to create racial boundaries or to shift the residential placement of African American families. And they included choosing school sites to force families to move to segregated neighborhoods if they wanted education for their children. Taken in isolation, we can easily dismiss such devices as aberrations. But when we consider them as a whole, we can see that they were part of a national system by which state and local government supplemented federal efforts to maintain the status of African Americans as a lower caste, with housing segregation preserving the badges and incidents of slavery.[347]

[344] Rothstein 2017.
[345] Rothstein 2017, 127.
[346] Massey and Denton 1993, 57.
[347] Rothstein 2017, 122.

Rothstein insists upon the singularity of Black segregation, which he thinks Americans have a habit of denying: "When we wish to pretend that the nation did not single out African Americans in a system of segregation specifically aimed at them, we diffuse them as just another *people of color.* I try to avoid such phrases."[348]

The phobic hatred of Blackness could be disguised by the FHA's technocratic maps and the boosterish euphemisms of "urban renewal," but on the ground in white neighborhoods, there was no mistaking the phenomenon. Thomas Sugrue's 1995 study, "Crabgrass-Roots Politics: Race, Rights, and the Reaction against Liberalism in the Urban North, 1940–1964," presents postwar Detroit as a site where blue-collar white workers met the second wave of the Great Migration with all-out resistance. Officials catalogued "over two hundred incidents against Blacks attempting to move into formerly all-white neighborhoods, including mass demonstrations, picketing, effigy burning, window breaking, arson, vandalism, and physical attacks." Speaking of "the colored problem," one white resident opined: "Eighty percent of [Black people] are animals. If they keep them all in the right place there wouldn't be any trouble." Sixty-eight percent of whites said they favored residential segregation, with many citing Jim Crow as a model. Between 1943 and 1965, whites in Detroit formed at least 192 "civic associations," "protective associations," "improvement associations," and "homeowners' associations" to oppose the siting of public housing projects and resist the entry of Black people into white neighborhoods. Beneath the concern about property values and crime was a deeper anxiety.[349] Sugrue writes:

> The most commonly expressed fear was not of "riotous living" or crime, but of racial intermingling. Black "penetration" of white neighborhoods posed a fundamental challenge to white racial identity. Again and again, neighborhood groups and letter writers referred to the perils of rapacious Black sexuality and race mixing. The politics of family, home, and neighborhood were inseparable from the containment of uncontrolled sexuality and the imminent danger of interracial liaisons.[350]

Living in the same neighborhood connoted social equality, which led to miscegenation and the contamination of the white race. Whites were overtaken by this fear of "the pollution of [symbolic and literal] intercourse" with Black people. It was the same phobic fear that forbade the

---

[348] Rothstein 2017, xvii.
[349] Sugrue 1995, 560, 556, 556, 558.
[350] Sugrue 1995, 561.

"commingling" of the races in the *Plessy* decision and moved lynch mobs to savage their victims, even after death, with a violence unmatched by that of any other species.

XVII JAPANESE AMERICAN MOBILITY

Until the Second World War, white homeowners in the U.S., with assistance from every level of government and numerous private interests, tended to eschew both Black people and Asian Americans as neighbors.[351] Racially restrictive covenants, for example, often prohibited both by name or contained a blanket prohibition on all who were not "Caucasian." At the same time, Black people and Asian Americans have been disfavored differentially in U.S. housing markets, and with different degrees of vehemence, and this gap expanded significantly during the postwar period. White supremacy *and* anti-Blackness. Many whites who preferred to exclude Asian Americans from their neighborhoods were willing to let them in, and even embrace them, over time, as an alternative to letting Black people in. Thus the Asian–Black gap has been inscribed into the geography of urban housing. Here, as elsewhere, Asian Americans have been seen as the lesser of two evils, and their mobility has been powered by the phobic hatred of Blackness.

In the middle of the Second World War, the War Relocation Authority initiated various programs to promote the post-camp resettlement of Japanese Americans, as narrated in its publication, *The Relocation Program*:

Early in 1943 the agency began at the centers a long and arduous effort to stimulate relocation which was to last until the early fall of 1945. Almost every conceivable device was used to build up confidence among the evacuees and create in their minds a desire to take up residence outside the centers. Pamphlets and releases were prepared in practically all the field offices describing the particular localities involved and outlining the general relocation prospects for evacuees. Periodic newsletters were sent out to keep evacuees at all centers constantly informed of specific job opportunities and other changing features in the relocation picture in each major community. Special teams made up of employees from the Washington office and field offices were sent to centers to describe relocation

[351] Prior to the 1920s, Japanese Americans were often excluded from white neighborhoods in California by racially restrictive covenants. As the Japanese exclusion movement gained momentum in the 1920s, Japanese Americans who purchased homes in the white neighborhoods of Rose Hill and Pico Heights in Los Angeles faced opposition from alliances of white homeowners, realtors, and nativist activists (Brooks 2009). Little Tokyo in Los Angeles emerged out of these dynamics.

prospects and hold interviews with individual evacuees who might be interested. Photographs and motion pictures giving the evacuees the visual impression of living conditions in some of the outside communities were sent into the centers and widely exhibited.[352]

Referring to "centers" instead of internment camps and "evacuees" instead of prisoners, the WRA cast itself, misleadingly, as a protector rather than a carceral authority. Still, it is significant that the federal government, within a year of commencing internment, had launched a sustained effort to promote Japanese American resettlement outside the camps.

Until the Western Defense Command revoked the West Coast general exclusion order for Japanese Americans on December 17, 1944, internees were instructed not to return to the West Coast. Thus the WRA opened field offices in cities throughout the East and Midwest, where its staff worked with universities, civic leaders, and clergy to assist tens of thousands of Japanese Americans, connecting them with housing opportunities, jobs, and social networks. Modest relocation assistance grants, supplemented by Social Security resettlement assistance grants, were administered through local welfare agencies. Before the end of the war, anticipating their own closure, WRA field offices set up local organizational alliances to continue their work. The stated policy was to disperse or scatter internees—President Roosevelt suggested "one or two families per county"—to prevent the (re)formation of Little Tokyos, address labor shortages, and reduce local opposition on the part of whites.[353]

The solicitude and assistance extended by the WRA should not blind us to the coerciveness of its actions, as it prevented Japanese Americans from returning home to the West Coast, steered them to other parts of the country, and discouraged them from living in proximity to each other—and all of this after forcibly evacuating and interning them and their families for a protracted period. Nor were WRA programs in any sense a meaningful compensation for the individual and community devastation wrought by internment. Still, it is worth noting that the federal government's aim was not only to assist Japanese Americans in resettling, but to help them integrate into white society. Japanese Americans who moved to cities like Chicago were encouraged to find housing in integrated, transitional, or white areas. They were not expected to live in the Black ghettos that had emerged there. Nor, for the most part, were they willing to do so.

[352] *The Relocation Program*, n.d., 141.
[353] Howard 2008, 224.

Nisei who resettled in Chicago found that their not-Blackness was as much of a boon in the housing market as it was in the workplace. As of 1941, 80 percent of Chicago residential properties were covered by racially restrictive covenants, and the segregation of Black people was well established.[354] Charlotte Brooks notes that whites resisted Japanese American neighbors less vigorously than they did Black neighbors:

> The white resistance that occasionally accompanied the appearance of *Nisei* in a neighborhood never reached the fever pitch of antiblack sentiment. No tradition of Japanese American segregation bolstered resistance, and no blockbusting real estate agents preceded the resettlers. As a result, hostility toward *Nisei* neighbors remained sporadic and generally nonviolent.[355]

Initially "[f]orced into transition zones because of their race, Japanese Americans hesitated to remain in such areas once they became mostly African American." Adopting the language of white Chicagoans, *Nisei* responded with dismay when Black people moved in next door—"I imagine they're going to dirty up the place"—and joined whites in their flight from the South Side to the North Side and the suburbs.[356] Cultivating their not-Blackness was an investment in future opportunities. By way of reward, *Nisei* were admitted to whites-only establishments such as restaurants, nightclubs, theaters, and dance halls. Their social acceptance by whites—as coworkers, neighbors, and friends—accelerated after the war's end.

In her article, "Nisei and Race Prejudice: Jim Crow Tendencies among Japanese American Evacuees May Hamper Resettlement," published in the JACL's paper, *Pacific Citizen*, on January 1, 1944, Marie Pulley, a liberal white homeowner in an integrated Chicago neighborhood, told of her encounters with prospective *Nisei* tenants:

> [T]o my amazement, which led me to look into the matter beyond our own experience, it was discovered that the *Nisei* maintain an extremely rigid and well-developed racial prejudice against brother Americans who are Negroes. When they came to our street, for instance, and saw children of Negro professional people (all of them of higher cultural status than the ordinary *Nisei*) playing quietly in some of the yards in the neighborhood, they looked no further for our welcome home .... There are doubtless two reasons for the strong *Nisei* prejudice against associating themselves with American Negroes. The first is that of expediency. They do not, as a group already meeting with racial prejudices, wish

---

[354] Brooks 2000.
[355] Brooks 2000, 1677.
[356] Brooks 2000, 1675, 1676.

to align themselves with another minority group .... This reaction of expediency of the *Nisei* is, however, a minor one. I have found upon intense and wide investigation among the *Nisei* an actual feeling of superiority of themselves over the American Negro citizen .... The *Nisei* now stands at a crossroad in American life, and he has a dangerous and vital choice to make .... The people who are most kindly disposed towards the *Nisei*, and who will do all in their power to aid him personally, as well as socially, politically, economically, are those advanced, liberal souls who have long been working for better inter-racial conditions. They hold every sympathy for the tense Negro situation of segregation; they will not take kindly to helping a group of *Nisei*, no greater culturally than the Negro, to perpetuate the prejudice among them that they are working to eradicate in white groups. Thus the *Nisei*, by his racial prejudices against his suffering fellow American, the Negro, is alienating the energies and interests of the only really friendly group in this country. Who can bring this point home to them before it is too late?[357]

Pulley's commentary did not go unnoted. In the same edition of *Pacific Citizen*, an editorial entitled "Nisei and Jim Crow" references her article and calls upon *Nisei* to resist racial prejudice against Black people and speak up in their defense: "It is not enough to insist upon equality of treatment for the *Nisei*."[358]

Black migration to San Francisco had soared during the war. Between 1940 and 1945, San Francisco's Black population had increased more than 600 percent, as jobs in the defense industry, and especially Bay Area shipyards, had drawn Black migrants to the area.[359] In 1940, the city's Black population was less than 5,000. A decade later, it had grown almost ninefold to 43,460.[360] The white phobic response was to accelerate the ghettoization of Black people. Thus the San Francisco Housing Authority (SFHA) established racial segregation in its public housing units, a so-called "neighborhood pattern policy" where Black people were confined to one development (Westside Courts in the Western Addition) and excluded from all others.[361]

---

[357] Pulley 1944, 4.
[358] "Nisei and Jim Crow" 1944, 4.
[359] Broussard 1993, 4.
[360] Broussard 1993, 133.
[361] Pursuant to an NAACP-supported lawsuit (*Banks* v. *SFHA*) in 1953, the SFHA eventually allowed Black people to apply to other public housing developments, but the supply of units citywide did not meet the demand. In the *Banks* case, the District Court of Appeal, First Division, in California held that the SFHA's segregation of public housing was unconstitutional. Chinese Americans reacted with dismay because they did not want Black residents moving into the Ping Yuen public housing project in Chinatown, which they made clear in community meetings, and they did not want access to faraway public housing projects themselves. The local English-language Chinese newspaper *The*

Racially restrictive covenants were still in place in California after the war, but as not-white groups tried to move into white areas covered by such agreements, they discovered that whites almost never went to court to enforce the covenants unless prospective Black buyers/renters were involved. In other words, whites tolerated Asian Americans who bought or rented covenanted homes, for the most part, but not Black people.[362] Mark Brilliant writes: "[A]s inclusive as they were in print, in practice during the 1940s in California racially restrictive housing covenants were enforced overwhelmingly in courts [against Black people]."[363] When the JACL considered filing an amicus brief in relation to a group of housing segregation cases Loren Miller was handling for the NAACP, they realized that of the thirty to forty cases pending in front of the California Supreme Court at the time, not one involved a Japanese American.[364] Furthermore, when white Californians used violence to keep their neighborhoods white, their targets were almost exclusively Black.[365] All of which is to say, "Asian Americans now moved to places where African Americans could not follow."[366] One neighborhood in the Richmond district of San Francisco had had only three "minority" families in 1950. By 1957, realtors estimated that 15 to 20 percent of that neighborhood's homes were owned by "minorities," predominantly Asian Americans.[367]

Something similar was unfolding on the employment front. Asian Americans in San Francisco enjoyed increased job opportunities after

Chinese Press supported the "neighborhood pattern policy" that had segregated public housing in the first instance (Schiller 2015). The JACL endorsed the desegregation of public housing in San Francisco.

[362] Similarly, whites did not typically bring enforcement cases against Mexican Americans. Some judges refused to enforce restrictive covenants against them on the grounds that they were in fact white. Some Mexican Americans signed restrictive covenants themselves, promising to exclude Black people from the neighborhood.

[363] Brilliant 2010, 92.

[364] Brilliant 2010. Individual Asian Americans joined efforts such as the Los Angeles Committee Against Restrictive Covenants, and the JACL joined the NAACP-led legal fight for fair housing. In 1947, the California Supreme Court upheld the enforceability of racially restrictive covenants in two Los Angeles cases involving Asian Americans (Chinese American Tommy Amer and Korean American Yin Kim). These were among the cases the U.S. Supreme Court agreed to review in the lead-up to *Shelley* v. *Kraemer* (1948), where the court fatally weakened racially restrictive covenants by ruling that they were unenforceable. The court agreed to review these two cases, among other cases, and ultimately decided to only hear four cases in *Shelley*, all involving Black plaintiffs (Cheng 2013).

[365] Brooks 2009.

[366] Brooks 2009, 224.

[367] Tang 2008, 232.

the war, especially relative to Black people. A 1946 report from the Committee on Fair Employment Practice observed that the Chinese American employment scenario looked strong, but that anti-Black discrimination was already erasing the wartime gains of Black workers.[368] While Black workers suffered from the scaling down of the wartime economy, Chinese Americans were finding jobs outside the ethnic economy of Chinatown for the first time, for example in shipbuilding factories and downtown offices.[369] Meanwhile, a Council for Civic Unity survey in the mid-1950s showed that private employment agencies had given up on referring qualified Black applicants for jobs, as the effort had proved fruitless. One respondent said her agency in San Francisco made calls for qualified Asian American applicants, but automatically placed qualified Black applicants in the "inactive file."[370]

What accounts for the increasing acceptance of Asian Americans as neighbors and employees in the postwar period? Many scholars say it was the Cold War that incentivized white Americans to change their ways.[371] By the late 1940s, the U.S. state faced intense race-related criticism from the Soviet Union abroad and from the rising Black civil rights movement at home.[372] As noted above, U.S. officials approached the matter as a public relations problem. Penny Von Eschen writes: "[N]either the Truman nor the Eisenhower administration acted decisively on civil rights. Instead, the preoccupation of the Truman administration with America's 'Achilles' heel' led to frenetic efforts to shape the world's *perceptions* of race in America."[373] How to conceal structural anti-Blackness with a convincing performance of racial democracy?

---

[368] Tang 2008, 232.

[369] R. Lee 1999.

[370] Tang 2008, 232.

[371] Cheng 2013; Kurashige 2008; Tang 2008. Tang argues that Black people became "new objects of racial scorn" in the postwar era, a place formerly occupied by Asian Americans, whose status rose after the war. Kurashige argues that Japanese Americans and Black people were comparably oppressed before the war, Black people were elevated over Japanese Americans during the war, and that Japanese Americans were elevated over Black people during the Cold War. My argument is that the respective racial positions of Asian Americans and Black people remained the same over time. The status of Asian Americans improved in the sense that anti-Blackness helped to increase their socioeconomic mobility after the war, but they remained not-white and above all not-Black.

[372] In 1950, Republican Senator Henry Cabot Lodge referred to race as "our Achilles' heel before the world." Quoted in Borstelmann 2001, 76.

[373] Von Eschen 1997, 121. Italics in original.

Under Truman, the State Department's programs in psychological warfare and propaganda were geared toward improving the nation's image abroad. The United States Information Service (USIS) developed radio, film, and print material to convey positive images of Black life in the U.S., and Voice of America broadcasts carefully curated race stories for international audiences. The general approach was to acknowledge the existence of racial discrimination, but at the same time insist that it was disappearing and that it was not determinative of life outcomes in any case. Meanwhile State Department personnel stationed around the world monitored, reported, and worked to counteract negative local press coverage of U.S. race relations.[374] By promoting an upbeat, sanitized view of racial issues and pushing back against negative media reporting, officials sought to gain the upper hand in the Cold War struggle for the "hearts and mind" of the unaligned.

The USIS pamphlet, "The Negro in American Life" (1952), was a product of this public relations campaign. The opening line—"Perhaps the single aspect of the United States that is most disconcerting to her friends and most frequently cited by her enemies is the position of the Negro"— clarified the stakes up front. The good news, the pamphlet averred, was that "progress [was occurring] on every front—social, economic, educational—at a tremendous pace." While the U.S. government had encouraged this progress, it had not "issued commands from a central source" or "attempted to alter psychology by fiat" like Soviet communists would have. Rather, like a proper democratic government, it understood that racism is "essentially a question of evolving human relations" that cannot be rushed. Happily, discrimination "diminishe[d] every year, for democracy contain[ed] within itself the resources for eradicating this evil from the hearts of its people."[375] In support of these claims, the pamphlet cited rising Black school enrollment rates and literacy rates, the growing Black presence in music and the arts, Black participation in industrial workplaces and unions, and Black voting and political power—even in the South. Unlike the first Reconstruction, the pamphlet stated, this "second Reconstruction," this gentle and gradual correction of segregated institutions, was about nurturing equality rather than imposing it. *All things in their own time.* In a text supposedly dedicated to celebrating Black advancement, this jab at the first Reconstruction struck an incongruous and revealing note.

---

374 Von Eschen 1997.
375 U.S. Information Service, "The Negro in American Life" (1952), 2.

It was in this geopolitical context that performing racial democracy came to be seen as an act of patriotism. Many white Californians were willing to compromise the whiteness of their neighborhoods in order to do their part. The Sing Sheng case seemed to exemplify these dynamics. Sheng, a Chinese American, bought a home in Southwood, a white neighborhood in San Francisco. When he learned of his neighbors' objections, he asked Southwood to hold a formal vote on whether to allow him into the neighborhood. In a letter to residents, Sheng made his case in Cold War terms, referencing "the present world conflict" between "Communism and Democracy."[376] In February 1952, 174 residents voted no, 28 voted yes, and 14 had no opinion. A wave of public outrage followed. Political leaders and organizations—including California Governor Earl Warren, the San Francisco Board of Supervisors, the city attorney, the mayor, U.S. senators, the National Committee for Free Asia, and local church and civic groups—issued public statements supporting Sheng and linking his case to the Cold War. Media (print, television, radio) from around the nation covered the story through this frame as well. *The San Francisco Chronicle* said it received more letters on Sheng than it had on any other issue in months. When it tallied the letters in a mock vote, the results were 266 for Sheng, 16 against.[377] Some letters were from white homeowners who invited Sheng to buy their homes.[378] Even though Sheng lost the battle, in other words, he won the war, as the episode indicated that "the cost of preserving Asian American segregation was too high for the nation to bear."[379] By incentivizing whites to perform racial democracy, therefore, the Cold War created new opportunities for Asian American mobility.

But there is more to the story. Bringing structural anti-Blackness back into the picture enables us to recognize the sleight of hand that occurred. Sing Sheng was embraced by white San Franciscans, including the city's elite, as a way of speaking back to worldwide criticism of *the oppression of Black people in the U.S.* As with the citation of *Yick Wo* in *Plessy*, white Americans had Sheng stand in as a false substitute for the paradigmatically segregated Black person. In this way, Sheng, as an Asian American, was weaponized against the Black struggle. Whites dramatized their acceptance of Asian Americans as proof of their anti-racism,

---

[376] Cited in Cheng 2013, 75.
[377] Cheng 2013, 81.
[378] Cheng 2013.
[379] Brooks 2009, 203.

when in reality they were willing to accept Asian Americans *so that they would not have to accept* Black people. Asian Americans were the lesser of two evils. Their advancement did not *represent* Black advancement, it *substituted* for it. *Whiteness is best but the most important thing is not-Blackness. Better Asians than Blacks.*

Charlotte Brooks notes that Sheng received an outpouring of support from politicians, journalists, and the public, while Black San Franciscans subjected to *physical violence* by white neighbors received none. Contemporaneous instances of whites attacking the properties of Black renters or homeowners in San Francisco—including at least one that involved a cross burning and the Ku Klux Klan—received little or no media coverage and awakened no public outrage.[380] It was Sheng's Asian Americanness, his constitutive not-Blackness, that made him the ideal prop for the theater of white performative anti-racism. It was not the Cold War alone, but also the imperative of reproducing structural anti-Blackness, that lifted Asian Americans up during this period.

A 1955 study on housing discrimination in San Francisco, based on interviews with realtors, verified not only that Black people were the most abjected group, but that Asian Americans were lifted up by their presence. Realtors' comments included:

"Generally, the feeling is against non-Caucasians, but most people will qualify this by saying they mind Orientals less than Negroes."

"Mexicans are often not considered a minority and Orientals are generally accepted, but the Negro is a special problem."

"It is easier for Orientals than Negroes to buy .... Japanese and Chinese are often accepted almost like whites."[381]

One real estate broker in San Francisco spoke of a white woman home-owner who had rejected a Black doctor's offer on her home for $24,000 and accepted a Chinese family's offer for $22,000, because she had "less feeling against the Chinese than she did against negroes."[382] This wording is revealing: she had an aversion to both, but her aversion to Black people was stronger. By 1961, 67 percent of the city's rental vacancies were open to Asian Americans, while only 33 percent were open to Black people.[383]

Black ghettoization and Japanese American mobility, then, were not parallel and independent processes, but mutually imbricated ones. Prior

---

[380] Brooks 2009.
[381] Tang 2008, 233.
[382] Tang 2008, 233.
[383] Tang 2008, 233.

to the war, the threat of Asian American groups had loomed large in the white Californian's imagination, in part because the Asian American population was relatively large there and the Black population was relatively small. But the influx of Black migrants during the war created a scenario more like postwar Chicago, where the phobogenic presence of Black people helped to clarify the not-Blackness of Asian Americans. In these circumstances, Asian Americans were invited into adjacency with whites, the better to keep Black people in their place. Reflecting on Los Angeles in the early 1960s, a *Nisei* Protestant minister conjectured "that white sellers viewed Japanese Americans as a tolerable alternative to Blacks who, they feared, would trigger a neighborhood 'invasion.'"[384] He continued:

A lot of us are congratulating ourselves on working for and securing wide acceptance in the community at large. But I suspect that we have been bailed out by the Negroes. They moved in and frightened the whites, who then found that we Japanese weren't so bad after all. They could stop hating us and start hating the Negroes.[385]

The boundary between whites and Asian Americans was relaxed in order to shore up the one between Black people and everyone else. By 1961, the report to the U.S. Commission on Civil Rights from its California Advisory Committee declared that the minority housing crisis in the state was almost exclusively a Black issue, and that "there is a far greater degree of housing mobility for Orientals and Mexican-Americans in California than exists for Negroes."[386] Chinese and Japanese Americans, Charlotte Brooks writes, were achieving "unprecedented residential and social mobility throughout the state."[387]

As in Chicago, some *Nisei* in California cultivated their not-Blackness as valuable property. Scott Kurashige notes: "Making racial generalizations, some *Nisei* parents believed that protecting their children from the ravages of urban society necessitated shielding them from intimate contact with Blacks."[388] Kurashige quotes JACL leader Kats Kunitsugu observing ruefully in 1958: "A great many *Nisei* mirror the prejudices of the white majority. They harbor preconceptions about Negroes, and it takes only one case of seeing a Negro spit on the street … and they are

[384] Kurashige 2008, 245.
[385] Kurashige 2008, 245.
[386] Brilliant 2010, 172.
[387] Brooks 2009, 1.
[388] Kurashige 2008, 254.

convinced with thin lip certainty that all Negroes are that way."[389] In 1963, the Rumford Fair Housing Act was signed into law in California, prohibiting racial discrimination in the sale or leasing of housing units over a certain size. In response, the California Real Estate Association, in tandem with conservative organizations and white supremacist groups, mobilized to put Proposition 14 (repealing the Rumford Act) on the ballot the following year. The JACL organized against the ballot initiative, but many Japanese Americans supported it nevertheless, citing "their desire to escape or protect themselves from the Negro influx" as the main reason.[390] In a column for *Pacific Citizen* entitled, "Are You Being Played for a Sucker?" (October 2, 1964), Larry Tajiri wrote: "It is astounding to learn that there are some Japanese Americans who are currently supporting Prop. 14, for the narrow and selfish reason that repeal of the fair housing act will mean that they will not be forced to rent or sell property to Negroes or to members of other minorities."[391] Proposition 14 passed by a landslide, and the Rumford Act was repealed.

XVIII AN ALIBI FOR ANTI-BLACKNESS

By the mid-1960s, the issue of widespread and persistent Black urban poverty was a prominent topic of debate among U.S. policy makers. The emergent Black Power movement, influenced by Malcolm X, cited racial and economic oppression, but white elites favored other explanations. In 1965, Daniel Patrick Moynihan, assistant secretary of labor under President Lyndon B. Johnson, released a report entitled *The Negro Family: The Case for National Action* (1965). The Moynihan report attributed Black urban poverty to the "tangle of pathology" in the ghetto, the diseased Black culture in which female-headed families prevented Black men from exercising their proper authority as heads of households. Jobs, vocational training, and educational programs were needed, Moynihan argued, to help Black men regain their rightful position within their own families and become successful breadwinners.

Although Moynihan did not discuss Asian Americans in *The Negro Family*, they played an important role in his thinking about the impact of racial discrimination. In a private memo to President Johnson, dated

[389] Kurashige 2008, 254.
[390] Robinson 2012a, 237.
[391] Robinson 2012b, 261.

March 5, 1965, he expressed optimism about solving the Negro problem "once and for all," citing what had happened with Asian Americans:

A quarter-century ago Japanese Americans were subject to the worst kind of racial discrimination and mistreatment. All of which has practically disappeared before our eyes. The reason is that Japanese (and the Chinese) have become a prosperous middle-class group. They now send twice as large a proportion of their children to college as do whites. Have twice as large a proportion of professional persons. Having solved the class problem, we solved the color problem. One of the reasons it was possible to do the former is that Japanese and Chinese have probably the most close knit family structure of any group in America.[392]

Proper family structure led to class mobility, which in turn led to overcoming racial discrimination. In other words, it was not racial discrimination that made Black people persistently poor—they, too, could do an end run around racial discrimination and prosper, if only they had the right (i.e., heteronormative, patriarchal) family structure.[393] Structural anti-Blackness and the Asian–Black gap were disavowed, and Asian Americans were presented as a group that suffered "the worst kind of racial discrimination" and succeeded anyhow.

Moynihan continued his reflections on Asian Americans at a conference on "the Negro American" in 1965, sponsored by *Daedalus* and the American Academy of Arts and Sciences. When one of his interlocutors, Mr. Berry, mentioned the stigma placed upon Black people, Moynihan responded:

[T]here may be something that we can learn from a nonwhite group—it is right before our eyes and is really rather astonishing—along the lines of the strategy we discussed of making the stigma dysfunctional and perhaps finding that the problem of color disappears. I think it can be done in this country much more readily than we think—and I did not come here to be optimistic. I had been vaguely aware of this but had never thought much about it. I ran into it simply in trying to correct the "nonwhite" figure, which we use in the Labor Department, to produce the Negro figure. There is a racism in our statistics: A person is white; or there is something he does not have, and then he is nonwhite. That is how we divide everybody. But that nonwhite group contains one group of people whom, it seems to me, we should know more about than we do. I think it has to be said

---

[392] Wu 2014, 171.

[393] In 1970, Japanese Americans had a median education of 12.5 years, as compared with 12.2 years for whites and 9.9 years for Black people. Ten percent of the total U.S. population were professionals; nineteen percent of Japanese Americans were professionals. The median Japanese American family income was almost $3,000 higher than the median white family income (Murray 2008, 191).

that no ethnic group in this country has ever been the subject of as much formal, federal, racist oppression as the Chinese or Japanese.[394]

The fallacy of minority equivalence—that Asian Americans were treated comparably to (or even worse than) Black people—is the unsubstantiated premise of Moynihan's comments. He continued:

One fascinating thing is that the proportion of Chinese and Japanese with no education—zero years—is ten times the proportion of white people with no education. And that exact same set of people, in the exact same year, had more than twice the proportion of their population in college or graduate school as had whites, had twice the proportion of their population employed in professional capacities as had whites, and had more than twice the proportion of their population employed in managerial or proprietary positions as had whites. As a matter of fact, we in Washington have thought how useful it would be in this country if we broke down our statistics and reminded ourselves now and then that there is a group that is not Caucasian that is twice as smart and twice as successful. The Japanese and Chinese have one-half the unemployment rate of the whites. They have one-half the marriage-dissolution rate, divorce rate, broken-family rate of the whites. I do not know what the truth is, but I have the impression that twenty-five years ago these people were colored. They were so colored that they were a race apart, and when World War II started, for example, we put the Japanese behind barbed wire. Those who protested were not heard because they were, after all, colored people. Twenty-five years later, it seems to me, they are not colored anymore, except in terms of our census data. Am I wrong that they have ceased to be colored? They are Japanese; but if daughter brings home a Japanese, father is more likely to see the high energy physicist than the Japanese. In any event, I think that having solved the class problem, we have solved a color problem.[395]

Again, economic advancement has the power to nullify racial discrimination, transforming "colored" people into those who have "ceased to be colored."

At this point, Moynihan's interlocutors joined in:

MR. GEERTZ: It is just as easy to argue that they [Asian Americans] never had the stigma [that was imposed on Black people], despite the formal oppression.
MR. HUGHES: The statistics that Mr. Moynihan speaks of—the number of Japanese children in college, their unemployment, and all the other things—would have been essentially the case in 1920.
MR. MOYNIHAN: I do not see how that could be.

---

[394] *Transcript of the American Academy Conference on the Negro American: May 14–15, 1965, 1966, 342.*
[395] *Transcript of the American Academy Conference on the Negro American: May 14–15, 1965, 1966, 343.*

MR. HUGHES: It was, though. I know because I happened to have been interested in the Orientals in the twenties. Their marriages were not broken up. They were in business. There was a stigma, but they were in college just the same. And they were not in juvenile court.

MR. HANDLIN: Yes, but the stigma was there. The resistance to intermarriage was strong. The barriers to social contact were formidable.

UNIDENTIFIED: They were different, though.

MR. PETTIGREW: The Chinese and Japanese were never slaves.

MR. GEERTZ: That is right. It is not the same.[396]

Moynihan's interlocutors were inclined to think that Asian Americans had always had it better than Black people, not least because they were never slaves. Yet he dismisses such observations out of hand.

A few moments later, another interlocutor, Mr. Wilson, returned to Moynihan's argument:

I would like to return to our friends the Chinese and Japanese, whom Mr. Moynihan so auspiciously threw in. I suppose I return to them because I was raised in California where the Chinese and Japanese were *the* colored minority, in sufficient numbers and concentration in San Francisco and in Los Angeles, where I lived, that color bias and oppression were directed at them. There were no Negroes at that time .... The discrimination was rigid. It was sanctified by law .... [The Chinese and Japanese] were excluded from almost all aspects of life: economic, political, and social .... Now, after only one or two generations, while there are undoubtedly traces of discrimination, Chinese and Japanese move about with almost complete freedom in California. Things have even gone to the absurd point that in California last year, when the state put on the ballot a proposition that would make open-occupancy ordinances unconstitutional, some Chinese and Japanese voted for it. They did not want "colored" people—that is, Negroes—moving into their neighborhoods. This is an enormous change in one generation. It seems to me that if we had begun to analyze the problem a couple of years ago in terms of *stigma* (whatever this means), we would not have been able to predict this outcome. I do not think that the concept *stigma*, left undefined, is very helpful. What we are talking about here are *behaviors* .... It seems to me that, when we talk about the stigma of the Negro, it is easy to make references to slavery, 300 years, Africa, or color. But it seems to me it is more appropriate now to talk about behaviors and how much these behaviors differ in one group that is "colored" from those in another group that is "colored."[397]

Asian Americans had risen from the bottom on their own efforts and were now displaying their own phobic avoidance toward Blackness—a sure

[396] *Transcript of the American Academy Conference on the Negro American: May 14–15, 1965*, 1966, 343.

[397] *Transcript of the American Academy Conference on the Negro American: May 14–15, 1965*, 1966, 346. Italics in original.

sign of having arrived. Their success showed that even "colored" groups could make it in the U.S. if they acted properly, which meant that all of the talk about "slavery, 300 years, Africa" was but a distraction. As in the citation of *Yick Wo* in *Plessy*, as in the "rehabilitation" of Japanese Americans during and after the war, as in the Sheng housing case in Cold War San Francisco, whites called Asian Americans to stand in for Black people as part of the ongoing disavowal and reproduction of structural anti-Blackness.

Other writings from this period figured Asian Americans in much the same way. Ronald Haak's article "Co-opting the Oppressors: The Case of the Japanese-Americans" (1970) opened with a question: "The oppressed minority, against overwhelming odds and with little hope their efforts would do them any good, induced the white majority to erase the stigmata. How did it happen?" Noting that Japanese Americans were respected and yet held down before the war, Haak, channeling the War Relocation Authority, credited their "wartime record of camp cooperation and combat valor" with "finally [breaking] down the accusations against [them]."[398] He wrote:

What helped them [Japanese Americans] most in the long run was the way they chose to earn recognition by performance, rather than by claiming it on principle. They steered clear of demands for radical revisions in the national power structure, in the distribution of wealth, in the ethnic composition of political and policy-making bodies. They simply worked and endured until their performance overwhelmed, without contentiousness, society's negative definitions of their worth.[399]

Rather than demanding recognition, Japanese Americans earned it by performing so well that whites had no choice but to grant it to them. This argument is strongly reminiscent of Mike Masaoka's "Japanese American Creed." As in Masaoka's piece, the barely absent referent, the essential counterpoint to Japanese American virtue, is obstreperous, voracious Blackness.

In *Japanese Americans: Oppression and Success* (1971), William Petersen wrote: "Asked which of America's ethnic minorities has been subjected to the most discrimination, the worst injustices, few persons would even think to answer, 'The Japanese Americans.' Yet if the question refers to those now alive, that is the correct response." Citing a constitutional law expert, Petersen claimed that internment involved the

---

[398] Haak 1970, 24, 25.
[399] Haak 1970, 30–31.

"most drastic invasion of the rights of citizens of the United States by their own government that has thus far occurred in the history of our nation."[400] Then, commenting on the intergenerational problems afflicting "problem minorities," he observed:

[S]ince Negroes constitute the country's largest and most visible racial minority, the pessimistic conclusions derived from their history have been generalized into a theory of race relations .... [Yet] the Japanese case constitutes the outstanding exception to the generalization that past oppression blocks present progress. By almost any criterion of good citizenship that we choose, not only are Japanese Americans better than any other segment of American society, including native whites of native parents, but they have realized this remarkable progress by their own almost unaided effort. In the early years they got some support from Japan's consuls; but this assistance, seldom very effective in any case, became of more and more questionable value as Japanese Americans increasingly recognized that their fate, whatever it might be, was tied to that of the United States. In their new homeland, they were neither the hapless beneficiaries of social welfare nor the cause of militant placard-bearers. Out of the elements of American democracy—universal education, the free labor market, citizenship for all native-born residents, color-blind justice—to the sometimes slight degree that these were available to them, the Japanese themselves fashioned their identity as the nation's prize sub-nation .... Every attempt to hamper the progress of Japanese Americans, in short, has resulted only in enhancing their determination to succeed. Even in a country whose patron saint is Horatio Alger's hero, there is no parallel to this success story.[401]

Despite seeing "substantial improvements" in the last two decades, Black people were, according to Petersen, "aggressively dissatisfied that they ha[d] not yet achieved full equality with whites." Civil rights reforms had only made matters worse by "exacerbat[ing] racial conflict" and "encourag[ing] the rise of black violence and white backlash."[402] In this chaotic context, Asian Americans provided decisive proof that state intervention was not the answer. *Black people had to stop protesting and pull themselves up, like everyone else.*

According to the standard Asian Americanist critique of such discourse, Haak, Petersen and their ilk are peddling the "model minority myth," which exaggerates how well Asian Americans are doing in order to use them as a wedge against Black people. However, as mentioned before, this critique overlooks what is really going on: how Asian Americans are given the boon of not-Blackness and thus allowed certain

---

[400] Petersen 1971, 3, 6.
[401] Petersen 1971, 4–5.
[402] Petersen 1971, 218.

kinds of mobility denied to Black people, and how this structural favoritism is then disavowed so that Asian Americans can be weaponized to alibi the system and discredit the Black freedom struggle. Insisting that "Asian Americans are bona fide minorities, too"—as many Asian Americanists do—is counterproductive because it actually recapitulates the fallacy of minority equivalence that weaponization depends upon. What we need is an analysis that recognizes that Asian Americans are always already positioned above and against Black people, and that the favoritism toward Asian Americans as the lesser of two evils is not just a fleeting *discursive* event but also a centuries-old *structural* feature of this anti-Black order.

As mentioned above, Japanese racial discourse was notably anti-Black by the postwar period, and Japanese immigrants to the U.S. thus met anti-Blackness coming and going. We should not be surprised that a kind of ideological convergence emerged between white narratives about Japanese Americans and the latter's narratives about themselves. The story of Japanese Americans as a model minority who transcended Blackness was *co-fashioned*, as it were.[403] Without losing sight of the disparate power of the two parties, it is important to consider the ways in which some *Nisei*, including prominent figures, responded to the incentives and pressures of the anti-Black order by cultivating their not-Blackness as an identity and property right.

In his article "Rhetorics over Racial Discrimination," (*Pacific Citizen*, November 10, 1961), Clifford Uyeda, president of the JACL's San Francisco chapter, responded to a speech in which JACL national president Frank Chuman had urged Japanese Americans to be morally consistent and fight against anti-Black discrimination, too:

Two obstacles, one intellectual and one emotional, seem to lie between complete identification with the problems of Negro minority. [First] [t]hat Negroes are discriminated against because of their race, and that their excessive crime rate is attributable to their sense of uselessness and hopelessness which was inevitably bred in their poor socio-economic status are statements that do not make complete sense. The *Nisei* cannot help but recall that our parents faced social and economic discriminations far more severe than do most of the present day Negroes in the United States. On top of this, they were foreigners, barred from U.S. citizenship and reminded of this in no uncertain terms .... [Second] because of the high crime rate among Negroes, the *Issei* and *Nisei* became frequent victims.

---

[403] There were dissenting Asian American voices, particularly among leftists, in every era. However, as far as I can ascertain, these were in the minority.

Uyeda continued:

The present day trend seems to be for equality through legislation—a fine thing, but a more dedicated effort toward deserving this equality through self-improvement seems to have become secondary. A large segment of the Negro community is conscientiously striving to improve the status of their people. But aside from the general public education on the problems of minority groups, the re-education of the minority groups themselves toward better citizenship will go a long way toward decreasing minority discrimination .... Better housing is desirable but this does not automatically bring about improvement in character or conduct.[404]

Japanese Americans succeeded even though they were more discriminated against than Black people and were noncitizens to boot. On top of this, they were victimized by Black criminals. Civil rights and fair housing were all well and good, but Black people would do better to focus on improving their own "character or conduct" rather then playing the victim. *Nisei* leaders like Uyeda could not conceal their pride at having supposedly bested Black people in the competition of life. When the JACL ran a national, multigenerational survey of Japanese Americans from 1964 to 1967 as part of the Japanese American Research Project, it included this question: "Negroes are interested in bettering their position in American society. What advice would you give Negroes, as a race, to achieve their goals?"[405]

Two years after Uyeda's piece came out, *Nisei* journalist Howard Imazeki published "To Our Negro Neighbor, This Is Our Voice" (June 29, 1963) in the San Francisco-based, Japanese-language newspaper *Hokubei Mainichi*. He wrote:

We have had the pleasure of meeting some outstanding Negro leaders. We are sad to confess, however, that we have had more occasions to come in contact with lesser Negroes, who make a great number of our people afraid to come out to Nihonmachi [the Japanese quarter] at night. Some of our respected Negro leaders, too, often present themselves as being small. They will tell you the reason that there is a large number of crimes being committed by the Negroes is because the colored people are not equally treated. They will tell you that the reason there are more Negro dropouts from high schools is because the colored children are not given an opportunity to follow the kind of work they want after graduation. They blame society for their womanfolks giving birth to illegitimate children and living on welfare checks. They blame society for the petty thefts and rapes being perpetrated by their manfolks in Nihonmachi. In short, they blame all of their antisocial habits and cultural maladjustment on the "unjust" community in

[404] Uyeda 1961, 2.
[405] Wu 2014, 174.

which they live. We have yet to hear any Negro voice "blaming" themselves for their social maladjustment. We once told a prominent San Francisco Negro leader at a NAACP gathering that one doesn't have to have a penny in his pocket to check himself from stealing or raping a woman, for that was what he had implied in his chip-on-the-shoulderish defense of Negro misbehavior. What we are trying to say most sincerely is that the Negro community leaders should do a little soulsearching of their own today and see if their backyards couldn't be tidied up a bit, find if their children couldn't be given a little more community push and encouragement for education, and examine if there is not one rock too many on their shoulders needlessly. From the looks of the Negro papers in San Francisco there is an apparent lack of this sort of leadership, this sort of self-reflection.[406]

The piece attracted a good deal of interest, both positive and negative. Clifford Uyeda, in "This Is Our Voice," hastened to concur with Imazeki, urging Black people to demonstrate good citizenship and allegiance to the nation, as Japanese Americans did.[407] But Bill and Yuri Kochiyama, two prominent Japanese American leftists involved in both the Asian American movement and the Black liberation struggle, denounced the piece, observing that there was no comparison between the wartime internment of Japanese Americans and 300 years of slavery and its aftermath.[408] On July 24, 1963, less than a month after the piece was published, U.S. Representative Joe Waggoner Jr., a Louisiana segregationist, read it into the *Congressional Record* as part of his argument against pending civil rights legislation:

Mr. Speaker, as I have said many times before and as many others have echoed the statement, the civil rights proposals which have been sent to us by the administration are not, as some would have us believe, concerned with the so-called rights of the minorities, but are concerned solely with giving one minority, the Negro, special and preferential treatment. That this is true has not escaped the attention of another minority group in this country, the Japanese-Americans. The Japanese American newspaper *Hokubei Mainichi* of San Francisco had some telling words for the Negroes in an editorial when they advised the Negro to "do a little soul searching." Because they too are a minority group, their words are worth a thousand of many others who have spoken on this subject. I commend the article to the attention of all my colleagues.[409]

As whites continued to weaponize Asian Americans against the Black freedom struggle, they could rely on the fact that some *Nisei* were intent on weaponizing themselves.

[406] Imazeki 1963, n.p.
[407] Uyeda 1963, 3.
[408] Robinson 2012a.
[409] Masaoka 1963, 2.

Greg Robinson noted that *Nisei* "remained largely aloof from the black freedom struggle as it developed in the years after Brown."[410] Some Japanese Americans supported the civil rights movement, including Larry Tajiri, who wrote and ran numerous sympathetic stories and editorials in the *Pacific Citizen*. "However, these positive statements were largely overshadowed by a number of more hostile remarks," Robinson observed. Furthermore, the Imazeki article, as Bill and Yuri Kochiyama observed at the time, "may [have been] representative of the thinking of many *Nisei* in California and across the country."[411] In 1963, the JACL had an internal debate over whether to send representatives to the March on Washington organized by Martin Luther King Jr. and colleagues. Mike Masaoka thought they should, but officials from local chapters disagreed, arguing that the civil rights issue was controversial, that it alienated white allies, and that it was not their (the *Nisei*'s) fight, in any case. The JACL decided not to participate in the march as an organization, although individual members were permitted to attend. Japanese American academic Daniel Okimoto remarked drily: "The *Nisei* community is in little danger of winning medals for social crusading on behalf of those outside its circle."[412]

Japanese immigrants were positioned as Asiatics in the U.S. racial order from their first arrival in the late nineteenth century, dynamically constituted at the juncture between white supremacy and anti-Blackness. Across the vicissitudes of their historical experience—they were tolerated at first, then persecuted and interned, and then "rehabilitated" and mostly accepted—they always remained not-white but above all not-Black. Even at the nadir of their historical trajectory, wartime internment, not-Blackness was a boon that mitigated their plight. And it was not-Blackness that won them a starring role in the U.S. state's performances of anti-racism during and after the war, wherein Japanese American (re-)entry into the society and polity was staged as a paean to the nation and a rebuke to the Black struggle. Then, in the late 1960s, young Americans of Asian descent, including Japanese Americans, changed the course of history by forming a movement that denounced white supremacy and called for solidarity with other communities of color. This is the subject of Part Three.

[410] Robinson 2012a, 224.
[411] Robinson 2012a, 226, 229.
[412] Robinson 2012a, 239.

Part Three

Solidarity/Disavowal

I INTRODUCTION

The Asian American movement of the 1960s and 1970s is conventionally narrated as a historic moment when activists forged an Asian American subjectivity and politics for the first time. The movement not only brought multiple Asian national origin groups together under a single panethnic rubric, but also redefined their relation to the Black freedom struggle. Emulating the Black Power movement, and the Black Panther Party in particular, Asian American activists rejected assimilation, embraced their Asian heritage, and declared themselves part of the Third World United Front—alongside Black, Chicano, and Indigenous peoples—against global white supremacy and imperialism. To this day, Asian American thinkers and activists invoke the Asian American movement nostalgically as a highpoint of radical, cross-racial alliance building and an example of what Asian Americans' politics once were and could be again.

Bringing structural anti-Blackness back into the picture, however, casts these events in a new light. What becomes clear is that most Asian American activists did not engage the concept or reality of anti-Blackness to any meaningful extent. Alongside other Third World United Front groups, they co-produced a keen analysis of white supremacy, but they did not theorize the *other* force that shapes the racial order by abjecting Black people and lifting up all others.[1] They emphasized the subordination of all not-white groups but overlooked the unevenness of their statuses relative to one another. What came out of the movement, then, was *an indictment of white supremacy coupled with a silence about anti-Blackness*—a half-finished critique, in other words. The constitutive not-Blackness of Asian Americans remained unthought and unspoken.

To be clear, the other not-white, not-Black groups mobilizing during this period—including Puerto Ricans, Chicanos, and American Indians—were also silent about anti-Blackness. Fanon's *Black Skin, White Masks* had just been published in 1952 and translated into English in 1967. The Black Panther Party itself did not theorize anti-Blackness per se, although it did center the oppression of Black people in its political analysis. Scholarly articulations of the concept of anti-Blackness, moreover, were decades in the future. My point in Part Three, therefore, is not to blame Asian American activists and thinkers for not being ahead of their time, but rather to think through, retrospectively, the ways in which their political critique was incomplete and how this incompleteness generates an ethical and interpretive crisis in Asian American thought and politics that remains unresolved to this day.

Lacking a cogent critique of anti-Blackness, Asian Americans have trouble responding effectively to urgent events within their own communities. When Korean immigrant storeowners claimed they were scapegoated by whites and Black people alike in the Los Angeles uprising of 1992, many liberal and progressive Asian Americans knew there

---

[1] Susan Koshy writes: "Based on an implicit construct of *parallel minoritization* rather than *stratified minoritization*, the racial politics of the sixties challenged white supremacy by positing the opposition between white and nonwhite positionality and strategically deferred theorizing the relationship between racial minorities outside this framework" (2001, 155). Italics in original.

was more to the story but failed to provide a plausible counternarrative. When conservative Chinese immigrant professionals joined forces with conservative whites and in the attack on race-conscious admissions, beginning in the 1990s, liberal and progressive Asian Americans objected but could not define a compelling alternative position. When NYPD officer Peter Liang killed Akai Gurley in 2014, and when Minneapolis officer Tou Thao participated in the murder of George Floyd in 2020, many liberal and progressive Asian Americanists were again at a loss. In each instance, events on the ground gave the lie to the notion of Third World unity and raised troubling questions about Asian American investments in the regimes of private property and carcerality that subtend structural anti-Blackness. In each instance, Asian Americans across the political spectrum failed to recognize their own not-Blackness, which meant they could not effectively analyze or critique the dynamics at hand.

In addition, Asian Americans sometimes pursue a go-it-alone political approach that ignores and therefore tends to reinforce structural anti-Blackness. When they request specific anti-discrimination measures tailored to their circumstances, they offer the U.S. state another opportunity to grant remedies to Asian Americans instead of granting them to Black people—*so that* it does not have to grant them to Black people. *Better Asians than Blacks.* Staging anti-racism efforts on behalf of Asian Americans provides the state some cover from Black critique, with the added bonus of devaluing Blackness relative to Asian Americanness. We can see this with the passage of two pieces of legislation widely hailed as victories for Asian Americans—the Civil Liberties Act of 1988 (granting Japanese Americans reparations for internment) and the COVID-19 Hate Crimes Act of 2021 (condemning "hate crimes" against Asian Americans and dedicating resources to law enforcement solutions). Both statutes commanded significant support from white conservatives. Both granted Asian Americans a kind of recognition being withheld from Black people. All of which is to say, the phobic hatred of Blackness continues to fuel the advancement of Asian Americans, who provide an alibi to the U.S. state in exchange for mobility.[2]

---

[2] It is important to emphasize that this is a structural situation where a group designated as not-white but above all not-Black is powerfully induced to go along with whites in maintaining and reproducing anti-Blackness. Asian Americans are not the only group put in this position, and there is nothing about them as Asian Americans per se that makes them more likely than anyone else to follow these inducements. In other words, what Part Three describes is not, for the most part, a failure of integrity on the part of individual Asian Americans as much as a set of structural arrangements in which not-Black groups are strongly encouraged to play along with and refrain from challenging the imperatives of an anti-Black order.

In Jordan Peele's 2017 film *Get Out*, the one Asian American character is an unnamed man of Japanese descent played by Hiroki Tanaka. He is an invited guest at the cocktail party the Armitages throw in honor of Chris's visit. During the party he approaches Chris and asks if being African American is "an advantage or a disadvantage." (This is his only line in the film.) Shortly thereafter, Tanaka's character sits among the white guests at what turns out to be a modern-day slave auction, where he, along with the others, places a bid on Chris's body. What does it mean for an Asian American man to ask this question of a Black man moments before trying to appropriate his body by force? One possible interpretation is that the Asian American man is disavowing his own structural advantage, his not-Blackness, even as he is enacting it. He pretends not to know that being Black is a disadvantage even as he prepares to bid on a Black man's body at the auction. In other words, he asks the question in bad faith, not so much seeking an answer as taking the opportunity to dissemble his own racial status to Chris and to himself. What Peele gestures toward, unforgettably, is Asian American implicatedness in an anti-Black world. Which again raises the question: What kind of ethical crisis does structural anti-Blackness generate for Asian Americans? And what are the possibilities for how they might address it?

II THE BLACK PANTHERS AND CARCERALITY

According to Loïc Wacquant, the urban ghetto that emerged in the twentieth-century U.S. is a "peculiar institution" that is genealogically and functionally linked to two predecessors, slavery and Jim Crow. All three institutions served the dual purpose of "labor extraction and social ostracization," functioning "to recruit, organize, and extract labor out of African Americans ... and to demarcate and ultimately seclude them so that they would not 'contaminate' the surrounding white society."[3] The fourth and final "peculiar institution," Wacquant continues, is prison in the era of mass incarceration. When the shift from manufacturing to the service sector produced surplus Black labor and the urban rebellions of the 1960s showed the incapacity of the ghetto to contain the Black threat, the prison emerged as a solution to both developments.[4] It did

---

[3] Wacquant 2001, 99.
[4] Jordan Camp (2016) argues that the dialectical confrontation between Black protest and state repression has been an important driver of the shift toward mass incarceration, with Black critique in the form of urban and prison revolts creating political legitimacy crises which the state responds to by doubling down on carcerality.

not replace the urban ghetto but rather formed a "deadly symbiosis" with it, such that the ghetto and prison make up "a single *carceral continuum* which entraps a redundant population of younger black men (and increasingly women) who circulate in a closed circuit between its two poles in a self-perpetuating cycle of social and legal marginality with devastating personal and social consequences."[5]

Members of the Black Panther Party, formed in Oakland in 1966 by Huey Newton and Bobby Seale, were familiar with this closed circuit between the ghetto and the prison. From the armed patrols that monitored police conduct to the numerous campaigns on behalf of political prisoners, the Panthers kept the carceral system in their sights. The Free Huey campaign that grew out of Huey Newton's encounter with police in October 1967 transformed the organization into a recognizable brand, boosting fundraising and coalition building and raising Newton's stature. With a steady stream of stories about police violence, trials, and fugitives, the Black Panther Party newspaper suggested an endless war with the carceral state. Indeed the first draft of the Panthers' Ten Point Platform, circulated in 1967, put carceral reform at the center of the discussion: Point 7 called for an end to police brutality and the murder of Black people; Point 8 called for freedom for all Black men in jails and prisons; and Point 9 affirmed the right to a trial by a jury of one's peers.

For the Black Panthers, calling the police an occupying army was more than a metaphor. Following the Revolutionary Action Movement, they theorized the ghetto as an internal colony created and maintained by the violence of the U.S. state. By this view, the patrol car in the Oakland ghetto was part and parcel of the racial and economic violence that U.S. imperialists inflicted upon Third World peoples all over the globe in the search for power and profits. Embracing a revolutionary nationalism informed by Marx, Lenin, and Mao, the Black Panthers understood themselves as part of a global anti-capitalist, anti-fascist, anti-imperialist alliance. This is captured in Emory Douglas's image of a pig labelled "U.S. Imperialist" being strangled by four hands labelled "Get Out of the Ghetto," "Get Out of Africa," "Get Out of Asia," and "Get Out of Latin America."[6]

Like earlier radical Black internationalists, the Black Panthers thought racial oppression nullified Black people's obligations to the U.S. state, rendering them effectively stateless. Point 10 of the Ten Point Platform,

---

[5] Wacquant 2002, 52–53. Italics in original.
[6] *The Black Panther*, January 4, 1969, 9. https://collections.vam.ac.uk/item/O102220/get-out-of-the-ghetto-poster-douglas-emory.

which included a quotation from the Declaration of Independence, expressed their rejection of U.S. political authority. Governments were created to secure inalienable rights, they wrote, and

[w]henever any form of government becomes destructive of these ends, it is the right of people to alter or to abolish it, and to institute new government, laying its foundation on such principles and organizing its powers in such form as to them shall seem most likely to effect their safety and happiness.[7]

Born in a revolution against tyranny, the U.S. had become a tyrannical power itself, and it was now being called to account by a new kind of revolutionary. As bearers of a world-historical tradition of freedom fighting, the Black Panthers took their case to a higher political authority. In addition to calling for a United Nations-supervised plebiscite "in which only black colonial subjects will be allowed to participate for the purpose of determining the will of black people as to their national destiny,"[8] they submitted a petition to the U.N. in 1973, in which they condemned the U.S. for "flagrantly violat[ing]" the Genocide Convention, called on the U.N. Human Rights Commission to sanction the U.S., and demanded that the U.S. make reparations for its "racist and genocidal practices."[9]

The Black Panthers forcefully opposed the Vietnam War as a racist and imperialist venture. They were especially critical of the racially disparate impact of the U.S. military draft. Point 6 of the Ten Point Platform stated:

We believe that Black people should not be forced to fight in the military service to defend a racist government that does not protect us. We will not fight and kill other people of color in the world who, like Black people, are being victimized by the White racist government of America. We will protect ourselves from the force and violence of the racist police and the racist military, by whatever means necessary.[10]

In a similar vein, an image from the Black Panther Party newspaper shows a Black soldier affirming that his true comrade is the humble Vietnamese peasant, not the white American soldier-capitalist pig lying face down in a pool of his own blood. Like Cyril Briggs decades earlier, the Black Panthers resisted the ruse of nationality and recognized that it was rather race and class that defined friend and foe.

The Black Panthers walked a tightrope between emphasizing the specificity of the status of Black people and embracing the Third World

---

[7] Bloom and Martin 2013, 72. Italics in original.
[8] This was Point 10 of the platform as of May 1968; it was later removed.
[9] Martin and Yaquinto 2007, 606–607.
[10] Bloom and Martin 2013, 72.

solidarity that flowed from their anti-capitalist and anti-imperialist com-mitments. (It is worth noting that their alliances with not-Black groups put them at odds with many other Black Power groups.) Black people were clearly centered in the party's thought and practice, but if the dis-tinctive position of Blackness was everywhere implied, it was nowhere explicitly theorized. Thus the Black Panthers did not name structural anti-Blackness or analyze how other not-white groups are weaponized against the Black struggle. Successive iterations of the Ten Point Platform showed their attempts to finesse these issues. As Laura Pulido notes, the 1972 version of this document included new language such as "our Black and oppressed communities" and "people of color" for the first time.[11] Point 3, which had previously been changed from "We want an end to the robbery by the white man of our Black community" to "We want an end to the robbery by the capitalist of our Black community," was now "We want an end to the robbery by the capitalist of our Black and oppressed communities." At the same time, though, Point 3 discussed "40 acres and 2 mules" as "restitution for slave labor and mass murder of Black people," with no mention of other groups of color.

Consider, too, "In Defense of Self-Defense: Executive Mandate Number One," a speech written by Huey Newton and delivered by Bobby Seale in Sacramento on May 2, 1967:

The Black Panther Party for Self-Defense calls upon the American people in general and the Black people in particular to take careful note of the racist California Legis-lature, which is now considering legislation aimed at keeping the Black people dis-armed and powerless at the very same time that racist police agencies throughout the country are intensifying the terror, brutality, murder and repression of Black people. At the same time that the American government is waging a racist war of genocide in Vietnam, the concentration camps in which Japanese Americans were interned during World War II are being renovated and expanded. Since America has historically reserved the most barbaric treatment for nonwhite people, we are forced to conclude that these concentration camps are being prepared for Black people, who are determined to gain their freedom by any means necessary. The enslavement of Black people from the very beginning of this country, the genocide practiced on the American Indians and the confining of the survivors on reserva-tions, the savage lynching of thousands of Black men and women, the dropping of atomic bombs on Hiroshima and Nagasaki, and now the cowardly massacre in Vietnam, all testify to the fact that towards people of the color the racist power structure of America has but one policy: repression, genocide, terror, and the big stick. Black people have begged, prayed, petitioned, demonstrated and everything else to get the racist power structure of America to right the wrongs which have

[11] Pulido 2006.

historically been perpetrated against Black people .... The Black Panther Party for Self-Defense believes that the time has come for Black people to arm themselves against this terror before it is too late .... A people who have suffered so much for so long at the hands of a racist society, must draw the line somewhere. We believe that the Black communities of America must rise up as one man to halt the progression of a trend that leads inevitably to their total destruction.[12]

Linking the oppression of Black people to that of other not-white groups, the Panthers at the same time suggested the unique status of Black people and their special role in revolutionary politics. Note that with the exception of internment, the Asians mentioned are victims of U.S. militarism and imperialism abroad. If Asian Americans stood in an ambiguous relation to the U.S. state, Asian communist nations (China, Vietnam, and North Korea) did not.

In August 1967, the FBI launched a new offensive against what they called "black hate groups," a category that included organizations as varied as the Student Nonviolent Coordinating Committee, the Nation of Islam, Revolutionary Action Movement, and the Southern Christian Leadership Conference. The following year, the House Un-American Activities Committee published a report that accused the Soviet empire of stoking Black discontent and fanning the flames of Black nationalism in the U.S.[13] Once again, U.S. intelligence agencies conjoined the threats of communism and Blackness, denouncing Black activists as Bolshevik pawns and justifying their repression as a national security imperative. FBI COINTELPROs, or counterintelligence programs, which had emerged in the 1950s as an instrument against leftists, were retooled in the 1960s as an instrument against the Black struggle. According to an internal FBI memo from 1968, COINTELPROs sought to prevent Black Power activists from forming coalitions, to discredit them in the eyes of the public, and to thwart the emergence of a Black "Messiah."[14] FBI Director J. Edgar Hoover announced in July 1969 that "the Black Panther Party, without question, represents the greatest threat to the internal security of the country."[15] Of the 295 COINTELPRO initiatives undertaken to destabilize Black nationalist organizations during this period, 233 of them (79 percent) targeted the Black Panthers.[16]

---

[12] Foner 1995, 40–41.
[13] Plummer 2012.
[14] Camp 2016; Rhodes 2017.
[15] The source here is an *Oakland Tribune* article, dated July 15, 1969, quoted in Bloom and Martin 2013, 3.
[16] Bloom and Martin 2013, 210.

In the fall of 1968, the FBI, working closely with the Chicago Police Department, set up a COINTELPRO targeting the Chicago chapter of the Black Panther Party. They recruited William O'Neal from prison to infiltrate the chapter and act as an informant. O'Neal, who became chief of security for the chapter, provided the FBI and CPD with information about which weapons the Panthers had, who was coming and going in the apartment of Fred Hampton, the head of the chapter, and the exact layout of the apartment, including the location of Hampton's bed and nightstand. At 4:30 a.m. on December 4, 1968, fourteen officers of the Cook County Special Prosecutions Unit burst into Hampton's apartment, guns blazing. Joshua Bloom and Waldo Martin wrote: "They did not bring the standard raiding equipment they had used in previous Chicago Panther raids, such as tear gas or sound equipment; instead, they carried a Thompson submachine gun, five shotguns, a carbine, nineteen .38 caliber pistols, and one .357 caliber pistol."[17] Fred Hampton, drugged with secobarbital, possibly by O'Neal, was shot twice through the head as he lay in bed; Mark Clark, another Panther, was also killed, and four others were wounded. The FBI paid O'Neal a $300 bonus for his efforts.[18]

The FBI and CPD claimed they had killed the Panthers in a shoot out, but "[m]ost of the rooms and walls appeared to be free of scars, pockmarks, and bullet holes. There were clusters of bullet holes and the gouges of shotgun blasts in the places where the Panthers said the two men had been killed and four others had been wounded .... There were no bullet marks in the area of the two doors through which the police said they entered."[19] In May 1970, a special federal grand jury investigating the raid found that law enforcement had "grossly exaggerated" Panther resistance in the incident, that at least eighty-two shots had been fired into the apartment, that only was shot was fired from inside, that the police lab made "serious and repeated errors" with the evidence, and that the Chicago Police Department internal inquiry was "so seriously deficient that it suggests purposeful malfeasance."[20]

To create "Fred Hampton's Door 2" (1975), Black activist and artist Dana Chandler took a door he found in an empty lot, painted it red and

---

[17] Bloom and Martin 2013, 238.
[18] Bloom and Martin 2013.
[19] The source here is a *New York Times* article, dated December 6, 1969, quoted in Bloom and Martin 2013, 239.
[20] Quoted in Rhodes 2017, 292. In May 1970, all charges were dropped against the seven surviving Panthers, as there was no proof they had fired at police. The state paid the estates of Hampton, Clark, and survivors $1.8 million to settle the case.

green, attached it to a black base (the three colors of the Pan-African flag), shot multiple bullet holes in it, and splattered it with red paint.[21] In addition, he wrote "FRED HAMPTON Chairman Black Panther Party" where the mail slot should have been and placed a red, white, and blue stamp saying "U.S. APPROVED" on the upper right quadrant. Why did Chandler choose to tell Hampton's story with a door? The best-known images of the murderous raid on Hampton's apartment came from photographs of the after-scene inside the apartment, including the blood-soaked mattress where Hampton's body had lain. In an interview, Chandler remarked: "[S]ometimes you create symbols of things as opposed to imagery that speaks realistically to things. And these officers had the audacity to blow the door open. An image of his body would be one of hundreds, of thousands of images of dead Black bodies."[22] Like Kerry James Marshall's "Heirlooms and Accessories" (discussed in Part One), Chandler's art refuses to show more violated Black bodies. The bullet-pocked door stands in for the body but also denies the viewer the sight of the body, calling out the secret fascination with Black death and forcing the gaze instead to the violence that causes it.

Doors were key to law enforcement's coverup. The FBI and CPD claimed that the Black Panthers had shot at the officers as they entered the front door, but the forensic evidence belied this claim. A CPD photograph shows Hampton's bloody, half-dressed body face down on the ground, sprawled across the threshold of the bedroom door.[23] After assassinating him, they dragged his corpse to the door threshold to conceal the fact that they shot him while he was in a drug-induced stupor in bed. The door, interface between outside and inside, carries contradictory meanings—threshold, confinement, protection, exclusion, escape. Fred Hampton's front door could not protect him from the police onslaught because the structural violence against Black people cannot be contained. There was a reason Hampton had predicted he would not die of old age. In an anti-Black order, the door to a Black home cannot hold.[24]

---

[21] Originally Dana Chandler created "Fred Hampton's Door" as a painting (of a door riddled with bullet holes) that was exhibited in a one-person show at Galerie Amadeus in Boston in October 1970. The painting was stolen from Expo '74 (the World's Fair) in Spokane in 1974 (Cook 2019). See "Fred Hampton's Door 2" at this link: https://wsimag.com/culture/68590-black-power-in-print.

[22] Chandler was speaking here of the painting "Fred Hampton's Door," but the point is pertinent to the second iteration as well (Cook 2019).

[23] Bloom and Martin 2013, fig. 31.

[24] Hampton's pregnant partner, Akua Njeri, survived the raid, but Hampton's ties to her and their unborn son were severed that night.

In another sense, though, Fred Hampton's door did hold, as Chandler's artwork attests. The police broke it down but all of their hardware and murderous intent could not stamp out the Black threat within and without. Hampton's apartment was cluttered with political posters, manifestos, flyers, pamphlets, and record albums. Frantz Fanon's *The Wretched of the Earth* and Malcolm X's *Autobiography* were among the items found. Sampada Aranke writes: "[T]he political life of the objects left for us ... alert us to the living and viable threat radical black practitioners pose to the sanctity of state power."[25] As Fred Hampton said, "You can kill a revolutionary but you can't kill the revolution." The door as threshold to the new and portal to the future.

III THE ASIAN AMERICAN MOVEMENT

Asian Americans came into being denouncing white supremacy and who they themselves had been under white supremacy. As campus and community groups rallied under the label "Asian American" in the late 1960s, they followed Stokely Carmichael's logic and said every Oriental is a potential Asian American.[26] If the Oriental was passive, compliant, assimilationist, and brainwashed into believing in white superiority, the Asian American was militant, fearless, proud of their Asian heritage, and committed to the struggle against white supremacy and imperialism. Asian Americanness was as much about embracing a certain kind of left, Third World politics as it was about being of Asian descent. Larry Kubota's article "Yellow Power!" (1969) declared that "Yellow Power [wa]s a call for all Asian Americans to end the silence that has condemned us to suffer in this racist society and to unite with our Black, Brown, and Red brothers of the Third World for survival, self-determination, and the creation of a more humanistic society."[27]

During the Third World Liberation Front's (TWLF) 1968 strike at San Francisco State College, Asian Americans joined other activists of color in a fight to establish ethnic studies. The TWLF strikers expressed support for George Murray, the Black Panther Party Minister of Education, who had been fired from his campus teaching job for political reasons. In this racially fraught context, the college appointed S. I. Hayakawa, a *Nisei* linguist and English professor, as interim president. Hayakawa had

---

[25] Aranke 2013, 131.
[26] Carmichael: "Every negro is a potential black man." (Marable 2015 [1983], 80)
[27] Kubota 1969, 4.

no prior administrative experience—he "had never served on important university committees or held an administrative post"[28]—and his main qualifications for the job seemed to be his minority status, his assimilationist fervor, and his outspoken opposition to the strike. In one speech he declared, "We [Asian Americans] are a colored race of non-whites—we've been through the same thing but we've been able to come through it better than the Negroes have."[29] Black people, he added, should emulate Asian Americans if they want to get ahead. After declaring a state of emergency on campus, Hayakawa sent police to break up protests, suspended student leaders, and threatened to suspend faculty who showed support for the strike. His right-wing commentary and fondness for the police made him a perfect Oriental foil for the emerging Asian American movement—not to mention a darling of white conservatives.[30]

Except for the tam-o'-shanter he favored, Hayawaka was not an anomaly. He represented a *Nisei* mindset that dated back at least to Mike Masaoka's "Japanese American Creed."[31] Many *Nisei* expressed fulsome support for his actions and comments as San Francisco State College president. *Hokubei Mainichi*, the newspaper where Howard Imazeki served as editor, named Hayakawa "*Nisei* of the Year" in 1968. The Community Interest Committee of Nihonmachi (CICN), organized and co-chaired by three former presidents of the Japanese American Citizens League (George Yamasaki, Clifford Uyeda, and Steven Doi), praised Hayakawa, and a pro-Hayakawa petition circulated by the *Nisei* Junior Chamber of Commerce was signed by Uyeda, Doi, Imazeki, and other *Nisei* leaders.[32] According to a spokesperson for the *Nisei* Junior Chamber of Commerce, 85 percent of the Japanese American community supported Hayakawa. While there was internal disagreement within the community, a "sizeable portion of San Francisco's Japanese American community stood behind Hayakawa."[33]

In *Chains of Babylon: The Rise of Asian America* (2009), Daryl Maeda praises Asian American activists for defying Hayakawa and charting a

---

[28] Maeda 2009, 58.

[29] Maeda 2009, 57.

[30] See Maeda 2009.

[31] See the discussion of this in Part Two.

[32] Maeda 2009.

[33] Maeda 2009, 62–63. Hayakawa later switched his affiliation to the Republican Party and was elected U.S. senator for California for one term (1977–1983). In that office, he urged the U.S. Supreme Court to rule in favor of Bakke in *Regents of the University of California* v. *Bakke* (1978) and opposed the passage of a reparations bill for Japanese Americans (Maeda 2009).

new path: "If in the period after World War II Asian Americans faced new racial possibilities, the choice of some to reject whiteness and instead practice a politics of multiethnic unity, interracial solidarity, and transnational anti-imperialism seems all the more remarkable."[34] Yet this formulation of Asian Americans choosing the more ethical path obscures two critical points. First, the fact that Asian Americans *were in a position to choose* between assimilationism and Third Worldism reflects their structurally advantaged position over Black people, who were not offered this choice. Second, there were more than two paths to choose from. We can imagine a third path where Asian Americans theorized structural anti-Blackness, recognized their own not-Blackness, and condemned the Asian–Black gap. This was a path not taken.

There was a brief moment in the movement when it seemed like it might be. In "The Emergence of Yellow Power in America" (1971), Amy Uyematsu observed that even though Asian Americans were denied equal opportunities with whites, they were also, on the whole, better off than other groups of color, enjoying economic mobility and "token acceptance" by whites.[35] "[T]he fact is that the white power structure allowed Asian Americans to succeed through their own efforts," Uyematsu wrote, "while the same institutions persist in denying these opportunities to black Americans."[36] She continued:

Their [Asian Americans'] passive behavior serves to keep national attention on the black people. By being as inconspicuous as possible, they keep pressure off of themselves at the expense of the blacks. Asian Americans have formed an uneasy alliance with white Americans to keep the blacks down. They close their eyes to the latent white racism toward them which has never changed. Frightened "yellows" allow the white public to use the "silent Oriental" stereotype against the black protest: The presence of twenty million blacks in America poses an actual physical threat to the white system. Fearful whites tell militant blacks that the acceptable criterion for behavior is exemplified in the quiet, passive Asian American.[37]

As Asian Americans played this game for strategic advantage, Uyematsu explained, they came to believe it themselves, "nurs[ing] their own feelings of inferiority and insecurity by holding themselves as superior to the blacks."[38]

[34] Maeda 2009, 17.
[35] Uyematsu 1971, 9.
[36] Uyematsu 1971, 11.
[37] Uyematsu 1971, 11.
[38] Uyematsu 1971, 9.

In "The Oriental as a 'Middleman Minority,'" Alan Nishio, too, high-lighted the ways in which whites weaponized Asian Americans against the Black struggle. He wrote: "As Black and Brown communities push for equal rights and opportunities, the Oriental is used to 'integrate' previously all-white communities or organizations." Then, borrowing a metaphor from Malcolm X, he added: "[Y]ellow Uncle Toms like Hayakawa ... act as the 'well-fed' houseboys of the Establishment, defending the planta-tion from the 'lowly' field slaves."[39] Anticipating the concept of structural anti-Blackness, Uyematsu and Nishio expressed powerful insights that complicated the movement's positions in productive ways, but their ideas were sidelined as the ideology of Third Worldism became ascendant.

The structural advantage of Asian Americans was an open secret in the movement era, hampering the work of Third World organizing at the grassroots level. BPP Chairman David Hilliard called Chinese Americans "the Uncle Toms of the non-white people of the U.S." and urged them to get closer to the Panthers by first getting closer to communist China.[40] Amy Uyematsu noted: "The middle-class attainment of Asian Americans has also made certain blacks unsympathetic to the yellow power move-ment. In the words of one B.S.U. member, it looks like Asian Americans 'just want more of the money pie.' It is difficult for some blacks to relate to the yellow man's problems next to his own total victimization."[41] Filipina American student activist Liz Del Sol, too, observed "that there was a strong sentiment by Black and Latino/Chicano students that they were more oppressed than Asians," even as Asian American students complained "that their interests were not given the same attention as the Black and Latino/Chicano students."[42] In *Black, Brown, Yellow, and Left: Radical Activism in Los Angeles* (2006), Laura Pulido wrote: "Asian Americans, who occupied a relatively more privileged place within the racial hierarchy, were the last sought after in terms of coalitions and part-nerships. In fact, Asian Americans were largely absent [from historical documents and interviews with Black and Chicanx people]."[43]

It was in this context that Richard Aoki, field marshal in the Black Panther Party and member of the Third World Liberation Front at University of California, Berkeley, became a towering figure in the Asian

[39] Nishio 1969, 280.
[40] Maeda 2009, 77.
[41] Uyematsu 1971, 12.
[42] Del Sol 2014, 143.
[43] Pulido 2006, 153–154.

American movement. His ties to the Black Panthers gave him a unique kind of street cred and political capital: the most radical Black activists had vetted him, an Asian American, and proclaimed him to be a genuine revolutionary. Decades later, his biographer Diane Fujino wrote that Aoki was "the [single] most iconic figure of the Asian American movement."[44]

The Red Guards, too, gained credibility through their association with the Black Panthers. It was the Panthers who urged a group of leftist Chinese American youth in San Francisco to form their own organization in 1969 and invited them to weekly study sessions on revolutionary theory. It was the Panthers whom the Red Guards chose to imitate in terms of style, ideology, rhetoric, programming (free breakfast program, health testing, legal services) and political platform.[45] Fred Hampton invited the Chicago Red Guards to join his Rainbow Coalition against police and gang violence, while David Hilliard invited Alex Hing of the San Francisco Red Guards to accompany him and other Black Panthers on a trip to North Korea, Vietnam, and Algeria.[46] Much of the Red Guards' Ten Point Platform copied the Panther's platform point for point and word for word, simply substituting "Yellow" for "Black."[47]

Consider the following passages:

[Point 8 of the Black Panther Party Ten Point Platform]
We Want Freedom For All Black Men Held In Federal, State, County And City Prisons And Jails. We believe that all Black people should be released from the many jails and prisons because they have not received a fair and impartial trial.

[Point 6 of the Red Guards' Ten Point Platform]
We want freedom for all Yellow men held in federal, state, county and city prisons and jails. We believe that all Yellow people should be released from the many jails and prisons because they have not received a fair and impartial trial.

---

[44] Fujino 2012, xiii. See below for discussion of Richard Aoki.

[45] See Maeda 2009.

[46] The other Asian American activist invited on this trip was Pat Sumi. See Wu 2013.

[47] The Red Guards platform changed the order of some of the points, left out some of the points, and added a new Point 8 ("We want adequate and free medical facilities available for the people in the Yellow community") and Point 10 ("We demand that the United States government recognize the People's Republic of China ..."), as well as the following quotation by Mao Zedong: "The Socialist system will eventually replace the Capitalist system; this is an objective law independent of Man's will. However much the reactionaries try to hold back the wheel of history, sooner or later revolution will take place and will inevitably triumph."

The Red Guards learned Mao from the Black Panthers, as Chinatown leaders at this time were firmly pro-Kuomintang. Alex Hing commented: "They [the Panthers] were our role models, and the Panthers introduced us to revolutionary struggles going on in Asia" (Wang 2014).

In a 2014 interview, Alex Hing said: "[We Chinese Americans] were all facing the same thing that other people were facing. The same kinds of situations due to capitalism, U.S. imperialism, as it applies to minorities ... [W]e advocated uniting with African Americans because our fight is the same as theirs. And I still think that's the case."[48] But Asian Americans were and are not targeted by the carceral state in the way Black people were and are. When do emulation and identification border on erasure and displacement? The textual move of ~~Black~~ Yellow literally erases Black and puts Yellow in its place, rather than leaving Black where it is and understanding Yellow in relation to it.[49]

Playwright Frank Chin ridiculed the Red Guards' imitation of the Black Panthers, calling them "yellow minstrels" who "perform[ed] blackness."[50] Since Asian Americans were not victimized by the carceral system, Chin observed, it was inauthentic to suggest an equivalence with Blackness. Once more, the themes of blackface, racial substitution, swapping, inhabitation, and body snatching pop up in Asian American history. Daryl Maeda countered that the Red Guards were not engaged in blackface minstrelsy because their intent was adulation rather than denigration. Yet, as Eric Lott and others have shown, desire and longing have always been an integral a part of blackface minstrelsy, along with aggression and hatred.[51] Rather than focusing solely on *intent*, in any case, we might consider the *impact* and *meaning* of the Red Guards' actions. What did the Red Guards have to gain by putting on Blackness, politically speaking, and what were the broader implications of such a performance in an anti-Black order? If, per Chin, they put on Blackness without having earned it, how did this advantage them in the context of the movement era? Did it bolster their claims to victimhood? Did it create an aura of righteousness around their cause? Did it help Chinese Americans *at the expense of* the Black struggle? Did it erase, dilute, or otherwise compromise Black people's claims about the specificity of their abjection? Did it emphasize white supremacy and obscure structural anti-Blackness? Solidarity *and* disavowal. Solidarity *as* disavowal.

---

[48] Wang 2014.
[49] See Dylan Rodríguez's call for an understanding of "whether and how Asian American studies and its corresponding Asian Americanisms are structurally entangled with, and actively complicit in, the genesis and expansion of the carceral state" (2005, 242).
[50] Frank Chin says his uncle was raised in a Chinese Baptist home for boys during the Great Depression. The home raised money through blackface minstrelsy shows (Terkel 1992).
[51] Lott 1995.

IV ASIAN AMERICANS AS AFFIRMATIVE ACTION SPOILERS

Affirmative action in the U.S. was never not controversial. The moment it emerged as a modest means of redressing racial discrimination and promoting Black incorporation, it sparked intense white anger and resistance. The first U.S. Supreme Court case to address affirmative action in higher education, *Regents of the University of California* v. *Bakke* (1978), set the terms for how the debate in this area would unfold. Although the court upheld affirmative action here, it constricted the policy, fatefully shifted its rationale, and planted the seeds for its ultimate collapse. In a way that has not been fully appreciated, the court's figuration of Asian Americans as affirmative action spoilers in *Bakke* played a critical role in these developments.

Justice Powell's *Bakke* decision draws heavily on the "Memorandum for Mr. Justice Powell" (August 29, 1977) authored by Powell's clerk, Bob Comfort.[52] Powell handwrote "Excellent memo" at the top and affirmed his clerk's arguments in extensive handwritten margin notes throughout, indicating that the memo closely shaped and/or reflected his views on the case. In the memo, Comfort notes that Respondent (Bakke) argues that all racial classifications, even supposedly "benign" ones, must be treated as suspect and trigger strict scrutiny, lest courts be faced with the impossible task of adjudicating innumerable claims of group injury in an effort to determine which classifications are "benign" and which are not. He writes:

Most of the ethnic groups comprised by American society have faced and to some extent still face prejudice and hostility. Courts will be called upon to explain why classifications disadvantaging some groups will trigger strict scrutiny and those dealing with others will not. Principled bases for such racial distinctions, says Respondent, are hard to imagine. Presumably, courts would be required to establish rankings of those groups that have been harmed the most by exclusion from various institutions. Courts have done little of this sociometric analysis in the past.[53]

Concurring with Respondent, Comfort opines that the court should decide matters on an individual basis, rather than attempting to judge relative group desert and "delving into the intractables, catalogued by Respondent and his allies, of deciding whose ox has been gored more often and for how long."[54] The "sociometric analysis" that the court has rightly avoided would be beyond its purview in any case, he argues,

---

[52] Comfort 1977. See also "The Harvard Plan that Failed Asian Americans" 2017.
[53] Comfort 1977, 26.
[54] Comfort 1977, 32.

because there is no "principled" way to make such distinctions, no objective way to ascertain who has been harmed, how much and by whom, and what is owed to them as a result. Moreover, such judgments would inevitably vary according to "political frame of reference" and time period. Depicting U.S. society as a noisy competition of comparably situated "ethnic" groups, Comfort throws a pluralistic veil over an anti-Black social order. Black abjection is disappeared in a sea of equivalences.

Comfort's rejection of sociometry is more apparent than real, however, since his judgment that there are too many comparably situated groups to adjudicate among is *itself* a sociometric conclusion. Comfort's covert sociometry presumes that there is no persistent structural (dis)advantage or group positionality—no foundational anti-Blackness—but only fluidity, variation, and complexity. *Society as a cacophony of competing, self-interested voices.* Since most "ethnic groups" (a designation that Comfort applies to white "ethnics" as well) face discrimination, there is no justification for burdening any groups with race-conscious remedies designed to help other groups. While the Equal Protection Clause of the Fourteenth Amendment was passed to help Black people, Comfort notes, "it is too late in the day to restrict that Amendment to some narrow class of historical 'wards.'"[55] Citing *Yick Wo*, he observes that Asian Americans and other groups have long benefited from heightened scrutiny as well.

Petitioner (UC Regents), Comfort notes, suggests that courts could simply begin with the obvious—that Black people have been disadvantaged in society—and go from there, perhaps including a few other groups as well. Comfort responds:

The prejudice faced by every distinct racial and ethnic group entering this country makes each a potential candidate for compensatory legislation. Concensus [sic] as to who needs it and who should bear the burden will be lacking. (Witness the nearly 60 briefs filed in this case.) The attempt to separate competing claims may well confound judicial ingenuity .... Benign scrutiny could be reserved, of course, for a few groups said to be harmed more than most—blacks, Puerto Ricans, Indians. But it is not immediately clear how one draws a bright line between those groups and, say, Jews or orientals [sic]. Both of those groups faced almost hysterical prejudice for decades after first arrival in this country. Both face a quieter, subtler form of prejudice today. A decision that the prejudice facing blacks has been quantitatively more disabling would amount to a judicial leap of faith, I think, rather than a judicial expression of social concensus [sic].[56]

---

[55] Comfort 1977, 27.
[56] Comfort 1977, 36–37.

Comfort brings Asian Americans ("orientals") into the picture (along with Jews) for the specific purpose of undercutting Petitioner's suggestion. Asian Americans are spoilers here, a wrench in the works. Because they, too, are racial minorities subjected to racial discrimination, albeit a "quieter, subtler form" than that inflicted upon other minorities, they complicate attempts to decide who deserves remedial consideration and who does not. Asian Americans are invoked, in other words, to thwart Petitioner's attempted specification of Black subjection and to help maintain the legal nonrecognition of Black suffering. A thoughtful sociometry would short circuit this move by demonstrating that the abjection of Black people is historically unique and distinguishable from the racism that Asian Americans face, but this is precisely the kind of analysis that Comfort has ruled out a priori. As indicated in this passage, he will not admit to a "quantitative" difference, let alone a qualitative one, between the discrimination faced by Black people and that faced by other groups.

Comfort continues:

There are three objections to [Petitioner's suggestion]. First, it would require the same judicial leap of faith, discussed above, to conclude that the prejudice confronting blacks or chicanos [sic] has been more disabling than that initially faced by Jews, orientals, or the Irish. Certainly there is no objective way to prove it. Second, it is not at all clear that the institutional obstacles presently confronting blacks (and other select groups) are significantly more debilitating than those facing Italians, Poles, etc., in certain contexts. Third, and perhaps most important, acceptance of this response would entail the creation of more of ... "Black Law." "Black Law" is law that is inexplicable and probably wrong except in the context of the courts' desire to aid the black drive for social parity .... [R]isk inheres in the creation of an "exclusion remedy" doctrine for blacks alone. Inevitably, other groups, whose perceptions of prejudice are no doubt quite strong, will demand explanations as to why they cannot avail themselves of this unique doctrine ... [and] racial and ethnic divisiveness would be perpetuated by the Constitution rather than assuaged.[57]

Affirmative action threatens to corrupt the law in the name of Black advancement and foment racial division to boot. According to Comfort, "Black Law" is what happens when Blackness is allowed to derange the law. This brings to mind what Christina Sharpe calls "anagrammatical blackness," or "the ways that meaning slides, signification slips, when words ... abut blackness."[58] Put "Black" before "Law" (or any other word such as "rights," "freedom," or "citizenship"), and the latter's integrity

---

[57] Comfort 1977, 49–50.
[58] Sharpe 2016, 80.

and meaning begin to dissolve. As Justice Bradley did in *The Civil Rights Cases* (1883) a century earlier, Comfort inverts reality, reading the law's special targeting of Black people as the law's special favoritism toward Black people. In other words, he has gotten it precisely backward (it is the law that degrades Blackness, not the other way around) and upside down (the law persecutes rather than coddles Black people). Nevertheless, Justice Powell accepts Comfort's view on the matter unequivocally. His hand-written comment on this section of Comfort's memo reads: "[Petitioner's] argument that blacks are different is not logically supportable."[59]

The U.S. government's Amicus Brief in Support of Petitioner (UC Regents) again figures Asian Americans as a potential problem for race-conscious admissions. Declaring that "properly designed minority-sensitive programs" are necessary "to overcome the effects of years of discrimination," the brief lays out statistical evidence of discrimination against Black people and those of "Spanish heritage," including higher poverty and unemployment rates, lower rates of educational attainment, and concentration in low paying and low-status jobs.[60] Footnote 39 then states obliquely, "The figures for Asian Americans (Japanese, Chinese, and Filipino only) are somewhat different."[61] Various statistics are provided—indicating that Asian Americans look more similar to whites than to other "minority" groups—with no accompanying explanation. Later, during a discussion of the paucity of Black and other not-white students in medical schools, footnote 51 states: "There is no apparent under representation of Asian-American persons," and then:

At the same time, no one can doubt that this racial group has been the subject of discrimination in this country .... Nor is it clear that discrimination against Asian-American persons is a thing of the past .... Discrimination may take subtle forms, and the admission of large numbers of Asian-American students does not preclude the possibility of discrimination.[62]

---

[59] Comfort 1977, 49.

[60] U.S. government's Amicus Brief in Support of Petitioner (UC Regents), 3. Those of "Spanish heritage" were also considered underrepresented minorities in the UC Davis Medical School's admissions program. This brief, however, focuses primarily on Black students, with Latinx folks brought in as a secondary example. Black students are seen as the paradigmatic beneficiaries of race-conscious admissions. Where Latinx people stand in an anti-Black social order—how they are positioned in this order relative to Black people, whites, and Asians and what this means for their status as beneficiaries of race-conscious admissions—is a matter that has not been addressed in affirmative action jurisprudence, only momentarily rising to the surface in the *Fisher* case (to be discussed below).

[61] U.S. government's Amicus Brief in Support of Petitioner (UC Regents), 42.

[62] U.S. government's Amicus Brief in Support of Petitioner (UC Regents), 46, 47.

Since Asian Americans are a "minority" who are (probably still) discriminated against, the brief stops just short of asking: how are they able to gain admission in "large numbers" without special consideration?[63] The subtextual tension built through these footnote commentaries then breaks into the main text when the issues left unresolved by the trial court are enumerated:

> It is not clear from the record why Asian-American persons are included in the special program. There is no doubt that many Asian-American persons have been subjected to discrimination. But although we do not know the application rates for Asian-Americans at Davis, the available evidence suggests that Asian-American applicants are admitted in substantial numbers even without taking special admissions into account .... Although it may well be that disadvantaged Asian-American persons continue to be in need of the special program to overcome past discrimination, the record is silent on that question.[64]

Asian Americans pose a problem for affirmative action because they seem to disrupt the assumed connection between discrimination and injury/need. They are discriminated against, but they succeed anyway, the brief suggests, which could potentially cast doubt on the remedial rationale for affirmative action.

Writing for the plurality on the court, Justice Powell responds to Petitioner's argument that discrimination against the white majority is not suspect if it has a benign purpose:

> [T]he difficulties entailed in varying the level of judicial review according to a perceived "preferred" status of a particular racial or ethnic minority are intractable. The concepts of "majority" and "minority" necessarily reflect temporary arrangements and political judgments. As observed above, the white "majority" itself is composed of various minority groups, most of which can lay claim to a history of prior discrimination at the hands of the State and private individuals. Not all of these groups can receive preferential treatment and corresponding judicial tolerance of distinctions drawn in terms of race and nationality, for then the only "majority" left would be a new minority of white Anglo-Saxon Protestants. There is no principled basis for deciding which groups would merit "heightened judicial solicitude" and which would not. Courts would be asked to evaluate the extent of the prejudice and consequent harm suffered by various minority groups. Those whose societal injury is thought to exceed some arbitrary level of tolerability then would be entitled to preferential classifications at the expense of

---

[63] Between 1970 and 1974, the total number of Asian Americans admitted to the UC Davis Medical School through general admissions was forty-one. The number of Black and Chicano students admitted through general admissions during those five years was one and six, respectively. See footnote 6 in *Regents of the University of California* v. *Bakke* (1978).

[64] U.S. government's Amicus Brief in Support of Petitioner (UC Regents), 70–71.

individuals belonging to other groups. Those classifications would be free from
exacting judicial scrutiny. As these preferences begin to have their desired effect,
and the consequences of past discrimination were undone, new judicial rankings
would be necessary. The kind of variable sociological and political analysis to
produce such rankings simply does not lie within the judicial competence—even
if they otherwise were politically feasible and socially desirable.[65]

Drawing heavily upon the spirit and wording of Comfort's memo, Powell
asserts that an objective sociometry is impossible because most, if not
all, groups have been harmed by prejudice, and there is no non-arbitrary
way to decide who should get "preferential treatment" as a result, and
who should not. Indeed, the very terms "minority" and "majority" have
little purchase, Powell avers, as the white "majority" is but a composite
of white "minorities" that have each faced discrimination, and once we
subtract them, the remainder, white Anglo-Saxon Protestants, become,
lo and behold, a "new minority." *We are all minorities now.* (Note the
sleight of hand here, shifting from a racial-political definition of "minority" to a numerical one.)

Justice Powell's vision of intergroup relations—his sociometry that
refuses to call itself sociometry—turns out to be highly impactful: it
directly underwrites his momentous finding that the "societal discrimination" Petitioner claims to be redressing through race-conscious
admissions is an excessively "amorphous concept of injury" that does
not justify the use of racial classifications (as a finding of a specific constitutional or statutory violation, by contrast, would).[66] It paves the
way, that is, for Powell to *substantially delink affirmative action from
its original remedial rationale for Black people.* Powell then offers an
alternative rationale for race-conscious admissions: diversity. Under the
First Amendment, he argues, universities have wide latitude to use race-
conscious measures to create diversity in the student body in order to
secure the educational benefits that flow therefrom, including, among
other things, a "robust exchange of ideas."[67] With this, race-conscious
admissions survives *Bakke*, but the hope of using it to remedy persistent
patterns of racial domination does not.[68]

Justice Powell flags Asian Americans no fewer than three times in
his effort to discredit the "societal discrimination" rationale. That he

[65] *Regents of the University of California* v. *Bakke* (1978), 2751–2752.
[66] *Regents of the University of California* v. *Bakke* (1978), 2757.
[67] *Regents of the University of California* v. *Bakke* (1978), 2760, quoting from *United States* v. *Associated Press*, D.C., 52 F.Supp. 362, 372.
[68] See Lawrence 2001.

discusses them exclusively in the footnotes reinforces the sense that Asian Americans are secret spoilers, the repressed truth of affirmative action waiting to be exposed. First, in footnote 36, Powell observes that Justices Brennan, White, Marshall, and Blackmun (in their opinion concurring in part and dissenting in part) argue that Black people would have gotten better test scores absent "societal discrimination," but "nothing is said about Asians"—the suggestion being that Asian Americans disrupt the presumed link between discrimination and poor performance. In footnote 37, Powell again expresses his concern that the "societal discrimination" rationale will lead to "first the schools, and then the courts ... [being] buffeted with competing claims." Here he mentions the University of Washington, which includes Filipinos but excludes the Chinese and Japanese from positive racial consideration in admissions:

> But what standards is the Court to apply when a rejected applicant of Japanese ancestry brings suit to require the University of Washington to extend the same privileges to his group? ... [T]he Court could attempt to assess how grievously each group has suffered from discrimination, and allocate proportions accordingly; if that were the standard, the current University of Washington policy would almost surely fall, for there is no Western State which can claim that it has always treated Japanese and Chinese in a fair and evenhanded manner.[69]

Japanese and Chinese Americans were discriminated against, too, but do not need help getting in to the University of Washington, which should give the architects of affirmative action pause.[70] Finally, in a passage where Powell argues that a finding of specific constitutional or statutory violations is necessary to justify racial classifications which burden innocent whites, he notes in footnote 45: "[T]he University [University of California, Davis] is unable to explain its selection of only the four favored groups—Negroes, Mexican-Americans, American Indians, and Asians—for preferential treatment. The inclusion of the last group is especially curious in light of the substantial numbers of Asians admitted through the regular admissions process."[71] Why include Asian Americans in an affirmative action program when they do not need help getting in? Why do Black people and other groups need help getting in when Asian Americans do not?

---

[69] *Regents of the University of California* v. *Bakke* (1978), 2752.
[70] Powell indirectly raises but does not explore the question of intra-Asian diversity here. It is not uncommon for universities to differentiate Asian national origin groups and offer some but not others special consideration, depending upon their enrollment numbers, although the discourse about race-conscious remedies has tended to treat Asian Americans as a homogeneous group.
[71] *Regents of the University of California* v. *Bakke* (1978), 2758.

Why do Asian Americans appear to disrupt the link between discrimination and injury/need? The Asian American movement's own political critique offers little clarification here because it addresses only white supremacy. Bringing structural anti-Blackness back into the picture is illuminating. It is not that Asian Americans make it despite discrimination and Black people do not, but that the generic concept of "discrimination" fails to distinguish between the racism that Asian Americans face and the foundational abjection inflicted upon Black people. It fails to account for the fact that Asian Americans are not-white, but above all not-Black and thereby beneficiaries of a structural Asian–Black gap. The relevant question, therefore, is not "how do Asian Americans start out in the same place as Black people and end up farther ahead?" but rather "how does Asian Americans' not-Blackness constitute a structural advantage that helps them get ahead, despite the discrimination they face?" A sociometry that explored this question would undercut the Asian-Americans-as-spoilers trope by exposing the fallacy of minority equivalency upon which it rests. It would create space to re-specify the status of Black people (and, by extension, other groups) and bring back the very issues of compensatory justice that Justice Powell banished in *Bakke*.

Powell concludes that diversity is a compelling state interest that justifies race-conscious admissions in higher education, but cautions that race can only be considered as one factor among many. Harvard's "holistic" review, Powell intones, is an exemplary program that uses race as a plus factor only. On the other hand, UC Davis Medical School's special admissions program, which sets aside 16 out of 100 slots for "minorities," generates a racial "quota" in violation of the Equal Protection Clause of the Fourteenth Amendment and Title VI of the 1964 Civil Rights Act.[72] In a dissenting opinion, Justice Thurgood Marshall challenges Powell's finding that the UC Davis Medical School's special admissions program violates the Equal Protection Clause of the Fourteenth Amendment. After briefly touching on various historical events (including slavery, *Dred Scott*, Black Codes, Reconstruction, and Jim Crow) and present-day statistics (concerning, among other things, Black maternal death rates, infant mortality, poverty, and unemployment), Marshall writes:

---

[72] The highly fractured set of opinions in *Bakke*—one bloc of four justices joined parts of Powell's decision; another bloc of four joined other parts; the nine justices issued a total of six different opinions—raised questions about the precedential weight of the case going forward.

"At every point from birth to death, the impact of the past is reflected in the still disfavored position of the Negro."[73] Even in the absence of a finding of a constitutional violation or specific harm to an individual, he avers, racial classifications are necessary and permissible when a group is in need of remedy because of past discrimination. Responding to Powell's rejection of the "societal discrimination" rationale, he writes:

[I]t is more than a little ironic that, after several hundred years of class-based discrimination against Negroes, the Court is unwilling to hold that a class-based remedy for that discrimination is permissible. In declining to so hold, today's judgment ignores the fact that for several hundred years, Negroes have been discriminated against not as individuals, but rather solely because of the color of their skins. It is unnecessary in 20th-century America to have individual Negroes demonstrate that they have been victims of racial discrimination; the racism of our society has been so pervasive that none, regardless of wealth or position, has managed to escape its impact. *The experience of Negroes in America has been different in kind, not just in degree, from that of other ethnic groups.* It is not merely the history of slavery alone, but also that a whole people were marked as inferior by the law. And that mark has endured. The dream of America as the great melting pot has not been realized for the Negro; because of his skin color, he never even made it into the pot.[74]

The burden of malignant racial classifications has fallen most heavily on Black people for hundreds of years, with enduring and "pervasive" effects, and Powell can only judge "societal discrimination" to be too "amorphous" a concept because he "ignores [this] fact." Bob Comfort, commenting to Justice Powell on the first draft of Justice Marshall's decision, writes, "As always, the fact that we have Asians thrown into this case is unexplained."[75] What Comfort failed to notice was that Marshall had already inoculated his argument against the Asian American spoiler effect by clarifying the singularity of Black abjection.

---

[73] Justice Thurgood Marshall's dissent in *Regents of the University of California* v. *Bakke* (1978), 2802.

[74] Justice Thurgood Marshall's dissent in *Regents of the University of California* v. *Bakke* (1978), 2804. Italics added.

[75] See Bob Comfort's handwritten comments to Justice Powell on the first draft of Justice Marshall's opinion in *Bakke*, circulated by Marshall on June 23, 1978. 76–811 *Regents of University of California* v. *Bakke*—Opinion drafts—Marshall (1 of 2). http://law2.wlu.edu/powellarchives/page.asp?pageid=1322. In folder 14 of this same archive of Powell's papers, Powell's memo "Fullilove v. Kreps" (January 28, 1980), relating to a case on minority business contracting, states: "We also need a footnote dealing with the sticky problem of Chinese and other 'minorities' being bracketed indiscriminately with Negroes" (4–5). Although no such footnote appears in Powell's concurring opinion in *Fullilove* v. *Klutznick*, it is clear that Powell continued to reflect on "Asian spoilers" after *Bakke*.

V JAPANESE AMERICAN REPARATIONS

A decade after the *Bakke* decision, the U.S. Congress passed the Civil Liberties Act of 1988, in which the U.S. government apologized for wartime internment and promised $20,000 to each survivor. Japanese American activists who had fought for this legislation for years celebrated their victory. But a persistent question haunted the entire process, usually whispered rather than spoken aloud: In making this gesture to Japanese Americans, was the U.S. state further denigrating Black people? After all, Black individuals and organizations had pressed the case for reparations for slavery since before the Civil War, to no avail. Granted that the victims of wartime internment deserved an apology and compensation for what they suffered, what did it mean to give reparations to them and not to Black people? For wartime internment and not for slavery and Jim Crow?

By the time the Japanese American redress and reparations movement began in the 1970s, the struggle for Black reparations had been going on for over 100 years. Black emigrationists asked for redress in the 1850s, and the end of the Civil War renewed calls for compensation for former slaves. Sojourner Truth petitioned the U.S. government to give public lands to freedpeople, and General William Sherman's Special Field Order 15 initiated a land redistribution project (under the promise of "40 acres and a mule") on the South Carolina coast and the Sea Islands—until President Andrew Johnson, entering office after Lincoln's assassination, called a halt to it and ordered the land returned to former Confederate leaders. In the late 1800s, the National Ex-Slave Mutual Relief, Bounty, and Pension Association formed to petition the U.S. government for pensions for freedpeople, and Bishop Henry McNeal Turner of the African Methodist Episcopal Church called for $40 billion in reparations for freedpeople and the cession of several Southern states to enable them to form an independent Black nation.[76]

Starting in the 1950s, reparations became a central focus for Black (inter)nationalist groups. Queen Mother Audley Moore founded the Reparations Committee of Descendants of United States Slaves, which did grassroots organizing around the issue, in addition to petitioning the United Nations. In May 1969, at a conference on Black economic development, James Forman issued his Black Manifesto, which accused U.S. churches of complicity in global racism, colonialism, and slavery, and

---

[76] Biondi 2003; Kelley 2007.

demanded reparations, a southern land bank, and other resources for Black communities.[77] Point 3 of the Black Panthers' Ten Point Platform called for reparations, and in 1973, the Panthers submitted a petition to the U.N. arguing that the U.S. had violated the Genocide Convention of 1948 and thus owed reparations "to those who have suffered the damages of racist and genocidal practices."[78] In the 1980s, N'COBRA (National Coalition of Blacks for Reparations in America) emerged, calling for a plebiscite to create a New Afrikan nation supported by $3 billion of annual reparations.[79]

It was in this context of Black reparations long denied that the Japanese American redress and reparations movement began. According to Alice Yang Murray, the movement was comprised of three interwoven strands led by, respectively, the JACL, the National Coalition for Redress/Reparations (NCRR), and the National Council for Japanese American Redress (NCJAR).[80] As the JACL lobbied Congress to establish a commission to study wartime internment and make policy recommendations, the other two organizations emerged as a corrective to what they saw as the JACL's conservatism and accommodationism. The NCJAR opted to fight for redress through class-action litigation, while the NCRR articulated a more militant critique of internment as an example of structural racism that culminated decades of anti-Japanese persecution.[81] Composed mostly of *Sansei* (third-generation Japanese Americans), the NCRR was inspired by the Asian American and Black Power movements and had a Third Worldist or people-of-color orientation.

The JACL's reparations campaign bore the same ideological imprint as its wartime efforts had. In the spirit of Mike Masaoka's "Japanese American Creed," the JACL pamphlet "Redress! The American Promise" stated:

Unable to become citizens, they [Japanese Americans] worked to create exemplary communities up and down the coast, particularly as far as public records were concerned. They generally took care of their own problems so that the public records showed the Japanese had hardly a person on the public welfare

---

[77] Aiyetoro and Davis 2010; Kelley 2007. A later version of the manifesto pointed the finger at synagogues as well as churches.
[78] Martin and Yaquinto 2007, 607.
[79] Yamamoto 1998.
[80] Murray 2008.
[81] In 1983, NCJAR brought a class-action suit against the U.S. government on behalf of all former evacuees and internees, citing twenty-two causes of action and fifteen violations of constitutional rights. The case made its way through the appellate process until 1988, when the U.S. Supreme Court denied certiorari. See Hatamiya 1993.

list or police blotters. After enduring the hardships of life behind barbed wire and sending their sons off to war, they left camp "with characteristic determination, patience, and hard work" to "climb back to normalcy." When they finally became eligible for naturalization in 1952, they rushed to take citizenship exams. These immigrants still prized citizenship after enduring "harassment and even violence from organized hate groups," confinement in "detention camps," and the loss of "everything they had worked for" .... Who else would, or even could, continue to have faith in a nation that had treated them so shabbily for so long?[82]

Japanese Americans deserved redress as a reward for staying faithful to the nation despite decades of abuse. And for being a good minority that eschewed "public welfare" and did not show up on "police blotters." As in the "Japanese American Creed," the not-so-absent referent is Black people, the bad minority whose supposed indolence, criminality, and sense of entitlement provide an ideal foil for Japanese American personal and political virtue.

Formed by Congress, the Commission on Wartime Relocation and Internment of Civilians (CWRIC) began holding public hearings in the early 1980s. At a hearing on August 4, 1981, Vice Chairman Daniel Lungren, a conservative Republican congressman from California, raised the slippery slope problem, pressing two JACL officials to explain how the government could help them without opening the door to Black reparations. *Tell us how we can do x without having to do y.*

Vice Chairman Lungren:
If the panel were to decide that redress were appropriate, and there were a question of the amount involved, would you be so insistent on the fact that heirs of internees receive funds? I ask you that question for this reason: obviously, any monies that come, come from taxpayers now. Do you think it's appropriate that taxpayers now, some of whom were not even born when these things took place, ought to be required by the government to take money from their pockets and give it to heirs of internees .... The only reason I bring this up, I did receive a letter in my office over the last two weeks from someone who identified himself as a black American, saying that he as a black American had never received compensation for the wrongs done his ancestors by virtue of officially sanctioned discrimination all the way to the point of slavery. And he put it rather forcefully. He said, "If this award is going to be made, I'm going to demand that I get my acre and two mules" or whatever the slogan was back there.

Mr. Kawahara:
40 acres and one mule.

[82] Murray 2008, 370.

Vice Chairman Lungren:
All right, 40 acres and a mule, whatever. How do you—and I'm not just asking this as a rhetorical question—I'm saying how do you precisely suggest that this is such a unique situation it ought to be treated differently than the experience of the black American?

Mr. Kawahara:
I don't think we should speak for other minority groups who have felt oppressed. I think our task is to present our case as American citizens who were incarcerated during World War II. So if black Americans or other oppressed Americans feel that they have a judgment against the government in the form of a commission, or whatever else. I think that is their prerogative, and that should be given to them.

Mr. Shigekuni:
I believe that the chair, the national chair for JACL Redress Committee had a good answer for that on the nationally televised show, when he mentioned that in the case of black Americans, the government was not responsible for what happened to them. But in the case of Japanese Americans, it was the government's action directly that caused the problems that were faced at that time and we're facing now.

Commissioner Goldberg:
Not exactly, no.

Vice Chairman Lungren:
Our constitution specifically defined blacks as less than full human beings, and officially countenanced slavery by a Supreme Court decision, and you can't more directly do that than write it into the constitution and then, in fact, put the full strength of the government behind it. But I don't want to get into a full-blown argument here. We've got more witnesses here.[83]

Lungren mocks the struggle for Black reparations ("40 acres and a mule, whatever"), maneuvers Shigekuni into dissociating from it, and then questions the latter's assertions.

When conservatives made it clear they would only support reparations for internment if it did not open the door to reparations for slavery, JACL officials made a proactive, concerted effort to distance themselves from the Black fight for reparations. Phil Tajitsu Nash, a lobbyist for the redress movement, wrote:

Once the CWRIC had its hearings, the JACL lobbyists were very conscious of the problem that any reparations for Japanese Americans could be used to argue for "40 acres and a mule" (slavery reparations) by African Americans.

[83] Public Hearing, Commission on Wartime Relocation and Internment of Civilians, Los Angeles, August 4, 1981, 191–194.

Indeed, both JACL and non-JACL activists had been influenced by Yale Law School Professor Boris Bittker's 1973 classic, "The Case for Black Reparations," which gave serious consideration to the legal and political issues raised by righteous demands for reparations. Thus, myself and everyone I knew of in the lobbying effort were careful to mention the factual differences between the Japanese American and African American grievances, so that fiscal and social conservatives could be assured that we were pushing only for the limited case of redress for Japanese Americans unfairly incarcerated during World War II. Rep. Newt Gingrich and other conservatives supported us because he agreed that property rights of American citizens should not be violated, but his support might have waned if African American property rights had been introduced into the equation.[84]

If Japanese Americans wanted reparations, they would have to symbolically throw Black people under the bus to get them. They would have to reinforce the justifications the government used to deny Black reparations, which amounted to denying the historical truth of slavery.

Not all Japanese American activists endorsed the JACL's approach. With their Third World orientation, NCRR members preferred to directly analogize internment to African slavery and Native American reservations, arguing that all three groups deserved reparations.[85] However, analogizing, too, denied the singularity of Black abjection and erased the Asian–Black gap. In addition, the NCRR, like the JACL, offered no rationale for why Japanese Americans should be allowed to jump ahead in the queue and receive reparations before other groups did. Thus they had no effective response when Clarence Reynolds, president of a Black emigrationist group in Chicago, testified at a November 1981 CWRIC hearing in New York that Black people had been treated even worse than Japanese Americans and were thus more deserving of reparations.

During congressional debates over the reparations bill, when conservatives warned that the proposed legislation would entail Black reparations as well, Japanese American legislators followed the JACL in arguing that internment was a singular wrong uniquely deserving of remediation. Senator Matsunaga stated:

Mr. President, the greatness of any nation can be accurately measured by the laws under which its people are governed. This year we celebrate the bicentennial of that greatest of documents ever written by mortals which we have adopted as the

[84] Email from Phil Tajitsu Nash (a lobbyist for the redress movement) to Greg Robinson, May 28, 2012, cited in Robinson 2016, 169–170.
[85] Murray 2008.

supreme law of our land. In so doing, I am extremely pleased ... [that] [m]embers of the august body have joined together in introducing legislation to remove that one ugly blot which has marred our National Constitution over the past 45 years.[86]

This legislation had the power to literally wipe clean the nation's entire postwar record, Matsunaga suggested. It could alibi the nation and the Constitution and presumably erase the history of Jim Crow. Could lawmakers pass up a chance to purchase national redemption so cheaply? Here Matsunaga moved past distinguishing Japanese American reparations from Black reparations ("you can do x without doing y") to proposing the former as a more palatable alternative to the latter ("you can do x *instead of* y"). There had to be a buy-in for conservative white legislators, and this was it.

Senator Inouye sounded the same note later in the debate:

Mr. President, I am pleased to join my colleagues as we the people celebrate the 200th birthday of our Constitution, to address what has been described as "The Ugly Blot" on U.S. constitutional democracy .... The Japanese-American case is unique in the constitutional history of our country in that there was a total abrogation of constitutional guarantees inflicted against a single group of citizens and resident aliens solely on the basis of ethnicity.[87]

Pace Inouye, internment's "total abrogation of constitutional guarantees" on the basis of ethnicity or race was not in any way unique but rather par for the course in U.S. history, as demonstrated most vividly by centuries of slavery, lynching, Jim Crow, de facto segregation, mass incarceration, and police violence. Indeed, the only way Inouye could make the case for the singular gravity and egregiousness of "The Ugly Blot" was to redact structural anti-Blackness in toto.

In her book *Righting a Wrong: Japanese Americans and the Passage of the Civil Liberties Act of 1988* (1993), Leslie Hatamiya writes: "The crucial question is how a small and politically incohesive minority group was able, at a time of massive federal budget deficits, to secure passage of a potentially controversial bill, authorizing $1.25 billion in redress payments, by members of Congress who would gain no electoral advantage by supporting that bill."[88] Hatamiya credits Japanese American activists for packaging and selling reparations in a way that flattered the ideological commitments of the right wing. Rather than talking about civil rights,

---

[86] *Congressional Record*, 100th Congress, 1st Session, U.S. Senate, April 10, 1987, 8957.

[87] *Congressional Record*, 100th Congress, 1st Session, U.S. Senate, April 10, 1987, 8963.

[88] Hatamiya 1993, 2. The Civil Liberties Act also made reparations to Aleuts who had been removed from the Aleutian and Pribilof islands and interned.

special interests, and handouts, activists emphasized individual rights, liberty, equal opportunity, the Constitution, and American institutions and values—even quoting Ronald Reagan on occasion. Hatamiya mentions Representative Mineta's decision to arrange for the vote on H.R. 442 (named after the famed *Nisei* combat unit) to be held on September 17, 1987 (the exact bicentennial date), as a "symbolic statement that redress was not simply a Japanese American issue, but an American issue, because when one group is deprived of its constitutional rights, the freedom of all Americans is threatened."[89]

Yet the archive suggests there was more to the story. What Hatamiya overlooks is that Japanese American activists and lawmakers traded on their not-Blackness, weaponized themselves, and offered a payout in anti-Blackness that outweighed the financial cost of the bill. Conservatives did not receive a convincing answer to the slippery slope problem, but some of them voted for the bill anyway because, contra Hatamiya, they did get something out of it—something greater than "electoral advantage." Granting Japanese American reparations *in the absence of Black reparations, instead of Black reparations* was an unmistakable symbolic statement that Black lives were worth less than other lives. Rendering Japanese American suffering legible deepened the illegibility of Black suffering. Like Justice Brown invoking *Yick Wo* in *Plessy* almost a century earlier, lawmakers drew on Asian Americans to "prove" that the U.S. state *recognized and corrected its racist lapses*—as if passing the Civil Liberties Act somehow addressed slavery and its afterlife. This was the politics of racial substitution in its most cynical form.

The passage of the Civil Liberties Act was a moment of high political theater where government officials once again invoked Asian Americans as an alibi for prevailing power arrangements, thus weaponizing them against the Black struggle. The idea was to lift Asian Americans up (at relatively little cost), the better to nail down Black abjection. Some Japanese American community leaders recognized the game that was afoot and played along to achieve their legislative goal. Afterwards, amid the general celebrations, a few Asian American commentators expressed concern. In two separate essays published in 1992 and 1998, Eric Yamamoto, for example, reflected that the social meaning and legacy of Japanese American reparations were wide open and still to be determined, depending upon how Japanese Americans acted in the future in relation to other racially subordinated groups. He asked: "Would we

---

[89] Hatamiya 1993, 153.

[Japanese Americans] draw upon the lessons of the reparations movement and work to end all forms of societal oppression, or would we
close up shop because we got ours?"[90] If Japanese Americans supported
other struggles, he suggested, it could be said retrospectively that the
Civil Liberties Act contributed to institutional restructuring for all.
Furthermore, Yamamoto wrote,

The inquiry into intergroup relations may also require digging into and beyond
the pervasive effects of white supremacy, into the extent to which Japanese Americans (and Asian Americans) have been complicit in the subordination of African
American communities over the last fifty years. In present-day America, depending on the circumstances, racial groups can be simultaneously disempowered and
empowered, oppressed and complicit in oppression, liberating and subordinating. Do Asian Americans, themselves subject to continuing discrimination and
negative stereotyping, have an obligation to aid in the healing of African American communities culturally, spiritually, and economically?[91]

Here Yamamoto provided a salve for those worried about the righteousness of Japanese American reparations. Reparations could be retroactively redeemed if, going forward, Japanese Americans reversed their own
complicity in Black oppression. In this way, reckoning with the policy's
meaning is pushed forward to an indeterminate future time and space.
Japanese American reparations will not have been unfair if ...

VI *OBADELE V. UNITED STATES*

In the eyes of some Black scholars, the meaning of Japanese American
reparations was plain right away. Arguing that Black people had suffered
more severe injuries than Japanese Americans, Vincene Verdun wrote:

Granting reparations to Japanese Americans without granting similar compensation to African Americans sends the latter yet another message declaring that they
are on the bottom of society's ladder, and this exclusion confirms their sense of
futility in the quest for justice in the United States. Amelioration of one ill has
made a previously tolerable condition seem degrading.[92]

In other words, Black people were actually rendered worse off than before
by the Civil Liberties Act. J. Angelo Corlett made a similar argument:

[W]ould it not also be true that what Japanese Americans experienced at the
hands of the U.S. government was not nearly as harmful as what African

[90] Yamamoto 1998, 480; Yamamoto 1992.
[91] Yamamoto 1998, 486.
[92] Verdun 1993, 659.

Americans experience(d), both in terms of the very kinds of racist oppression and in terms of duration? And would not such facts suggest that, just as the United States willingly apologized and provided reparations to certain Japanese Americans, so too ought the United States to do so to African Americans? Moreover, should not the amount of reparations to African Americans be substantially larger than that which has been provided to certain Japanese Americans? This would follow from both the kinds of anti-African American racist oppression and the duration of it .... It is obvious that U.S. citizens do not believe that African Americans deserve reparations .... [The Civil Liberties Act] seems to be a blatant instance of simply expressing significant respect to those whom most citizens feel respect, while denying significant respect to those whom most citizens believe are not worthy of it.[93]

The Civil Liberties Act demonstrated the racial hierarchy of mattering: Japanese Americans mattered, Black people did not. Japanese American suffering demanded redress, Black suffering did not. Both Verdun and Corlett raise the issue of *comparative desert*.[94] If non-comparative desert is what one deserves absolutely, comparative desert is what one deserves in comparison with others. This latter concept recognizes the fact that justice is irreducibly comparative and public. For Black people, not getting slavery reparations is a violation of non-comparative desert, and Japanese Americans getting reparations is a violation of comparative desert in addition—an injury on top of an injury on top of an injury.[95]

All of this was on Dr. Imari Obadele's mind when he renewed his pursuit of Black reparations in the wake of the Civil Liberties Act. Obadele had cofounded Republic of New Afrika (RNA), a radical Black internationalist group, in Detroit in the late 1960s. Calling for five states (Louisiana, Mississippi, Alabama, Georgia, and South Carolina) to be ceded by the U.S. and reconstituted as a new Black nation built upon the Tanzanian model of African socialism, the RNA linked the demand for reparations to principles of sovereignty and self-determination.[96] From its perspective, the Fourteenth Amendment had not so much *granted* U.S. citizenship to Black people as it had *imposed* it upon them, thus

---

[93] Corlett 2007, 186–187.
[94] See Kagan 1999.
[95] Some state and local governments have apologized for slavery and legal segregation, as have some corporations and universities. In 2019, the Georgetown University student body voted to pay fees toward slavery reparations. The U.S. House of Representatives passed an official apology for slavery on July 29, 2008, and the U.S. Senate followed suit on June 18, 2009 (Wenger 2018). However, neither apology nor reparations have issued from the White House on behalf of the nation as a whole.
[96] Kelley 2007.

denying them the right to self-determination.[97] The RNA was targeted by FBI COINTELPROs through the 1970s, and Obadele served two prison terms related to his political work, after which he earned a PhD in political science from Temple University and began teaching and writing about Black reparations and revolutionary nationalism.

In 1987, as the House of Representatives debated H.R. 442, Obadele and colleagues formed the National Coalition of Blacks for Reparations in America (N'COBRA).[98] That same year, Obadele presented to the U.S. Congress "An Act to Stimulate Economic Growth in the United States and Compensate, in Part, for the Grievous Wrongs of Slavery and the Unjust Enrichment Which Accrued to the United States Therefrom," in which he asked that Congress pay $3 billion annually to Black organizations and families and to the RNA (whose leaders were to be democratically elected under United Nations supervision). Echoing the Black Panther Party, he also proposed a U.N.-supervised plebiscite to determine the political will of the Black community in each of the five former states. These moves, as well as his call for European colonial powers to pay reparations to African nations, placed him in the long tradition of Black internationalist organizing.[99]

Like William Patterson and Paul Robeson before them, Obadele and colleagues sought to bring global attention to the status of Black people in the U.S. The U.S. government tried to thwart them at every turn. N'COBRA was one of several radical Black organizations that worked through the United Nations Human Rights Commission to organize the U.N. World Conference Against Racism, Racial Discrimination, Xenophobia, and Related Intolerances, held in Durban, South Africa, in 2001, with the interrelated goals of declaring slavery a crime against humanity, asserting the economic motive behind white supremacy, and calling for reparations. They had hoped to focus the conference exclusively on those of African descent, but the U.S. and the E.U. had insisted on adding "Xenophobia and Related Intolerances" to the title, a move that opened the event up and despecified the status and experience of Black people. When the conference nonetheless issued the Durban Declaration and Programme of Action, which pronounced that "slavery and the transatlantic slave trade are a crime against humanity,"[100] 168

[97] Aiyetoro 2003.
[98] Aiyetoro 2003.
[99] Biondi 2003.
[100] Biondi 2003, 5.

nations signed it, but the U.S. refused. The U.S. also opposed all calls for slavery reparations at the conference.[101]

N'COBRA suggested, without stating directly, that Black people were owed more reparations than other racialized groups. In "The Reparations Campaign" (2000), they wrote:

> We cannot allow anyone to offer, or accept on our behalf, some arbitrary figure based on some other peoples' reparations settlement. For example, the four year internment of Japanese in America, or the five year holocaust of Jewish people in Europe may require a different set of remedies than the 500 years holocaust of Africans in America. The nature and extent of the damage and the number of people impacted will dictate the type, duration, and amount of reparations owed.[102]

However, when Obadele initiated a lawsuit against the U.S. government, charging that the exclusion of Black people from the Civil Liberties Act was a violation of the Equal Protection Clause of the Fourteenth Amendment, some N'COBRA members declined to join, perhaps because of a concern that the lawsuit might set a precedent for undermining Black reparations in the future, as well as a reluctance to create further tensions between Black and Asian American communities.

In 1998, Obadele and Kuratibisha X Ali Rashid submitted claims with the Office of Redress Administration (ORA) to receive reparations payments under the Civil Liberties Act. Lawmakers had specified that eligibility was restricted to "individual[s] of Japanese ancestry" who were U.S. citizens or permanent resident aliens and had been "confined, held in custody, relocated, or otherwise deprived of liberty or property as a result of" a number of governmental orders arranging for evacuation and internment. Obadele and Rashid claimed that they, too, were "descendants of persons who were, confined, held in custody, relocated, or otherwise deprived of liberty or property ... by action taken by or on behalf of the United States or its agents, representatives, officers, or employees."[103] In a letter to the ORA, dated August 3, 1998, Obadele backed up this claim with a discussion of the Atlantic slave trade; the U.S. government's denial of self-determination to Black people; the *Plessy* Court's authorization of discrimination in jobs and housing; and the targeting of Black groups by the FBI COINTELPRO programs.[104]

---

[101] See Wareham (2003) for more on the international struggle for reparations for slavery and colonialism and an account of how the U.S. attempts to thwart this effort on the global stage.

[102] Martin and Yaquinto 2007, 625, 627.

[103] Brief of Appellants and Joint Appendix, U.S. Court of Appeals for the Federal Circuit, 14.

[104] Brief of Appellants and Joint Appendix, U.S. Court of Appeals for the Federal Circuit, 34–35.

Obadele's responses to an ORA form entitled "Declaration for Unique Cases" were revealing:

Citizenship:
"New Afrikan"

Address prior to evacuation and internment:
"Street and City are unknown because the relocation began with the forcible relocation of my forebears from Afrika beginning before 1865, under U.S. law, for purposes of enslavement and dehumanization"

Property loss from internment:
"Property losses include destruction of links to my ancestral family and heritage, including loss of names, community rights and family structure .... Loss includes deprivation of my liberty because of the denial of self-determination rights to me by the manner in which the U.S. Congress, the U.S. Supreme Court and U.S. Presidents ... interpret(ed) the Fourteenth Amendment insisting that me and other New Afrikans have no right to citizenship other than United States. This right belongs to me/us as descendants of persons wrongfully kidnapped from Afrika and wrongfully restrained in the U.S."[105]

Obadele thus used the U.S. government's own administrative procedures and language to illuminate the comparative injustice of redressing the smaller injury done to Japanese Americans and ignoring the larger injury done to Black people.

When the ORA declared that Obadele and Rashid were ineligible to submit claims under the Civil Liberties Act because they were not Japanese American, Obadele wrote a letter (October 13, 1998) to Acting Assistant Attorney General for Civil Rights, Bill Lan Lee, asking him to reverse this finding and to provide for New Afrikans "five times the $20,000 [paid to former internees] on the basis of the longer racist suffering of the members of the class, as compared with the suffering of the Japanese, who well deserved the small amount of money awarded them."[106] Japanese Americans deserved reparations, but Black people were owed a much larger amount because slavery lasted for much longer than (and was much more severe than) internment. The following year, Obadele and Rashid filed a joint complaint with the U.S. Court of Claims, arguing that the denial of payments under the Civil Liberties Act violated the Equal Protection Clause of the Fourteenth Amendment

---

[105] Brief of Appellants and Joint Appendix, U.S. Court of Appeals for the Federal Circuit, 40, 43.
[106] Brief of Appellants and Joint Appendix, U.S. Court of Appeals for the Federal Circuit, 15.

and the Due Process Clause of the Fifth Amendment.[107] The favoritism toward Asian Americans, in other words, was a constitutionally impermissible injury against Black people.

In *Obadele* v. *United States* (2002), Judge Lawrence Baskir denied the U.S. government's motion to dismiss on procedural issues but granted the government's motion for judgment on the administrative record. He wrote: "Make no mistake, the Plaintiffs have made a powerful case for redress as representatives of a racial group … who were enslaved, oppressed, and disenfranchised."[108] And the U.S. Supreme Court had ruled in *Adarand Constructors* v. *Peña* (1995) that all governmental racial classifications, even apparently benign ones, must be subjected to strict scrutiny. However, Baskir continued, the D.C. Circuit Court had already ruled in *Jacobs* v. *Barr* (1992)—a case where a German American who had been interned challenged the Civil Liberties Act on equal protection grounds—that this law did, in fact, survive strict scrutiny, and that it was narrowly tailored to achieve a compelling government interest (here, redressing national discrimination against Japanese Americans). Baskir saw this case as decisive for *Obadele* and thus rejected the plaintiffs' claims. But Baskir overlooked a key factual difference between the two cases. As a white man, Jacobs did not merit reparations because he was not subjected to racial discrimination as Japanese Americans had been. Thus he was not denied equal protection by being denied benefits under the Civil Liberties Act. But the facts were different for Obadele as a Black man.

Obadele's Appellant brief stated: "In the underlying case, the government presented no evidence to resolve the basic Constitutional question as to why, based solely upon racial preferences, 'the Congress sought to provide reparations to Japanese Americans, yet [the Congress] following the three hundred plus years of slavery and post slavery years, has never provided reparations to African Americans.'"[109] It also claimed that Judge Baskir of the Court of Claims failed to conduct a proper strict scrutiny exam that assessed whether the government interest in remedying Japanese American injury justified the infliction of injury on appellants, namely, the "denial of equal treatment" even though "they had suffered and continue to suffer similar and longer injury … than that suffered by

---

[107] Kalonji Tor Olusegun was also one of the group who filed the original complaint; he dropped out of the lawsuit when it was appealed.
[108] *Obadele* v. *United States* (2002), United States Court of Federal Claims, 14.
[109] Brief of Appellants and Joint Appendix, U.S. Court of Appeals for the Federal Circuit, 25.

the Japanese who were compensated under the Act."[110] In April 2003, the U.S. Court of Appeals for the Federal Circuit ruled against Obadele and Rashid, affirming the decision of the U.S Court of Claims. The U.S. Supreme Court then denied certiorari, bringing the litigation to a close. The *Obadele* lawsuit did not succeed in legal terms, and it received little public or scholarly attention, but it entered the historical record as a rare indictment of the structural favoritism shown to Asian Americans and an attempt to name the injury done to Black people through violations of comparative desert.

VII THE NOT-BLACKNESS OF SOON JA DU

During the 1970s and 1980s, the growing presence of Korean immigrant storeowners in poor urban Black neighborhoods became an unmistakable symbol of the Asian–Black gap. The scenario was strikingly reminiscent of the Mississippi Delta in the 1920s, where Gong Lum and other Chinese immigrant merchants with a Black customer base used their stores as a vehicle of upward mobility into near-whiteness. U.S. immigration policy after 1965 favored those with capital (human and otherwise), and Korean immigrants were from relatively advantaged backgrounds (many were middle or lower middle class, had held white collar jobs in Korea, and were college educated). They used a combination of personal savings and loans (from relatives, friends, banks, or rotating credit associations) to start up stores. Once in the U.S., their not-Blackness shaped their entry as small business owners into the racial capitalist order. Unlike Black people, they were not subjected to residential segregation, targeted by police violence, or swept up into the prison-industrial complex. Though excluded for the most part from the general labor market because of language and accent, they faced no major obstacles moving into white neighborhoods and purchasing stores in Black neighborhoods. Most importantly, their children enjoyed social and economic mobility, often entering professional occupations and becoming white-adjacent. At the same time, discrimination in employment and lending, residential segregation, overpolicing, and incarceration depressed Black entrepreneurship rates, rendering poor Black urban residents a captive customer base.[111] Korean immigrant mobility, in this sense, was premised on Black immobility, the former's accumulation of

---

[110] Brief of Appellants and Joint Appendix, U.S. Court of Appeals for the Federal Circuit, 23.
[111] Wacquant 2002, 52–53.

assets premised upon the latter's dispossession.[112] This is part of what Toni Morrison meant when she quipped that immigrants coming to the U.S. get ahead "on the backs of Blacks."

Like Chinese and Japanese immigrants before them, Korean immigrants in the 1970s and 1980s traveled global circuits of anti-Blackness.[113] As far back as the late 1800s, Japanese and Chinese texts informed by Western race science influenced Korean thought, and the influx of U.S. cultural products after the Second World War cemented the tendency toward negrophobia.[114] A 1992 survey of Korean immigrant storeowners in New York City showed that 70 percent believed Black people were more criminally oriented than whites, 61 percent thought they were less intelligent than whites, 45 percent viewed them as lazy, and only 13 percent thought they were poor because of racial discrimination.[115] Owning a store in a poor urban area was seen as status derogation precisely because of its proximity to Blackness, and Koreans only resorted to this when they "lack[ed] the financial and cultural capital necessary" to purchase stores in affluent white areas.[116] The ghetto was the temporary purgatory they endured for the sake of their children's future.

On March 16, 1991, two weeks after the beating of Rodney King by LAPD officers, ninth-grader Latasha Harlins, who was Black, walked into the Empire Liquor Stores in Compton to buy some orange juice. She took a carton of orange juice that cost $1.79 out of the refrigerator, stuck it in the top of her backpack, and approached the counter with two dollar bills in her hand. Korean immigrant storeowner Soon Ja Du confronted her and accused her of trying to steal the orange juice. She then attacked Latasha, grabbing her sweater and trying to wrest the backpack from her by force. Latasha struck her several times in the face, picked up the orange juice (which had fallen on the ground), placed it on the counter, and turned and started walking toward the door. Soon Ja Du picked up a stool from behind the counter and threw it at Latasha, then pulled out a gun, aimed it at Latasha, and killed her with a single shot to the back of the head. Police found the two dollar bills still crumpled in Latasha's hand.

At the trial, Soon Ja Du's defense attorney depicted the shooting as an act of self-defense against the threat of Blackness. In an anti-Black order,

---

[112] Sexton 2010a.
[113] Kim and Jung 2021; Kim and Jung 2019.
[114] J. Kim 2015.
[115] Min 1996, 121.
[116] Abelmann and Lie 1995, 138.

self-defense is a loophole which authorizes virtually unlimited violence against Black people, since the fear of Blackness is not only reasonable but the organizing principle of society. Immediately after the shooting, Soon Ja Du and her husband, Billy Du, told law enforcement that Latasha Harlins was trying to steal money from the cash register, which the store video later disproved. Billy Du said "my wife shoot the robber lady" to the 911 dispatcher and the first police on the scene. Asked about this under cross-examination, he first denied saying it and then was forced to admit it.[117] Soon Ja Du testified at length about how her family had been harassed by Crips gang members in the period leading up to the shooting, and how she thought Latasha was a gang member based on how she was dressed.

Assistant District Attorney Roxane Carvajal pointed out in her closing statement that two facts undermined the self-defense claim: first, Soon Ja Du was the original aggressor, and second, she could not have felt in imminent danger if Latasha had turned her back and started walking out of the store.[118] Regardless of the legal technicalities, though, the Black person is, by definition, the aggressor in an anti-Black society. Commenting on the acquittal of the police officers who beat Rodney King, Judith Butler wrote:

The visual representation of the black male body being beaten on the street by the policemen and their batons was taken up by that racist interpretive framework to construe King as the *agent* of violence, one whose agency is phantasmatically implied as the narrative precedent and antecedent to the frames that are shown. Watching King, the white paranoiac forms a sequence of narrative intelligibility that consolidates the racist figure of the black man: "He *had* threatened them, and now he is being justifiably restrained." "If they cease hitting him, he *will* release his violence, and now is being justifiably restrained" .... The police are thus structurally placed to protect whiteness against violence, where violence is the imminent action of that black male body. And because within this imaginary schema, the police protect whiteness, their own violence cannot be read as violence; because the black male body, prior to any video, is the site and source of danger, a threat, the police effort to subdue this body, even if in advance, is justified regardless of the circumstances.[119]

Even if Black aggression is not visible within the temporal frame, it is projected onto the past and imminent future to make sense of anti-Black violence in the present. Like Rodney King, Latasha Harlins is "the site

[117] Stevenson 2013.
[118] Stevenson 2013.
[119] Butler 1993, 16. Italics in original.

and source of danger, a threat," so any "effort to subdue this body, even if in advance, is justified regardless of the circumstances" and "cannot be read as violence." Soon Ja Du's not-Blackness, meanwhile, meant that she, too, like the police, was "structurally placed to protect" property, society, and order. Her zealousness in this role was forgiven in advance.

Another defense strategy was to argue that the gun, which had been briefly stolen and recovered prior to the shooting, had been tampered with so that it discharged too easily. Du claimed that she had no knowledge of guns and that she had not meant to shoot Latasha and had no memory of doing so because she fainted right after.[120] Consider this exchange between defense attorney Richard Leonard and Soon Ja Du:

Richard Leonard:
At any point in time, do you remember pointing this gun at the back of the head of that young lady and pulling the trigger?

Soon Ja Du:
I don't even know where the focus of the trigger is, and I don't know that I even touched it ...

Richard Leonard:
When was the first time you knew that the girl had been shot with the gun that you had in your hand?

Soon Ja Du:
After I went to the hospital.[121]

Under cross-examination from ADA Carvajal, Du refused to admit that she knew one had to pull the trigger in order to fire a gun, adding: "I do not recall even discharging the gun. I don't even remember the bullet going out of the gun."[122] She was in a mental fugue from Latasha's "iron fist," she claimed, and did not realize that she was getting the gun, pulling it out of the holster, aiming, and pulling the trigger. This was not the only time Du claimed to have lost consciousness. Doctors who examined her at the Martin Luther King Jr. Medical Center after the shooting reported to police that she feigned being more injured than she was, in addition to acting unconscious during the physical exam and then waking up and looking around when she thought she was alone.[123] As Patricia Dwyer, the Los Angeles County probation officer, wrote in

[120] Chae 2002.
[121] From the trial transcript, quoted in Stevenson 2013, 158.
[122] Stevenson 2013, 160.
[123] Stevenson 2013.

her report: "Psychomotor testing indicated that defendant was in fact conscious, and staff observed the defendant sitting up and alert when she believed she was not being watched by hospital personnel."[124]

Dwyer's report described Du as being in "an uncontrollable rage" when she shot Latasha Harlins and noted that she made no effort to help the girl after the shooting.[125] In "To Be Almost Like White: The Case of Soon Ja Du" (2002), Augustina Chae wrote: "Soon Ja's actions indicate more rage at Latasha than fear of her .... Her belief system dictated that she should not submit to a young black girl and should make Latasha obey her at all costs even if it meant killing her."[126] Did Du act out of a fury fueled by anti-Black contempt? This was in part about class: having belonged to the local elite in Korea, Du was thought by some to have a "sense that she was of a different class, of a higher class, than most of the people she met in Korea or Los Angeles."[127] But it was also about anti-Blackness. Would Du have confronted, accused and physically attacked a white teenage girl? Would she have been so enraged by a white girl's punches that she pulled out a gun and shot her in the back of the head? Or did she, like the Chinese grocer in the South during the civil rights movement (quoted in Part One), consider it her prerogative to lay her hands on a Black girl with impunity?

After a racially diverse jury convicted Du of voluntary manslaughter, both ADA Carvajal and probation officer Patricia Dwyer recommended the maximum sentence of sixteen years in prison. During her pretrial interview with Du, Dwyer had been "so struck by Soon Ja's apparent lack of remorse that she was certain it was because something was being lost in translation." Dwyer "concluded the meeting and asked that Du return with a different interpreter," Brenda Stevenson recounts, only to realize that the problem was not one of translation after all.[128] In the interview with Dwyer, Du had declared, "They [Blacks] look healthy, young ... big question why they don't work ... [they] got welfare money and buying alcoholic beverages and consuming them instead of feeding children."[129] She had also said "if she [Latasha] was born in a better family," she would not have acted as she did.[130] Dwyer thus concluded

---

[124] Cited in Chae 2002, 105.
[125] Chae 2002, 118.
[126] Chae 2002, 114–115.
[127] Stevenson 2013, 61.
[128] Stevenson 2013, 234.
[129] Stevenson 2013, 233.
[130] Stevenson 2013, 233.

that race played a role in Du's actions that day. When Du made these comments to Dwyer, she disregarded what Charles Lloyd, a Black attorney on her defense team, had cautioned about revealing her anti-Black prejudices to investigators. If this was how Du spoke when duly warned, when her freedom was on the line, how did she speak under less exigent circumstances?

Los Angeles Superior Court Judge Joyce Karlin, a white woman, gave Du a suspended ten-year sentence, five years' probation, and 400 hours of community service, and charged her a $500 fine plus funeral expenses for Latasha. Karlin cast Du as a hardworking wife and mother who was overwhelmed by circumstances, shot Latasha by accident, and would never do anything like it again. In the sentencing colloquy, Karlin declared that Du and other shopkeepers "lawfully possess firearms for their own protection"; that Du had no criminal record and had committed this crime only "under circumstances of great provocation, coercion and duress"; and that none of this would have happened "if the gun she [Du] grabbed for protection had not been altered."[131] Du, Karlin concluded, was not "a danger to society."

At the same time, Karlin cast Latasha Harlins as a violent criminal. Karlin stated: "Although Latasha Harlins was not armed with a weapon at the time of her death, she had used her fists as weapons just seconds before she was shot," and her "assault on Mrs. Du" was not justified.[132] Karlin conjectured: "Had Latasha Harlins not been shot and had the incident which preceded the shooting been reported, it is my opinion that the district attorney would have relied on the videotape and Mrs. Du's testimony to make a determination whether to file charges against Latasha."[133] Latasha would have been the one on trial if not for the intervening event of her death. When ADA Carvajal observed that the case was a test of whether Black lives mattered, Karlin angrily pushed back: "Statements by the district attorney, [which] suggest that imposing less than the maximum sentence will send a message that a black child's life is not worthy of protection, [are] dangerous rhetoric, which serves no purpose other than to pour gasoline on a fire."[134]

Karlin concluded: "Did Mrs. Du react inappropriately to Latasha? Absolutely. Was Mrs. Du's over-reaction understandable? I think so."[135]

---

[131] Gotanda 1996, 248–249.
[132] Gotanda 1996, 248.
[133] Gotanda 1996, 249.
[134] Sentencing colloquy quoted in Gotanda 1996, 247.
[135] Gotanda 1996, 250.

Shooting Latasha in the back of her head and killing her was ill-advised and intemperate, but relatable. If Karlin had a white fourteen-year-old daughter who went into a store to buy orange juice, was falsely accused of shoplifting, assaulted, and then shot in the back of the head and killed, would Karlin use words like "inappropriate" and "understandable?" Black death is ultimately illegible in an anti-Black society. *The killer was not a killer, the victim was not a victim, the crime was not a crime.* By virtue of her not-Blackness, Du stood in as a proxy for whites defending their property against Black aggression. The trial thus became another ritualized occasion for rearticulating what Asian Americanness and Blackness mean in the eyes of the law, and for reinstantiating the Asian–Black gap. It did not matter that Du was not particularly likeable. All she needed was not-Blackness.

Although many in the Korean community in Los Angeles thought that the killing was wrong and resented the negative attention Du had brought to them, they rallied behind her out of a sense of community self-interest. *The Korea Times* argued that Du was being scapegoated to deflect attention from the Rodney King beating.[136] It also accused the mainstream media of presenting all Koreans as violent and neglecting to mention the Korean storeowners who had been killed by Black robbers. Both the English-language weekly and Korean-language daily editions of *The Korea Times* repeated Du's false claims about Latasha's aggression and criminality without correcting them. On March 18, 1991, two days after the incident, the Korean-language daily edition ran an article with the headline "A Black Teenage Girl Demanded Money and Punched [the woman storeowner]."[137] This article set the tone for the paper's coverage of the trial, which shaped public opinion within the local Korean community. When Black leaders launched a recall drive to remove Karlin from the bench, Augustina Chae notes, Korean community leaders "sen[t] her support letters, formed a group to back her in the 1992 election, and to raise money for [her] re-election."[138] Karlin had their back, and they had hers.

VIII KOREAN AMERICAN INNOCENCE

Korean American activists, community leaders, filmmakers, and scholars have cast Korean merchants as innocent victims who are minding

---

[136] Stevenson 2013.
[137] Chae 2002.
[138] Chae 2002, 159.

their own business (literally) when they get caught up through no fault of their own in the race war between whites and Blacks. According to this narrative, Korean immigrants come to the U.S. to pursue the American Dream—"We came to America to spread our young dreams"—only to find themselves attacked by those at the bottom (Black people) and abandoned by those at the top (white people).[139] Korean American journalist K. W. Lee, for example, describes Koreans as a scapegoat: "For the power structure, 4/29 was a knee-jerk divide-and-rule way of successfully diverting black anger [about Rodney King]."[140] The terms of self-description used by many Korean Americans—scapegoat, human shield, sacrificial lamb, pawn, mascot, America's punching bag, etc.—emphasize the group's innocence and victimhood.

Korean Americans centered themselves in the Los Angeles rebellion story by naming the events "Sa-I-Gu," or April 29 in Korean. In Korean tradition, important political events are named by their date (e.g., the March 1 Movement of 1919, which protested Japanese colonial rule). The term "Sa-I-Gu" located the attacks on Korean-owned stores in Los Angeles within the narrative frame of the Korean national and diasporic experience. As K. W. Lee wrote, "[Sa-I-Gu was] the latest validation of our *Hahn* [suffering] embedded in our soul through an unending series of upheavals and oppressions, foreign and domestic, for nearly a millennium, thanks to the cursed geopolitics of the rabbit-shaped peninsula surrounded by covetous powers."[141] Asserting this frame effectively shut down the frame that viewed the acquittal of the four LAPD officers as yet another moment in the centuries-long abjection of Black people. Elaine Kim, for example, wrote: "[M]any Korean Americans have trouble calling what happened in Los Angeles an 'uprising.' At the same time, we cannot quite say it was a 'riot.' So some of us have taken to calling it *sa-i-ku*, April 29, after the naming of other events in Korean history."[142] Why do many Korean Americans have trouble calling the uprising an uprising? What is obscured or disavowed when the term "Sa-I-Gu" is used instead?

The scapegoating trope suggests that Korean Americans suffer the double burden of white *and* Black hostility—which is to say, they are even worse off than Black people, who are only targeted by whites.

---

[139] A line spoken by Jung Hui Lee in the film *Sa-I-Gu* (1993).
[140] K. W. Lee 2012a, 87. Note how this claim reproduces tropes of Black unreason and Black political immaturity/incapacity.
[141] K. W. Lee 2012b, 91.
[142] E. Kim 1993, 216.

In this way, the Asian–Black gap is not only denied but *inverted*. Sumi Cho writes about the "triple scapegoating" inflicted upon Korean Americans, as they were targeted for looting and arson by Black people, abandoned by white powerholders, and subjected to media sensationalization and stereotyping.[143] K. W. Lee invokes the Holocaust: "[Sa-I-Gu] was our made-in-America Warsaw, where ghetto Jews in the capital of Poland, under brutal Nazi boots, stood all alone against the world. Of all places on earth, we have met our own latter-day pogrom in the City of Angels."[144] If Korean Americans were ghettoized Jews on April 29, does this mean Black protesters were Nazis? For Koreans to be cast as the ultimate victims, Black people must be displaced from that status and fantasized into a position of power.

In "In Defense of Destroying Property" (2020), R. H. Lossin asks why dispossessed protesters are expected to be non-violent "in the face of overwhelming state brutality and structural economic and racial injustice." Lossin writes:

Property destruction [by protesters] is not synonymous with the violence that is being protested …. Property is itself a violent thing, especially in a poor black neighborhood. It is created through a combination of state-sponsored expropriation and exploitation and it is defended by various forms of state-sanctioned violence …. In light of the economic deprivation experienced by large portions of the population, the vandalizing of property and the theft of goods could just as easily be framed as the enforcement of a moral economy—the rightful appropriation of stolen wealth.[145]

If private property is a congealed form of violence, then looting and burning can be understood as a form of self-defense against that violence. Looters denaturalize capitalist inequalities in defiance of the police who reinforce them. Vicky Osterweil writes: "When rioters take territory and loot, they are revealing precisely how, in a space without cops, property relations can be destroyed and things can be had for free …. [They are] getting straight to the heart of the problem of the police, property, and white supremacy."[146]

"[A] space without cops" is precisely what the Korean storeowners in Los Angeles feared. Korean community leaders lamented that during the uprising the police went to guard Beverly Hills, a predominantly white,

[143] Cho 1993, 197.
[144] K. W. Lee 2012b, 91–92.
[145] Lossin 2020.
[146] Osterweil 2014.

affluent area, while leaving areas with Korean-owned stores unprotected. Even when LAPD officers were on the scene, they were observed standing by and watching while people looted and vandalized Korean-owned stores. (A moment like this is captured in the film *Sa-I-Gu*, discussed below.) Korean Americans felt abandoned by the U.S. state, and indeed they were, but there are different forms of abandonment. To be ignored by the police in moments of crisis is one kind of abandonment, to be systematically targeted, demeaned, harassed, beaten, imprisoned, and killed by the police is another. Korean Americans experience the first kind of abandonment because they are neither white nor wealthy *and escape the second kind of abandonment because they are not-Black.* Exemption from structural disadvantage, even if relative and incomplete, is a form of structural advantage.

In the vacuum created by police neglect, some Korean American storeowners armed themselves with shotguns and semiautomatic rifles and stood on the roofs of their stores. *Radio Korea* mobilized squads of Korean American men from throughout Southern California to assist them. During a radio interview, one Korean storeowner said that people engaged in looting were "like beasts ... [t]hey are not men."[147] Ironically, the one Korean American killed in the Los Angeles uprising, Edward Jae Song Lee, was shot accidentally by a Korean storeowner who mistook him for a looter. The movie *Sa-I-Gu* (1993) approaches Lee's killing as a tragedy to be lamented and never asks: Was it acceptable for the store-owner to shoot at people taking things from the stores? Would it still be a tragedy if he had killed one of them instead of Lee?

On May 11, 1992, *Newsweek* ran a story on the uprising that featured a photograph of a Korean American man with a tense expression walking on a streetcorner, holding up a semiautomatic pistol.[148] A firetruck is visible in the background, along with smoke from a burning store. The caption under the photo is from another Korean American interviewed for the story: "This is not America." The man with the gun wears a t-shirt with an iconic picture of Malcolm X, in which he is looking out the window while holding a shotgun at his side, ready to defend himself. Beneath the photo of Malcolm X, the t-shirt reads: "By Any Means Necessary." As David Palumbo-Liu observes, this visual image overflows with meaning. He asks: "How has an icon of Black Power been uprooted from its historical specificity and appropriated, so that it now seems to

---

[147] Stevenson 2013, 305.
[148] Palumbo-Liu 1994, 367.

sanction and even prescribe counterviolence against blacks and others who might *threaten* the dominant ideology?"[149]

By wearing the t-shirt during the uprising—surely not a coincidence—the Korean American man asserts an identification with Malcolm X. Except it is not whites coming for Black people, but Black (and Latinx) people coming for Koreans. Here Koreans displace Black people as innocent victims, and the latter morph into malevolent aggressors. As Palumbo-Liu suggests, Malcolm X's authority is then invoked to support shooting Black protesters, as if standing on one's store roof and shooting people who are taking your property were the same thing as defending one's life against government assassination—or as if being Asian American were the same thing as being Black in America.[150] The Black struggle is disavowed coming and going. We are left with the question: why is the Korean American man claiming to be Black—or, more precisely, putting Blackness on momentarily—while doing the work of the police?

Korean storeowners sustained almost half of the damage inflicted upon property during the Los Angeles rebellion of 1992.[151] The very presence of Korean immigrant storeowners in poor Black neighborhoods was a reminder of the structural advantage they enjoyed in an anti-Black order. The phobic hatred of Blackness that some demonstrated in their personal interactions with Black customers added insult to injury. When Judge Joyce Karlin spared Du prison time and offered a colloquy exonerating Du and demonizing Latasha, the message was clear: Korean immigrants, like whites, could murder Black people with impunity. Indeed, this was one of the defining prerogatives of not-Blackness. The targeting of Korean-owned stores in South Central and Koreatown in April 1992 was a collective indictment of Korean immigrants as beneficiaries of and participants in structural anti-Blackness.

IX *SA-I-GU*, THE MOVIE

Writer-director Dai Sil Kim-Gibson says the movie *Sa-I-Gu* (April 29) was "born in a hurry, full of raw emotion and the pain of Korean American

---

[149] Palumbo-Liu 1994, 368. Italics in original.
[150] When the restaurant of a Bangladeshi family in Minneapolis was destroyed by fire during the protests against George Floyd's murder, Ruhel Islam was overheard by his daughter on the phone, saying: "Let my building burn. Justice needs to be served." Later he said "We can rebuild a building, but we cannot rebuild a human" (Nierenberg 2020).
[151] Stevenson 2013.

women."[152] Three months after the Los Angeles uprising, Kim-Gibson, along with Christine Choy and Elaine Kim, borrowed filmmaking equipment and "rushed to Los Angeles in anger, fury, and sorrow."[153] In the film's opening segment, Kim-Gibson explains she wanted to make a movie to "give voice to the voiceless victims, i.e., the Korean American shopkeepers and shopowners who lost everything in the Los Angeles upheaval." From the start, then, the film centers Korean Americans as the true victims of the events—those who were "voiceless" and "lost everything." Black people are moved offstage, to return as silent malefactors later.

The film's organizing frame, symbolizing collective loss and grief, centers on the death of Eddie (Edward Jae Song Lee), the one Korean American who died in the uprising (after being shot by a Korean storeowner who mistook him for a looter). The film opens with his mother Jung Hui recalling that Eddie was agitated by the uprising and wanted to help other Koreans, so he rushed out to see how he could get involved. Photos of Eddie's childhood flash by as Jung Hui wistfully describes an immigrant family experience shaped by economic precarity. As the film proceeds, a handful of other Korean immigrant storeowners also tell their anguished stories, but we return again and again to the Lees, where the drama of Eddie's death is slowly spun out. The climactic moment occurs when Jung Hui realizes her son is dead. Shown the black and white photo of the unidentified man shot by the Korean storeowner, she thought it could not be Eddie because the man in the photo was wearing a dark shirt and Eddie was wearing a white shirt that day. But then she sees a color version of the photo and realizes that the man's t-shirt was not dark but blood-soaked. At Eddie's funeral, mourners weep and wail, and the soundtrack becomes assertively plaintive. The last scene shows the Lees standing in front of their house, looking forlorn, as Jung Hui says in a voiceover that she still waits for Eddie to come home even though she knows he never will.

Toward the end of the film, Jung Hui says: "At the time, I thought it was one man who shot him but if I think of it broadly, it was not an individual. It was not just an individual matter. Something is drastically wrong." Black–white racial conflict is raging out of control, she implies, and Eddie's death was collateral damage. The effect of her statement, affectively if not logically, is to transfer the viewer's mounting anger over Eddie's death to the Black people who participated in the uprising,

---

[152] J. Y. Kim 2014, 146.
[153] J. Y. Kim 2014, 146.

thus erasing the role of the Korean shooter and safeguarding the trope of Korean innocence. The gun was fired, Eddie was killed, but no one (individual) shot him. Indeed, the Korean shooter is given no time on screen. We never see him or hear him or learn his name. In diegetic terms, he does not exist. The situation was to blame for Eddie's death, not the shooter. *If it had not been for the riots, Eddie would be alive.* Having been displaced at the start of the film, Black people are brought back at the end to shoulder the blame. It is telling that not a single Black person speaks to the camera during the entire film. We see Black customers, Black looters, Black children playing in the street, but we never hear their voices. *Blackness is a mute and destructive force.*

When Jung Hui says "something is drastically wrong," what is she referring to? Structural anti-Blackness? The murder of Latasha Harlins? The fact that Soon Ja Du got no prison time? Judge Joyce Karlin's sentencing colloquy? The near-fatal beating of Rodney King? The acquittal of the four officers? The segregation, discrimination, and state violence that impoverish and oppress Black communities? The structural and functional linkages among slavery, Jim Crow, the ghetto, and the prison system? The illegibility of Black protest in an anti-Black society? Or how all of this landed on Korean storeowners and her family in particular?

One of the storeowners, Mrs. Han, says on camera:

To me, it is unfair that African American people attack Korean people at this time. From what I understand, they have accumulated all their problems and frustrations against white people, and now they express their anger against Koreans. When I think about it, I am most angry at white people. If the government had watched over the blacks better, this would not have happened to us.[154]

Black people scapegoated Koreans during the rebellion, though ultimately it was the fault of whites for not "watching over" them better. "Because we are Koreans," another storeowner added, "Americans and Blacks treat us like this." (Note that in this formulation, "Americans" and "Blacks" are mutually exclusive categories.) Choon Ah Song, another storeowner, recounts that her husband used to dress in a Santa costume and give Christmas gifts to (Black) neighborhood kids, and that after their store burned down, the kids asked them to reopen and give them a July 4 barbeque party. She declares: "I felt betrayed by the black kids. All my love for them turned to nothing." *We treated them so well, and this is what we get in return.* By reducing intergroup issues to an interpersonal

---

[154] Quoted in Song 2005, 161.

matter, Song erases the structural inequalities that fueled and shaped the conflict in the first place.

Watching *Sa-I-Gu*, one wonders how far the filmmakers went to conceal Korean women's anti-Black views. On the topic of editing, Elaine Kim, one of the filmmakers, stated in a media interview: "[T]here was one [Korean American] woman who really hated and feared African Americans. She was a wreck, watching African American children like a hawk, thinking they were all about to steal something from her store. We didn't include her comments."[155] Why did the filmmakers leave this woman out of the film? Were her beliefs unrepresentative of other storeowners? Or was the problem rather that she was too direct in expressing them? What difference would it have made if they had included her in the film? How much would it have undercut the narrative of Korean innocence and victimhood?

In an interview after the film's release, writer-director Dai Sil Kim-Gibson recounted the following incident:

> I was at the Human Rights Festival in New York City with *Sa-I-Gu* in 1993. During the Q&A—I will never forget this—an African American man raised his hand and said, "Do you have any fucking idea how many African American young people died that day? Why are you making such a big fucking deal about one person who died?" I've never experienced such a hostile, powerful question. Even though the way he put it was unfair, I think I understood his anger. I was just silent for two seconds. Then I told him I was twelve years old at the time of the Korean war. When I first saw a dead body, it was beyond shock. My brother was hit by shrapnel and I had to cross over dead bodies to find him a doctor. By that time, I had seen many dead bodies. I became numb. Can you imagine how many American kids and Americans parents for that matter sit in their living rooms watching the television? They see so many mass deaths, thinking nothing of it. If you want to humanize life, you also have to humanize death. This detailed story of Edward Lee is my way of telling people that for every death there is a grieving mother. The audience and my questioner were as quiet as if cold water had been poured on them. I was shocked and grateful and I didn't blame him because he had the right to be angry. Our age ignores death.[156]

The way Kim-Gibson evades the man's point here is symptomatic of how the film itself forgets, misunderstands, and overlooks Black suffering. The man's point is that the film elevates Eddie over Black victims, thus reinforcing the devaluation of Black lives. It is the *Obadele* principle: paying attention to Asian American suffering and not Black suffering,

[155] Quoted in Song 2004, 234.
[156] Quoted in Ratner 2011, 36.

when Black suffering is categorically worse, inflicts an additional injury on Black people. Though shaken by the man's "hostile" and "angry" words—she writes elsewhere: "[c]onfronted with a totally unexpected question, my legs went weak and my head was spinning"—Kim-Gibson refuses to hear him, covering over the specificity of anti-Blackness with generic observations about death.[157] What exactly triggered her vertigo? Was it being called out on that which she was repressing? Her statement "for every death there is a grieving mother" is especially ironic, since one of the hallmarks of slavery was "los[ing] your mother" and the denial of kinship ties.[158] *Partus sequitur ventrem* (that which is brought forth follows the belly/womb): the child follows the mother into slavery, where the mother–child bond is abrogated.

In 2004, Kim-Gibson released a new film, *Wet Sand: Voices from L.A.*, a sequel to *Sa-I-Gu*. As if still responding to the questioner at the Human Rights Festival, she said she had

decided to focus again on the victims, only this time, not just on Koreans, but on all the victims: African American, Latino, and white. As I mentioned, *Sa-I-Gu* was made in a hurry, and narrowly focused on Korean American women, but this time, I decided I needed to do more systematic research and explore the larger picture.[159]

Unlike *Sa-I-Gu*, *Wet Sand* discusses the Rodney King beating and the acquittal of the four officers, as well as the murder of Latasha Harlins. Kim-Gibson's desire to interview Black people this time was partly thwarted, however, by the distrust some showed toward her. (Some slammed their front doors in her face.) Significantly, Kim-Gibson chose to make Eddie's story the central frame once again. The film opens with Jung Hui brushing leaves off his grave and closes with her statement that "something is drastically wrong." After vowing to focus on "all the victims," Kim-Gibson is drawn irresistibly back to this one.

The Los Angeles rebellion was a wake-up call for many Korean Americans.[160] Being targeted by protesters was traumatic, as was being treated as not-whites by the U.S. state in a moment of crisis. The question is, how are Korean American trauma and grief to be addressed in an anti-Black world? In a world where Black trauma and grief are not episodic but structural features of the social order? How do we talk about the

[157] J. Y. Kim 2014, 149.
[158] Hartman 2007.
[159] J. Y. Kim 2014, 150.
[160] R. Kim 2012.

violence done to Korean Americans' property over the course of several days in relation to the violence done to Black people's bodies and souls over the course of hundreds of years of slavery and its afterlife? Can we acknowledge the loss of the Korean American dream and at the same time acknowledge that the dream was purchased, in James Baldwin's words, at the expense of the Black person? Can we recognize that Korean Americans suffered property losses during the rebellion, while remembering that in the end they still had "something to save"—namely, their not-Blackness?

X *BRIAN HO* V. *SFUSD*

The Asian spoilers line developed by Justice Powell in *Bakke* was resurrected a few decades later when the U.S. Supreme Court next took up the issue of affirmative action in higher education in *Grutter* v. *Bollinger* (2003). During the intervening period, an important development occurred that would influence the trajectory of anti-affirmative action politics in the U.S. In the 1990s, a group of conservative, affluent Chinese immigrants took up the Asian spoilers line themselves in an effort to end race-conscious admissions at Lowell High School, a prestigious alternative school in San Francisco. Their argument—that Lowell's affirmative action plan unfairly burdened Asian Americans in order to help Black and Latino students—reproduced right-wing discourses about meritocracy and equal opportunity, with a trenchant twist. As compared with white students, Asian American students had a more persuasive case to make precisely because they were racial minorities, too. If it was unfair to allow affirmative action to burden white students, it was even more unfair to allow it to burden Asian American students. The battle over Lowell marked the entry of conservative Chinese immigrant organizations into anti-affirmative action politics, where they have since become a formidable force on a national scale. Lowell served as a trial run that allowed these groups to hammer out the rhetoric and strategies they would deploy in subsequent anti-affirmative action campaigns.

By 1971, when parents of Black schoolchildren filed a lawsuit (*Johnson* v. *SFUSD*) against the San Francisco Unified School District, more than a century of de jure and de facto segregation had produced notable racial separation in San Francisco schools.[161] Finding that the city had intentionally maintained a system of de jure segregation in its

---

[161] *Facing Our Past, Changing Our Future*, Part I, 2020.

elementary schools, District Court Judge Stanley Weigel ordered it to come up with a desegregation plan.[162] The city then designed and implemented the Horsehoe Plan, which pursued "racial balance" by assigning students so that the percentage of each of four major subgroups differed by no more than fifteen points from the subgroup's districtwide percentage.[163] The main thrust of this plan was to mitigate Black exclusion from various schools, and it had measurable success in the dozen or so years it was in effect.

Opposition from white and Chinese American families, combined with white and Chinese American flight from the public school system, prompted the SFUSD to shift from the Horseshoe Plan to a new student assignment plan, Education Redesign, in 1978.[164] Instead of "racial balance," Educational Redesign sought "racial unidentifiability," mandating that each school have at least four of nine subgroups and that no one subgroup should exceed 45 percent of the student body (40 percent for alternative schools). This shifted the focus from rectifying Black exclusion to promoting diversity and ensuring that no one subgroup would become a majority.[165] Since there were no mandatory minimums for any particular subgroup, schools were not required to have any Black students at all. In addition, because Educational Redesign only required busing in neighborhoods that were not "naturally integrated," "Black students were disproportionately assigned to be bused compared to every other racial group in the district."[166]

In the spirit of *Bakke*, which was decided the same year, race-conscious admissions were shifting from redressing anti-Black discrimination to securing multiracial diversity as an end in itself. In June 1978, the San Francisco NAACP filed a lawsuit alleging that Educational Redesign would

[162] In June 1974, the Ninth Circuit Court of Appeals issued a ruling in *Johnson* v. *SFUSD*. The ruling held that the court's decision in *Keyes* v. *School District No. 1, Denver* (1973) required "segregatory intent" be shown in order to establish a finding of de jure segregation. Since the U.S. District Court for the Northern District of California had not taken this step, the case was remanded. It was also ordered that Chinese American intervenors (who were opposed to desegregation efforts) be heard at this point. No subsequent action was taken by either the plaintiffs or defendant, so District Court Judge Weigel dismissed the case in June 1978 without prejudice.

[163] Quinn 2020, 34. San Francisco voluntarily desegregated junior and senior high schools starting in September 1974 through Operation Integrate.

[164] *Facing Our Past, Changing Our Future*, Part II, 2020.

[165] The Black population in San Francisco in 1940 was 4,846. In 1970, it was 96,078. (Quinn 2020, 5). The white population of San Francisco began to decline in the 1960s, and the numbers of other not-white groups grew after 1965.

[166] *Facing Our Past, Changing Our Future*, Part II, 2020.

have a segregating effect on the city's schools. In 1983, the parties agreed to a court-supervised Consent Decree that retained Educational Redesign's formula for student assignment—known as Paragraph 13—and created new programs intended to enhance educational equality by (among other things) ending discriminatory disciplinary practices, diversifying faculty and staff, and creating high-quality schools in low-income areas.[167]

In 1992, the District Court commissioned a Committee of Experts to report on the status of the Consent Decree, eight years on. The report made three key observations. First, Chinese Americans had become the largest subgroup of students in the district, replacing Black students, who had been the largest subgroup when the Consent Decree started. (In 1967–1968, Chinese Americans were 13.5 percent of students. By 2007–2008, Chinese Americans comprised 31.4 percent of students, with Black students at 12.8 percent.[168]) Second, the report found that desegregation was proceeding, but Black and Latino students continued to struggle in terms of academic achievement. Third, the report flagged "the disparity in achievement scores between white and Chinese American students on the one hand and African American and Hispanic students on the other"— a disparity that was apparent despite the presence of low-income, LEP (limited English proficiency) Chinese students in the mix.[169] Henry Der, Executive Director of Chinese for Affirmative Action, lamented that San Francisco had created a two-tiered educational system where most Chinese students were paired with white students in better schools, and Black and Latino students were put together in worse schools.[170]

Similar findings were reported on a national scale in Gary Orfield's 1994 study of Asian American students and desegregation, which found that "Asian students are the most successful racial group in American schools."[171] Orfield wrote:

Theories are often put forward about the cultural norms that lead to hard work, values, family structure and other purported causes of better education. The assumption has often been that Asians, confronting the same challenges and

---

[167] Quinn 2020; Biegel 2008. Paragraph 13 specified nine racial groups: Spanish surname, other white, other non-white, Japanese, Chinese, Filipino, Korean, African American, and Native American. Each school was required to have four of these groups and no group was to be more than 40 percent of the student body (at alternative schools) or 45 percent of the student body at neighborhood schools (Fraga et al. 2005).

[168] Der 2008, 1087, 1092.

[169] Levine 2000, 52.

[170] Hong 1993.

[171] Orfield 1994, 1.

opportunities, were doing much better than other minority groups. This report examines whether or not the opportunities for contact with successful students and schools are equal for the various minority groups. It reports that, in general, Asians are far less likely than African Americans and Latinos to confront segregation either by race or poverty. Since racial and economic segregation are very strongly related to lower levels of school academic achievement, this means that most Asian students attend more competitive schools.[172]

Exposing the fallacy of minority equivalency—that they all "confron[t] the same challenges and opportunities"—Orfield showed that Asian Americans as a whole attended better schools than Blacks and Latinos, and had more contact with white students than these groups did, because they were less likely to be segregated and/or poor.[173] He wrote:

> Viewed on a national scale, Asians could much more appropriately be classified as an advantaged rather than a disadvantaged group of students and one that is far less segregated than African Americans and Latinos. Since, on average, Asian students score higher and come from families with higher average income than whites, and a great deal higher than other minority groups, both white and Asian students can be accurately described as coming from predominantly privileged groups (even though there are large numbers of both Asians and whites living in poverty and experiencing educational failure) .... Asians are in schools, on average, with two-thirds students from the groups with most success in U.S. education but Latinos and blacks, on average, attend schools with less than half this proportion of whites and Asians. To the extent that the background of other students in the school and school's level of academic competition contributes to student achievement, Asian students typically face a far more favorable school setting than other minority groups.[174]

Noting that "[i]t d[id] not make sense to treat very successful non-segregated groups of students as if they were segregated and disadvantaged," Orfield called for "a new concept of segregation" that acknowledged these complex multiracial dynamics.[175]

Admissions officers at Lowell High School set up differential required admissions scores for different subgroups in order to achieve a diverse incoming class where no one subgroup exceeded 40 percent (per the Consent Decree). Chinese American students, who constituted the largest single subgroup, had the highest required admissions score, followed

---

[172] Orfield 1994, 2.
[173] Orfield also acknowledges that some urban schools in cities receiving immigrants and/or refugees (for example, Minneapolis) have higher levels of Asian American segregation and more Asian American students in high-poverty schools.
[174] Orfield 1994, 14–15.
[175] Orfield 1994, 32.

by whites and other Asian subgroups, followed by Black and Latino students. Angered by the handicapping of their children, Chinese American parents decided to take action, but they were divided about how to proceed. Chinese for Affirmative Action (CAA) and the Chinese American Democratic Club (CADC) thought that the required admissions score for Chinese American students should be no higher than that of whites, but, at the same time, they were supportive of efforts to increase Black and Latino enrollment at Lowell.[176] By 1993, however, some members of the CADC had come out against race-conscious admissions altogether, and they planned a lawsuit to challenge the Consent Decree.

Since not all CADC members supported the lawsuit, those who did formed a separate organization for this purpose, the Asian American Legal Foundation (AALF). Claiming to be an "Asian American" as opposed to "Chinese American" organization accomplished a number of things. It not only implied that the organization and lawsuit were more panethnic and broad-based than they were (both were almost exclusively Chinese American), but also obscured the fact that the Lowell admissions system actually worked to the advantage of those Asian American groups who were underrepresented in Lowell's student body, including Filipino Americans and Southeast Asian Americans. In addition, the panethnic moniker linked the *Brian Ho* case to the Asian spoilers narrative that had emerged from the *Bakke* case and was being amplified in debates over race-conscious admissions in the University of California system.

Under the guidance of the AALF, a group of Chinese American students (Brian Ho et al.) initiated the lawsuit *Brian Ho* v. *SFUSD* in July 1994. On July 23, 1996, the plaintiffs filed a motion for summary judgment asking the District Court to end the Consent Decree.[177] The motion made three arguments. First, that the Lowell admissions program was unconstitutional because it violated the Equal Protection Clause of the Fourteenth Amendment. As a race-based classification scheme, it had to be subjected to strict scrutiny, and it failed to survive this test because there was no judicial finding of de jure segregation in San Francisco, which meant there was no "compelling government interest" to address. (Although District Court Judge Stanley Weigel had found de jure segregation in the city's schools in 1971, the Ninth Circuit Court of Appeals ruled a few years later that the standard for determining de jure segregation

---

[176] Quinn 2020.
[177] This was not the first time that Chinese Americans in San Francisco challenged desegregation efforts. See *Guey Heung Lee* v. *Johnson* (1971).

had become more exacting and remanded the case back to the District Court level, where no further action was taken.) Second, the plaintiffs' motion argued that the Lowell plan also failed the second prong of strict scrutiny in that the plan was not "narrowly tailored" to achieve its goals. Third, the motion argued that even if there had been de jure segregation in 1983, at the time the Consent Decree was established, the "vestiges" had since been eliminated "to the extent practicable."[178] There was no de jure segregation to speak of and thus the Consent Decree was unconstitutional. As in *Gong Lum*, Chinese American plaintiffs in *Brian Ho* made an equal protection argument that advanced their own interests and reinforced structural anti-Blackness.[179]

The San Francisco Unified School District submitted to the court an affidavit by Steve Phillips, president of the San Francisco Board of Education, in which he stated:

I am aware that all vestiges of the segregatory acts alleged by the San Francisco NAACP have not yet been eliminated .... We have not yet reached the level of achievement that would permit us to validly claim that the victims of prior segregatory acts are convinced that we have fully complied with the terms of the Consent Decree and that all vestiges of segregation have been removed .... Among the desegregation obligations referenced in the Consent Decree, which require our continued and focused attention are: (a) The over-representation of African-American males in Special Education; (b) Too many schools exceed Paragraph 13 guidelines; (c) Too many African-American and Latino students are in the bottom quantile in standardized achievement tests; (d) The grade point averages for African-American and Latino children are disproportionately low; and (e) The number of expulsions and suspensions of African-Americans, particularly males, is disproportionately high.[180]

This was a Board of Education official making a sworn statement that the segregation targeted by the Consent Decree had not yet been resolved. Supporters of the *Ho* plaintiffs offered a simple response: Even if "vestiges" of segregation persisted, Chinese American students should not be burdened by attempts to remedy them. The U.S. was a meritocracy, and because Chinese American students worked hard and achieved great things, they deserved the academic rewards in question. Disadvantaging them because of race—hurting one minority to help other minorities—was racist. As Rowena Robles wrote, the *Ho* plaintiffs and their supporters

---

[178] Plaintiffs' Motion for Summary Judgment, *Brian Ho* v. *SFUSD* (1996), 20.
[179] *Gong Lum* v. *Rice* (1927) is discussed at length in Part One.
[180] Quoted in *Brian Ho* v. *SFUSD*, ruling by United States Court of Appeals, Ninth Circuit, June 4, 1998, n.p.

"[took] advantage of the dominant construction of Asian Americans as the model minority and of the neoconservative discourse on reverse racism to portray themselves as victims of discrimination," relying as well on "contrasting constructions of African American and Latino students as undeserving and unqualified beneficiaries of race-based policies."[181]

Appropriating the language and imagery of the civil rights movement, Chinese American activists depicted the *Ho* plaintiffs as a subjugated class fighting bravely against the forces of segregation (a supposed alliance of Black people, state officials, and other powerful stakeholders). Amy Chang of the AALF declared: "The San Francisco school district, the state, and the NAACP have put themselves in the same position as George Wallace in the early 1960s—they are saying quotas then, quotas now, and quotas forever."[182] At a March 6, 1993 meeting of the San Francisco School Board, approximately 100 Chinese American adults and students took off their hats and shouted "No more caps! Jim Crow Must Go! Stop Discrimination Now!"[183] In this way, Chinese Americans displaced Black people from their own history and occupied it instead, borrowing the moral authority of the Black struggle to undercut a program that was the fruit of that struggle. Comparing their relatively affluent and advantaged children to Black victims of Jim Crow, they distorted historical truth in pursuit of their own goals.

District Court Judge Orrick denied the *Ho* plaintiffs' motion for summary judgment on May 6, 1997, prompting them to appeal the case to the Ninth Circuit Court of Appeals.[184] In June 1998, the Ninth Circuit Court dismissed the appeal for lack of jurisdiction, but not before stating that strict scrutiny did indeed apply in this case and detailing the questions left for trial: "Do vestiges remain of the racism that justified paragraph 13 of the consent decree in 1982? Is paragraph 13 necessary to remove the vestiges if they do remain?" Both sides readied expert witnesses and reports for the approaching trial. In February 1999, less than an hour before the trial was set to begin, the parties reached a

---

[181] Robles 2004, 73.

[182] Cited in Robles 2006, 50. The CADC said the Consent Decree scapegoated innocent Chinese children and was "San Francisco's own form of 'ethnic cleansing'" (quoted in Quinn 2020, 235).

[183] Lau 1993.

[184] Judge Orrick ruled that the Consent Decree was not unconstitutional under the standards that applied in 1983, and that even if there had been a problem, the *Ho* plaintiffs were barred from raising it now by *res judicata* because they were adequately represented when the Consent Decree was entered. See Levine (2000) for the issues left to be determined at trial.

settlement by which the Consent Decree would be amended to eliminate race/ethnicity as a basis for admission. The Chinese American
plaintiffs had won.

The impact of the *Ho* settlement was immediate.[185] For the fall 1999
freshman class at Lowell, Black and Latino admissions offers fell 50 percent from the previous year; fall 2000 saw another 15 percent decline, leaving Black students, who comprised 16 percent of the student population
citywide, as only 1.5 percent of Lowell's freshman class.[186] Stuart Biegel,
who was later hired as a monitor for the Consent Decree, described the
effect of the *Ho* settlement as "immediate resegregation."[187] According
to Biegel, the number of schools that were severely resegregated at one
or more grade levels went from 30 (out of 115) in 2001–2002 to 50 in
2005–2006.[188] During this period, the achievement gap between Black
and Latino students and other students grew larger—after it had diminished at various points under the original Consent Decree.[189] Biegel
wrote: "[T]he performance level at many severely resegregated schools
dropped dramatically during the post-1999 resegregation."[190] Black students, in particular, he pointed out, were "a community in crisis."[191]
Since the *Ho* case, the SFUSD has experimented with different student
assignment plans, but segregation has persisted at a high level. As of
September 2020, the SFUSD reported: "Despite the District's good intentions, San Francisco schools are more segregated now under the current
policy than they were thirty years ago."[192]

Progressive Asian Americans inside and outside the Chinese American
community took the *Ho* plaintiffs to task. Henry Der, Executive Director
of Chinese for Affirmative Action, opposed the *Ho* lawsuit from the start,
observing:

Chinese are at the best schools currently. Chinese dominate these schools, either
through academic admissions or neighborhood assignment .... [T]he assertions
and terms being used by CADC, such as "state-sponsored segregation," are not
based on fact or evidence .... The fact is Chinese are exercising choice and are as
mobile as any ethnic group in San Francisco high schools.[193]

---

[185] Der 2008.
[186] Hing 2001, 21.
[187] Biegel 2008, 187.
[188] Biegel 2008, 188.
[189] Biegel 2008, 192.
[190] Biegel 2008, 198.
[191] Biegel 2008, 195.
[192] *Facing Our Past, Changing Our Future*, Part II, 2020.
[193] Lim, July 1994.

The CADC, according to Der, "claim[ed] that Chinese are being victimized when it's the other way around. Chinese go to the best schools in significant numbers, they get bused the least, and they certainly exercise choice—what more do they want?"[194] In an article entitled "Asians Without Blacks and Latinos in San Francisco," Bill Ong Hing wrote:

Unfortunately, I think lessons of why we must be willing to make sacrifices for the common good have been cast aside. Instead, the Chinese American parents grabbed everything. Chinese American plaintiffs in *Ho* did not take the high road to do the right thing. In the process of fighting for what they believe would be just, they visited injustice on Latino and African American students in San Francisco.[195]

Emil Guillermo, writing in *The Filipino Express*, observed: "When the history of affirmative action is written, Chinese Americans will have a special place. They helped kill it." He continued:

This is what happens when a sense of balance between private desires and the public good is lost among many "successful" minorities. Chinese Americans, and many Asian Americans, are undergoing assimilation's debilitating impact. Acting as the selfish individual, it's easy to walk into a moral trap. Equal opportunity? Just for me, thank you. The DCALs [Denied Chinese Americans of Lowell] want it all, and they didn't seem to care about anyone else. Blacks? Latinos? Filipinos? If Lowell was the best, then they wanted it for their kids. If they were denied, then something was definitely wrong .... [This case] threatens to expose the existing holes in the artificial umbrella of a coalition we know as "Asian American" .... When the Chinese went rogue on the Lowell issue to look out for themselves, it was no different than a Clarence Thomas speaking out against the black civil rights mainstream.[196]

Both Hing and Guillermo lamented that *Ho* supporters showed no altruistic concern for other groups or the "public" or "common" good. In all of the progressive critique, however, a crucial question went unaddressed: is there a case to be made that Asian Americans as a whole, as well as whites and other not-Black groups, are *ethically obligated* to accept certain burdens *in order to offset the structural advantage of not-Blackness*?[197] Without an analysis of structural anti-Blackness and

[194] Lim, August 1994. The CAA proposed combining competitive admissions with a lottery system at Lowell, as well as removing group caps. The CADC insisted on "meritocracy" rather than a lottery. Other alternative schools in San Francisco have used a lottery system for admissions.
[195] Hing 2001, 27.
[196] Guillermo 1999.
[197] See Quinn (2020) for discussion of post-*Ho* efforts by Chinese American parents to challenge high school admissions plans in San Francisco.

the Asian–Black gap, progressives could not explore this question. Thus they could not offer the full-throated, historically grounded defense of race-conscious admissions that the moment required.

Buoyed by their success in the *Ho* case, conservative Chinese American groups began to think bigger. The Asian spoilers tack had succeeded in taking down affirmative action in the San Francisco public school system; would it work in higher education, too? Could Asian American students accomplish what white students had not been able to, namely forcing elite colleges and universities to end race-conscious admissions once and for all?

XI ASIAN/AMERICAN BLACKFACE

In April 2013, Lambda Theta Delta (LTD), the largest Asian American fraternity at University of California, Irvine, posted a YouTube video of four of its members singing Justin Timberlake and Jay-Z's "Suit and Tie." The member depicting Jay-Z was in blackface. At the bottom of the screen: "No racism intended. All fun and laughter." Ironically, the disclaimer both ruled out the ignorance defense (they knew they would appear racist) and demonstrated their ignorance (blackface minstrelsy was always about racism *and* fun, about racism *as* fun). Other evidence then emerged to confirm that this was not LTD's first spin around the minstrel stage. Local media picked up on the story and before long Vicki Vargas of NBC News was on campus asking how one minority group could do this to another. White fraternities have historically been avid practitioners of blackface, but what did it mean for an Asian American fraternity to black up?

The LTD episode seems less anomalous if we remember that blackface remains a worldwide phenomenon, an enduring expression of a collective, anti-Black unconscious. As the violent occupation and commodification of Black flesh, blackface serves as a go-to status affirmation for all not-Blacks. A century and a half after Admiral Perry marked the "opening" of Japan with minstrelsy shows, it is still a common cultural denominator between Asia and the West, a taken-for-granted platform for mutual engagement. The question, therefore, is not where LTD members were exposed to blackface, but rather, where, in the supranational circuitry of anti-Blackness, were they *not* exposed to blackface?

Japanese descriptions of Africans as subhumans and animals began some time after Portuguese and Dutch traders brought African servants to Japan in the 1500s. Japanese proverbs already valorized white skin as beautiful and associated Blackness with negative symbolic meanings, albeit unevenly.[198] In the early 1800s, Dutch scholars and missionaries introduced Johann Blumenbach's fivefold racial classification system to Japan, and the Japanese found Western race science dovetailed in most respects with their own racial mapping of the modern world. Hence U.S. cultural exports such as Stephen Foster's minstrel songs, Harriet Beecher Stowe's *Uncle Tom's Cabin*, Margaret Mitchell's *Gone with the Wind*, Edgar Rice Burroughs's *Tarzan*, and Sambo figures found a ready market Japan by the late 1800s.[199] Decades later, the Black American military personnel stationed in Japan during the postwar occupation "bore the brunt of both American and Japanese racism," as did their mixed-race children, whether raised in Japan or the U.S.[200]

In postwar Japanese capitalist culture, John Russell shows, blackface has been ubiquitous. Well into the 1980s, the Black figure with grossly exaggerated white lips was a staple of Japanese advertising, from the Calpis beverage company's minstrel trademark to the mannequins in Tokyo department stores.[201] At the same time, from music, to hairstyles, to fashion, to vernacular speech, to dance steps, Blackness has come to signify cool, serving as "a boundless reservoir of style and play from which [the Japanese] may borrow to perform their own acts of social resistance ... a medium through which some Japanese attempt to give voice to their own sense of alienation and rebellion against the restrictive social norms of their society."[202] "B-stylers" in the youth hip-hop scene tanned themselves as dark as possible to show their love for Blackness.[203] "Ganguro" girls wore blackface and Afro wigs in a similar spirit. All of these "black simulacra," Russell observes, "allow[ed] the Japanese to savor 'blackness' without the bother of having to deal with real black people or to make a place for them within their society."[204] Meanwhile, top-ranking Japanese officials have made repeated public statements demeaning Black people as unintelligent, irresponsible, and a drain on society, indicating that anti-Black affect runs the full gamut of Japanese society, from the person on the street to the highest echelons of power.[205]

---

[198] Russell, February 1991.
[199] Tajima and Thornton 2012.
[200] Russell 1997, 104. See also Thornton and Tajima 2018.
[201] Russell, February 1991.
[202] Russell 1997, 108.
[203] K. Lee 2015.
[204] Russell 1997, 109.
[205] Government officials contributed to the racial milieu. In 1986, Prime Minister Yasuhiro Nakasone, addressing a meeting of his Liberal Democratic Party, blamed Black people,

Black male sexuality, in particular, has been fetishized and commodified in Japan. The phenomenon of Japanese women seeking out Black men specifically for sex (but not as husbands or fathers for their children) has been the topic of Japanese novels, television shows, and essays.[206] Female novelists such as Yamada Eimi have built their careers on stoking the Japanese public's fascination with this topic. In *Beddotaimu* (*Bedtime Eyes*, 1987), she wrote:

Putting force into my lips, I tug his chest hairs, savoring his body odor. I recall a similar smell. A sweet and rotten smell like cocoa butter. From his arm pits came a strange smell. A corrupt odor, but definitely not unpleasant. As if by being assaulted by a dirty thing, I am made aware I am a pure thing. That kind of smell. His smell gives me a sense of superiority. It makes me yearn like a bitch in heat driven by the smell of musk.[207]

What turns the woman on is the man's Blackness, his utter abjection, his perverse power to lift her up and cleanse and redeem her. In November 1995, *Sapio*, a Japanese news magazine, interviewed a Japanese woman about why she preferred to date Black men. She reflected: "Blacks are like a drug .... Even if you want to quit you can't .... Their bodies give off pheromones. They're like walking penises. All they think about is sex .... Black penises are huge. Too big for the bodies of us Japanese women. I've heard that after having sex with them, the sheets are stained with blood."[208]

Blackface acts are routinely seen on Japanese television.[209] In 2015, to advertise an upcoming appearance together on Fuji TV, the girl band Momoiro Clover Z posed in blackface alongside two older singers who have been doing blackface performances since the 1980s. Baye McNeil, a Black American expatriate living in Japan, launched a Change.org petition to persuade Fuji TV not to air the segment. #StopBlackfaceJapan became a trending hashtag.[210] But habits are hard to change. In 2018, Japanese comedian Masatoshi Hamada appeared on a New Year's Eve television show, where he did a blackface impersonation of Eddie Murphy's character in *Beverly Hills Cop*. When the

---

Puerto Ricans, and Mexican Americans for declining "American intelligence levels." In 1988, Michio Watanabe, a leading politician, said Black people were not good at paying back their personal debts. In 1990, Minister of Justice Seiroku Kajiyama compared the influx of foreign prostitutes into Tokyo to the movement of Black people into white neighborhoods in the U.S. (Russell, October 1991).

[206] Russell, October 1991.
[207] Quoted in Russell, October 1991, 423.
[208] Russell 1998, 136.
[209] T. Jones 2018.
[210] K. Lee 2015.

skit drew criticism, Hamada's defenders shot back that he loved and respected Eddie Murphy and that there is no discrimination against Black people in Japan.[211]

Anti-Blackness has generated a blackface tradition in China as well. African slaves were brought to China as early as the ninth century. By the mid-1800s, in the Han Chinese imaginary, "Blackness equaled enslavement, a fate to be avoided by the Chinese."[212] After defeat in the Opium War of 1840–1842 forced China to open to Western powers, Western race science came to China through missionary teachings, reports from Chinese students who studied in the West, and Japanese translations of Western philosophy.[213] As noted in Part One, following the Republican revolution of 1911, which overthrew the Qing dynasty in the name of driving out Western imperialism, Chinese reformers articulated a racial ideology that asserted the superiority of the Han people and placed yellows and whites above blacks, browns, and reds. Kang Youwei's influential text *One World* (1913) argued that the Chinese and Westerners were the most fit for survival and would eventually become indistinguishable from one another, achieving "one world." The inferior races—and especially Africans, the most inferior group—would disappear through natural selection.[214] As in Japan, Western racial ideas, lightly edited, mapped onto Chinese racial ideas quite well.

After the communist revolution, the Chinese regime promoted several events—including the Bandung Conference (1955), Zhou Enlai's visits to Africa (1963–1964), and the building of the Tanzanian-Zambian railway (1965–1975)—as indicating a new approach to Africa born of the global struggle against Western capitalism and imperialism. In two proclamations supporting the African American struggle (1963 and 1968), Mao Zedong presented China as part of a global "people of color" formation. Although Sino-African solidarity discourse subsided from the late 1970s to the late 1990s, during which Deng Xiaoping's Open Door Policy reconnected China to the West, China turned again to Africa after this period, investing in massive infrastructural projects there, competing with Taiwan and Russia for influence on the continent,

[211] Specia 2018.
[212] Shih 2013, 158.
[213] Lan 2016.
[214] Shih 2013.

and becoming Africa's largest trading partner by the 2010s. Sensitive to criticism that it has established an imperialistic relationship with Africa, the Chinese government has resurrected Maoist Third Worldist discourses in its defense.[215] Shu-Mei Shih observes in China "an all-consuming nationalism that justifie[s] itself through a discourse of wounding: China was the victim of Western imperialism and the object of racism."[216] The result is that the Chinese, according to Yinghong Cheng, are "racially supersensitive and super-insensitive at the same time," ready to see China "as a victim of foreign racism while denying [their] own racism."[217] Focused on the West's racial depredations and not their own, the Chinese recapitulate Asian America's half-finished critique on a global scale.

As in Japan, commodity capitalism is an important driver of Black degradation in China. Put simply, (anti-)Blackness sells. Starting in the 1930s, the Shanghai-based company Hawley & Hazel manufactured a popular toothpaste called Darkie for the Chinese and other Asian markets. A grinning man in blackface graced each box. (The company's CEO had visited the U.S. in the 1920s and had been inspired by Al Jolson in the movie *The Jazz Singer*.) After acquiring half of the company in 1985, Colgate-Palmolive changed the name to Darlie and made the man racially ambiguous, but the Chinese characters on the product still said "Black Man Toothpaste." It took the global resurgence of Black Lives Matter following the murder of George Floyd to prompt the company to consider rebranding the product in 2020.[218] The backlash on Weibo, China's biggest social network, was immediate. One post said: "I got it. Next, even blackboards could not have the character 'black,' otherwise it would be disrespectful to Black people; neither could white boards have the word 'white,' otherwise it would be seen as white supremacy."[219] Others said rebranding was "American-style speech crime" and compared it to the Cultural Revolution's persecution of intellectuals in the 1960s.[220]

In 2016, a Chinese television advertisement for Qiaobi laundry detergent went viral. A young Chinese woman is doing laundry at home when a young Black man splattered with paint walks in. After they exchange

---

[215] Lan 2016.
[216] Shih 2013, 156.
[217] Cheng 2011, 575.
[218] Pham 2020.
[219] Li 2020.
[220] Li 2020.

suggestive looks, she puts a tab of detergent in his mouth and shoves him into the washing machine and turns it on. Muffled screams can be heard. He reemerges from the washer a fair-skinned Chinese man, and the woman is delighted. "Change begins with Qiaobi" flashes on the screen. The viewer, at first tantalized/alarmed by an imminent act of interracial sex, is relieved to find Blackness disappeared so that the Chinese negrophobic heteropatriarchal order can be reestablished. The commercial ran for months on Chinese television and in Chinese cinemas without incident until a U.S. expatriate shared it on social media.[221]

Relations between Chinese women and Black men were also at issue during Chinese protests against African students in the late 1980s. African students first traveled to China to study in 1960, during the Mao era, and by 1988 there were 1,500 African students (almost all men) enrolled in Chinese universities.[222] The Nanjing protest in 1988 was triggered by a dispute between a Chinese gatekeeper at Hehai University and two male African students who brought Chinese girls to their dorm rooms on Christmas Eve. After a rumor spread that an African man had abducted a Chinese woman, hundreds of Chinese students stormed the hall for foreign students, shouting "Black Devils! Kill the Black Devils!"[223] Violent attacks on African students ensued, and more than 100 of them fled to the railway station. Approximately 3,000 Chinese students gathered and started marching to the railway station, chanting slogans such as "Down with the niggers!" "Niggers go the hell home" and "Niggers! Kill the niggers!"[224] Before they could reach the railway station, the police forced the African students onto buses and transported them to a military guest house outside the city.[225]

The Chinese students complained that they were struggling financially while African students were given a free ride through scholarships. Yet they paid no attention to the white students, who were better off than the African students. Nor did they ask university officials for more funding or improved conditions for themselves. Instead, they demanded the expulsion of Africans from China.[226] The events in Nanjing sparked similar anti-African protests in other Chinese cities. Even though "no

---

[221] "What's behind China's 'Racist' Whitewashing Advert?" (2016). See also Huang 2020.
[222] Sautman 1994, 416. Cheng (2011) mentions that Chinese students staged anti-African protests in Shanghai (1979), Tianjin (1986), Nanjing (1988), and Beijing (1989).
[223] Sullivan 1994, 449.
[224] Cheng 2011, 562.
[225] Sullivan 1994.
[226] Sautman 1994.

fatalities were involved," Barry Sautman writes, "the 1988–1989 attacks on Africans had the makings of an incipient pogrom."[227]

There was a connection between the anti-African protests and the Chinese student democracy movement that emerged in the spring of 1989. In 1986, a group of Chinese students had sent a letter to all African embassies in Beijing expressing anger that the Chinese government provided economic aid to African students, including scholarships to study in China. They argued that China should not "feed uncultured Africa with the results of our efforts" or "allow any Negro to hang about our universities to annoy Chinese girls and to introduce on our academic grounds manner[s] acquired by life in tropical forests."[228] Drawing on stock tropes of Black primitivism, laziness, and sexual aggression, the students chastised Chinese leaders for wasting national resources on backward nations instead of trying to catch up with the West and improve the lives of their own people. This demand for more governmental responsiveness and accountability helped to fuel the student democracy movement.

Recent social media debates in China reveal a continuing preoccupation with the putative excesses of Black male sexuality. When former NBA star Shaquille O'Neal was invited to China to endorse the Chinese beer Harbin in the early 2010s, protest erupted on Tianya, a Chinese social media platform. Some called for a boycott of Harbin, others compared Black people to orangutans and said they spread HIV.[229] In this discourse, Kun Huang notes, African and African American men are "scapegoated as sources of contamination," and Chinese–Black marriages are figured as "a violation of 'Chineseness' and an affront to the national-reproductive community."[230] Hence the cyberattacks on Lou Jing, a biracial Chinese-Black woman who appeared on the Shanghai variety show *Let's Go! Oriental Angel*, and her Chinese mother. Anxieties about controlling Chinese women's bodies, their sexuality, and public health are expressed in this this distinctly anti-Black register of Chinese nationalism.[231]

---

[227] Sautman 1994, 420.
[228] Cheng 2011, 564. Cheng (2011) notes that these views about China's investments in Africa ignore both the negative impact of the investments upon Africa (supporting dictators, supporting unfair labor contracts, discouraging unionization, and more) and the benefits that accrue to China from these investments, including, among other things, oil and other natural resources.
[229] "What's behind China's 'Racist' Whitewashing Advert?" (2016).
[230] Huang 2020.
[231] Huang 2020.

As in Japan, blackface performances continue to appear regularly on Chinese television. In 2018, a blackface skit was shown on the nation's most-watched Lunar New Year television show, put on by state media. Meant to celebrate Chinese-African ties, the skit opens with African dancers in "tribal" clothing and people dressed as various wild African animals. A young African woman asks a Chinese man to pose as her husband so that she can escape her matchmaking mother, break free of African tradition, and go to China to study. Her mother is played by a Chinese woman in blackface with exaggerated buttocks, who walks onstage with a fruitplate on her head and a monkey (played by a human actor) by her side. When the young woman tells her mother of her plans, the latter shouts "I love the Chinese! I love China!"[232] As Roberto Castillo writes, the skit "presented a narrative in which China is seen as a solution to Africa's backwardness" and Africans feel love and gratitude toward the Chinese.[233] This is a not-atypical representation of the China–Africa relationship in the Chinese media.[234]

As Wen Liu observes, anti-Blackness traverses global space in the service of capitalism, justifying China's economic interventions in Africa and its treatment of African laborers.[235] A Chinese businessman who worked in Africa complained on China.com that Africans do not respect the Chinese because the Chinese did not colonize them like whites did. Online responses included: "Don't treat these niggers like humans, otherwise they won't see you as human"; "Only colonization can force these gorillas to respect you"; and "I have worked on construction engineering in Africa. These niggers are born subhuman."[236] Black people are necessary for business, but they must be kept in their place. This view has shaped the treatment of African migrants in China as well. The growth of China–Africa trade in recent decades has spurred increasing African migration to China, especially to Guangzhou, where African migrant communities have been dubbed "chocolate city" or "little Africa" by the local media.[237] These migrants, many of whom are traders serving a middleman function between African clients and Chinese factories and suppliers, complain that the Chinese police engage in racial profiling and target them for visa and passport checks.

---

[232] Castillo 2018.
[233] Castillo 2018. Also see "Lunar New Year: Chinese TV Gala Includes 'Racist Blackface' Sketch" (2018).
[234] In 2021, the Lunar New Year Show again featured blackface performance.
[235] W. Liu 2018.
[236] Cheng 2011, 570.
[237] Lan 2016.

In April 2020, reports circulated in China that COVID-19 was being imported by foreigners, triggering a wave of nativist actions which fell disproportionately on African migrants. Migrants were subjected to public harassment and shunning. They were turned away from restaurants, refused taxi rides, banned from stores, locked in hospital isolation rooms, and evicted from their apartments. Many of those evicted ended up sleeping on the streets and begging for food because stores and restaurants would not serve them. An image of a Chinese McDonalds employee holding up a sign saying "Black people are not allowed" went viral. When African governments protested the treatment of their nationals, the Chinese government denied racial discrimination but encouraged Chinese businesses to treat people equally and set up a hotline for foreigners who needed assistance.[238]

In May 2020, when a Black professional basketball player from the U.S. moved to China to play ball, a neighborhood WeChat post fretted about his arrival: "Is money more important than lives? African people are a high-risk group, and Guangzhou people are all not renting to them."[239] Black people who left the U.S. to escape anti-Blackness found no respite in China. One Black expatriate explained: "We feel like we don't have a home. Here [China] is not that comfortable right now or maybe it hasn't been for a while. And then also we can't really call America home anymore, either. So, it's just like, where do you go?"[240] There is no outside to the global circuitry of anti-Blackness.

In Korea, too, anti-Blackness emerged from the confluence of Western race science and strains of colorism, ethnocentrism, and racialism in the native culture. By the late 1800s, Korean writers, editors, and thinkers had begun to absorb Western racial ideologies via Japanese- and Chinese-language texts, a trend that continued during the half-century of Japanese colonial rule and the quasi-colonial relationship with the U.S. that followed.[241] Inoue Kakuguro, who was a pupil of eugenicist Fukuzawa Yukichi (who translated Western books on race into Japanese), acted as an advisor to editors at the Korean newspaper *Hanseongsunbo* in the late 1800s.[242] In 1897, the Korean newspaper *Dongnipsinmun* published a reflection on race:

---

[238] Kanthor 2020.
[239] Williamson and Wang 2020.
[240] Kanthor 2020.
[241] Kim and Jung 2019; J. Kim 2015. In 2014, the Korean Central News Agency of North Korea, in the aftermath of President Barack Obama's visit to South Korea, called him "a wicked black monkey" and "a crossbreed with unclear blood" (Kim and Jung 2019, 55).
[242] Kim and Jung 2019, 62.

Blacks are stupider than the East race and very inferior to whites .... Among all the races, since whites are the most brilliant, diligent, and courageous, they have gradually defeated other inferior races all around the world and acquired land and forests. Therefore, some races among the inferior, who cannot learn whites' knowledge and customs, should be gradually extinct .... The Australian natives are similar to blacks and no more enlightened than blacks, and thus their lives are not much different from animals.[243]

According to Jae Kyun Kim and Moon-Kie Jung, Koreans at the turn of the twentieth century embraced a "three-tier typology" in which Europeans were enlightened, Asian peoples were moving toward enlightenment at variable rates, and Africans and others were still in a state of savagery.[244] This much resonated with Japanese and Chinese racial beliefs, but Koreans, because of their history, also had a specific anxiety about being colonized by and becoming the slaves of other (Asian) peoples. Drawing on social-Darwinist logic, they viewed Black and Indigenous peoples as inferior races destined for slavery and resolved to use education to elevate themselves and remain a free people. Blackness allowed Koreans to imagine themselves in the middle tier of peoples, where they could focus on how to expand the gap between themselves and those below. In this sense, anti-Blackness was "vital to Koreans' sense of themselves and their place in the modern world"—indeed "the fundament, the bedrock, of Korean identity formation."[245]

Blackface performance has been commonplace in Korea during the last half-century. In 1975, as part of the "Korea Thank You Festival" for 1,000 U.S. troops near Camp Stanley in Uijeongbu, two Korean comedians did a blackface performance imitating Ray Charles and Louis Armstrong. From 1986 to 1987, Lee Bong-won performed in blackface on the KBS program "Show Video Jockey," only stopping because he did not want to offend the Africans coming to Seoul in 1988 for the Olympic Games. In 2012, the Lunar New Year special edition of MBC's "Quiz that Changes the World" featured comedians Lee Gyeong-sil and Kim Ji-seon in blackface and basketball jerseys.[246] When Korean comedians perform skits with Rastafari wigs and blackface, Gil-Soo Han writes, this is "generally taken at face-value and as 'normal' comedy by Korean audiences."[247]

[243] Kim and Jung 2019, 66.
[244] Kim and Jung 2019; J. Kim 2015.
[245] Kim and Jung 2019, 60–61.
[246] Van Volkenburg 2012; Van Volkenburg 2020.
[247] Han 2015, 2.

As in Japan, it is Black American expatriates living in Korea who are likely to call out the anti-Blackness there—at their own peril. In August 2020, a high school yearbook photo on TikTok went viral, sparking controversy. The Korean youth in the photo were in blackface and parodying the "dancing pallbearers" of Ghana, a tradition where dancers perform at the funeral to celebrate the life of the deceased. Sam Okyere, a Ghanaian entertainer who is living as a permanent resident in Korea, criticized the photo and the routine use of blackface in Korean culture: "You put in so much effort to educate people here in Korea and make them understand that you can appreciate a culture without making a mockery of the people …. This ignorance cannot continue."[248] The online backlash was swift and severe, with some Koreans calling for Okyere's deportation. Okyere quickly apologized, saying he did not mean to denigrate the students in the photo. Barely mollified, his critics reminded the world that blackface is fine as long as there are no bad intentions. *No racism intended. Just fun and laughter.*

The runaway phenomenon of K-pop, which first emerged in the 1990s, shows once again how well (anti-)Blackness sells in global capitalism. In K-pop performance, Blackness is figured ambivalently, as the object of fascination and hunger, on the one hand, and contempt and denigration, on the other. K-pop groups draw unapologetically and deeply from Black music, dance, fashion, hairstyles, and language. The CEO of Big Hit Entertainment, the parent company of the K-pop band BTS, acknowledged "Black music is the base" of the group's musical identity.[249] K-pop's relationship to Blackness runs the gamut from cultural appropriation—which some see as a soft form of blackface—to actually performing in blackface. Girls' Generation, BEAST/B2ST, Bubble Sisters, and Mamamoo all did blackface performances in the 2000s. In 2003, the Bubble Sisters posed for the cover of their debut album (and did the accompanying video) in blackface, accessorized with Afro wigs, cornrows, and curlers.[250] In a revealing interview, the group members said they were told by music executives that they were too ugly and fat compared with other K-pop girl bands, and since they perceived themselves to have vocal talent like Black people and to be unattractive like Black people, they chose to do blackface as a way of branding themselves for the market.[251] Other K-pop artists, too, have given high-profile blackface

[248] Yoon 2020.
[249] De Luna 2020.
[250] Han 2015, 12. See at: www.discogs.com/master/1406470-Bubble-Sisters-First-Impression.
[251] Han 2015.

performances—including Gikwang of BEAST/B2ST, who appeared on a variety show in 2012 sporting an Afro wig and exaggerated lips and eating watermelon, and girl group Mamamoo, who performed Mark Ronson and Bruno Mars's "Uptown Funk" in blackface in 2017.

During the 2020 protests following George Floyd's murder, some K-pop groups expressed support for Black Lives Matter. BTS donated $1 million to Black organizations in a #MatchAMillion campaign, and their fans matched the donation.[252] K-pop stans (dedicated fans) led the way at points, urging their favorite groups to get involved. When the Dallas Police department released the app "iWatch Dallas" to solicit videos of protesters for surveillance purposes, K-pop fans flooded the app by submitting hundreds of "fancams" (videos of K-pop performances) and causing the app to shut down. They also flooded right-wing hashtags on Twitter (such as #WhiteLivesMatter and #WhiteOutWednesday) with fancams and reserved tickets to Donald Trump's June 2020 rally in Tulsa, Oklahoma, so that the auditorium would have swathes of empty seats.[253] At the same time, Black K-pop fans consistently report the racial abuse they face in digital fan spaces. They are doxxed and harassed by not-Black fans, especially when they speak up about Black Lives Matter.[254] One Black K-pop fan reflected: "Even though Black K-pop stans are finding themselves stuck in this anti-Black fandom, they can't go anywhere else because every fandom has anti-Blackness in it."[255]

XII RICHARD AOKI'S TWO UNIFORMS

During the movement era, Richard Aoki embodied radical Asian Americanness in the U.S. The whispered doubts about Asian American political commitments seemed to be answered by his ascension to the office of Field Marshal in the Black Panther Party and his leadership roles in the Asian American Political Alliance and the Third World Liberation Front at UC Berkeley. Aoki, who befriended Huey Newton and Bobby Seale at Merritt College, was one of a handful of Asian Americans who joined the Black Panthers in the early years. He became known for providing Newton and Seale with their first guns—an M-I Garand rifle and a 9mm pistol (both designed for military use), and later a .357 Magnum—and giving them basic training in cleaning and handling firearms, which

---

[252] Elba 2020.
[253] Elba 2020.
[254] Haasch 2020.
[255] Haasch 2020.

he had learned during his stint in the U.S. military.[256] Aoki proved that a cool Asian cat could be accepted as a bona fide race warrior by the most radical Black revolutionaries of the era. His association with the Black Panthers gave him automatic standing in Asian American and Third World organizations. As biographer Diane Fujino writes, "[Aoki] gained activist credentials as the leading Asian American in the BPP. His rise to leadership in the Third World strike stemmed, in part, from his link to Black Power."[257] Generations of Asian American leftists have learned about Aoki's activism and seen the iconic photos of him in sunglasses, black leather jacket, and black beret.

Richard Aoki committed suicide in 2009, apparently because of declining health from a long illness. At his memorial, his involvement with the Black Panthers was emphasized, and many former Panthers attended the service. Some attendees found the showcasing of the U.S. flag and playing of Taps unsettling—wasn't patriotic loyalty to the U.S. state at odds with Aoki's political commitments? Diane Fujino writes: "But the memorial organizers recognized that in Aoki's closet, among the few material possessions kept all these years, hung two neatly maintained uniforms—his Black Panther leather jacket affixed with a Free Huey button and his U.S. Army uniform with an American flag in its pocket."[258] In other words, the organizers chose to reflect Aoki's truth, however idiosyncratic.[259] Questions remained, however: Why did Aoki hang a U.S. Army uniform next to his Black Panther uniform? What did it mean that he carefully preserved this pair of items?

In 2012, just months after Fujino published her biography, *Samurai among Panthers: Richard Aoki on Race, Resistance, and a Paradoxical Life*, journalist Seth Rosenfeld announced that his research on the FBI and student radicalism revealed that Richard Aoki had been an FBI informant from 1961 to 1977. Based upon an interview with an FBI official and documentary evidence from the FBI, Rosenfeld said that Aoki was recruited after finishing high school, when he was an ardent anti-communist, and over the next sixteen years provided information to the FBI about

---

[256] Bloom and Martin 2013, 48.

[257] Fujino 2012, xviii.

[258] Fujino 2012, 276.

[259] In her biography of Aoki, Fujino suggests she doubted the veracity of some of what he said during interviews. "Did Aoki use vague and indirect language to insinuate a greater involvement in the BPP than he actually had? Was Aoki committed to factual accuracy? 'Probably yes' is the answer to both questions, suggesting that narratives are more than simple truths or falsehoods" (Fujino 2012, xxv). She also says his tendency to embellish "aroused [her] suspicions" (Fujino 2012, xxv).

the Communist Party, the Socialist Workers Party, the Asian American Political Alliance, the Red Guards, the Third World Liberation Front, and the Black Panther Party. He filed more than 500 reports on these groups between 1961 and 1971. Aoki regularly named those who had membership in these groups and/or attended meetings. "As a result," Rosenfeld writes, "many were indexed in FBI files for future investigation."[260] Aoki's reports on the Black Panthers provided a mixture of innocuous or publicly known information, personal information on Huey Newton and Bobby Seale, and details about internal conflicts, leadership struggles, and discussions about guns. After Newton was involved in a police shootout that left Oakland officer John Frey dead, Aoki told the FBI the address of the woman Newton was living with and whose car he was driving that day. Aoki was paid between $100 and $400 per month by the FBI.

Rosenfeld's story sent shockwaves through Asian American political and academic circles. Aoki's defenders denied the veracity of the story, questioning Rosenfeld's timing, his motives, and inconsistencies and contradictions in his account.[261] They accused him of making up the story to create a buzz around his forthcoming book. They pointed out the absurdity of taking the FBI's word about Aoki, given its long history of snitchjacketing (identifying an innocent person as an FBI informant in order to create distrust and discord within an organization). As Rosenfeld released hundreds and then thousands of pages of Aoki's FBI reports, Aoki's supporters shifted from denying the story outright to offering a less damning interpretation of the evidence, namely, that he was an unwilling informant who was coerced into working with the FBI and provided them only with information that was publicly available and/or not harmful to the targets. The FBI's aims in disclosing Aoki's reports, his supporters insisted, included staining Aoki's reputation, fomenting Afro-Asian disunity, and undermining the revolution.

Scott Kurashige speculated that perhaps Aoki got involved with the FBI in good faith, became politically radicalized in the course of working for them, and was then forced to continue working for them because being exposed as an informant would jeopardize his reputation and even his life.[262] Harvey Dong, Aoki's friend and executor of

---

[260] Rosenfeld 2015.

[261] Ho, August 2012; Lew-Lee 2012; Howard 2012a; 2012b; Louie and Louie 2012; Ho, September 2012; Nishida 2012; Churchill et al. 2012.

[262] Kurashige 2012. Kurashige compares Aoki to Geronimo Pratt, who was a decorated U.S. soldier in Vietnam before joining the Black Panther Party. As a prominent leader in the Los Angeles chapter, he was framed for murder through an FBI COINTELPRO program and falsely imprisoned for twenty-seven years.

his estate, similarly argued that the two uniforms "represented two phases of [Aoki's] life when he shifted his loyalties from the U.S. military to becoming a Black Panther revolutionary."[263] "He was pressured, cajoled, and hounded by the FBI," Dong wrote, "and he learned to deal with it in his own way."[264] Here Dong raises the "likelihood that Richard Aoki was resisting and perhaps disseminating misinformation to the FBI on behalf of the BPP."[265] In the same spirit, Fred Ho "playfully assert[ed] a hypothetical argument" that "for 16 years, the genius and trickster Aoki continued to lead on the FBI. That Richard Aoki was handling THEM!"[266] Thus supporters resolved the contradiction of Aoki's life through temporal sequencing: he *was* an FBI informant who had a change of heart and *became* a revolutionary, after which he merely pretended to be an informant.

The furious defense of Aoki was more than loyalty to a revered leader and beloved friend. It spoke to the loss that Rosenfeld's story portended for progressive and left-leaning Asian Americans.[267] Richard Aoki embodied the possibility that Asian Americans could join the tide of revolutionary history alongside Black people. To find out that Aoki had been an FBI informant, whatever the circumstances, was to discover the worst possible thing: that he was an Asian American who had sold out Black (and other) people, that he was a traitor to the Black revolution, a man who had aided and abetted the U.S. state in its murderous destruction of the Black Panther Party and other left groups. Aoki's life, as previously conceived, was a powerful rejoinder to anxieties about the authenticity of Asian American radicalism. What would it represent now?

Some of the memos that the FBI field office in San Francisco sent to FBI headquarters in Washington, D.C., about informant Aoki are accessible online. These are forms with boilerplate language, and they are heavily redacted. The field office used them to show the success of its informants program, account for its use of resources, and justify its requests for more.[268] The memos tell of how the FBI initially became interested in Aoki, how they groomed him, their assessment of his personality, and their analysis, over time, of his evolving financial situation, educational

[263] Dong 2013, 110–111.
[264] Dong 2013, 111.
[265] Dong 2013, 113.
[266] Ho, September 2012. Capitalization in original.
[267] Rosenfeld 2012.
[268] Griffey 2012.

plans, and employment. They describe Aoki as submitting "complete and thorough reports, usually typewritten," providing "considerable information," and being "extremely helpful."

The memo dated November 8, 1963, states: "The informant gives every indication of being completely responsible in his responsibilities to the Bureau. He has given no indication of any unreliability or instability. He appears to be a very alert individual and is extremely cautious in avoiding any situations which might embarrass the Bureau so far as his relationship with the Bureau is concerned." Numerous memos testify to Aoki's dedication and usefulness: "Informant is eager to maintain his relation with the Bureau and to be of any service possible" (January 11, 1965); "Informant has furnished timely reports of urgently needed information" (October 29, 1965); "The informant has the ability to relate to all races and crosses the barriers between the ethnic movements with ease" (December 14, 1971); "Coverage furnished by this informant is unique and not available from any other source. Many activist individuals seek informant's advice and counseling since informant is considered as a militant who has succeeded within the establishment without surrendering to it" (July 2, 1973); "Coverage furnished by this informant is classified as high level and is not available from any other source" (July 2, 1973).[269] Aoki's handlers in the field office had their own reasons for praising his abilities as an informant and emphasizing the value of his contributions. Still, the fact that they kept him on as a paid informant for sixteen years suggests that his contributions were valuable to them. The memo sections that lay out exactly what information Aoki passed on remain heavily redacted. We are left to imagine what lies beneath the whiteout.

Tony Platt, assessing the responses to Rosenfeld's story, writes: "I think we also need to consider the possibility that Aoki was both an informant and a leftist, and that he both reported to and fought against the FBI."[270] Not one or the other, not one then the other, but both at the same time. Of course, this synopsis only opens up more questions. Is this just a story about one individual's peculiar trajectory or does it indicate something more broadly about where Asian Americans stand in relation to the anti-Black order? Is Aoki's story in fact a phenomenon we have seen before—namely, putting on Blackness while doing the work of the police?

[269] See at: https://s3.documentcloud.org/documents/423064/fbi-files-richard-aoki.pdf.
[270] Platt 2012.

XIII ASIAN AMERICANS AS SPOILERS IN *GRUTTER* AND *FISHER*

In *Bakke*, as discussed above, Asian Americans were figured by the U.S. Supreme Court as affirmative action spoilers, a group whose ability to thrive despite discrimination alibied American society and undercut the "societal discrimination" rationale for race-conscious admissions. In the years after *Bakke*, Asian American enrollment in U.S. higher educational institutions rose significantly, surpassing their rapidly growing percentage of the population. As a result, Asian Americans were, in many cases, removed from existing affirmative action programs or not included in the formation of new ones.[271] Yet their role as spoilers continued, with a twist. Instead of being figured as beneficiaries of affirmative action programs who cast doubt on them from the inside, they are now figured as putative victims who are excluded from the programs and cast doubt on them from the outside. This evolving weaponization of Asian Americans is apparent in the two U.S. Supreme Court cases that have dealt with race-conscious admissions in higher education since *Bakke*—*Grutter* v. *Bollinger* (2003) and *Fisher* v. *University of Texas I* and *II* (2013, 2016). Once again, conservative Chinese immigrant groups—including the Asian American Legal Foundation, which was formed to support the *Brian Ho* case in the 1990s—have been key players in these developments, and once again, liberal and progressive Asian American advocacy groups have struggled to mount an effective response.

But first, in the early to mid-1980s, liberal and progressive Asian American scholars and advocates observed that Asian American college enrollment rates, though rising, were not keeping pace with Asian American application rates. They formed a task force that charged numerous highly selective universities (Harvard, Brown, Princeton, Stanford, Yale, UC Berkeley, and UCLA) with intentionally discriminating against

[271] Asian Americans were included in affirmative action programs at Boalt Law School (UC Berkeley) in the 1960s, but by the mid-1970s, faculty started to reconsider this as Asian numbers under regular admissions became more robust. Their reconsideration met with resistance, foreshadowing the tensions captured in *Bakke*. In 1984, UC Berkeley excluded Asian Americans from race-conscious admissions (S. Lee 2008). UCLA Law School did not include Asian Americans in its race-conscious admissions program initially, and when Asian American students asked for inclusion in 1969, faculty resisted, "arguing that Asian Americans had suffered less socioeconomic and educational disadvantages than blacks, Chicanos, and Native Americans" (Muratsuchi 1995, 97). Black and Mexican American law students offered to each give up one slot to create a total of two slots for Asian Americans in the special admissions program. Conflict over the issue continued at UCLA Law School in the 1980s.

and/or imposing illegal ceilings on Asian American applicants. University officials denied the charges and offered a range of responses, from arguing that Asian Americans were overrepresented (relative to their proportion of the population)[272] to arguing that they were not as qualified because they were not as well-rounded as other applicants. The Asian American task force challenged both of these claims, arguing that the implied use of proportionality measures as well as the emphasis on supplemental criteria (criteria other than grade point averages [GPAs] and test scores) were discriminatory against Asian applicants. Federal and state investigations, in addition to in-house reviews, produced mixed results. Harvard, for example, announced that its internal review showed no bias and that the difference between Asian American and white admissions rates was fully explained by the fact that white applicants were more likely to be "legacies" and strong on extracurricular activities. The Chancellor of UC Berkeley, on the other hand, publicly apologized to Asian Americans for "disadvantaging" them in the admissions process and promised reform. The Department of Education's Office of Civil Rights cleared Harvard of wrongdoing, but ordered UCLA to admit five Asian Americans who had been unfairly rejected from the graduate program in mathematics.[273]

Asian American scholars and activists took pains to distinguish between admissions ceilings, which they opposed, and affirmative action, which they supported. Thus legal scholar Jerry Kang explained that he denounced "negative action" (disadvantaging Asian applicants relative to white applicants), while supporting "affirmative action" (advantaging applicants from certain not-white groups relative to the general applicant pool).[274] There was no necessary connection between the two: schools could legitimately use affirmative action to raise the floor of Black and Latinx enrollment without imposing an arbitrary and unfair ceiling on Asian enrollment. Furthermore, as Goodwin Liu demonstrates, it is a "causation fallacy" to assume that affirmative action itself has a significant adverse effect on Asian American acceptance rates, or that ending affirmative action would redound primarily to the benefit of Asian Americans, since the number of slots involved in affirmative action programs is too small to affect Asian American admissions rates in any notable way. Liu writes: "In a selection process where there are far more

[272] Since 1974, the University of California has been governed by a state legislative resolution calling for the ethnic mix of the student body to match that of state high school graduates.

[273] Takagi 1992.

[274] Kang 1996. Also see West-Faulcon 2017.

applicants than available opportunities, the likelihood of success for *any* candidate is low, even under race-neutral criteria. Reserving a small number of seats for minority applicants, relative to the total number of seats, will not decrease that low likelihood very much."[275]

Nevertheless, in a harbinger of things to come, at the height of the Asian American admissions controversy in the 1980s, Reagan's attorney general William Reynolds opined in a speech that the ceiling on Asian Americans was the "inevitable result" of a floor for other favored racial groups.[276] White conservatives, recognizing that Asian Americans' discrimination claims carried more weight presumptively than whites' discrimination claims, were cultivating Asian Americans as a long-term weapon against race-conscious admissions. Pursuing this strategy would likely raise the number of Asian Americans on college campuses, but this was an acceptable price to pay for dismantling affirmative action. *White is best but the most important thing is not-Blackness. Better Asians than Blacks.*

Asian American task force members joined with university officials to defend race-conscious admissions against Reynolds's attack, but the problem, Dana Takagi noted, was that his speech drew upon the task force's own arguments and data.[277] And the problem went beyond this. Consider the parameters of the task force's mission: rather than advancing a critique of how racial inequity, broadly conceived, is baked into multiple levels of university admissions, the task force focused narrowly on the question of discrimination against Asian American applicants. It challenged the use of supplemental admissions criteria as discriminatory against Asians, but endorsed the use of nonsupplemental admissions criteria (GPAs and Scholastic Assessment Test [SAT] scores), which have been shown to discriminate against Black students.[278] Notably, the task force did not question the pervasive racial segregation and economic inequality that shape K-12 education, systematically skewing educational

---

[275] G. Liu 2002, 1054. Italics in original. See also Kidder 2005–2006.

[276] Cited in Takagi 1992, 104.

[277] Takagi 1992.

[278] SAT scores have been shown to reflect parents' education and income more than student merit. See Wong and Silver 2018; Selingo 2018. Also see Au (2016) on how standardized tests have been used as a "racial project" in the U.S. for over a century. Au writes: "The logic of test-based structural denial works thusly: If standardized tests provide for the fair and objective measurement of individuals, then standardized testing holds the promise that every test taker is objectively offered a fair and equal chance at educational, social, and economic achievement. Problems like racism and class privilege are thus supposedly neutralized through testing .... As such, with the empirical evidence provided by presumptively 'objective' standardized tests, Whites and wealthy

outcomes against students who are Black, Latinx and/or poor, or the "school-to-prison-pipeline" that extends hyperpolicing into schools and funnels Black students in particular into the prison system. Nor did it discuss the myriad factors that Devon Carbado, Kate Turetsky, and Valerie Purdie-Vaughns have identified as disadvantaging Black students in the college admissions process, including explicit racial bias, implicit racial bias, stereotype threat, racial isolation, and negative institutional cultures.[279] In other words, the task force probed the status and power differential between whites and Asian Americans *but ignored the status and power differential between Asian Americans and Black people*. It is not entirely surprising, therefore, that William Reynolds found its report useful in his broadside against race-conscious admissions.

By the time of *Grutter* v. *Bollinger* (2003), the notion that affirmative action victimized Asian Americans was quite familiar, thanks to anti-affirmative action efforts that had unfolded in California during the 1990s, including the *Brian Ho* case.[280] In the first U.S. Supreme Court case to address race-conscious admissions since *Bakke*, Barbara Grutter, a white woman who had been rejected by the University of Michigan Law School, filed suit, claiming that the law school's affirmative action program discriminated against her in violation of the Fourteenth Amendment and Title VI of the Civil Rights Act of 1964.[281] The Brief for Petitioner directly challenged the coherence of the diversity rationale laid out in Justice Powell's "lone analysis" decades earlier, arguing that only a remedial program narrowly tailored to respond to a specifically identified racial injury should pass strict scrutiny.[282] Once again, Asian Americans

---

elites could mask their own structural advantages, deny the existence of systemic racism, justify racial hierarchies, and structure specific racial groups as less intelligent and inferior, all under the guise of 'naturally' occurring aptitude among individuals competing within a meritocratic framework" (Au 2016, 46–47).

[279] Carbado et al. 2016. See Wong and Silver (2018) on how Black and Latino high school graduates are less likely to enroll in college than Asian Americans and whites, less likely to attend elite, private four-year higher educational institutions than Asian Americans and whites, more likely to experience substandard schooling and poverty than Asian Americans and whites, and less likely to be referred to gifted programs than Asian Americans and whites.

[280] *Grutter* v. *Bollinger* (2003).

[281] A parallel lawsuit, *Gratz* v. *Bollinger*, challenged the University of Michigan's undergraduate admissions program. That program, which gave an automatic twenty-point advantage to "underrepresented minorities," was struck down at the same time that the law school's program was upheld.

[282] Brief for the Petitioner (2003), 29. To be distinguished from the broader "societal discrimination" rationale that Justice Powell rejected as too "amorphous" in *Bakke*.

were figured as spoilers: "[D]isadvantage on the basis of race [in race-conscious admissions] works not only against Caucasian Americans, but also against other groups, including minority groups historically discriminated against, especially Asian Americans."[283]

The Brief for Respondents, which defended the law school's affirmative action program as modelled on the Harvard plan and thus compliant with *Bakke*, dealt with Asian Americans by shifting them out of the "minority" category. According to the Brief for Respondents, the law school aimed for a "critical mass" of students "from groups which have been historically discriminated against, like African-Americans, Hispanics, and Native Americans."[284] Footnote 5 here simply stated: "Members of these groups are referred to as 'minority' students."[285] Note the omission of Asian Americans from this list. The three named groups deserved special attention, the brief stated, because they are "the groups most isolated by racial barriers in our country."[286] The brief then juxtaposed "minority" students and "white and Asian" students, reinforcing the designation of Asian Americans as nonminorities. Footnote 80 in this passage noted that while Asians and Jews also have unique experiences because of their ethnicity, they are already admitted to the law school in significant numbers according to race-neutral criteria.

The Asian American Legal Foundation (AALF), the conservative Chinese American group that emerged out of the *Brian Ho* case in the 1990s, filed an Amicus Brief in Support of Petitioner. The brief aimed to depict race-conscious admissions as a policy that *produced* rather than alleviated racial discrimination. To this end, the brief suggested an equivalence between the statuses of Asian Americans and Black people, emphasized white discrimination against the Chinese, overlooked the not-Blackness that advantages Chinese Americans, and minimized anti-Black discrimination.[287] The brief charged the University of Michigan

---

[283] Brief for the Petitioner (2003), 39.
[284] Brief for Respondents (2003), 4.
[285] Brief for Respondents (2003), 4.
[286] Brief for Respondents (2003), 50.
[287] Asian American conservatism on this issue has been primarily championed by Chinese Americans, although some Indian Americans and Korean Americans have been involved, too. White plaintiffs advance the argument that affirmative action occurs against a "colorblind" background and thus constitutes "reverse discrimination." See Gotanda 1991. Depicting Asian Americans as affirmative action's "victims" is a related move. It is important to note that many whites view *any* race-conscious remedial action as discriminatory against them, and that this dates back to the backlash against the Freedmen's Bureau after the Civil War, where programs to help Black people emerging

Law School with "plac[ing] barriers before Chinese Americans and other 'non-preferred' individuals that are unjustified by any remedial purpose." Echoing Justice Powell's dystopic ruminations in *Bakke*, the brief depicted state actors, "freed from the constraints of any remedial purpose," as running amok with their racial schemes, arbitrarily designating certain groups "preferred" and others "non-preferred." Negative action and affirmative action get conflated in the brief without explanation: "There is ample reason to look askance at any program that classifies people by ethnicity to achieve some 'ideal' racial composition. There is no difference between a policy of admitting some people because there are 'not enough' of their race and a policy of excluding others because there are 'too many' of theirs." The court must heed the lesson of the *Brian Ho* case, the brief warned—namely, the "the modern-day dangers of Kafkaesque social engineering in a multiracial society."[288]

What made the University of Michigan Law School's admissions program especially repugnant, the brief argued, was that it ignored the long, ugly history of discrimination against the Chinese, including the so-called "queue ordinance," the persecution of Chinese laundries that culminated in the *Yick Wo* decision, and school segregation. Here the brief mentioned *Gong Lum* v. *Rice* (1927) and *Guey Heung Lee* v. *Johnson* (1971), two cases involving Chinese American resistance to state-imposed racial classifications, and quoted Justice Douglas from the latter case: "*Brown* v. *Board of Education* was not written for blacks alone. It rests on the Equal Protection Clause of the Fourteenth Amendment, one of the first beneficiaries of which were the Chinese people of San Francisco." Then, riffing off Justice Marshall's separate opinion in *Bakke*, the brief stated: "[I]t would be ironic indeed were Chinese Americans to find themselves classified as a 'non-preferred' ethnicity in the 21st century, when a dominant theme of their history in this country has been one of *de jure* discrimination." The brief closed with this striking passage:

It is simplistic to assume that any given African American candidate has suffered adversity and disadvantage, thereby gaining valuable perspective or experience,

from slavery were castigated as unfair to whites (Schnapper 1985; Ross 1990). Today, polls suggest that many (perhaps most) white Americans feel that they are discriminated against on the basis of race, and a major theme of white nationalism today is the threat of "white genocide."

[288] Brief of the Asian American Legal Foundation as Amicus Curiae in Support of Petitioners (2003), 2, 5, 5, 4.

while assuming that the opposite is true for any given Chinese American candidate .... [Given] the example of two random African American and Chinese American candidates, a statement that the person has experienced adversity might be true for both, either, or neither of the two. All that can be known *a priori* is that both individuals deserve to be considered on their own merits, undistorted by the prism of a diversity scheme.[289]

With this explicit denial of structural anti-Blackness and Asian American not-Blackness, the AALF paved the way for its ultimate claim: that the University of Michigan Law School's program unfairly burdened Asian Americans as an already disadvantaged racial group, making them the worst-off group of all.

There is a kind of forgetting insisted upon in the AALF brief, a willed suppression of historical truth. Consider the citation of *Gong Lum* v. *Rice* and *Guey Heung Lee* v. *Johnson* as proof that Chinese Americans have fought educational segregation. In the former case, attorneys for Chinese American Martha Lum argued that she should be allowed to attend white rather than "colored" schools in Jim Crow Mississippi, on the grounds that the Equal Protection Clause protected the Chinese, too, *from the dangers of associating with Black students.* In the latter case, attorneys for Chinese American children in San Francisco argued that they should not have to obey a desegregation busing order designed to promote Black integration, on the grounds that busing would disrupt Chinese cultural instruction and community cohesion.[290] Chinese Americans fought against racial classification in education in both cases—*but in ways that directly reinforced structural anti-Blackness and the segregation of Black students.*

Led by the National Asian Pacific American Legal Consortium (NAPALC), progressive Asian American advocacy groups submitted an Amicus Brief in *Grutter* for the specific purpose of countering the AALF argument that race-conscious admissions harm Asian Americans.[291] The NAPALC brief laid out two arguments: first, Asian Pacific Americans (APAs) are not harmed by the University of Michigan's affirmative action programs, and they benefit, as all students do, from a diverse student body; and second, APAs should be treated by affirmative action programs as underrepresented minorities where appropriate, especially

---

[289] Brief of the Asian American Legal Foundation as Amicus Curiae in Support of Petitioners (2003), 17, 3, 29.

[290] Chinese Americans were unsuccessful in both cases.

[291] The Amicus Brief (in support of Respondents Grutter/Gratz) was also sponsored by the Asian Law Caucus and the Asian Pacific American Legal Center.

in employment and public contracting.[292] Concerned that the model minority myth disguises APA disadvantage relative to whites, the brief attempted to set the record straight by describing APA poverty rates, limited returns on education, employment barriers, stereotypes, and more. *We are minorities, too.* But the brief did not address the elephant in the room—namely, what distinguishes Asian Americans from other minorities. Why are Asian Americans the only "minority" to break the link between discrimination and injury/need? Why are they doing well in undergraduate admissions without affirmative action? Ironically, by insisting that Asian Americans are a bona fide "minority," focusing exclusively on their disadvantage relative to whites, and neglecting to discuss their advantage relative to Black people, the brief reinforced the AALF's fallacious assertion of minority equivalency.

The U.S. Supreme Court ruled for the defendants 5–4 in *Grutter*, affirming that diversity was a compelling state interest and that the University of Michigan Law School was justified in using race as one factor in a holistic review of individual applicants. Aiming for a "critical mass" of "underrepresented" students in the name of diversity, the majority held, did not constitute illegitimate "racial balancing" via the use of specific numerical quotas.[293] A decade later, with significant funding from right-wing donors, right-wing white activist Ed Blum launched another major challenge to race-conscious admissions in higher education. Under Blum's tutelage, Abigail Fisher, a white woman applicant who had been rejected by University of Texas, Austin, sued the university, charging that its affirmative action program discriminated against her in violation of the Fourteenth Amendment. In *Fisher* v. *University of Texas at Austin* (*I* and *II*), the most recent U.S. Supreme Court case(s) on this issue, the Asian spoilers narrative reached a new level of prominence, setting the stage for the Harvard anti-affirmative action case examined in the next section.[294]

[292] "Asian Pacific American" (APA) and "Asian Pacific Islander" (API) are terms that capture a moment in time when Asian Americans and Pacific Islanders were considered one racial category under the U.S. Census. To highlight their specific needs and grievances, Pacific Islanders, who have a markedly lower socioeconomic status profile than most Asian national origin groups, requested their official recognition as a separate entity. The U.S. Census now reflects this reality by making "Asian" and "Native Hawaiian and Pacific Islander" separate categories.

[293] Chief Justice Rehnquist's dissent, joined by Justices Scalia, Kennedy, and Thomas, argues that "critical mass" is a concept meant to conceal "racial balancing." Justice Kennedy's separately filed dissent repeats this argument.

[294] *Fisher* v. *University of Texas at Austin* (2013) is known as *Fisher I*, and *Fisher* v. *University of Texas at Austin* (2016) is known as *Fisher II*. For more on Asian Americans and this case, see Poon and Segoshi 2018.

In the Brief for Petitioner in *Fisher I*, Asian Americans occupied center stage. To begin with, the brief observed that officials at the University of Texas, Austin recognized Asian Americans as a "minority" when it suited them, but not in undergraduate admissions:

[A]lthough UT includes Asian Americans as minorities in its diversity statistics, marketing materials, and classroom analysis, it employs race in admissions decisions to the detriment of Asian Americans, thus subjecting them to the same inequality as White applicants.[295]

In addition, the brief continued, UT Austin pursued unconstitutional "racial balancing" with an eye to the state's demographics. Why did UT Austin consider Asians "overrepresented" and Hispanics "underrepresented," when there are fewer of the former than the latter enrolled? Because "UT uses state racial demographics as its baseline for determining which minority groups should benefit from its use of race," and

[t]his differing treatment of racial minorities based solely on demographics provides clear evidence that UT's conception of critical mass is not tethered to the "educational benefits of a diverse student body" …. UT has not (and indeed cannot) offer any coherent explanation for why fewer Asian Americans than Hispanics are needed to achieve the educational benefits of diversity.[296]

UT Austin should admit a roughly equal number of Asians and Hispanics, the brief suggested, since both were "minorities" who contribute to "diversity."[297] To do anything else was discriminatory against Asian Americans.

The Brief for Respondents in *Fisher I* explained that UT Austin followed the *Grutter* Court's reasoning on why only "underrepresented" minorities like Black people and Hispanics deserve special consideration. Unlike the University of Michigan Law School, UT Austin did count Asian Americans as a "minority"—just not an underrepresented one. Asian Americans were fully 18 percent of the UT Austin freshmen class (while constituting only 3 percent of the population of Texas) in 2004.[298]

---

[295] Brief for Petitioner, *Fisher I* (2012), 7.
[296] Brief for Petitioner, *Fisher I* (2012), 7, 28.
[297] In 2008, Asian Americans were 19 percent of the UT Austin freshman class and 3.4 percent of the state population; Hispanics were less than 20 percent of the class and 36 percent of the state population; and African Americans were 6 percent of the class and 12 percent of the state population. That is, Asian American enrollment that year was more than five times their percentage of the population, Hispanic enrollment was less than two-thirds of their percentage of the population, and African American enrollment was half of their percentage of the population. *Fisher v. Texas* (2009), 607.
[298] Brief for Respondents, *Fisher I* (2012), 45.

That is, they were admitted at six times their proportion of the state population that year. And Asian American enrollment numbers actually increased after UT Austin implemented its race-conscious admissions program in 2005, undermining the plaintiff's argument that the program burdened Asian Americans.

The AALF filed an Amicus Brief in support of Petitioner in *Fisher I*, reprising the central themes of their *Grutter* brief.[299] Condemning "racial balancing" and the diversity rationale as discriminatory against an already burdened group, the brief stated:

Efforts to manipulate the racial composition of schools necessarily come with a steep cost—borne in the first instance by individuals on the wrong side of the racial balancing act because their racial groups lack political or social clout. Schools in general, and highly competitive universities in particular, have a limited number of slots. Every slot allocated to someone who would not have been admitted but for their race is a slot *denied* to someone else who would have been admitted but for their race. The costs of such racial gerrymandering fall not merely on members of a supposedly privileged racial majority, but on individuals belonging to *any* non-preferred or "overrepresented" race that must be displaced in order to increase the numbers of a preferred or "underrepresented" race or ethnicity.[300]

By translating "underrepresented" as "preferred," the AALF inverted reality, recasting the most disadvantaged students as the special favorites of the power structure. It was as if college admissions were a spoils system that rewarded Black students (who supposedly possess "political or social clout") and burdened Asian Americans (who supposedly lack such clout). In this counterfactual fantasy scenario, Black people had captured the state and were "gerrymandering" college admissions to benefit themselves, turning Asian Americans into the paradigmatic victims of racial injustice.

And then, the climactic line of the AALF brief in *Fisher I*: "*Grutter* will be seen as the *Plessy* of its generation."[301] Unforgettably, the case that affirmed race-conscious university admissions in the name of diversity

---

[299] This brief was coauthored by the Judicial Education Project.

[300] Brief for the Asian American Legal Foundation and the Judicial Education Project as Amici Curiae in Support of Petitioner (May 29, 2012), 6.

[301] Brief for the Asian American Legal Foundation and the Judicial Education Project as Amici Curiae in Support of Petitioner (May 29, 2012), 36. *Plessy v. Ferguson* (1896) was the single most important U.S. Supreme Court case upholding Jim Crow in the American South. Here the court ruled that segregated railway cars in New Orleans, Louisiana, did not violate the Equal Protection Clause of the Fourteenth Amendment because "separate but equal" facilities were still equal. See Part One for discussion of this case. *Brown v. Board of Education* (1954) overturned *Plessy*, finding that "separate but equal" facilities were inherently unequal.

was likened to the case that nailed down Jim Crow segregation in the U.S. South. A program that was designed to temper segregation was equated with the most impactful pro-segregation judicial opinion in the nation's history. Black people were cast as malevolent legislators in Jim Crow Louisiana, and Asian Americans as Homer Plessys courageously defying segregation laws. In this way, Asian Americans displaced Black people from their own history while simultaneously donning the Black struggle's mantle of righteousness.[302] *Asians are the new Blacks*. In this sociometry, the Asian–Black gap is not only denied but turned on its head.

Progressive Asian American advocacy groups again responded by arguing that Asian Americans were "minorities" who favored affirmative action, too. Asian American Legal Defense and Education Fund's Amicus Brief emphasized that Asian Americans benefit from affirmative action and are not harmed by it. Asian American Center for Advancing Justice's Amicus Brief noted that "[l]ike other minority groups, AAPIs [Asian American Pacific Islanders] have suffered racial prejudice, and race-conscious admissions programs have helped counteract that prejudice."[303] Overall, the brief continued, select Asian subgroups stood to benefit directly from race-conscious admissions, all Asians stood to benefit from diversity, many Asians stood to benefit from affirmative action in other contexts, and Asians as a whole were not demonstrably harmed by UT Austin's program. As such, "[t]he undersigned *Amici* reject these unfounded claims [by Petitioner and her amici] that AAPIs are harmed by such programs, and categorically oppose such efforts to use the AAPI community as a wedge group to curtail opportunities for racial minorities."[304] What the brief did *not* do was attempt to countermand the AALF's suspect sociometry with a more accurate portrayal of Asian American and Black positionalities.

In *Fisher I*, the U.S. Supreme Court vacated and remanded the Fifth Circuit Court of Appeals's ruling upholding UT Austin's program, saying that the lower court had not applied strict scrutiny correctly.[305] After the Fifth Circuit Court of Appeals upheld the university's plan, Abigail Fisher

---

[302] Frank Wilderson (2010; 2021) argues that in an anti-Black world, Black suffering is illegible and, at the same time, serves as a vehicle for making the suffering of others legible.

[303] Brief of Amici Curiae Asian Americans Advancing Justice in Support of Appellees and Affirmance, United States Court of Appeals for the Fifth Circuit (November 1, 2013), 7.

[304] Brief of Amici Curiae Asian Americans Advancing Justice in Support of Appellees and Affirmance, United States Court of Appeals for the Fifth Circuit (November 1, 2013), 4.

[305] Justice Thomas wrote a concurring opinion in *Fisher I*, in which he declares, without commentary or explanation, "There can be no doubt that the University's discrimination injures white and Asian applicants who are denied admission because of their race." See his concurring opinion in *Fisher I* (2013), 2431. Echoing the AALF brief,

appealed, and the Supreme Court, in *Fisher II*, upheld the lower court's ruling by a 4–3 vote. Writing for the majority, Justice Kennedy cited the district court's finding that all groups, including whites and Asians, can potentially benefit from racial considerations in holistic review, as well as the Asian American Legal Defense and Education Fund's amicus brief argument that UT Austin's program does not discriminate against Asian Americans.

In his dissenting opinion, Justice Alito, joined by Chief Justice Roberts and Justice Thomas, quoted the AALF's claim that UT Austin views Asian Americans as less valuable than Hispanics in promoting diversity and criticized the court majority and the Fifth Circuit Court of Appeals for "act[ing] almost as if Asian-American students do not exist."[306] The Fifth Circuit Court was wrong when it claimed that ending race-conscious admissions would produce a nearly "all-white" student body, Alito noted, as this ignored the fact that Asian Americans were already admitted without special consideration. Indeed the Fifth Circuit Court, in his view, showed a "willful blindness" to Asians that was "absolutely shameless."[307] Alito then cited the AALF Amicus Brief a second time (when he argued that the court's tolerance of discrimination against Asians was "particularly troubling" because of their long struggle with discrimination) and a third time (when he wrote that UT Austin should pay attention to intraracial diversity among Asian Americans).[308] Nearly forty years after *Bakke*, the Asian spoilers trope was going strong, nurtured by a distinctive ideological alliance of conservative Chinese immigrant professionals and conservative whites.[309]

XIV *STUDENTS FOR FAIR ADMISSIONS* V. *HARVARD*

Fresh off his momentous victory in *Shelby County* v. *Holder* (2013)—in which the U.S. Supreme Court effectively eviscerated the Voting Rights Act of 1965 and opened the door to widespread voter suppression efforts at the state level—conservative white activist Ed Blum turned his attention back to affirmative action. Reflecting on the *Fisher II* decision, he hit upon a new strategy for attacking race-conscious admissions—using

Thomas also compares University of Texas at Austin to slaveholders who said slavery was a "positive good" and segregationists who said segregation protected Black students from white racism.

[306] Justice Samuel Alito's dissent in *Fisher II* (2016), 2227.
[307] Justice Samuel Alito's dissent in *Fisher II* (2016), footnote 5.
[308] Justice Samuel Alito's dissent in *Fisher II* (2016), 2228.
[309] See Garces and Poon 2018.

Asian American instead of white plaintiffs. Blum declared, "I needed plaintiffs; I needed Asian plaintiffs … so I started … *HarvardNotFair. org*."[310] Featuring pictures of downcast Asian American students, this website recruited Asian American plaintiffs by asking: "Were You Denied Admission to Harvard? It may be because you're the wrong race …. TELL US YOUR STORY."[311]

In July 2014, Blum's new organization, Students for Fair Admissions (SFFA), was incorporated in preparation for filing suit against Harvard. Its board of directors consisted of three members: Ed Blum (president), Abigail Fisher of *Fisher* v. *Texas* (secretary) and Abigail's father, Richard Fisher (treasurer).[312] William Consovoy, who clerked for Justice Thomas and was second author on the Brief for Petitioner in *Fisher I* and lead author on the Brief for Petitioner in *Fisher II*, was second author on the SFFA's first filed complaint against Harvard. The lawsuit filed by SFFA against Harvard in the district court in Massachusetts was the first one in the nation's history where the plaintiffs challenging race-conscious admissions in higher education were Asian American. This was the predictable if not inevitable culmination of the Asian spoilers narrative that had first emerged in *Bakke* a half-century before.

The SFFA's initial complaint, filed in November 2014, echoed the AALF's amicus briefs in *Grutter* and *Fisher*.[313] It argued that Harvard's "holistic" admissions plan had always been an "elaborate mechanism for hiding Harvard's systematic campaign of racial and ethnic discrimination against certain disfavored classes of applicants."[314] Harvard violated Title VI of the Civil Rights Act of 1964 in four ways, the complaint alleged: engaging in invidious discrimination against Asian American applicants, pursuing "racial balancing," using race as a dominant factor rather than just a "plus" factor, and not pursuing available race-neutral alternatives. Like Jews in the past, the complaint averred, Asian Americans were a "disfavored" group suffering mistreatment in the admissions process. Indeed, Harvard had a history of discriminating against Asian Americans in particular, the complaint insisted. In

---

[310] Memorandum in Support of Defendant's Motion for Summary Judgment on All Remaining Counts (June 30, 2018), 10.

[311] See at: http://harvardnotfair.org. Capitalization in original.

[312] Memorandum in Support of Defendant's Motion for Summary Judgment on All Remaining Counts (June 30, 2018), 10.

[313] The AALF submitted an amicus brief in the Harvard case. Since this brief substantially reprises the AALF's briefs in *Grutter* and *Fisher*—except for a discussion of the racial disparity in Harvard's personal ratings (see below)—I do not discuss it here.

[314] Complaint (November 17, 2014), 3.

the 1970s, the university had denied Asians "minority" status (on the grounds that they were not underrepresented) and refused to grant them special consideration in race-conscious admissions; in the 1980s, Asian American advocates had charged the university with imposing a ceiling on Asian admissions; and recently, "decisive statistical evidence"[315] had emerged to prove that the university was discriminating against Asian applicants once again.[316]

Although the SFFA complaint focused on the question of a ceiling for Asians and made no argument connecting this issue to affirmative action for other groups, it nevertheless asked the court to issue "a permanent injunction prohibiting Harvard from using race as a factor in future undergraduate admissions decisions," and a declaratory judgment that "any use of race or ethnicity in the educational setting violates the Fourteenth Amendment and Title VI of the Civil Rights Act of 1964."[317] No explanation is offered as to why SFFA's request of the court is this broad. Instead, there is this passage:

[T]he proper response is the outright prohibition of racial preferences in university admissions—period .... Harvard and other academic institutions cannot and should not be trusted with the awesome and historically dangerous tool of racial classification. As in the past, they will use any leeway the Supreme Court grants them to use racial preferences in college admissions—under whatever rubric—to engage in racial stereotyping, discrimination against disfavored minorities, and quota-setting to advance their social-engineering agenda. Strict scrutiny has proven to be no match for concerted discrimination hidden behind the veil of "holistic" admissions. There may be times when social problems can be solved democratically. But massive resistance to racial equality is not one of them. See *Brown v. Bd. of Educ. of Topeka, Kan.*, 349 U.S. 294 (1955).[318]

---

[315] Complaint (November 17, 2014), 43.
[316] The complaint cites, among other sources, Espenshade and Radford's 2009 study of admissions data from several elite public and private colleges, which argued that Asian applicants generally suffer an "Asian penalty" of 140 points on the SAT compared with whites—that is, they need an SAT score 140 higher than whites do to get into these schools, all other things being equal. Espenshade and Radford's book is extensively cited by opponents of affirmative action. However, critics have noted that it has at least one serious methodological flaw: it looks only at GPAs and SAT scores, leaving out all other supplemental criteria used in admissions. Espenshade and Radford have since written: "It is likely that incorporating in our models an even fuller range of academic performance measures as well as these other nonacademic factors would cast the effect of coming from an Asian background in a different light" (cited in West-Faulcon 2017, 635). In addition, they emphasize that their book is "not able to settle the question of whether Asian applicants experience discrimination in elite college admissions" (cited in West-Faulcon 2017, 635).
[317] Complaint (November 17, 2014), 119.
[318] Complaint (November 17, 2014), 6–7.

Here the complaint nearly ventriloquized the AALF Amicus Brief in *Fisher*. Again the reference to Jim Crow segregation, and again the historical script was flipped to create a more serviceable alternative reality. The persistent truth of Black subjection, the integrationist intent of Harvard's plan, and the immunities and advantages that accrue to Asian Americans as not-Blacks—each of these factors was turned on its head. Black people and their allies, the complaint asserted, were die-hard segregationists who used the levers of power to oppress innocent, "disfavored" Asians and build "massive resistance" to integration. Asian Americans, meanwhile, were innocent Daisy Bateses braving hateful crowds to integrate American schools for the good of all.

In a motion for summary judgment submitted in June 2018, the SFFA argued that documents gleaned during discovery showed that Harvard had conducted its own internal investigation (through the Office of Institutional Research) in 2013 that indicated bias against Asian Americans in the admissions process, and that the university had concealed the findings.[319] Even without a "smoking gun," the motion added, plaintiffs could prove that the facially neutral Harvard plan had a discriminatory purpose through circumstantial evidence and the elimination of other plausible explanations. Here the motion presented a report by the plaintiffs' expert, Peter Arcidiacono, whose statistical analysis of six years of Harvard's admissions data found that the admissions plan "disproportionately harm[ed]" Asian applicants.[320]

Harvard's admissions plan rates students along four dimensions: academic, extracurricular, athletic, and personal. Then each student receives an overall rating, which takes into account but is not mechanically determined by the other four ratings. Arcidiacono's report argued that the university discriminated against Asian applicants in three ways: in the personal rating, where Asians received the lowest scores of all groups (here applicants are assessed on traits such as "positive personality," "others like to be around him or her," "likeability … helpfulness, courage [and] kindness," "attractive person to be with," "widely respected," and "good person");[321] in the overall rating, which, like the personal

---

[319] Plaintiff's Memorandum of Reasons in Support of Its Motion for Summary Judgment (June 15, 2018).

[320] Expert Report of Peter S. Arcidiacono (2018), 7.

[321] Expert Report of Peter S. Arcidiacono (2018), 7–8. The personal rating score is composed of one personal rating by the admissions office and one by an alumnus/an interviewer. Alumni interviewers give Asian applicants personal ratings that are comparable to whites and higher than those for Black and Latinx people. However, the admissions office gives Asian applicants lower personal ratings than all other groups.

rating, is subjective;[322] and in selection for admission. On this last point, Arcidiacono argued that Asians faced a "ratings penalty"—meaning their chances of admission would go up if they were white.[323] On August 30, 2018, President Trump's Department of Justice formally declared its support for SFFA's lawsuit, extending Attorney General Jeff Sessions's broader assault on affirmative action and deepening the alliance of white and Chinese American conservatives on this issue.

Harvard's motion for summary judgment, also filed in June 2018, began by challenging the SFFA's standing to file the suit. The first line of the motion states: "This case is the latest salvo by ideological opponents of the consideration of race in university admissions." Then: "Although SFFA purports to be an organization dedicated to vindicating the interests of Asian-American applicants, it is nothing of the sort—it is merely a vehicle to litigate the ideological preferences of its founder Edward Blum, and does not have standing to bring this lawsuit."[324] The motion then argued that the university's admissions plan passed strict scrutiny: it pursued a compelling governmental interest in creating a diverse student body; it was narrowly tailored; it considered race flexibly along with other factors rather than using a quota or engaging in "racial balancing"; and it could not be effectively replaced by race-neutral alternatives.[325] Indeed, Harvard conducted a flexible and individualized "whole person evaluation" that considered:

information about the applicant's extracurricular and athletic participation, teacher recommendations, guidance counselor recommendations that frequently discuss much more than academic qualifications, the applicant's essays, an evaluation from a Harvard graduate in the applicant's community who interviewed the applicant, information reflecting the applicant's socioeconomic background,

---

[322] Again, the admissions office gives Asian applicants lower overall ratings than other groups, but alumni interviewers do not.

[323] Expert Report of Peter S. Arcidiacono (2018), 10.

[324] Memorandum in Support of Defendant's Motion for Summary Judgment on All Remaining Counts (June 15, 2018), 1, 3. The motion says SFFA amended its bylaws once it realized that Harvard would challenge its standing, but even then, the motion avers, members say they have not attended meetings and refuse to testify about whether they have voted in any SFFA elections. And only a "tiny fraction" of its 20,000 supposed members have paid dues, while unidentified donors gave the organization nearly $2 million in 2015–2016. The motion explores other measures by which SFFA lacks standing as well, concluding that SFFA plaintiffs do not fulfill the "core requirement that [students] suffer a concrete injury, traceable to the defendant's conduct, that would be redressed by the relief sought." See Memorandum in Support of Defendant's Motion for Summary Judgment on All Remaining Counts (June 15, 2018), 12–15.

[325] Memorandum in Support of Defendant's Motion for Summary Judgment on All Remaining Counts (June 15, 2018).

parental education and occupation, an expression of the applicant's likely academic and extracurricular interests at Harvard, any academic or artistic work the applicant has submitted, and much more.[326]

In addition, the admissions plan paid attention to many other kinds of diversity other than racial diversity, including socioeconomic background, academic interests, experiences of hardship, passions, public service, and more.[327]

Finally, the Harvard motion denied that Harvard's admissions plan discriminated against Asian Americans, whose percentage of the admitted class had increased by 29 percent over the past decade to nearly 23 percent.[328] To prove the charge, the motion pointed out, SFFA had to show Harvard "discriminated on the basis of race, the discrimination was intentional, and the discrimination was a substantial or motivating factor for [Harvard's] actions."[329] On this point, the internal review by Harvard's Office of Institutional Research in 2013 was not designed to detect *intentional* discrimination and did not in fact do so. Its analysis was also "incomplete, preliminary, and based on limited inputs."[330] As months of discovery produced "no documentary or testimonial support" for the charge that Harvard used quotas and pursued "racial balancing," the motion continued, the plaintiffs' case was "entirely statistical," and, as such, had to demonstrate "gross disparities" in order to meet the bar of evidence. Far from finding such "gross disparities," the statistical analysis of Harvard admissions data conducted by the university's expert, David Card, found "no negative effect of Asian-American ethnicity."[331]

---

[326] Memorandum in Support of Defendant's Motion for Summary Judgment on All Remaining Counts (June 15, 2018), 4.

[327] According to the motion, for the class of 2019, Harvard received 26,000 domestic applications for 1,600 slots. Of the 26,000, 3,500 had perfect SAT math scores, 2,700 had perfect SAT verbal scores, and more than 8,000 had perfect converted GPAs. Memorandum in Support of Defendant's Motion for Summary Judgment on All Remaining Counts (June 15, 2018), 3–4.

[328] Memorandum in Support of Defendant's Motion for Summary Judgment on All Remaining Counts (June 15, 2018), 2. According to Harvard's website, the class of 2021 is 14.6 percent Black, 22.2 percent Asian American, 11.6 percent Hispanic, 2.5 percent Native American or Pacific Islander. The remainder of students are white.

[329] Memorandum in Support of Defendant's Motion for Summary Judgment on All Remaining Counts (June 15, 2018), 35, citing *Goodman* v. *Bowdoin College* (2004).

[330] Memorandum in Support of Defendant's Motion for Summary Judgment on All Remaining Counts (June 15, 2018), 38.

[331] Memorandum in Support of Defendant's Motion for Summary Judgment on All Remaining Counts (June 15, 2018), 35, 38, 39. Dr. David Card produced an original report and a rebuttal report responding to Dr. Peter Arcidiacono's report.

Arcidiacono's report, on the other hand, was marred by "fatal defects."[332] Arcidiacono's sample excluded recruited athletes, "legacies," and other "special category" students, on the grounds that they were evaluated under a separate process (which is not true); and it excluded personal ratings from its analysis, on the grounds that these are biased against Asian Americans (which has not been demonstrated).[333] Personal ratings are in fact too complex to be modelled statistically, Harvard's motion argued, as they involve multiple components that are statistically unobservable, or impossible to measure. "Where so much relevant information is statistically unobservable, it is methodologically unsound to conclude that intentional discrimination is the cause of the perceived association between race and personal ratings."[334] A proper statistical analysis (i.e., Card's rebuttal report) shows no discernible discrimination *at all* against Asian American applicants, let alone "gross disparities."[335]

On September 30, 2019, U.S. District Court Judge Allison Burroughs ruled in favor of Harvard, finding that its "holistic review" admissions plan passed strict scrutiny. Moreover, the court found "no persuasive documentary evidence of any racial animus or conscious prejudice against Asian Americans."[336] White applicants were significantly more likely to have "made strong high school contributions to athletics, and this disparity counteract[ed] the effect that Asian American applicants' relative academic and extracurricular strength would otherwise have on their admission rate."[337] "Strength across multiple dimensions," Judge Burroughs wrote, is "highly correlated with admission to Harvard and results in fewer admitted Asian American applicants."[338] While Harvard

---

[332] Memorandum in Support of Defendant's Motion for Summary Judgment on All Remaining Counts (June 15, 2018), 41.

[333] "Special category" students include recruited athletes, children of faculty and staff, "legacies," and applicants on the Dean's List or Director's List. The admit rate for "legacies"—students who have a parent or two parents who are Harvard alumni—is as much as five times higher than that for non-legacies (Franklin and Zwickel 2018).

[334] Memorandum in Support of Defendant's Motion for Summary Judgment on All Remaining Counts (June 15, 2018), 43. According to the motion, Dr. Arcidiacono also errs in pooling admissions data across six admissions cycles instead of analyzing each cycle separately.

[335] For his part, Dr. Arcidiacono argues that Dr. Card's analysis is wrong because he refuses to exclude "special category" applicants, who must be excluded in order to determine whether similarly situated applicants are treated differently because of race. He also faults Dr. Card for refusing to exclude personal ratings in his model, when they should be excluded, he claims, because they are discriminatory against Asians.

[336] Findings of Fact and Conclusion of Law (September 30, 2019), 17.

[337] Findings of Fact and Conclusion of Law (September 30, 2019), 60.

[338] Findings of Fact and Conclusion of Law (September 30, 2019), 60.

admissions officers did assign Asian American applicants slightly lower personal ratings than other groups, teacher and guidance counselor recommendations accounted for some of this disparity. Still, Judge Burroughs allowed, the disparity between white and Asian American personal ratings "ha[d] not been fully and satisfactorily explained," and it was "possible, though unsupported by any direct evidence before the court, that part of the statistical disparity resulted from admissions officers' implicit biases that disadvantaged Asian American applicants in the personal rating relative to white applicants."[339] She wrote:

Taking account of all of the available evidence, it is possible that implicit biases had a slight negative effect on average Asian American personal ratings, but the Court concludes that the majority of the disparity in the personal rating between white and Asian American applicants was more likely caused by race-affected inputs to the admissions process (e.g., recommendations or high school accomplishments) or underlying differences in the attributes that may have resulted in stronger personal ratings.[340]

Asian American applicants were accepted at the same rate as other applicants and comprised more than 20 percent of admitted classes, up from 3.4 percent in 1980, Judge Burroughs pointed out. "Although Asian Americans can and do bring important and diverse perspectives to Harvard, because only about 6 percent of the United States population is Asian American compared to nearly a quarter of Harvard's class, it is reasonable for Harvard to determine that students from other minority backgrounds are more likely to offer perspectives that are less abundant in its classes and to therefore primarily offer race-based tips to those students."[341] Pursuing meaningful diversity on campus and in the classroom did not constitute discrimination against Asian Americans.

In November 2020, the First Circuit Court of Appeals upheld the district court's ruling, and SFFA promptly appealed the case to the U.S. Supreme Court.[342] In January 2022, the Court granted certiorari; in fall 2022, the Court heard the case. Supporters of affirmative

---

[339] Findings of Fact and Conclusion of Law (September 30, 2019), 72.

[340] Findings of Fact and Conclusion of Law (September 30, 2019), 72–73.

[341] Findings of Fact and Conclusion of Law (September 30, 2019), 126. Black people and Hispanics make up about 20 percent of domestic applicants to Harvard, though together the two groups constitute more than 30 percent of the national population. Asian Americans make up roughly 22 percent of applicants recently, while being less than 6 percent of the national population. See Findings of Fact and Conclusion of Law (September 30, 2019), 10–11.

[342] *Students for Fair Admissions, Inc.* v. *President and Fellows of Harvard College*, United States Court of Appeals, First Circuit, November 12, 2020.

action are gravely concerned. With the Trump administration's three recent appointments (Gorsuch, Kavanaugh, and Barrett), the court is more conservative than it has been in decades, and several justices are on record as opposing affirmative action. A 6–3 vote against Harvard is a likely outcome. Will Ed Blum's latest gambit pay off? Will SFFA persuade the court that a ceiling on Asian Americans exists, that it is inextricably tied to a floor for other minority groups, and that the consideration of race in admissions should therefore be prohibited altogether? Will the notion that Asian Americans are "minorities," too, undermine the argument for race-conscious admissions and give this conservative Court an occasion for banning it altogether? It remains to be seen whether the Asian spoilers narrative, deployed by an alliance of right-wing whites and Chinese immigrants, will accomplish what white charges of "reverse racism" have not been able to: the dismantling of affirmative action in American institutions of higher education.

XV BLACK LIVES MATTER AND THE ASIAN AMERICAN POLICEMAN

Galvanized by the July 2013 acquittal of George Zimmerman in the murder of Trayvon Martin, #BlackLivesMatter began as a hashtag and became a movement. In July 2014, Eric Garner was murdered via a police chokehold in Staten Island, New York. *I can't breathe.* Less than a month later, in August 2014, Michael Brown was murdered via police bullets in Ferguson, Missouri. *Hands up, don't shoot.* And the murders of Black people kept coming, each a grim data point in a centuries-long series with no end in sight. The most expansive Black mobilization in the nation's history has had a simple but powerful point to make: a century and a half after Emancipation, "Black Lives Matter" is still an aspiration and a demand rather than a reality. Violence against Black people, by both the U.S. state and private actors, is a systemic problem, and the first Black presidency in U.S. history not only failed to mitigate, but actually functioned to dissemble, this bitter truth. Like earlier waves of the Black freedom struggle, Black Lives Matter has succeeded, through various forms of civil disobedience, in producing "a crisis of authority and legitimacy for US policing," and, by extension, for the U.S. state.[343]

[343] Camp and Heatherton 2016, 4. Black Lives Matter advances a systematic critique of police, prisons, and power that goes beyond ideas of liberal incorporation. It also emphasizes grassroots democracy and decentralized politics, as opposed to the NAACP

In "A Herstory of the #BlackLivesMatter Movement" (2014), Alicia Garza, one of the founders of Black Lives Matter, writes:

[W]e understand that when Black people in this country get free, the benefits will be wide reaching and transformative for society as a whole. When we are able to end hyper-criminalization and sexualization of Black people and end the poverty, control, and surveillance of Black people, every single person in this world has a better shot at getting and staying free .... This is why we call on Black people and our allies to take up the call that Black lives matter. We're not saying Black lives are more important than other lives, or that other lives are not criminalized and oppressed in various ways. We remain in active solidarity with all oppressed people who are fighting for their liberation and we know that our destinies are intertwined. And, to keep it real—it is appropriate and necessary to have strategy and action centered around Blackness without other non-Black communities of color, or White folks for that matter, needing to find a place and a way to center themselves within it.

Invoking the Combahee River Collective's celebrated Black feminist statement of 1977, Garza explains why the specification of Black oppression is both necessary and nonexclusionary. She then calls out not-Black progressives for homogenizing the statuses and experiences of different communities of color:

Progressive movements in the United States have made some unfortunate errors when they push for unity at the expense of really understanding the concrete differences in context, experience and oppression ... [and when they engage in the] worn out and sloppy practice of drawing lazy parallels of unity between peoples with vastly different experiences and histories .... [T]he state apparatus has built a program of genocide and repression mostly on the backs of Black people—beginning with the theft of millions of people for free labor— and then adapted it to control, murder, and profit off of other communities of color and immigrant communities. We perpetuate a level of White supremacist domination by reproducing a tired trope that we are all the same, rather than acknowledging that non-Black oppressed people in this country are both impacted by racism and domination, and simultaneously, BENEFIT from anti-black racism.[344]

It is not just that not-Black groups like Asian Americans are not as oppressed as Black people, it is also that *they gain something from the oppression of Black people*. There are complex dynamics at play, in other

---

model of hierarchical authority, membership, and official platforms. The BLM project was founded by queer Black women and focuses more on queer, trans, undocumented, disabled, and nonbinary gender issues than prior instantiations of the Black freedom movement. How radical it is in terms of its stance on capitalism is yet to be determined through internal struggle (Rickford 2015).

[344] Garza 2014. Capitalization in original.

words, that belie the simple fantasy of Third World groups standing shoulder to shoulder against white supremacy.

In July 2013, Asian Americans Advancing Justice, a national coalition of prominent advocacy groups, commented on the acquittal of George Zimmerman:

> As a civil rights organization, we believe the [Trayvon Martin] case illustrates the pervasiveness of racial prejudice in our society and our legal system and the unique history and ongoing struggle of African Americans against racism and oppression. For the Asian American community, this painful tragedy echoes the infamous case of Vincent Chin.[345]

What is striking about this statement is that it recognizes the "unique history and ongoing struggle" of Black people and then promptly likens it to the murder of Chinese American Vincent Chin. Black singularity is noted for a moment and then quickly disappeared through the habit of equivalencing. The Trayvon–Vincent comparison was made frequently in Asian American commentary at the time. Ironically, repeatedly invoking Chin some thirty years after his murder had the opposite effect from that intended: it emphasized how few Asian Americans, as compared with Black people, become victims of racially motivated murder.

In August 2014, after the police killing of Michael Brown in Ferguson, Missouri, the National Council of Asian Pacific Americans released this statement:

> The tragedy in Ferguson is not an isolated incident. Racial suspicion of black men, especially by law enforcement, has become an epidemic in many parts of the country. Thus, we urgently call upon the White House, the Department of Justice and congressional leaders to review and address the ongoing pattern and practice of racial violence and systemic discriminatory treatment by law enforcement of our communities of color. As people of color and immigrants, our own communities' histories in the United States include violence and targeting, often by law enforcement. From the killing of 19-year-old Fong Lee by a Minneapolis police officer in August of 2010, to the ongoing targeting and surveillance of South Asian, Muslim and Sikh communities in the post-9/11 climate, our communities have experienced the impact of suspicion and discriminatory treatment based on race, national origin and faith.

The statement begins by emphasizing the specificity of police violence against Black men, after which every passing sentence moves farther away from this topic and toward a universal or generic sense of what

---

[345] "How the Asian American Community Relates to the Trayvon Martin Case," *Asian Americans Advancing Justice*, July 2013.

"discriminatory treatment" means. The rhetorical pattern we see in both organizational statements is symptomatic of the difficulty that Asian American advocacy groups have in holding open space to talk about the distinctiveness of Black abjection. There are at least two reasons why this occurs. First, there is an organizational and affective investment in moving Asian Americans to or near the center of the stage. Second, the people-of-color framework of contemporary racial advocacy mandates equivalencing and analogizing as supposed steps toward solidarity. The negative impact of the Asian American movement's half-finished critique is apparent here: by challenging only white supremacy, Asian American activists end up reproducing anti-Blackness.

In November 2014, a new phase opened in the relationship of Asian Americans to Black Lives Matter. The name of another Black person was added to the series of police murder victims: Akai Gurley. This time, in a twist, the police officer who pulled the trigger was Chinese American rather than white. NYPD officer Peter Liang and his partner were conducting a "vertical patrol" in a stairwell of the Louis Pink Houses in East New York, Brooklyn, when he fired his weapon—inadvertently, he claimed. The bullet ricocheted off the walls and struck Akai Gurley some floors below. Liang stood over Gurley and argued with his partner over who would inform their supervisor; neither called an ambulance or performed CPR. The friend whom Gurley had been visiting tried to administer first aid with the help of a 911 operator, but to no avail. Gurley died on the scene. Liang was charged, indicted, and convicted of second-degree manslaughter and official misconduct (for not helping Gurley or calling for help). The charges carried up to fifteen years of prison time, but Liang got no jail time. In an echo of the Soon Ja Du case, he was sentenced to five years' probation and 800 hours of community service.

In revelatory language, NYPD Commissioner William Bratton described what happened in the stairwell as an "accidental discharge." There was no intent to kill, Bratton averred, Liang had simply made an error. Here again "intent" creates a capacious loophole. If the Jerome camp blackface performers did not intend to denigrate Black people, if Japanese American activists did not intend to undermine the fight for Black reparations, if Soon Ja Du did not intend to shoot Latasha in the back of the head, if the Asian American Legal Foundation did not intend to lower Black and Latinx enrollment at Lowell High School, if Lambda Theta Delta blackface performers did not intend to be racist, if K-pop bands in blackface did not intend to demean Black performers, and so on. "Intent" focuses on *individual* malice and distracts us from the inescapably structural dynamics of anti-Blackness.

Does the absence of clear individual intent mean an act is necessarily accidental? As was the case with Soon Ja Du and the unnamed Korean storeowner who shot Edward Jae Song Lee, there is more to the phrase "accidental shooting" than meets the eye. Peter Liang claimed that he kept his finger off the trigger, and then a loud sound in the dark stairwell (the ceiling light bulb was broken) surprised him and his finger twitched, causing the gun to discharge: "The gun just went off, after my body tensed up."[346] Like Soon Ja Du, Liang distances himself from the discharge of the weapon, almost as if it fired on its own. The Glock used by NYPD officers has more than double the trigger resistance of the model available to the public, however, and it has a Safe Action System designed to prevent an accidental slip of the finger. The jurors in Liang's trial asked to hold his Glock pistol, to touch the metal slide, to squeeze the 11.5-pound trigger. After this sensory experiment, the jurors decided he had lied. One juror said: "It was very hard to pull the trigger ... [so] we knew his testimony wasn't completely true."[347]

Did Liang fire his gun because of his fear of the Blackness lurking in the stairwell below? (Fanon: the Black is "phobogenic."[348]) Whether it is a teenager returning from the convenience store with Snapple Iced Tea and Skittles, or a man driving with a broken taillight, or a child playing with a toy gun in the park, or a woman sleeping in her own bedroom, Blackness itself seems sufficient cause for the police (and their surrogates) to open fire. After which there is nothing to forgive.

Did Peter Liang kill Akai Gurley by "accident"? How do we assess the magnitude of the injury done to Black people under the cover of the word "accidental"? Consider the scene of the killing. The Louis Pink Houses, like other low-income public housing units in New York City and across the nation, show that race is indeed, in Ruth Wilson Gilmore's words, "differential vulnerability to premature death." Public housing projects are physical nodes in which intense poverty, inadequate health care, underemployment, substandard and dilapidated housing, unequal education, exposure to environmental toxins and overpolicing converge. They exemplify the U.S. system of urban hypersegregation that racial

---

[346] Liang testifying in his trial, from the documentary film *Down a Dark Stairwell* (Liang 2020).
[347] Phippen 2016.
[348] Fanon 1986 [1952], 117.

capitalism has sculpted for the past century. Debunking the conventional wisdom that residential segregation outside the South has been random, unintentional, and *accidental*, Richard Rothstein's *The Color of Law: A Forgotten History of How Our Government Segregated America* (2017) shows that it has been the result of decades of explicit and coordinated public and private decision making by government agencies, courts, banks, realtor associations, homeowners associations, white mobs, police, and others. No other racial group in the U.S., Rothstein emphasizes, has been segregated as severely, systematically, and deliberately as Black people have.

Consider, too, what Liang was doing in the Louis Pink Houses. Initiated by the NYPD in 1991, "vertical patrols" or "vertical sweeps"— where officers start on the roof of public housing buildings and work their way down, floor by floor, via the stairwells—entail (1) stopping anyone and everyone in hallways, stairwells, rooftops, landings, elevators, and other common areas without probable cause; (2) conducting searches of these persons; (3) demanding proof that they live there or are visiting a resident; (4) arresting them for violating trespass laws, often without trying to ascertain whether or not they are bona fide residents or visitors; and (5) holding them in custody for a period of one night to weeks (which sometimes results in loss of employment and other adverse consequences). An example of aggressive overpolicing, vertical patrols are of questionable legality. Adam Carlis observes that vertical patrols "violate state search and seizure jurisprudence because their systematic nature precludes the requisite suspicion state law requires before a police officer can approach and question a suspect."[349]

Vertical patrols had claimed the lives of at least two Black men in New York City before Akai Gurley, but it was their quotidian effects on all residents that were the subject of *Davis* v. *City of New York* (2012), a class-action lawsuit filed by the Legal Aid Society on behalf of public housing residents. The initial complaint argued that vertical patrols constituted unlawful search and seizure and racial discrimination, in violation of the Fourth and Fourteenth Amendments, respectively. In addition, it documented the ways in which vertical patrols terrorized residents' family and friends and deterred them from visiting, thus preventing residents from "maintaining and fostering close familiar and personal relationships" and deepening their social isolation. Residents said it felt like they were living in "penal colonies" where they were treated like suspects,

[349] Carlis 2009, 2004.

surveilled, harassed, and subjected to abuses of power.[350] Keeping in mind Loïc Wacquant's (2002) analysis of the structural and functional linkages among slavery, the ghetto, and the prison, one is struck by the *non-randomness* and *non-accidentalness* of Akai Gurley's violent death, the predictability and overdeterminedness of it, by how Black life is lived in adjacency to death. When is an accident not only not an accident, but evidence of its obverse—that is, structure?

There is a non-random congruence here between the argument that Liang's killing of Gurley was "accidental" and the argument that Korean immigrant storeowners had nothing to do with the dispossession and violence that marked Black life in South Central Los Angeles at the time of the 1992 Los Angeles rebellion. Both arguments seek to establish Asian Americans' moral innocence in an absolute way, to deny that they are entangled in structural anti-Blackness, to insist that they come away clean. What does it mean for Asian immigrants to enter the scene of Black urban segregation and impoverishment and open stores as vehicles for their own upward mobility? What does it mean for an Asian American police officer to enter public housing and conduct vertical patrols with a gun drawn and his finger on the trigger? More generally, what does it mean to conduct business as usual or enforce law and order in a social order that is a "state of emergency" for Black people?[351] Is the line between innocence and complicity straightforwardly observable?

Liang's Chinese American supporters thought he was being scapegoated by the system and Black protesters alike. Like Dai Sil Kim-Gibson in the film *Sa-I-Gu*, they argued that white officials were misdirecting Black rage at Asian Americans in order to save their own skin. As one young Chinese American woman put it, Liang "took the fall for the sins of a country."[352] (It bears noting that Black people here are assumed to be incapable of independent political action and easily controlled by white masterminds.) Akai Gurley, from this perspective, was merely a victim of an accidental shooting—it was Peter Liang who was the true victim of racial injustice. On February 20, 2016, in the largest mobilization of Americans of Asian descent since the Asian American movement a half-century earlier, more than 100,000 Chinese Americans rallied in Brooklyn

---

[350] Complaint/Demand for Jury Trial, *Davis v. The City of New York* (2010), United States District Court for the Southern District of New York, 4.

[351] See Wilderson 2010.

[352] Kuo 2019, 48, quoting a widely circulated video interview with a Chinese American woman that was viewed 4 million times and translated and shared on Chinese-language media.

and in forty cities across the country to complain that the system was forcing "Peter Scapegoat" to pay for the sins of others. Why, they asked, was Liang the first NYPD officer to be convicted in the on-duty killing of a civilian since 2005? Why was he indicted and convicted while white officers who killed Black people were not? The 120,000 signatories of a WhiteHouse.gov petition decried the system's "selective prosecution" of the Chinese, a tradition they traced back to *Yick Wo* v. *Hopkins* and San Francisco's persecution of Chinese laundry operators in the 1800s.

The allusion to *Yick Wo* v. *Hopkins* was ironic, since the U.S. Supreme Court invoked this case in *Plessy* v. *Ferguson* to alibi Jim Crow and the U.S. state, thus initiating the official practice of weaponizing Asian Americans against the Black struggle (see Part One). How far were Liang's defenders willing to go in disavowing the Black struggle? As critics noted, the WhiteHouse.gov petition amounted to a demand that Liang be granted the same dispensation as white officers *to kill Black people with impunity*. Reflecting on the pro-Liang rallies, Jay Caspian Kang writes: "[N]o amount of nuance or qualification or appeal to Martin Luther King will change the fact that the first massive, nationwide Asian-American protest in years was held in defense of a police officer who shot and killed an innocent black man."[353] Were Liang's defenders pressing for racial equality broadly conceived? Or simply to be made equal shareholders with whites in this anti-Black order?

Pro-Liang rallies were organized by conservative Chinese immigrant professionals, most of whom had emigrated from mainland China since the mid-1980s.[354] This was a class of actors who had been victorious in the *Brian Ho* case in the 1990s and were by this time emerging onto the national scene as a highly disciplined anti-affirmative action fighting force. Earlier in 2014, the pro-affirmative action Senate Constitutional Amendment 5 (SCA 5) had been sailing through the California legislature when groups of conservative Chinese immigrants mobilized to derail it, in part by persuading Democratic Asian American legislators to change their positions.[355] As a result, SCA 5 went down, and the preexisting ban on affirmative action in the state university systems remained in place. Conservative Chinese immigrant activists were sending a clear message that they rejected the Third World solidarity model. Instead, it was Asian Americans first and last—or, more precisely, Chinese Americans first and last.

[353] Kang 2016.
[354] Feng and Tseng-Putterman 2019, 240.
[355] Song 2020.

Chinese nationalism was a powerful driver in the pro-Liang protests. Wen Liu, an ethnographer who embedded as a participant-observer, notes that protesters often wore red and played Chinese music as if the events were an extension of the Lunar New Year festival.[356] WeChat and other Chinese social media platforms were used to mobilize support for Liang, and sometimes rallies in U.S. cities were organized by individuals living in China.[357] (With more than a half billion Chinese users, WeChat has thrived in the vacuum created by the Chinese government's ban on Facebook, Twitter, and other foreign platforms.) China's CCTV covered the pro-Liang events extensively, and the state-run New China News Agency sent journalists to several U.S. cities to report on them.[358] An op-ed piece in the *Global Times*, a Chinese Communist Party newspaper, complained about "the obvious double standards toward different races that has [sic] made people furious" and pointed out that Chinese Americans are "a model group in the U.S." who are nonetheless "easily overlooked or discriminated against."[359] Another party newspaper, the *People's Daily*, denounced the U.S. for its racial problems and its hypocrisy in criticizing China's human rights record.[360]

Ideologically, this variant of Chinese nationalism converged with white nationalism in a number of ways. Both embraced neoliberal capitalism and the American Dream, rejected Black claims of racial oppression, and denounced race-conscious remedies as reverse racism and state-sponsored social engineering. Both built their claims upon racial buzzwords such as "meritocracy" and "law and order." A first-generation Chinese lawyer/ engineer who helped to organize both pro-Liang rallies and the anti-SCA 5 mobilization declared: "When we [Chinese] came to this country, most of us did not have anything. We made it because we are hard working, hard studying .... I would almost take offense to say that we should be united with Latinos and African Americans just for the sake of getting benefits, because that's not where our values are."[361] The national

[356] W. Liu 2018.
[357] Feng and Tseng-Putterman 2019. Feng and Tseng-Putterman write of WeChat: "Known as China's 'super app,' the combined messaging, social media, and mobile payment app has over 1.1 billion users, the large majority of whom are of Chinese heritage" (2019, 239). WeChat serves as a "staging grounds" (2019, 241) of sorts where Chinese and Chinese diasporic subjects discuss issues among themselves before strategizing about how to reach out to mainstream social media like Twitter and Facebook.
[358] Makinen 2016.
[359] Makinen 2016.
[360] W. Liu 2018.
[361] Quoted in J. C. Wong 2016.

WeChat group that organized the February 20, 2016, rallies was formed by David Tian Wang, founder and president of Chinese Americans for Trump.[362] Wen Liu writes, "A right-wing alliance developed between conservative Chinese and white Americans, who share a deep investment in preserving class privileges and status, in the name of 'racial justice.'"[363] Liang supporters were known to declare "All Lives Matter" and express strong support for the police.[364]

Many liberal and progressive Asian American advocates seemed unsure of how to respond to the emergence of right-wing Chinese immigrant organizations whose politics were decidedly at odds with theirs. Aside from questioning the reflexive defense of Liang as an Asian American, they did not offer a coherent approach to or interpretation of the scenario. Again, the non-theorization of structural anti-Blackness was a stumbling block. One striking exception to this trend was Asians4BlackLives, a collective that formed in the Bay Area in 2014 to support Black Lives Matter.[365] On December 15, 2014, a month after Peter Liang fatally shot Akai Gurley, they posted a statement that read in part:

As Asians, we recognize the ways in which we've been used historically to prop up the anti-Black racism that allows this violence to occur. We are an extremely diverse community. Some of us have been targeted, profiled, and killed by U.S. government institutions. Many of us came to the U.S. as a result of the devastation and displacement caused by the U.S. military and its "partners" in Asia, only to find a country uses police to devastate and displace black communities. However, we also recognize the relative privilege that many of us carry as Asians living in the U.S.[366]

What distinguishes this statement from those of other liberal and progressive Asian American advocacy groups is how it opens up space to discuss Asian Americans' structural advantage—and then *holds this space open* rather than allowing it to collapse. Asian American *positionality* and *functionality* in an anti-Black order are frankly discussed. Insights proffered by thinkers like Amy Uyematsu and Alan Nishio back in the 1960s are recuperated here, a half-century later.

---

[362] Feng and Tseng-Putterman 2019.
[363] W. Liu 2018, 430.
[364] See Liang 2020.
[365] Another exception to the trend was CAAAV: Organizing Asian Communities. CAAAV stands for Committee Against Anti-Asian Violence. This New York City group has a long history of opposing police violence against people of color, supported Akai Gurley's family, and criticized Liang's defenders. As a result, CAAAV members were accused of being race traitors and were even subjected to rape and death threats. See Liang 2020.
[366] Kuo 2019, 49.

As one observer noted, Asians4BlackLives believes "Asian American activism does not need to be AAPI-focused in order to achieve liberation for AAPI people."[367] Indeed the group centers Black leadership and the Black struggle in its thinking and activism. The mission statement declares: "We understand that the path to liberation for all communities travels through the liberation of Black communities in America. When Black people have justice and liberation, we all move one big step closer to real freedom."[368] Asians4BlackLives-NYC, which formed in 2016 in response to Liang's non-sentence, enacted this politics by supporting Akai Gurley's family, criticizing Liang supporters, and protesting *Sing Tao Daily* (the Chinese-language newspaper which many Chinese immigrants read for local news) for its inflammatory, anti-Black coverage of the case.[369]

Several years later, on May 25, 2020, four police officers murdered George Floyd on the streets of Minneapolis. Officer Tou Thao, who is Hmong American, played an active role in Floyd's murder by shielding Derek Chauvin and the other two officers from the bystanders who were trying to intervene and save Floyd's life. Thao was charged with aiding and abetting Chauvin's commission of second degree murder and second degree manslaughter.[370] On June 2, 2020, in an interview with special agents of the Minnesota Bureau of Criminal Apprehension and the FBI, Thao was asked if he could have done something differently, to which he responded: "I guess I would be more observant toward Floyd."[371] In their August 2020 filing with the attorney general's office, prosecutors wrote:

In the first five minutes Floyd was on the ground, he told the officers at least 20 times that he could not breathe. He told them nearly 10 times that he was dying. And then he fell silent …. As Floyd lost consciousness, a crowd of bystanders pleaded with Thao. They told him that the officers were killing Floyd. They screamed that Floyd had stopped moving. They alerted Thao that Floyd had stopped breathing. And they begged Thao almost 30 times to take Floyd's pulse. But instead of intervening on Floyd's behalf, Thao continued to push the crowd of bystanders back to the sidewalk, allowing the other officers to continue to pin

---

[367] "Asians 4 Black Lives" n.d. See https://blogs.brown.edu/ethn-1890v-s01-fall-2016/asians-for-black-lives.

[368] See at: https://a4bl.wordpress.com/who-we-are.

[369] Fu et al. 2019.

[370] In February 2022, Tou Thao and the two Minneapolis police officers who helped Chauvin murder George Floyd were all convicted on federal charges of violating Floyd's civil rights. They now await state trial on the criminal charges of aiding and abetting second-degree murder and second-degree manslaughter.

[371] Raiche 2020.

Floyd to the ground—with Chauvin on Floyd's neck, Kueng on Floyd's back, and Lane on Floyd's legs.[372]

In the paradigmatic scene where the white officer tells the Black man to assume the position, is this what the Asian American is doing?

In response to George Floyd's murder, Asians4BlackLives released the statement "Uplift Black Resistance, Help Build Black Power" (June 1, 2020), in which they wrote: "We, as Asians4BlackLives (A4BL), join our comrades in denouncing these gross displays of state-sanctioned police violence, and renew our call to all non-Black people of Asian descent to move in solidarity with Black communities for Black liberation and resistance." Tou Thao, they observed, was "not just a damning symbol for Asian American complicity in the death of Black people, but also a direct manifestation of anti-Blackness in our communities." Lifting up the demands of the Black struggle—including but not limited to defunding the police and abolishing the carceral system—they reminded Asian Americans: "In all these struggles, follow the leadership and center the perspectives of those most affected."[373] In a second statement, "Structural Racism Is the Pandemic, Interdependence and Solidarity Is the Cure" (July 9, 2020), Asians4BlackLives wrote:

> What [Asian Americans] have in common is that we're incentivized by capitalism and racism, particularly anti-Blackness, to hold up the dual evils of white supremacy and American imperialism …. That means [we must] understan[d] how we've been asked to buy into this system and to uphold ideas, policies, and practices that ultimately go against our interests. That also means being active and vocal supporters of Black liberation, and taking responsibility to end our anti-Blackness. We must acknowledge that anti-Blackness is at the core of all racism and that non-Black Asians have benefited—conditionally—from a system of anti-Blackness politically, economically, and socially.[374]

Going along with the racial system secures only temporary benefits for Asian Americans. In the long run, their liberation, too, depends on its dismantling. Which is to say, their liberation depends on the progress achieved by the Black struggle. Ethics and self-interest point in the same direction. By taking up the theorization of structural anti-Blackness, Asians4BlackLives illuminates a path forward out of the ethical crisis bedeviling Asian American politics today.

[372] "Prosecutors Depict Ex-Officer Tou Thao As Complicit in George Floyd's Death" 2020.
[373] See at: https://a4bl.tumblr.com/post/619777369649102848/asians-4-black-lives-uplift-black-resistance.
[374] See at: https://a4bl.tumblr.com/post/623193309907730432/asians-4-black-lives-structural-racism-is-the.

XVI   THE COVID-19 HATE CRIMES ACT OF 2021

As the COVID-19 pandemic unfolded in 2020, acts of anti-Asian harassment and violence multiplied across the country, triggered by President Trump referring to the disease as "Kung Flu" or "the Chinese flu." With this rhetoric, Trump authorized Americans to vent their pandemic-related anxiety and anger upon those (who looked like they could be) of Chinese descent. A video of an elderly Thai man being knocked to the ground in San Francisco's Chinatown by a Black man went viral, stoking panic among Asian Americans.[375] Were Asian Americans in danger? Were Black people coming for Asians? A wave of mainstream media stories, many written by Asian American journalists, reported that Asian Americans were afraid to walk in public, that they were buying guns, that youth groups were forming to escort the elderly in public. Headlines reported enormous spikes of up to 800 percent in anti-Asian hate crimes, and #StopAsianHate formed to name the specificity of the events and demand government action.

The attacks on Asian Americans are a sobering reminder that anti-Asian animus is a continuous undercurrent in U.S. culture, ready to be brought to the surface in exigencies like global war or a global pandemic. It can be relatively quiet for decades, but it does not disappear. No matter how closely Asian Americans may approach whiteness, they remain not-white and thus vulnerable to such historical vicissitudes. At the same time, because anti-Asian violence is largely contingent upon global events, and not a structural necessity—that is, the social order is not constructed upon a foundation of Asian abjection—it reflects Asian Americans' specific positionality relative to Black people. Even at the low points of their experiential path, when white supremacy is bearing down on them with particular force, Asian Americans are always already lifted upwards by anti-Blackness.

Consider the claim that Asian Americans no longer feel safe in public. The logical predicate to this claim is that they *did* feel safe in public prior to the pandemic. In other words, many Asian Americans traversed public spaces (restaurants, public transportation, shops, parks, and more) without undue worry about being attacked verbally or physically by strangers—until the pandemic hit. This sense of security, even if provisional and

---

[375] The man died from his injuries. It is still not clear that this was a racial attack. According to a journalist who wrote a piece on this case and spoke to me off the record, the assailant appeared to have a mental illness, as he was pacing and shouting on the street for nearly an hour before the elderly Thai man appeared.

revocable, is part of the boon of not-Blackness. It is precisely what is always denied to Black people in an anti-Black order. The phobic avoidance of Blackness fuels an insatiable drive toward segregation in both public and private spaces, and in the remaining spaces where Black people continue to interact with whites, they do so at their own peril. In the afterlife of slavery, white mob violence and state-sanctioned police violence have created an atmosphere of terror for Black people in the ordinary spaces of daily life. A century and a half after Emancipation, this is still true. This is what the Black Lives Matter movement calls out—the impossibility of driving while Black, playing in the park while Black, walking with Skittles while Black, sleeping in one's bed while Black, barbequing in the park while Black, bird-watching while Black, waiting for a friend in Starbucks while Black, taking a nap in a dorm common room while Black, pausing in the stairwell while Black. The impossibility of living when one is the subject of structurally necessary violence. At no point during the pandemic—indeed at no point in history—have Asian Americans been in this position.

In "What the Media Gets Wrong about Anti-Asian Hate" (June 23, 2021), Janelle Wong examined data on anti-Asian hate crimes over the past year and a half, as reported by nine credible sources, in order to "put anti-Asian violence in perspective." Contrary to media stories, the data showed that "while there has been an increase in anti-Asian hate since the start of the pandemic, it is mostly not physical attacks, not more widespread than that faced by other racial groups, not targeted at the elderly, and does not mostly involve Black offenders." Stop AAPI Hate, for example, reported that 65 percent of the anti-Asian incidents were verbal harassment, 18 percent were shunning, and just over 12 percent were physical assaults. In other words, the vast majority (83 percent) of incidents did not involve physical attacks. Similarly, the Virulent Hate Project at the University of Michigan found 80 percent of incidents consisted of a verbal assault or avoidance, and 17 percent were physical harassment, including spitting, coughing, sneezing. Headlines reporting dramatic increases in anti-Asian attacks were misleading, Wong noted, because they did not point out that the overall numbers started and remained low. In New York City, for example, an 833 percent increase was observed between 2019 and 2020, but the jump was from three incidents to twenty-eight incidents. In 2020, anti-Asian hate crimes were only 11 percent of all reported hate crimes in New York City, and Asian Americans make up 14 percent of the population there.[376]

---

[376] J. Wong 2021.

Putting anti-Asian violence "in perspective" also means noting that Black people are, in ordinary times, much more frequently the target of hate crimes than Asian Americans are. According to Wong, in 2019, Black people were the most frequent target of hate crimes in the U.S. (58 percent of reported cases), while Asian Americans were the target in only 4 percent of the cases. During the pandemic, Black people and Asian Americans reported experiencing hate crimes or incidents at comparable rates. From January 2021 to early March 2022, 17 percent of Black adults and 16 percent of Asian American adults reported such an experience.[377] Every racially motivated attack on Asian Americans must be condemned. At the same time, it is important to be clear as to the nature of the attacks, the overall numbers, and the frequency of the attacks as compared with attacks on other groups, including Black people.[378]

These facts make it all the more remarkable that President Joe Biden signed the COVID-19 Hate Crimes Act into law in May 2021. The text of the law reads in part:

Congress finds the following:

(1) Following the spread of COVID-19 in 2020, there has been a dramatic increase in hate crimes and violence against Asian-Americans and Pacific Islanders.

(2) According to a recent report, there were nearly 3,800 reported cases of anti-Asian discrimination and incidents related to COVID-19 between March 19, 2020, and February 28, 2021, in all 50 States and the District of Columbia.

(3) During this time frame, race has been cited as the primary reason for discrimination, making up over 90 percent of incidents, and the United States condemns and denounces any and all anti-Asian and Pacific Islander sentiment in any form.

(4) Roughly 36 percent of these incidents took place at a business and more than 2,000,000 Asian-American businesses have contributed to the diverse fabric of American life.

(5) More than 1,900,000 Asian-American and Pacific Islander older adults, particularly those older adults who are recent immigrants or have limited English proficiency, may face even greater challenges in dealing with the COVID-19 pandemic, including discrimination, economic insecurity, and language isolation.

(6) In the midst of this alarming surge in anti-Asian hate crimes and incidents, a shooter murdered the following 8 people in the Atlanta, Georgia region, 7 of whom were women and 6 of whom were women of Asian descent ....

(7) The people of the United States will always remember the victims of these shootings and stand in solidarity with those affected by this senseless tragedy and incidents of hate that have affected the Asian and Pacific Islander communities.[379]

---

[377] Wong and Ramakrishnan 2022.

[378] J. Wong 2021. After the publication of the article, Professor Wong received hate mail from Chinese Americans accusing her of being a race traitor.

[379] See at: www.congress.gov/bill/117th-congress/senate-bill/937/text.

Rather than putting anti-Asian hate crimes in perspective, this text isolates them and decontextualizes them so that they appear singularly severe, the better to present the federal government as the avenging angel of justice. Although the statute, in substantive terms, streamlines the prosecution of hate crimes generally, the text suggests that Department of Justice officials will have Asian Americans top of mind when they set about enforcing it. Introduced by two Asian American lawmakers (Senator Mazie Hirono and Representative Grace Meng), the COVID-19 Hate Crimes Act passed the House with strong bipartisan support and passed the Senate *94 to 1*—a remarkable event in this era of unprecedented political polarization. The media announced the passage of the law approvingly as a sign of the federal government's concern for Asian American communities and commitment to stemming anti-Asian attacks.

What explains the extraordinary level of support for this statute? To answer this question, we need to look at the statute in relation to two other contemporaneous political projects. The first is a report—entitled *Report of the International Commission of Inquiry on Systemic Racist Police Violence against People of African Descent in the United States*—that was released in March 2021 by an international team of human rights experts. The second is the George Floyd Justice in Policing Bill, which aims to reduce police violence against marginalized communities and was, at that time, stalled in the U.S. Senate.[380] If we look at the COVID-19 Hate Crimes Act in relation to the human rights report and the congressional bill, what do we learn?

Let us start with the human rights report, in which human rights experts from around the world documented the systematic violation of Black Americans' rights by the police and associated institutions in the U.S. They concluded that police violence toward Black people is so severe and extensive that it constitutes a "Crime against Humanity," a concept developed in international law after the Second World War to address state-sponsored atrocities. The report called upon international bodies to investigate and demanded that the U.S. government also acknowledge that slavery and colonialism were "Crimes against Humanity" and establish a congressional commission to study reparations. In the tradition of Malcolm X and the Black Panther Party, as well as earlier Black internationalists like William Patterson and Paul Robeson, the report attempted to bring international opinion to bear on the treatment of Black Americans

---

[380] The bill failed to make it out of the Senate.

by the U.S. state. Despite the gravity and importance of its subject, the report was largely ignored by the U.S. media and government.[381]

Relatedly, the George Floyd Justice in Policing Bill was inspired by the resurgence of the Black Lives Matter movement after the murder of George Floyd by four Minneapolis police officers on May 25, 2020. The bill seeks to curb racial violence and discrimination on the part of the police by banning certain police practices that are used disproportionately on Black people (including the chokehold and the carotid hold) and making it easier to hold violent officers accountable in court. Although it asks for much less than what the human rights report calls for, the bill is vigorously opposed by police unions and Republican senators. After passing the House in a close vote along party lines, it became bogged down in the Senate over whether or not police officers should continue to enjoy "qualified immunity" from civil prosecution.

The COVID-19 Hate Crimes Act sailed through Congress and was greeted with fanfare, while the international human rights report on police violence was ignored by the U.S. media and government, and the bill to curb police violence stalled in the Senate. It is significant that the

---

[381] The *Report of the International Commission of Inquiry on Systemic Racist Police Violence against People of African Descent in the United States* was sponsored by the National Conference of Black Lawyers, the International Association of Democratic Lawyers, and the National Lawyers Guild. The commission was composed of judges, lawyers, professors, and experts from Barbados, India, South Africa, France, the U.K., Costa Rica, Pakistan, Japan, Antigua and Barbuda, Jamaica, and Nigeria. "Crimes against humanity" were first defined by the Nuremberg principles after World War II. The Rome Statute of the International Criminal Court (Rome Statute) sets forth this formulation: "For the purpose of this Statute, 'crime against humanity' means any of the following acts when committed as part of a widespread or systematic attack directed against any civilian population, with knowledge of the attack: (a) Murder; (e) Imprisonment or other severe deprivation of physical liberty in violation of fundamental rules of international law; (f) Torture; (h) Persecution against any identifiable group or collectivity on political, racial, national, ethnic, cultural, religious, gender as defined in paragraph 3, or other grounds that are universally recognized as impermissible under international law, in connection with any act referred to in this paragraph or any crime within the jurisdiction of the court; (k) Other inhumane acts of a similar character intentionally causing great suffering, or serious injury to body or to mental or physical health." *Report of the International Commission of Inquiry on Systemic Racist Police Violence against People of African Descent in the United States* 2021, 119. The report calls on the U.S. president to sign the Rome Statute and the U.S. Congress to ratify it. It also calls upon the U.S. president to accept the jurisdiction of the International Criminal Court. Among numerous other recommendations, the report asks the U.S. government to "acknowledge that the transatlantic trade in Africans, enslavement, colonization and colonialism were Crimes against Humanity" and to establish a congressional commission to study reparations (2021, 18).

Hate Crimes Act expands the power of law enforcement, while the other two seek to curb it, but there is more to the story than the strength of police unions. It seems gratuitous and almost perverse to address anti-Asian hate in the middle of a Black-led movement that is calling out the more extensive problem of anti-Black hate. Why do something for Asians and not Black people in the middle of a Black Lives Matter resurgence triggered by yet another police murder of a Black person?

Both the human rights report and the bill to curb police violence put pressure on the U.S. government to address the singular oppression of Black people, and the U.S. government responded, as it has before, *by doing something for Asian Americans instead*. The pattern of substitution-cum-weaponization is by now familiar (see the section on Japanese American reparations above). Faced with mounting Black critique, the U.S. state invoked what it was doing for Asian Americans to alibi itself. The appearance of anti-racism is secured on the cheap without disrupting structural anti-Blackness. The unspoken message here is that Asian American lives matter more than Black lives. The U.S. government will act decisively to protect Asian Americans but refuses to protect Black Americans—even in the face of domestic and international pressure to do so, and even though racial violence against Black people is both more frequent and more deadly than racial violence against Asian Americans. Sometimes a law is not just a law but also a lesson in racial positionality.

In any event, the COVID-19 Hate Crimes Act is a hollow victory for Asian Americans. There is no evidence that labelling attacks "hate crimes," streamlining prosecutions, and funding more law enforcement trainings reduces the incidence of anti-Asian violence. These moves give the appearance of taking action—and thus help politicians, police officers, and the corporations involved in the prison industrial complex—but they do nothing for the average Asian American except give them a false sense of security while implicating them even more deeply in the reproduction of structural anti-Blackness. What if the safety and well-being of Asian Americans depends not upon quick-fix carceral solutions but upon moving toward a society where color and class no longer organize the distribution of life chances? What if Asian Americans cannot escape exclusion, harassment, and violence as long as the architecture of racial capitalism still stands? What if Asian Americans cannot be free until Black people are free?

Coda

Asian Americans and Anti-Blackness

As I complete this book, the Select Committee continues its investigation into the January 6, 2020, attack on the U.S. Capitol. For years prior to this event, white supremacism was given a notable boost by Donald Trump, who appointed white nationalists to office, trumpeted their talking points, enacted their fantasies as policy, and hung Andrew Jackson's portrait in the Oval Office for good measure. At the same time, the Confederate flags and nooses borne by the Capitol mob remind us vividly that the phobic hatred of Blackness was also an organizing principle in these events. Indeed, we can read January 6 not only as an expression of resurgent white nationalism, but also, and perhaps more fundamentally, as an expression of negrophobia, a wave of collective hysteria generated by eight years of a Black presidency. Emerging in 2008, with the election of Barack Obama, the wave gathered size and speed until it broke over the Capitol building that January day, leaving numerous bodies in its wake, literally and figuratively. For the whites who always disapproved of Obama because he is Black, his occupation of the Oval Office produced a profound disorientation. Drastic action was required to set things right again.

More than a century ago, whites in Houston—white military commanders, white military police, white soldiers, white police, white streetcar conductors, white residents—could not abide the sight of young Black men in uniform at Camp Logan. Their relentless and vicious aggression against the all-Black 24th Infantry Regiment led to the Houston Rebellion of 1917, after which nineteen Black soldiers were put to death and forty-one imprisoned for life for the crime of defending their lives against white violence. During the Second World War, the lynching of

Black soldiers in uniform made the same point: whites had too much to lose to let Black men put on uniforms and pick up guns. These historical scenes form an essential part of the backdrop for current events. What we are seeing today is not just the Republican Party fomenting racial conflict as an electoral strategy—although this is happening, too—but also, at a deeper level, the structural need to reassert Black abjection over and over again. Following David Marriott, it is still a question of who gets to hold the knife and who gets cut.

In this context, Asian Americans, especially younger cohorts, are seeking to understand their relationship to structural anti-Blackness in the U.S. with a sense of urgency. When I give talks around the country, I am frequently asked to comment on how Asian Americans might be better "allies" to the Black freedom struggle. For Asian Americans, the events of the pandemic era—in particular the racial reckoning brought on by the police murder of George Floyd in Minneapolis in May 2020—have raised a long-standing ethical dilemma with new force. How can they fight for their own protection and empowerment qua Asian Americans and also support Black liberation? What happens when the two objectives seem to conflict in the real world? What, if anything, is owed by Asian Americans to Black people?

In this book I offered some theoretical tools for thinking through these issues. If we understand that Asian Americans are always already seen as not-white but above all not-Black, as the lesser of two evils, then it becomes clear how they are lifted up by structural anti-Blackness in an ongoing way. From here we can see how Asian Americans get weaponized, and how some Asian Americans weaponize themselves, against the Black freedom struggle. A deepening alliance between right-wing whites and right-wing Asian Americans indeed seems to be on the horizon. But there is still an opening for progressive Asian Americans to counter this alliance by finally completing the critique left unfinished by the Asian American movement a half-century ago and theorizing their own not-Blackness in an anti-Black order. Armed with this framework, they can challenge the false sociometry advanced by conservative Asian Americans in the public sphere and persuade ordinary Asian Americans that the fight for Black liberation deserves their dedicated support.

Such a shift among Asian Americans could have a significant political impact right now. Take the issue of affirmative action in American higher education. As discussed in Part Three, the U.S. Supreme Court heard the case *Students for Fair Admissions* v. *Harvard College* (consolidated with its companion suit, *Students for Fair Admissions* v. *University of North Carolina*) in the fall of 2022, with a ruling expected by June 2023. The court is moving forward despite the Biden administration's official opinion that the court should not take up these cases, and despite the fact that the U.S. Court of Appeals for the Fourth Circuit has not yet ruled on the *University of North Carolina* case. Conservative forces, who have been attacking race-conscious admissions since its inception a half-century ago, hope for a 6–2 vote in their favor.[1] If this happens, Asian Americans will have played a critical role—both as props and as active agents—in the dismantling of programs that benefit all students, especially students of color, and especially Black, Latinx, and Indigenous students. If it is too late for progressive Asian American activists and thinkers to influence the court's ruling on this case, they may still be able to influence how the ruling is interpreted, what precedent it is taken to set, and what it ultimately comes to mean in a social and political sense. By countermanding the court's inevitable disavowal of structural anti-Blackness, they can go on record challenging the court's reasoning and make it clear that many Asian Americans disagree with both how the group was weaponized on this issue and the substantive outcome of dismantling race-conscious admissions at Harvard.

Asian Americans can also make a robust show of support for Black reparations. Although efforts to create a national task force on Black reparations have failed thus far, California recently became the first state to appoint a state-level task force to study reparations for slavery and anti-Black discrimination. The task force released an interim report in June 2022. Once it releases a final set of findings and recommendations and the state legislature begins to debate these, the question of comparative desert among not-white groups will almost certainly arise, as it did during deliberations over the Civil Liberties Act in 1988. Conservative legislators will ask: Why should Black people be given reparations for discrimination when other not-white groups, including Asian Americans, are not being offered the same? This query will resonate with particular force in California, which has been the hotbed for anti-Asian agitation in the U.S. for nearly two centuries. While conservative Asian Americans will likely use this question to try to derail Black reparations, progressive Asian Americans can make a powerful, unforgettable intervention by testifying that Asian Americans were always already seen as the lesser

---

[1] Justice Ketanji Brown has recused herself from the case because of her prior association with Harvard University.

of two evils and that prioritizing Black reparations therefore makes good historical sense, even in California. Asian Americans themselves must make this argument for it to be persuasive.

A commitment to challenging structural anti-Blackness would also change how many Asian Americans approach the issue of anti-Asian attacks, which have increased dramatically during the pandemic. Currently many advocates focus on isolating and naming the problem as something that is happening to Asian Americans specifically, even though "hate crimes" have also increased against Black people, who remain the principal targets of such violence. As discussed in Part Three, the COVID-19 Hate Crimes Act of 2021 is a product of this approach. But Asian Americans should not be satisfied with a symbolic sop thrown their way by elected officials, one that not incidentally bolsters the carceral state and reinforces the devaluation of Black lives. Instead, they can not only refuse outright to be weaponized against the Black struggle but also join Black thinkers and activists in condemning structural anti-Blackness, which creates the racial differentiations that fuel "hate crimes" in the first place. It may seem counterintuitive, but it is only by situating anti-Asian attacks in the broader context of the phobic hatred of Blackness that Asian Americans will move toward safety. For it is only by supporting the Black freedom struggle's efforts to dismantle structural anti-Blackness and racial capitalism and build a new world that we can address racially targeted violence at its roots.

Finally, Asian Americans must take responsibility for generating a misbegotten critique of the so-called model minority myth and correct it in a definitive way. Asian Americanists have made this critique the centerpiece of their intellectual agenda for a half-century (and I include my earlier work here, too), and the result has been a highly consequential mystification of white-Afro-Asian dynamics. As discussed in the book, when whites valorize Asian Americans over Black people, Asian Americanists have said *we are minorities too* and accused whites of constructing a "myth" that exaggerates Asian Americans' well-being and drives a wedge between them and Black people. In this way, Asian Americanists have reinforced the logic of minority equivalencing that underlies white practices of relative valorization and helped whites to obfuscate the central issue at hand: the structural positioning of Asian Americans as not-Black, which allows Asian Americans a kind of social and economic mobility largely denied to Black people. Once they acknowledge structural anti-Blackness, though, Asian Americans are uniquely positioned to advance a different critique, one that cuts through the mystification rather than reinforcing it: *The valorization of Asian Americans as a model minority is not just a myth or rhetorical construction; it reflects a deeply embedded structural favoritism that is the real explanation for why Asian Americans fare better than Black people in an anti-Black society.*

Thus many possibilities open up if Asian Americans choose to develop a politics antagonistic to anti-Blackness and racial capitalism instead of weaponizing themselves and allowing themselves to be weaponized in defense of these structural arrangements. This would involve risking their current social and economic status in the short term for the sake of building a just world for all in the long term. How all of this unfolds would of course depend upon the vagaries and contingencies of political struggle, all conditioned now by the time horizon of ecological catastrophe. Asian Americans cannot take down structural anti-Blackness and racial capitalism on their own, but precisely because they participate in their fortification, they can contribute to their demolition. In the paradigmatic scene where the white officer commands the Black person to assume the position, what would happen if Asian Americans supported the latter by all means necessary, buoyed by the conviction that the Black freedom struggle represents the most promising path to a new and better world? Whether or not Asian Americans choose to do this, and with how much conviction, will be the defining issue in Asian American politics in the twenty-first century.

References

COURT CASES

Adarand Constructors, Inc. v. *Peña* 515 U.S. 200 (1995).
Banks v. *Housing Authority of City and County of San Francisco* 120 Cal.App.2d 1 (1953).
Barbier v. *Connolly* 113 U.S. 27 (1885).
Brian Ho v. *San Francisco Unified School District* (1994).
Brown v. *Board of Education of Topeka* 347 U.S. 483 (1954).
Buchanan v. *Warley* 245 U.S. 60 (1917).
Chae Chan Ping v. *United States* 130 U.S. 581 (1889).
Cherokee Nation v. *Georgia* 30 U.S. 1 (1831).
Civil Rights Cases 109 U.S. 3 (1883).
Corrigan v. *Buckley* 271 U.S. 323 (1926).
Davis v. *City of New York* 902 F. Supp. 2d 405 (S.D.N.Y. 2012).
Dred Scott v. *Sanford* 60 U.S. 393 (1857).
Elk v. *Wilkins* 112 U.S. 94 (1884).
Fisher v. *University of Texas at Austin* 645 F. Supp. 2d 587 (2009).
Fisher v. *University of Texas at Austin* (I) 57 U.S. 297 (2013).
Fisher v. *University of Texas at Austin* (II) 579 U.S. 365 (2016).
Gong Lum v. *Rice* 275 U.S. 78 (1927).
Gratz v. *Bollinger* 539 U.S. 244 (2003).
Grutter v. *Bollinger* 539 U.S. 306 (2003).
Guey Heung Lee v. *Johnson* 404 U.S. 1215 (1971).
In re Tiburcio Parrott 1 F. 481 (1880).
In re Quong Woo 13 F. 229 (1882).
Jacobs v. *Barr* 959 F. 2d 313 (1992).
Johnson v. *San Francisco Unified School District* 339 F. Supp. 1315 (N.D. Cal. 1971).
Obadele v. *United States* 52 Fed. Cl. 432 (2002).
People v. *George Hall* 4 Cal. 399 (1854).
Plessy v. *Ferguson* 163 U.S. 537 (1896).

Prigg v. *Pennsylvania* 41 U.S. 539 (1842).
Regan v. *King* 49 F. Supp. 222 (N.D. Cal. 1942).
Regents of the University of California v. *Bakke* 438 U.S. 265 (1978).
Rice v. *Lum* 139 Miss. 760 (1925).
Scott v. *Emerson* 15 Mo. 576 (1852).
Shelley v. *Kraemer* 334 U.S. 1 (1948).
Somerset v. *Stewart* 98 Eng. Rep. 499 (1772).
Soon Hing v. *Crowley* 113 U.S. 703 (1885).
Students for Fair Admissions v. *Harvard College* 397 F. Supp. 3d 126 (D. Mass. 2019).
Students for Fair Admissions v. Harvard Coll., 980 F.3d 157 (1st Cir. 2020)
Takao Ozawa v. *United States* 260 U.S. 178 (1922).
Tape v. *Hurley* 66 Cal. 473 (1885).
The Slaughter-House Cases 83 U.S. 36 (1873).
United States v. *Wong Kim Ark* 169 U.S. 649 (1898).
Yick Wo v. *Hopkins* 118 U.S. 356 (1886).

PUBLIC HEARINGS

Hearings before the House Select Committee Investigating National Defense Migration, 77th Congress, 1st Session, U.S. House of Representatives, February 21, 23, 1942 [Tolan Hearings].
Hearings Regarding Communist Infiltration of Minority Groups—Part I, Committee on Un-American Activities, 81st Congress, 1st Session, U.S. House of Representatives, July 13, 14, 18, 1949.
Public Hearing, Commission on Wartime Relocation and Internment of Civilians, Los Angeles, California, August 4, 1981, National Archives, Record Group 220.

CONGRESSIONAL DEBATES

Congressional Globe, 39th Congress, 1st Session, U.S. House of Representatives, March 1, 1866.
Congressional Globe, 41st Congress, 2d Session, U.S. Senate, 1870.
Congressional Record, 64th Congress, 2d Session, U.S. Senate, December 11–13, 1916.
Congressional Record, 67th Congress, 2d session, U.S. House of Representatives, January 4, 1922.
Congressional Record, 68th Congress, 1st Session, U.S. Senate, March 13, 1924.
Congressional Record, 68th Congress, 1st Session, U.S. House of Representatives, April 1–14, 1924.
Congressional Record, 68th Congress, 1st Session, U.S. Senate, April 11, 1924.
Congressional Record, 68th Congress, 1st Session, U.S. Senate, April 14, 1924.
Congressional Record, 68th Congress, 1st Session, U.S. House of Representatives, May 9, 1924.
Congressional Record, 100th Congress, 1st Session, U.S. Senate, vol. 133, part 7, April 9–24, 1987.

STATE GOVERNMENTAL PROCEEDINGS

Official Journal of the Proceedings of the House of Representatives of the State of Louisiana, Second Regular Session of the Third General Assembly, May 12, 1890.

GOVERNMENT REPORTS

Chinese Immigration: Its Social, Moral, and Political Effect. Report to the California State Senate of its Special Committee on Chinese Immigration. Sacramento: State Office, F. P. Thompson, Supt. State Printing, 1878, v-302.

Congressional Record, 36th Congress, 1st Session, U.S. House of Representatives, April 16, 1860, Report No. 443 [on the coolie trade].

House Select Committee Investigating National Defense Migration, 77th Congress, 2d Session, U.S. House of Representatives, House Report No. 1911, *Preliminary Report and Recommendations on Problems of Evacuation of Citizens and Aliens from Military Areas*, March 19, 1942. Washington, D.C.: United States Government Printing Office [Tolan Committee Report].

Metcalf, Victor. *Japanese in the City of San Francisco, Cal.: Message from the President of the United States, Transmitting the Final Report of Secretary Metcalf on the Situation Affecting the Japanese in the City of San Francisco, Cal*. San Francisco: R. and E. Research Associates, 1971.

Report of the Commission Sent by China to Ascertain the Condition of Chinese Coolies in Cuba. Taipei: Ch'eng Wen Publishing, 1970 [1876].

Report of the Joint Special Committee to Investigate Chinese Immigration. Washington, D.C.: Government Printing Office, 1877. Senate Report No. 689, produced for the 44th Congress, 2d Session.

The Chinese Question. Report of the Special Committee on Assembly Bill No. 13. Sacramento, Calif.: D. W. Gelwick's, 1870.

MISCELLANEOUS DOCUMENTS, REPORTS, AND PUBLICATIONS

An Analysis of the Chinese Question, Consisting of a Special Message of the Governor and, in Reply Thereto, Two Letters of the Chinamen and a Memorial of the Citizens of San Francisco. San Francisco: Office of the San Francisco Herald, 1852, 1–14.

APM Research Lab. *The Color of Coronavirus: COVID-19 Deaths by Race and Ethnicity in the U.S.* August 5, 2020, see at: www.apmresearchlab.org/covid/deaths-by-race.

Asians4BlackLives. "Structural Racism Is the Pandemic, Interdependence and Solidarity Is the Cure." July 9, 2020, see at: https://a4bl.tumblr.com/post/62319 3309907730432/asians-4-black-lives-structural-racism-is-the.

Asians4BlackLives. "Uplift Black Resistance, Help Build Black Power." June 1, 2020, see at: https://a4bl.tumblr.com/post/619777369649102848/asians-4-black-lives-uplift-black-resistance.

"Asians 4 Black Lives." *Asian American Activism: The Continuing Struggle*, n.d., see at: https://blogs.brown.edu/ethn-1890v-s01-fall-2016/asians-for-black-lives.

Avins, Alfred, ed. *The Reconstruction Amendments' Debates: The Legislative History and Contemporary Debates in Congress on the 13th, 14th, and 15th Amendments*, vol. 1. Virginia Commission on Constitutional Government, 1967.

"Blackface in the Camps." *No No Boy Project*. n.d., see at: https://nonoboymusic .tumblr.com/post/162451820733/blackface-in-the-camps.

Comfort, Bob. "Memorandum for Mr. Justice Powell." August 29, 1977. 78–11 *Regents of University of California* v. *Bakke*, folder 2, see at: https://law2 .wlu.edu/deptimages/powell%20archives/Bakke76-811folder2.pdf.

Facing Our Past, Changing Our Future, Part I: *A Century of Segregation in San Francisco Unified School District (1851–1971)*, www.sfusd.edu. September 16, 2020, see at: www.sfusd.edu/facing-our-past-changing-our-future-part-i-century-segregation-san-francisco-unified-school-district.

Facing Our Past, Changing Our Future, Part II: *Five Decades of Desegregation in SFUSD (1971–today)*. www.sfusd.edu. September 16, 2020, see at: www .sfusd.edu/facing-our-past-changing-our-future-part-ii-five-decades-deseg regation-sfusd-1971-today.

FBI Memos on Informant Richard Aoki, see at: https://s3.documentcloud.org/ documents/423064/fbi-files-richard-aoki.pdf.

Hayes, Everis A., Rep. "Treaty-Making Power of the Government and the Japanese Question." Speech delivered in the U.S. House of Representatives, January 23, 1907.

"Letter to Clara Breed from Fusa Tsumagari." Arcadia, California, August 20, 1942. Japanese American National Museum Collection (Gift of Elizabeth Y. Yamada, 93.75.31JB), see at: www.janm.org/collections/item/93.75.31JB.

Letters for Black Lives: An Open Letter Project on Anti-Blackness, see at: www .lettersforblacklives.com.

Masaoka, Mike. "The Japanese American Creed." May 9, 1941, see at: https:// calisphere.org/item/780473cb012ec2e77ae82e140da139a2.

McClatchy, V. S., "Japanese Immigration and Colonization: Skeleton Brief." Washington, D.C.: Government Printing Office, 1921.

National Archives at College Park, Central Photographic File of the War Relocation Authority, 1942–1944, Record Group 210.

National Coalition of Blacks for Reparations in America. "The Reparations Campaign." In *Redress for Historical Injustices in the United States: On Reparations for Slavery, Jim Crow, and Their Legacies*, eds. Michael Martin and Marilyn Yaquinto, 625–628. Durham, N.C.: Duke University Press, 2007.

National Conference of Black Lawyers, International Association of Democratic Lawyers, and the National Lawyers Guild. *Report of the International Commission of Inquiry on Systemic Racist Police Violence against People of African Descent in the United States*, March 2021, 1–188.

"New Neighbors among Us." Wartime Relocation Authority, Department of the Interior, Washington, D.C., 1945, see at: https://rucore.libraries.rutgers.edu/ rutgers-lib/4114.

"Nisei in the War against Japan." Wartime Relocation Authority, Department of the Interior, Washington, D.C., April 1945, see at: https://calisphere.org/item/ac63eb5e532e1a7738824c1a24eb175b.

"Philadelphia, 1945." Philadelphia Nisei Council, 1945, see at: https://ddr.densho.org/media/ddr-densho-35/ddr-densho-35-412-mezzanine-0a3c7588ca.pdf.

Proceedings of the United States Senate, on the Fugitive Slave Bill,—the Abolition of the Slave-Trade in the District of Columbia,—and the Imprisonment of Free Colored Seamen in the Southern Ports (1850). In *From Slavery to Freedom: The African-American Pamphlet Collection*, Library of Congress, United States, 2000, 1–60, see at: www.loc.gov/item/lcwaN0019560.

Remarks of the Chinese Merchants of San Francisco upon Governor Bigler's Message, and Some Common Objections; with Some Explanations of the Character of the Chinese Companies, and the Laboring Class in California. San Francisco: The Office of the "Oriental," by Whitton, Towne & Co., 1855.

Republic of New Afrika. "Declaration of Independence." In *Redress for Historical Injustices in the United States: On Reparations for Slavery, Jim Crow, and Their Legacies*, eds. Michael Martin and Marilyn Yaquinto, 588–591. Durham, N.C.: Duke University Press, 2007.

Speer, Reverend William. *An Answer to the Common Objections to Chinese Testimony; and an Earnest Appeal to the Legislature of California for Their Protection by Our Law.* San Francisco: Chinese Mission House, 1857.

Stop AAPI Hate. *2020–2021 National Report.* March 16, 2021, see at: https://stopaapihate.org/2020-2021-national-report.

"The No-No Boy Project and the JA Incarceration Mobile Workshop." April 12, 2018. John Nicholas Brown Center for Public Humanities and Cultural Heritage, see at: www.brown.edu/academics/public-humanities/events/no-no-boy-project-and-ja-incarceration-mobile-workshop.

The Relocation Program. United States Department of the Interior, War Relocation Authority. Washington, D.C.: U.S. Government Printing Office, n.d.

Transcript of the American Academy Conference on the Negro American: May 14–15, 1965, Daedalus 95, no. 1, The Negro American 2 (Winter 1966): 287–441.

U.S. Information Service. "The Negro in American Life." 1952, see at: www.pbfa.org/books/the-negro-in-american-life.

"When You Leave the Relocation Center." War Relocation Authority, Department of the Interior, n.d., see at: https://encyclopedia.densho.org/media/encyc-psms/en-ddr-densho-274-15-1.pdf.

WRA, A Story of Human Conservation. United States Department of the Interior, War Relocation Authority. Washington, D.C.: U.S. Government Printing Office, 1946.

Wright, Henry Clark. "No Rights, No Duties, or Slaveholders, as Such, Have No Rights; Slaves, as Such, Owe No Duties." January 1, 1860. Cornell University Library Digital Collection, see at: www.amazon.com/rights-duties-Slaveholders-such-slaves/dp/1429717866.

GENERAL REFERENCES

Aarim-Heriot, Najia. *Chinese Immigrants, African Americans, and Racial Anxiety in the United States, 1848–82.* Champaign, Ill.: University of Illinois Press, 2003.

Abelmann, Nancy, and John Lie. *Blue Dreams: Korean Americans and the Los Angeles Riots.* Cambridge, Mass.: Harvard University Press, 1995.

Aiyetoro, Adjoa. "The National Coalition of Blacks for Reparations in America (N'COBRA): Its Creation and Contribution to the Reparations Movement." In *Should America Pay? Slavery and the Raging Debate on Reparations*, ed. Raymond Winbush, 209–225. New York: HarperCollins, 2003.

Aiyetoro, Adjoa, and Adrienne Davis. "Historic and Modern Social Movements for Reparations: The National Coalition of Blacks for Reparations in America (N'COBRA) and Its Antecedents." *Texas Wesleyan Law Review* 16 (2010): 687–766.

Allerfeldt, Kristofer. "Wilsonian Pragmatism? Woodrow Wilson, Japanese Immigration, and the Paris Peace Conference." *Diplomacy and Statecraft* 15:3 (2004): 545–572.

Ancheta, Angelo. *Race, Rights, and the Asian American Experience.* New Brunswick, N.J.: Rutgers University Press, 2006.

Anderson, Carol. *Eyes Off the Prize: The United Nations and the African American Struggle for Human Rights, 1944–1955.* Cambridge: Cambridge University Press, 2003.

Apel, Dora. *Imagery of Lynching: Black Men, White Women, and the Mob.* New Brunswick, N.J.: Rutgers University Press, 2004.

Aranke, Sampada. "Fred Hampton's Murder and the Coming Revolution." *Trans-Scripts* 3 (2013): 116–139.

Asaka, Ikuko. "'Colored Men of the East': African Americans and the Instability of Race in US–Japan Relations." *American Quarterly* 66:4 (December 2014): 971–997.

Au, Wayne. "Meritocracy 2.0: High-Stakes, Standardized Testing as a Racial Project of Neoliberal Multiculturalism." *Educational Policy* 30:1 (2016): 39–62.

Azuma, Eiichiro. *Between Two Empires: Race, History, and Transnationalism in Japanese America.* New York: Oxford University Press, 2005.

Bailey, Thomas. "California, Japan, and the Alien Land Legislation of 1913." *Pacific Historical Review* 1:1 (March 1932): 36–59.

Bascara, Victor. "'In the Future to Any Third Power': 'Most Favored Nations,' Personhood, and an Emergent World Order in *Yick Wo v. Hopkins.*" *Asian American Law Journal* 21 (2014): 177–208.

Batzell, Rudi. "Free Labour, Capitalism and the Anti-Slavery Origins of Chinese Exclusion in California in the 1870s." *Past and Present* 225 (November 2014): 143–186.

Bearden, Russell. "The Internment of Japanese Americans in Arkansas, 1942–1945." Master's thesis, University of Arkansas, 1986.

Berard, Adrienne. *Water Tossing Boulders: How a Family of Chinese Immigrants Led the First Fight to Desegregate Schools in the Jim Crow South.* Boston, Mass.: Beacon Press, 2016.

Berlin, Ira. *Slaves without Masters: The Free Negro in the Antebellum South*. New York: The New Press, 1974.

Bernstein, David. "The Supreme Court and 'Civil Rights,' 1886–1908." *Yale Law Journal* 100:3 (December 1990): 725–744.

"Revisiting *Yick Wo* v. *Hopkins*." *University of Illinois Law Review* 2008:5 (2008): 1393–1403.

Biegel, Stuart. "Court-Mandated Education Reform: The San Francisco Experience and the Shaping of Educational Policy after Seattle-Louisville and *Ho* v. *SFUSD*." *Stanford Journal of Civil Rights & Civil Liberties* 4 (2008): 159–215.

Biondi, Martha. "The Rise of the Reparations Movement." *Radical History Review* 87 (Fall 2003): 5–18.

Bittker, Boris, and Roy Brooks. "The Constitutionality of Black Reparations." In *Redress for Historical Injustices in the United States: On Reparations for Slavery, Jim Crow, and Their Legacies*, eds. Michael Martin and Marilyn Yaquinto, 143–159. Durham, N.C.: Duke University Press, 2007.

Blackmon, Douglas. *Slavery by Another Name: The Re-Enslavement of Black Americans from the Civil War to World War II*. New York: Anchor Books, 2008.

Bloom, Joshua, and Waldo Martin, Jr. *Black against Empire: The History and Politics of the Black Panther Party*. Berkeley: University of California Press, 2013.

Borstelmann, Thomas. *The Cold War and the Color Line: American Race Relations in the Global Arena*. Cambridge, Mass.: Harvard University Press, 2001.

Bow, Leslie. *Partly Colored: Asian Americans and Racial Anomaly in the Segregated South*. New York: New York University Press, 2010.

Brilliant, Mark. *The Color of America Has Changed: How Racial Diversity Shaped Civil Rights Reform in California, 1941–1978*. New York: Oxford University Press, 2010.

Briones, Matthew. *Jim and Jap Crow: A Cultural History of 1940s Interracial America*. Princeton: Princeton University Press, 2012.

Brooks, Charlotte. "In the Twilight Zone between Black and White: Japanese American Resettlement and Community in Chicago, 1942–1945." *Journal of American History* 86:4 (March 2000): 1655–1687.

Alien Neighbors, Foreign Friends: Asian Americans, Housing, and the Transformation of Urban California. Chicago: University of Chicago Press, 2009.

Broussard, Albert. *Black San Francisco: The Struggle for Racial Equality in the West, 1900–1954*. Lawrence: University Press of Kansas, 1993.

Buell, Raymond. "The Development of the Anti-Japanese Agitation in the United States." *Political Science Quarterly* 37:4 (December 1922): 605–638.

Burden-Stelly, Charisse. "Constructing Deportable Subjectivity: Antiforeignness, Antiradicalism, and Antiblackness during the McCarthyist Structure of Feeling." *Souls: A Critical Journal of Black Politics, Culture, and Society* 19:3 (2017): 342–358.

"Modern U.S. Racial Capitalism." *Monthly Review*, July 1, 2020.

Burin, Eric. *Slavery and the Peculiar Solution: A History of the American Colonization Society*. Gainesville, Fla.: University Press of Florida, 2005.

Burke, W. M. *The Japanese School Question*. San Francisco: Rincon, 1907, 1–15.

Butler, Judith. "Endangered/Endangering: Schematic Racism and White Paranoia." In *Reading Rodney King, Reading Urban Uprising*, ed. Robert Gooding-Williams, 15–22. New York: Routledge, 1993.

Caldwell, Dan. "The Negroization of the Chinese Stereotype in California." *Southern California Quarterly* 53:2 (1971): 123–131.

Camp, Jordan. *Incarcerating the Crisis: Freedom Struggles and the Rise of the Neoliberal State*. Berkeley: University of California Press, 2016.

Camp, Jordan, and Christina Heatherton, eds. *Policing the Planet: Why the Policing Crisis Led to Black Lives Matter*. London: Verso, 2016.

Capeci, Dominic, Jr. *The Lynching of Cleo Wright*. Lexington: University Press of Kentucky, 1998.

Carbado, Devon W. "Yellow by Law." *California Law Review* 97:3 (June 2009): 633–692.

Carbado, Devon W., Kate M. Turetsky, and Valerie Purdie-Vaughns. "Privileged or Mismatched: The Lose-Lose Position of African Americans in the Affirmative Action Debate." *UCLA Law Review Discourse* 64 (2016): 174–229.

Carlis, Adam. "The Illegality of Vertical Patrols." *Columbia Law Review* 109:8 (December 2009): 2002–2043.

Castillo, Roberto. "What 'blackface' Tells Us about China's Patronizing Attitude towards Africa." *The Conversation*, March 6, 2018.

Chae, Augustina. "To Be Almost Like White: The Case of Soon Ja Du." Master's thesis, University of Nebraska, December 2002, see at: https://digitalcommons.unomaha.edu/studentwork/451.

Chang, Thelma. *"I Can Never Forget": Men of the 100th/442nd*. Honolulu: Sigi Productions, 1991.

Chen, Jian Neo. "#Blacklivesmatter and the State of Asian/America." *Journal of Asian American Studies* 20:2 (June 2017): 265–271.

Cheng, Cindy. *Citizens of Asian America: Democracy and Race during the Cold War*. New York: New York University Press, 2013.

Cheng, Yinghong. "From Campus Racism to Cyber Racism: Discourse of Race and Chinese Nationalism." *China Quarterly* 207 (September 2011): 561–579.

Chin, Gabriel. "The *Plessy* Myth: Justice Harlan and the Chinese Cases." *Iowa Law Review* 82 (1996–1997): 151–182.

"Unexplainable on Grounds of Race: Doubts about Yick Wo." *University of Illinois Law Review* 2008:5 (2008): 1359–1391.

Cho, Sumi. "Korean Americans vs. African Americans: Conflict and Construction." In *Reading Rodney King, Reading Urban Uprising*, ed. Robert Gooding-Williams, 196–211. New York: Routledge, 1993.

Choy, Christine, Worth Long, and Allen Siegel, dirs. *Mississippi Triangle*. New York: Third World Newsreel, 1983.

Chuman, Frank. *The Bamboo People: The Law and Japanese-Americans*. Del Mar, Calif.: Publisher's Inc., 1976.

Churchill, Ward, Kathleen Cleaver, and Natsu Taylor Saito. "Distorting the Legacy of Richard Aoki." *San Francisco Bay View*, September 9, 2012.

Cohen, Lucy. *Chinese in the Post-Civil War South: A People without History.* Baton Rouge: Louisiana State University Press, 1984.

Cohn, David. *Where I Was Born and Raised.* Notre Dame, Ind.: University of Notre Dame Press, 1967.

Collins, Donald. *Native American Aliens: Disloyalty and the Renunciation of Citizenship by Japanese Americans during World War II.* Westport, Conn.: Greenwood Press, 1985.

Cook, Greg. "How Dana Chandler Brought Black Power to Boston Art, Murals and Museums." *Wonderland,* January 21, 2019.

Corlett, J. Angelo. "Reparations to African Americans?" In *Redress for Historical Injustices in the United States: On Reparations for Slavery, Jim Crow, and Their Legacies,* eds. Michael Martin and Marilyn Yaquinto, 170–198. Durham, N.C.: Duke University Press, 2007.

Daniels, Roger. "Japanese Immigrants on a Western Frontier: The Issei in California, 1890–1940." In *Historical and Sociological Studies of Japanese Immigration and Assimilation,* eds. Hilary Conroy and T. Scott Miyakawa, 76–91. Santa Barbara: American Bibliographical Center-Clio Press, 1972.

Davies, Elizabeth Jordie. "Everybody Wants to Be Black but Nobody Wants to Be Black." *Politics, Groups, and Identities,* forthcoming.

Davis, Angela. "From the Prison of Slavery to the Slavery of Prison: Frederick Douglass and the Convict Lease System." In *The Angela Davis Reader,* ed. Joy James, 74–95. Oxford: Blackwell, 1998.

Davis, Thomas. "More than Segregation, Racial Identity: The Neglected Question in *Plessy* v. *Ferguson.*" *Washington & Lee Race & Ethnic Ancestry Law Journal* 10:1 (2004): 1–41.

Dawson, Michael. "Hidden in Plain Sight: A Note on Legitimation Crises and the Racial Order." *Critical Historical Studies* 3:1 (Spring 2016): 143–161.

De Luna, Elizabeth. "'They Use Our Culture': The Black Creatives and Fans Holding K-pop Accountable." *The Guardian,* July 20, 2020.

Del Sol, Liz. "Finding Our Common Interests: Personal Reflections about the Asian Movement." In *Asian Americans: the Movement and the Moment,* eds. Steve Louie and Glenn Omatsu, 139–145. Los Angeles: UCLA Asian American Studies Center, 2014.

Der, Cynthia. "A Chinese American Seat at the Table: Examining Race in the San Francisco Unified School District." *University of San Francisco Law Review* 42 (Spring 2008): 1077–1113.

Dies, Martin. *The Trojan Horse in America.* New York: Dodd, Mead & Company, 1940.

Dikötter, Frank. "Racial Identities in China: Context and Meaning." *China Quarterly* 138 (June 1994): 404–412.

Dong, Harvey. "Richard Aoki's Legacy and Dilemma: Who Do You Serve?" *Amerasia Journal* 39:2 (2013): 102–115.

Dower, John. *War without Mercy: Race and Power in the Pacific War.* New York: Pantheon, 1986.

Dray, Philip. *At the Hands of Persons Unknown: The Lynching of Black America.* New York: Random House, 2002.

Du Bois, W. E. B., ed. *An Appeal to the World: A Statement on the Denial of Human Rights to Minorities in the Case of Citizens of Negro Descent in the United States of America and an Appeal to the United Nations for Redress.* Baltimore: NAACP, 1947.

Black Reconstruction in America, 1860–1880. New York: The Free Press, 1998 [1935].

Dubow, Saul. "Smuts, the United Nations and the Rhetoric of Race and Rights." *Journal of Contemporary History* 43:1 (2008): 43–72.

Duus, Masayo. *Unlikely Liberators: The Men of the 100th and 442nd.* Honolulu: University of Hawai'i Press, 1987.

Elba, Mariam. "K-pop Fans Are Getting Involved in U.S. Politics. Are They Activists?" *The Intercept*, July 1, 2020.

Eng, Aimee. "The Japanese Question: San Francisco Education in 1906." Stanford Graduate School of Education Case Library, Case 2006–3, December 14, 2006, 1–11.

Esthus, Raymond. *Theodore Roosevelt and Japan.* Seattle: University of Washington Press, 1966.

Fanon, Frantz. "The Fact of Blackness" (1952). In *Theories of Race and Racism: A Reader*, eds. Les Back and John Solomos, 257–265. London: Routledge, 2000.

Black Skin, White Masks, trans. Charles Lam Markmann. London: Pluto Press, 2008 [1952].

Fehrenbacher, Don. *The Dred Scott Case: Its Significance in American Law and Politics.* Oxford: Oxford University Press, 1978.

Feng, Yuanyuan, and Mark Tseng-Putterman. "'Scattered Like Sand' WeChat Warriors in the Trial of Peter Liang." *Amerasia Journal* 45:2 (2019): 238–252.

Ferguson, Edwin. "The California Alien Land Law and the Fourteenth Amendment." *California Law Review* 35:1 (March 1947): 61–90.

Finkle, Lee. "The Conservative Aims of Militant Rhetoric: Black Protest During World War II." *Journal of American History* 60:3 (December 1973): 692–713.

Finkelman, Paul. "Slavery in the United States: Persons or Property?" In *The Legal Understanding of Slavery*, ed. Jean Allain, 105–134. Oxford: Oxford University Press 2012.

Foner, Eric. *Reconstruction: America's Unfinished Revolution, 1863–1877.* New York: Harper & Row, 1988.

Foner, Philip, ed. *The Black Panthers Speak.* New York: Da Capo Press, 1995.

Foucault, Michel. *"Society Must Be Defended": Lectures at the Collège de France, 1975–1976*, eds. Mauro Bertani and Alessandro Fontana, trans. David Macey. New York: Picador, 1997.

Fraga, Luis, Nick Rodriguez, and Bari Erlichson. "Desegregation and School Board Politics: The Limits of Court-Imposed Policy Change." In *Besieged: School Boards and the Future of Education Politics*, ed. William Howell, 102–128. Washington, D.C.: Brookings Institution, 2005.

Franklin, Delano, and Samuel Zwickel. "Legacy Admit Rate Five Times that of Non-Legacies, Court Docs Show." *The Harvard Crimson*, June 20, 2018.

Franklin, John Hope. "The Enforcement of the Civil Rights Act of 1875." *Prologue* 6, no. 4 (Winter 1974): 225–235.

Fredrickson, George. *The Black Image in the White Mind: The Debate on Afro-American Character and Destiny, 1817–1914*. New York: Harper & Row, 1971.

Fu, May, Simmy Makhijani, Anh-Thu Pham, Meejin Richart, Joanne Tien, and Diane Wong. "#Asians4BlackLives: Notes from the Ground." *Amerasia Journal* 45:2 (2019): 253–270.

Fujino, Diane. *Samurai among Panthers: Richard Aoki on Race, Resistance, and a Paradoxical Life*. Minneapolis: University of Minnesota Press, 2012.

"The Indivisibility of Freedom: The *Nisei* Progressives, Deep Solidarities, and Cold War Alternatives." *Journal of Asian American Studies* 21:2 (June 2018): 171–208.

Fujitani, Takashi. *Race for Empire: Koreans as Japanese and Japanese as Americans During World War II*. Berkeley: University of California Press, 2011.

Gallichio, Marc. *The African American Encounter with Japan and China: Black Internationalism in Asia, 1895–1945*. Chapel Hill: University of North Carolina Press, 2000.

Gans, Herbert. "The Possibility of a New Racial Hierarchy in the Twenty-First Century United States." In *The Cultural Territories of Race*, ed. Michèle Lamont, 371–390. Chicago: University of Chicago Press, 1999.

Garces, Liliana and OiYan Poon. "Asian Americans and Race-Conscious Admissions: Understanding the Conservative Opposition's Strategy of Misinformation, Intimidation & Racial Division." The Civil Rights Project, UCLA, see at https://escholarship.org/uc/item/3560g5qq

Garza, Alicia. "A Herstory of the #BlackLivesMatter Movement." *The Feminist Wire*, October 7, 2014.

Gilmore, Ruth Wilson. *Golden Gulag: Prisons, Surplus, Crisis, and Opposition in Globalizing California*. Berkeley: University of California Press, 2007.

Goldsby, Jacqueline. *A Spectacular Secret: Lynching in American Life and Literature*. Chicago: University of Chicago Press, 2006.

Golub, Mark. "*Plessy* as 'Passing': Judicial Responses to Ambiguously Raced Bodies in *Plessy* v. *Ferguson*." *Law & Society Review* 39:3 (September 2005): 563–600.

Gordon, James. "Was the First Justice Harlan Anti-Chinese?" *Western New England Law Review* 36, no. 3 (2014): 287–370.

Gordon, Lewis. *Her Majesty's Other Children: Sketches of Racism from a Neocolonial Age*. Lanham, Md.: Rowman & Littlefield, 1997.

Gotanda, Neil. "A Critique of 'Our Constitution is Color-Blind.'" *Stanford Law Review* 44 (1991): 1–68.

"Multiculturalism and Racial Stratification." In *Mapping Multiculturalism*, eds. Avery Gordon and Christopher Newfield, 238–252. Minneapolis: University of Minnesota Press, 1996.

Gould, Stephen Jay. *The Mismeasure of Man*. New York: W. W. Norton, 1996.

Gressman, Eugene. "The Unhappy History of Civil Rights Legislation." *Michigan Law Review* 50:8 (June 1952): 1323–1358.

Griffey, Trevor. "When a Celebrated Activist Turns Out to Be an FBI Informant." *Truthout*, November 5, 2012.

Guillermo, Emil. "The Best Victims." *The Filipino Express*, March 14, 1999, 11.

Guterl, Matthew. "After Slavery: Asian Labor, the American South, and the Age of Emancipation." *Journal of World History* 14:2 (June 2003): 209–241.

Gyory, Andrew. *Closing the Gate: Race, Politics, and the Chinese Exclusion Act.* Chapel Hill: University of North Carolina Press, 1998.

Haak, Ronald. "Co-opting the Oppressors: The Case of the Japanese-Americans." *Trans-Action*, October 1970, 23–31.

Haasch, Palmer. "K-pop Stans Have Been Heralded as Digital Heroes for Fighting Racists Online, but Black Fans Are Still Getting Left Out of the Conversation." *Insider*, June 12, 2020.

Haller, John. *Outcasts from Evolution: Scientific Attitudes of Racial Inferiority, 1859–1900.* Carbondale, Ill.: Southern Illinois University Press, 1972.

Han, Gil-Soo. "K-pop Nationalism: Celebrities and Acting Blackface in the Korean Media." *Continuum* 29:1 (2015): 2–16.

Harris, Cheryl. "Whiteness as Property." *Harvard Law Review* 106:8 (June 1993): 1707–1791.

Harris, Robert. "Racial Equality and the United Nations Charter." In *New Directions in Civil Rights Studies*, eds. Armstead Robinson and Patricia Sullivan, 126–148. Charlottesville: University Press of Virginia 1991.

Hartman, Saidiya. *Scenes of Subjection: Terror, Slavery, and Self-Making in Nineteenth-Century America.* Oxford: Oxford University Press, 1997.

Lose Your Mother: A Journey Along the Atlantic Slave Route. New York: Farrar, Straus & Giroux, 2007.

"The Belly of the World: A Note on Black Women's Labors." *Souls: A Critical Journal of Black Politics, Culture, and Society* 18:1 (2016): 166–173.

Hatamiya, Leslie. *Righting a Wrong: Japanese Americans and the Passage of the Civil Liberties Act of 1988.* Stanford: Stanford University Press, 1993.

Hellwig, David. "Afro-American Reactions to the Japanese and the Anti-Japanese Movement, 1906–1924." *Phylon* 38:1 (1977): 93–104.

"Hilarious Antics of 'Nuthouse Gang' Keep Tuleans Screaming for More." *The Daily Tulean Dispatch*, September 16, 1942, 2.

Herbert, Lenese. "On Precedent and Progeny: A Response to Professor Gabriel J. Chin's Doubts about Yick Wo." *University of Illinois Law Review* 5 (2008): 1415–1426.

Hing, Bill Ong. "Asians without Blacks and Latinos in San Francisco: Missed Lessons of the Common Good." *Amerasia Journal* 27:2 (2001): 19–27.

Hirobe, Izumi. *Japanese Pride, American Prejudice: Modifying the Exclusion Clause of the 1924 Immigration Act.* Stanford: Stanford University Press, 2001.

Ho, Fred. "Fred Ho Refutes the Claim that Richard Aoki Was an FBI Informant." *San Francisco Bay View*, August 21, 2012.

"An Analysis of Seth Rosenfeld's FBI Files on Richard Aoki." *San Francisco Bay View*, September 8, 2012.

Hoffer, William James. *Plessy v. Ferguson: Race and Inequality in Jim Crow America.* Lawrence: University Press of Kansas, 2012.

Holden-Smith, Barbara. "Lynching, Federalism, and the Intersection of Race and Gender in the Progressive Era." *Yale Journal of Law and Feminism* 8 (1996): 31–78.

Hong, Grace Kyungwon. "Comparison and Coalition in the Age of Black Lives Matter." *Journal of Asian American Studies* 20:2 (June 2017): 273–278.

Hong, Lisa. "Debate Running Deep over Integration Consent Decree." *Asian-Week*, March 19, 1993, 28.

Horan, Michael. "Political Economy and Sociological Theory as Influences upon Judicial Policy-Making: The Civil Rights Cases of 1883." *American Journal of Legal History* 16:1 (January 1972): 71–86.

Horne, Gerald. *Black and Red: W. E. B. DuBois and the Afro-American Response to the Cold War, 1944–1963.* Albany: SUNY Press, 1986.

Race War: White Supremacy and the Japanese Attack on the British Empire. New York: New York University Press, 2004.

"How the Asian American Community Relates to the Trayvon Martin Case." *Asian Americans Advancing Justice*, July 2013.

"How Dana Chandler Brought Black Power to Boston Art, Murals and Museums." *Wonderland*, January 21, 2019.

Howard, Elbert (Big Man [pseud.]). "Richard Aoki, an American Revolutionary." *San Francisco Bay View*, August 23, 2012a.

"My Comrade, Richard Aoki." *San Francisco Bay View*, August 24, 2012b.

Howard, John. *Concentration Camps on the Home Front: Japanese Americans in the House of Jim Crow.* Chicago: University of Chicago Press, 2008.

Hsu, Immanuel. *China's Entrance into the Family of Nations: The Diplomatic Phase, 1858–1880.* Cambridge, Mass.: Harvard University Press, 1960.

Hu-Dehart, Evelyn. "Chinese Coolie Labor in Cuba in the Nineteenth Century: Free Labour or Neoslavery?" *Slavery and Abolition* 14:1 (1993): 67–86.

Huang, Kun. "'Anti-Blackness' in Chinese Racial-Nationalism: Sex/Gender, Reproduction, and Metaphors of Pathology." *positions politics*, June 29, 2020.

Hughes, Langston, and Arnold Rampersad. *The Collected Poems of Langston Hughes.* New York: Vintage, 1995.

Ichioka, Yuji. "The Early Japanese Immigrant Quest for Citizenship: The Background of the 1922 Ozawa Case." *Amerasia Journal* 4:2 (1977): 1–22.

The Issei: The World of the First Generation Japanese Immigrants, 1885–1924. New York: The Free Press, 1988.

Ignatiev, Noel. *How the Irish Became White.* London: Routledge, 2009 [1995].

Imazeki, Howard. "To Our Negro Neighbor, This Is Our Voice." *Hokubei Mainichi*, June 29, 1963.

Inui, Kiyo. "The Gentlemen's Agreement. How It Has Functioned." *ANNALS of the American Academy of Political and Social Science* 122:1 (November 1925): 188–198.

Iriye, Akira. *Pacific Estrangement: Japanese and American Expansion, 1897–1911.* Chicago, Ill: Imprint Publications, 1994.

Irons, Peter. *Justice at War: The Story of the Japanese-American Internment Cases.* Berkeley: University of California Press, 1993.

Irving, Michael. "Enormous Extragalactic Void Is Pushing on the Milky Way." *New Atlas*, January 31, 2017.

Jacobson, Matthew Frye. *Whiteness of a Different Color: European Immigrants and the Alchemy of Race.* Cambridge, Mass.: Harvard University Press, 1998.

Janken, Kenneth. "From Colonial Liberation to Cold War Liberalism: Walter White, the NAACP, and Foreign Affairs, 1941–1955." *Ethnic and Racial Studies* 21:6 (1998): 1074–1095.

Jefferson, Thomas. *Notes on the State of Virginia.* New York: Penguin Books, 1998 [1785].

Johnson, Howard. "The Anti-Chinese Riots of 1918 in Jamaica." *Immigrants & Minorities* 2:1 (1983): 50–63.

Johnson, Miranda. "Blackface Minstrelsy and the Theater of Empire, 1838–1860." Senior thesis, Bryn Mawr College, 2019. See at: http://scholarship.tricolib.brynmawr.edu.

Jones, Martha. *Birthright Citizens: A History of Race and Rights in Antebellum America.* Cambridge: Cambridge University Press, 2018.

Jones, Tracy. "I'm Raising a Biracial Daughter in Japan, Where She's Surrounded by Blackface." *Huffington Post*, March 5, 2018.

Joo, Thomas. "New Conspiracy Theory of the Fourteenth Amendment: Nineteenth-Century Chinese Civil Rights Cases and the Development of Substantive Due Process Jurisprudence." *University of San Francisco Law Review* 29:2 (Winter 1995): 353–388.

"*Yick Wo* Re-Revisited: Nonblack Nonwhites and Fourteenth Amendment History." *University of Illinois Law Review* 2008:5 (2008): 1427–1440.

Jun, Helen. *Race for Citizenship: Black Orientalism and Asian Uplift from Pre-Emancipation to Neoliberal America.* New York: New York University Press, 2011.

Jung, John. *Chopsticks in the Land of Cotton: Lives of Mississippi Delta Chinese Grocers.* N.p.: Yin & Yang Press, 2008.

Jung, Moon-Ho. *Coolies and Cane: Race, Labor, and Sugar in the Age of Emancipation.* Baltimore: Johns Hopkins University Press, 2008.

Kagan, Shelly. "Equality and Desert." In *What Do We Deserve? A Reader on Justice and Desert*, eds. Louis Pojman and Owen McLeod, 298–314. Oxford: Oxford University Press, 1999.

Kang, Jay Caspian. "How Should Asian-Americans Feel About the Peter Liang Protests?" *New York Times Magazine*, February 23, 2016.

Kang, Jerry. "Negative Action against Asian Americans: The Internal Instability of Dworkin's Defense of Affirmative Action." *Harvard Civil Rights-Civil Liberties Law Review* 31 (1996): 1–47.

Kanthor, Rebecca. "Racism against African Americans in China Escalates amid Coronavirus." *The World*, June 12, 2020.

Kearney, Reginald. "Japan: Ally in the Struggle against Racism, 1919–1927." *Contributions in Black Studies* 12:14 (1994): 117–128.

Kelley, Robin. "'A Day of Reckoning': Dreams of Reparations." In *Redress for Historical Injustices in the United States: On Reparations for Slavery, Jim Crow, and Their Legacies*, eds. Michael Martin and Marilyn Yaquinto, 203–221. Durham, N.C.: Duke University Press, 2007.

"Beyond Black Lives Matter." *Kalfou* 2:2 (Fall 2015): 330–337.

Kettner, James. *The Development of American Citizenship, 1608–1870.* Chapel Hill: University of North Carolina Press, 1978.

Kidder, William. "Negative Action versus Affirmative Action: Asian Pacific Americans Are Still Caught in the Crossfire." *Michigan Journal of Race & Law* 11 (2005–2006): 605–624.

Kim, Claire Jean. "The Racial Triangulation of Asian Americans." *Politics & Society* 27:1 (March 1999): 105–138.

"Playing the Racial Trump Card: Asian Americans in Contemporary U.S. Politics." *Amerasia Journal* 26:3 (2001): 35–65.

"Asian Americans Are People of Color, Too … Aren't They?" *AAPI Nexus* 2:1 (Winter/Spring 2004): 19–47.

Dangerous Crossings: Race, Species, and Nature in a Multicultural Age. Cambridge: Cambridge University Press, 2015.

"Murder and Mattering in Harambe's House." *Politics and Animals* 2:1 (2017): 1–15.

"Are Asians the New Blacks? Affirmative Action, Anti-Blackness, and the 'Sociometry' of Race." *Du Bois Review* 15:2 (Fall 2018): 1–28.

"Asian Americans and Anti-Blackness." *Politics, Groups, and Identities,* forthcoming.

Kim, Dae Shik. "Why Be a 'Model Minority' When You Could Dismantle White Supremacy?" *The Nation,* June 30, 2020.

Kim, Elaine. "Home Is Where the *Han* Is: A Korean-American Perspective on the Los Angeles Upheavals." In *Reading Rodney King, Reading Urban Uprising,* ed. Robert Gooding-Williams, 215–235. New York: Routledge, 1993.

Kim, Jae Kyun. "Yellow over Black: History of Race in Korea and the New Study of Race and Empire." *Critical Sociology* 41:2 (2015): 205–217.

Kim, Jae Kyun, and Moon-Kie Jung. "'The Darker to the Lighter Races': The Precolonial Construction of Racial Inferiors in Korea." *History of the Present: A Journal of Critical History* 9:1 (Spring 2019).

"'Not to Be Slaves of Others': Antiblackness in Precolonial Korea." In *Antiblackness*, eds. Moon-Kie Jung and João Costa Vargas, 143–167. Durham, N.C.: Duke University Press, 2021.

Kim, Ju Yon. "Remembering SA-I-GU: An Interview with Dai Sil Kim-Gibson." *Transition* 113 (2014): 144–152.

Kim, Rose. "Violence and Trauma as Constitutive Elements in Korean American Racial Identity Formation: the 1992 L.A. Riots/Insurrection/Saigu." *Ethnic and Racial Studies* 35:11 (2012): 1999–2018.

Kim-Gibson, Dai Sil, dir. *Sa-I-Gu.* San Francisco: Center for Asian American Media, 1993.

Wet Sand: Voices from L.A. San Francisco: Center for Asian American Media, 2004.

King, Gilbert. "What Paul Robeson Said." *Smithsonian Magazine,* September 13, 2011.

Konstantopoulos, Gina. "The Kamikaze Pilots and Their Image in World War II." Undergraduate thesis, Mount Holyoke College, April 2007.

Koppes, Clayton, and Gregory Black. "Blacks, Loyalty, and Motion-Picture Propaganda in World War II." *Journal of American History* 73:2 (September 1986): 383–406.

Kornweibel, Theodore, Jr. *"Seeing Red": Federal Campaigns against Black Militancy, 1919–1925.* Bloomington: Indiana University Press, 1998.

Koshy, Susan. "Morphing Race into Ethnicity: Asian Americans and Critical Transformations of Whiteness." *boundary 2* 28:1 (Spring 2001): 153–194.

Kozol, Wendy. "Relocating Citizenship in Photographs of Japanese Americans during World War II." In *Haunting Violations: Feminist Criticism and the*

Crisis of the "Real," eds. Wendy Hesford and Wendy Kozol, 217–250. Urbana: University of Illinois Press, 2001.

Kubota, Larry. "Yellow Power!" *Gidra* I:1 (April 1969): 3–4.

Kühl, Stefan. *The Nazi Connection: Eugenics, American Racism, and German National Socialism.* New York: Oxford University Press, 1994.

Kuo, Rachel. "Visible Solidarities: #Asians4BlackLives and Affective Racial Counterpublics." *Studies of Transition States and Societies* 1:2 (2019): 40–54.

Kurashige, Scott. *The Shifting Grounds of Race: Black and Japanese Americans in the Making of Multiethnic Los Angeles.* Princeton: Princeton University Press, 2008.

  "My Initial Thoughts on the Richard Aoki Controversy." *Twitlonger,* August 20, 2012, see at: www.twitlonger.com/show/iuop7v.

Kushner, Barak. *The Thought War: Japanese Imperial Propaganda.* Honolulu: University of Hawai'i Press, 2006.

Lake, Marilyn, and Henry Reynolds. *Drawing the Global Colour Line: White Men's Countries and the International Challenge of Racial Equality.* Cambridge: Cambridge University Press, 2008.

Lan, Shanshan. "The Shifting Meanings of Race in China: A Case Study of the African Diaspora Communities in Guangzhou." *City & Society* 28:3 (2016): 298–318.

Lau, Don. "CADC Protests Consent Decree at School Board Meeting." *AsianWeek,* March 12, 1993, 7.

Lauren, Paul Gordon. "First Principles of Racial Equality: History and the Politics and Diplomacy of Human Rights Provisions in the United Nations Charter." *Human Rights Quarterly* 5:1 (February 1983): 1–26.

Lawrence, Charles. "Two Views of the River: A Critique of the Liberal Defense of Affirmative Action." *Columbia Law Review* 101 (May 2001): 928–976.

Lee, Fred. "The Japanese Internment and the Racial State of Exception." *Theory & Event* 10:1 (2007).

Lee, Jennifer, and Frank Bean. "Reinventing the Color Line: Immigration and America's New Racial/Ethnic Divide." *Social Forces* 86:2 (December 2007): 562–586.

Lee, Julia. *Interracial Encounters: Reciprocal Representations in African and Asian American Literatures, 1896–1937.* New York: New York University Press, 2011.

Lee, K. W. "The Fire Next Time? Ten Haunting Questions Cry Out for Answers and Redress." *Amerasia Journal* 38:1 (2012a): 85–90.

  "Legacy of Sa-ee-gu: Goodbye Hahn, Good Morning, Community Conscience." *Amerasia Journal* 38:1 (2012b): 91–110.

Lee, Katy. "Japan's Blackface Problem: The Country's Bizarre, Troubled Relationship with Race." *Vox,* March 17, 2015.

Lee, Rose Hum. "Chinese in the United States Today." In *Unbound Voices: A Documentary History of Chinese Women in California,* ed. Judy Yung, 465–472. Berkeley: University of California Press, 1999.

Lee, Sharon. "The De-Minoritization of Asian Americans: A Historical Examination of the Representations of Asian Americans in Affirmative Action Admissions Policies at the University of California." *Asian American Law Journal* 15 (2008): 129–152.

Leong, Karen, and Myla Vicenti Carpio. "Carceral Subjugations." *Amerasia Journal* 42:1 (2016): 103–120.

Leroy, Justin. "Insurgency and Asian American Studies in the Time of Black Lives Matter." *Journal of Asian American Studies* 20:2 (June 2017): 279–281.

Leupp, Gary. "Images of Black People in Late Mediaeval and Early Modern Japan, 1543–1900." *Japan Forum* 7:1 (1995): 1–13.

Levine, David. "The Chinese American Challenge to Court-Mandated Quotas in San Francisco's Public Schools: Notes from a (Partisan) Participant-Observer." *Harvard Blackletter Law Journal* 16 (2000): 39–145.

Lew-Lee, Lee. "Field Marshal Aoki, Guy Kurose and Myself Were the Only Three Bona Fide Asian Members in the BPP." *San Francisco Bay View*, August 23, 2012.

Li, Jane. "'This Is Nuts': The Backlash to the Rebranding of 'Black Person Toothpaste' in China." *Quartz*, June 23, 2020.

Liang, Ursula, dir. *Down a Dark Stairwell*. New York: Kino Lorber, 2020.

Lim, Gerard. "SF's Chinese Students File Class Action Suit: Plaintiffs Claim Discrimination in Federal Consent Decree at Lowell High School." *AsianWeek*, July 15, 1994, 1.

"Lawsuit over Chinese American HS Enrollment: Class Warfare by the Bay?" *AsianWeek*, August 19, 1994, 1.

Litwack, Leon. *North of Slavery: The Negro in the Free States, 1790–1860*. Chicago: University of Chicago Press, 1961.

Liu, Goodwin. "The Causation Fallacy: *Bakke* and the Basic Arithmetic of Selective Admissions." *Michigan Law Review* 100 (March 2002): 1045–1107.

Liu, Haiming. "Chinese Exclusion Laws and the U.S.–China Relationship." *The Cal Poly Pomona Journal of Interdisciplinary Studies* 16 (Fall 2003): 151–156.

Liu, Wen. "Complicity and Resistance: Asian American Body Politics in Black Lives Matter." *Journal of Asian American Studies* 21:3 (October 2018): 421–451.

Loewen, James. *The Mississippi Chinese: Between Black and White*, 2nd ed. Prospect Heights, Ill.: Waveland Press, 1988 [1971].

Lofgren, Charles. *The Plessy Case: A Legal-Historical Interpretation*. New York: Oxford University Press, 1987.

Lossin, R. H. "In Defense of Destroying Property." *The Nation*, June 10, 2020.

Lott, Eric. *Love and Theft: Blackface Minstrelsy and the American Working Class*. New York: Oxford University Press, 1995.

Louie, Belvin, and Miriam Ching Yoon Louie. "Damn It, Richard, What the F**k?!" *San Francisco Bay View*, August 29, 2012.

Lowe, Lisa. *Immigrant Acts: On Asian American Cultural Politics*. Durham, N.C.: Duke University Press, 1996.

The Intimacies of Four Continents. Durham, N.C.: Duke University Press, 2015.

Lubet, Steven. *Fugitive Justice: Runaways, Rescuers, and Slavery on Trial*. Cambridge, Mass.: Belknap Press, 2010.

"Lunar New Year: Chinese TV Gala Includes 'Racist Blackface' Sketch." *BBC News*, February 16, 2018. www.bbc.co.uk/news/world-asia-china-43081218.

Lurie, Jonathan. "Reflections on Justice Samuel F. Miller and *The Slaughter-House Cases*: Still a Meaty Subject." *New York University Journal of Law & Liberty* 1:1 (2005): 355–369.

Lye, Colleen. "The Afro-Asian Analogy." *PMLA* 123:5 (2008): 1732–1736.

"Lynching in America: Targeting Black Veterans." Montgomery, Ala.: Equal Justice Initiative, 2017. https://eji.org/wp-content/uploads/2019/10/lynching-in-america-targeting-black-veterans-web.pdf.

Lyon, Cherstin. *Prisons and Patriots: Japanese American Wartime Citizenship, Civil Disobedience, and Historical Memory.* Philadelphia: Temple University Press, 2012.

Maeda, Daryl. *Chains of Babylon: The Rise of Asian America.* Minneapolis: University of Minnesota Press, 2009.

Makalani, Minkah. *In the Cause of Freedom: Radical Black Internationalism from Harlem to London, 1917–1939.* Chapel Hill: University of North Carolina Press, 2011a.

"Internationalizing the Third International: The African Blood Brotherhood, Asian Radicals, and Race, 1919–1922." *The Journal of African American History* 96, no. 2 (2011b): 151–178.

Makinen, Julie. "Chinese Social Media Platform Plays a Role in U.S. Rallies for NYPD Officer." *Los Angeles Times*, February 24, 2016.

Marable, Manning. *How Capitalism Underdeveloped Black America: Problems in Race, Political Economy, and Society.* Chicago, Ill.: Haymarket Books, 2015 [1983].

Marriott, David. *On Black Men.* New York: Columbia University Press, 2000.

Martin, Charles. "Internationalizing 'The American Dilemma': The Civil Rights Congress and the 1951 Genocide Petition to the United Nations." *Journal of American Ethnic History* 16:4 (Summer 1997): 35–61.

Martin, Michael, and Marilyn Yaquinto, eds. *Redress for Historical Injustices in the United States: On Reparations for Slavery, Jim Crow, and Their Legacies.* Durham, N.C.: Duke University Press, 2007.

Masaharu, Sato, and Barak Kushner. "'Negro Propaganda Operations': Japan's Short-Wave Radio Broadcasts for World War II Black Americans." *Historical Journal of Film, Radio, and Television* 19, no. 1 (March 1999): 5–26.

Masaoka, Mike. "NOT 'Our Voice.'" *Pacific Citizen*, August 2, 1963, 2.

Masaoka, Mike, with Bill Hosokawa. *They Call Me Moses Masaoka: An American Saga.* New York: William Morrow, 1987.

Massey, Douglas. "Still the Linchpin: Segregation and Stratification in the USA." *Race and Social Problems* 12 (2020): 1–12.

Massey, Douglas, and Nancy Denton. *American Apartheid: Segregation and the Making of the Underclass.* Cambridge, Mass.: Harvard University Press, 1993.

Matsuda, Mari. "We Will Not Be Used." *UCLA Asian American & Pacific Islands Law Journal* 79 (1993): 79–84.

Maxey, Edwin. "Exclusion of Japanese Children from the Public Schools of San Francisco." *Yale Law Journal* 16:2 (December 1906): 90–93.

McClain, Charles. *In Search of Equality: The Chinese Struggle against Discrimination in Nineteenth-Century America.* Berkeley: University of California Press, 1994.

McGuire, Phillip. "Desegregation of the Armed Forces: Black Leadership, Protest and World War II." *Journal of Negro History* 68:2 (Spring 1983): 147–158.

Taps for a Jim Crow Army: Letters from Black Soldiers in World War II. Lexington: University Press of Kentucky, 1993.

McWilliams, Carey. *Prejudice: Japanese-Americans: Symbol of Racial Intolerance.* Boston: Little, Brown, 1944.

Melamed, Jodi. "Racial Capitalism." *Critical Ethnic Studies* 1:1 (Spring 2015): 76–85.

Meriwether, James. *Proudly We Can Be Africans: Black Americans and Africa, 1935–1961.* Chapel Hill: University of North Carolina Press, 2002.

Metzger, Sean. "Ripples in the Seascape: The 'Cuba Commission Report' and the Idea of Freedom." *Afro-Hispanic Review* 27:1 (Spring 2008): 105–121.

Min, Pyong Gap. *Caught in the Middle: Korean Communities in New York and Los Angeles.* Berkeley: University of California Press, 1996.

"Minstrel Show Slated for Thursday." *The Denson Tribune*, May 2, 1944, 1. https://ddr.densho.org/ddr-densho-144/.

Mitchell, Koritha. *Living with Lynching: African American Lynching Plays, Performance, and Citizenship, 1890–1930.* Urbana: University of Illinois Press, 2011.

Molina, Natalia, Daniel Martinez HoSang, and Ramón A. Gutiérrez, eds. *Relational Formations of Race: Theory, Method, and Practice.* Berkeley: University of California Press, 2019.

Montgomery, Nancy. "When the Civil Rights Movement Became a Casualty of War." *Stars and Stripes*, November 9, 2014.

"Mother Country that Has Not Forsaken Us." Editorial. *The Tulean Dispatch*, November 11, 1943.

Muratsuchi, Albert. "Race, Class, and the UCLA School of Law Admissions, 1967–1994." *Chicana/o Latina/o Law Review* 16:1 (January 1995): 90–140.

Murray, Alice Yang. *Historical Memories of the Japanese American Internment and the Struggle for Redress.* Stanford: Stanford University Press, 2008.

Neu, Charles. "Theodore Roosevelt and American Involvement in the Far East, 1901–1909." *Pacific Historical Review* 35:4 (November 1966): 433–449.

Nierenberg, Amelia. "Their Minneapolis Restaurant Burned, but They Back the Protest." *New York Times*, May 29, 2020.

"Nisei and Jim Crow." Editorial. *Pacific Citizen*, January 1, 1944, 4.

Nishida, Mo. "Richard Lives! More Thoughts on My Friend, Richard Aoki." *San Francisco Bay View*, October 28, 2012.

Nishio, Alan. "The Oriental as a 'Middleman Minority.'" *Gidra* I:2 (May 1969). *Reprinted in Asian Americans: The Movement and the Moment*, eds. Steve Louie and Glenn Omatsu, 280. Los Angeles: UCLA Asian American Studies Center, 2014.

Nopper, Tamara. "Why Couldn't Richard Aoki Have Been an Informant?" *The New Inquiry*, August 30, 2012.

Nott, Josiah and George Gliddon. *Types of Mankind: Or Ethnological Researches, Based Upon the Ancient Monuments, Paintings, Sculptures, and Crania of Races.* Philadelphia: Lippincott, Grambo, 1854.

O'Brien, Robert. "Status of Chinese in the Mississippi Delta." *Social Forces* 19:3 (March 1941): 386–390.

Okada, Dave. "A Study of Male Nisei Workers in Two Chicago Industrial Plants under Wartime Conditions." Master's thesis, University of Chicago, June 1947.

Okamura, Raymond. "The American Concentration Camps: A Cover-Up through Euphemistic Terminology." *The Journal of Ethnic Studies* 10:3 (Fall 1982): 95–109.

Okihiro, Gary. *Margins and Mainstreams: Asians in American History and Culture*. Seattle: University of Washington Press, 1994.

Onishi, Yuichiro. "The New Negro of the Pacific: How African Americans Forged Cross-Racial Solidarity with Japan, 1917–1922." *The Journal of African American History* 92:2 (Spring 2007): 191–213.

Orfield, Gary, with Diane Glass. "Asian Students and Multiethnic Desegregation." The Harvard Project on School Desegregation, Harvard University, October 1994, see at: https://civilrightsproject.ucla.edu/research/k-12-education/integration-and-diversity/asian-students-and-multiethnic-desegregation/asian-students_orfield_glass.pdf.

Osterweil, Vicky. "In Defense of Looting." *The New Inquiry*, August 21, 2014.

Ozawa, Takao. "Naturalization of a Japanese Subject in the United States of America: A Brief In re Ozawa Case Now Pending the Decision in the Supreme Court of U.S.A." Printed for private circulation, October 1922.

Padover, Saul. "Japanese Race Propaganda." *Public Opinion Quarterly* 7:2 (Summer 1943): 191–204.

Palumbo-Liu, David. "Los Angeles, Asians, and Perverse Ventriloquisms: On the Functions of Asian America in the Recent American Imaginary." *Public Culture* 6 (1994): 365–381.

Patterson, Orlando. *Slavery and Social Death: A Comparative Study*. Cambridge, Mass.: Harvard University Press, 1982.

Patterson, William. *We Charge Genocide: The Historic Petition to the United Nations for Relief from a Crime of the United States Government against the Negro People*. New York: Emergency Conference Committee, 1951.

Peele, Jordan, dir. *Get Out*. Los Angeles: Universal Pictures, 2017.

Petersen, William. *Japanese Americans: Oppression and Success*. New York: Random House, 1971.

Pham, Sherisse. "Colgate is Still Selling 'Black Person Toothpaste' in China. Now that's under Review." *CNN Business*, June 19, 2020.

Phippen, J. Weston. "Why Was Officer Peter Liang Convicted?" *The Atlantic*, March 3, 2016.

Pirosh, Robert, dir. *Go for Broke*. Beverly Hills: Metro-Goldwyn-Mayer, 1951.

Platt, Tony. "The Case for and against Richard Aoki." *Social Justice*, September 17, 2012.

Plummer, Brenda Gayle. *Rising Wind: Black Americans and U.S. Foreign Affairs, 1935–1960*. Chapel Hill: University of North Carolina Press, 1996.

In Search of Power: African Americans in the Era of Decolonization, 1956–1974. Cambridge: Cambridge University Press, 2012.

Poon, OiYan and Megan Segoshi. "The Racial Mascot Speaks: A critical race discourse analysis of Asian Americans and *Fisher* vs. *University of Texas*." *The Review of Higher Education* 42:1 (Fall 2018): 235–267.

"Prosecutors Depict Ex-Officer Tou Thao as Complicit in George Floyd's Death." WCCO-TV. *CBS Minnesota*, August 25, 2020, see at: www.cbsnews.com/minnesota/news/prosecutors-depict-ex-officer-tou-thao-as-complicit-in-george-floyds-death.

Pulido, Laura. *Black, Brown, Yellow, and Left: Radical Activism in Los Angeles.* Berkeley: University of California Press, 2006.

Pulley, Marie. "Nisei and Race Prejudice: Jim Crow Tendencies among Japanese American Evacuees May Hamper Resettlement." *Pacific Citizen*, January 1, 1944, 5.

Quan, Robert. *Lotus among the Magnolias: The Mississippi Chinese.* Jackson: University Press of Mississippi, 1982.

Quinn, Rand. *Class Action: Desegregation and Diversity in San Francisco Schools.* Minneapolis: University of Minnesota Press, 2020.

Rable, George. "The South and the Politics of Antilynching Legislation, 1920–1940." *Journal of Southern History* 51:2 (May 1985): 201–220.

Raiche, Ryan. "Former MPD Officer Tou Thao Reveals to Investigators What He Could've Done Differently in Floyd Case." KSTP.com. *ABC 5 Eyewitness News*, August 14, 2020.

Ratner, Megan. "Dreamland and Disillusion: Interview with Dai Sil Kim-Gibson." *Film Quarterly* 65:1 (Fall 2011): 34–38.

Rhee, Jeannie. "In Black and White: Chinese in the Mississippi Delta." *Journal of Supreme Court History* 117 (1994): 117–132.

Rhodes, Jane. *Framing the Black Panthers: The Spectacular Rise of a Black Power Icon.* Urbana: University of Illinois Press, 2017.

Rickford, Russell. "Black Lives Matter: Toward a Modern Practice of Mass Struggle." *New Labor Forum*, December 8, 2015.

"Rights of the Japanese in California Schools." *Harvard Law Review* 20:4 (February 1907): 337–340.

Robinson, Cedric. *Black Marxism: The Making of the Black Radical Tradition.* Chapel Hill: University of North Carolina Press, 1983.

Robinson, Greg. *By Order of the President: FDR and the Internment of Japanese Americans.* Cambridge, Mass.: Harvard University Press, 2001.

    After Camp: Portraits in Midcentury Japanese American Life and Politics. Berkeley: University of California Press, 2012a.

    ed. *Pacific Citizens: Larry and Guyo Tajiri and Japanese American Journalism in the World War II Era.* Urbana: University of Illinois Press, 2012b.

    "The Paradox of Reparations: Japanese Americans and African Americans at the Crossroads of Alliance and Conflict." In *Minority Relations: Intergroup Conflict and Cooperation*, eds. Greg Robinson and Robert Chang, 159–187. Jackson: University Press of Mississippi, 2016.

Robles, Rowena. "The Asian American as Victim and Success Story: A Discursive Analysis of the *Brian Ho* v. *SFUSD* Lawsuit." *Asian American Policy Review* 8:13 (2004): 73–87.

    Asian Americans and the Shifting Politics of Race: The Dismantling of Affirmative Action at an Elite Public High School. New York: Routledge, 2006.

Rodríguez, Dylan. "Asian-American Studies in the Age of the Prison Industrial Complex: Departures and Re-narrations." *Review of Education, Pedagogy, and Cultural Studies* 27:3 (2005): 241–263.

Roediger, David. *The Wages of Whiteness: Race and the Making of the American Working Class.* London: Verso, 2007 [1991].

Rosenfeld, Seth. "FBI Files Reveal New Details about Informant Who Armed Black Panthers." *California Watch*, September 7, 2012.

"New FBI Files Show Wide Range of Black Panther Informant's Activities." *RevealNews.org*, June 9, 2015.

Ross, Michael. "Obstructing Reconstruction: John Archibald Campbell and the Legal Campaign against Louisiana's Republican Government, 1863–1873." *Civil War History* 49:3 (September 2003): 235–253.

Ross, Thomas. "Innocence and Affirmative Action." *Vanderbilt Law Review* 43:2 (1990): 297–316.

Rothstein, Richard. *The Color of Law: A Forgotten History of How Our Government Segregated America*. New York: Liveright, 2017.

Rouleau, Brian. "In the Wake of Jim Crow: Maritime Minstrelsy along the Transoceanic Frontier." *Common-Place* 12:4 (July 2012).

   With Sails Whitening Every Sea: Mariners and the Making of an American Maritime Empire. Ithaca, N.Y.: Cornell University Press, 2014.

Roxworthy, Emily. *The Spectacle of Japanese American Trauma: Racial Performativity and World War II*. Honolulu: University of Hawai'i Press, 2008.

   "Blackface behind Barbed Wire: Gender and Racial Triangulation in the Japanese American Internment Camps." *TDR: The Drama Review* 57:2 (Summer 2013): 123–142.

Russell, John. "Race and Reflexivity: The Black Other in Contemporary Japanese Mass Culture." *Cultural Anthropology* 6:1 (February 1991): 3–25.

   "Narratives of Denial: Racial Chauvinism and the Black Other in Japan." *Japan Quarterly* 38:4 (October 1991): 416–428.

   "The Other Other: The Black Presence in the Japanese Experience." In *Japan's Minorities: The Illusion of Homogeneity*, 2nd ed., ed. Michael Weiner, 84–115. New York: Routledge, 1997.

   "Consuming Passions: Spectacle, Self-Transformation, and the Commodification of Blackness in Japan." *positions* 6:1 (Spring 1998): 113–177.

Rzetelny, Xaq. "Milky Way Is Not Only Being Pulled—It's Also 'Pushed' by Void." *Ars Technica*, February 3, 2017.

Salyer, Lucy. "Baptism by Fire: Race, Military Service, and U.S. Citizenship Policy, 1918–1935." *Journal of American History* 91:3 (December 2004): 847–876.

Sautman, Barry. "Anti-Black Racism in Post-Mao China." *China Quarterly* 138 (June 1994): 413–437.

Saxton, Alexander. *The Indispensable Enemy: Labor and the Anti-Chinese Movement in California*. Berkeley: University of California Press, 1995 [1971].

Schiller, Reuel. "Conflict in the 'Tranquil Gardens': *Banks v. Housing Authority of San Francisco* and the Definition of Equality in Multi-Racial California." *UC Hastings Scholarship Repository*, 2015, 1–37.

Schnapper, Eric. "Affirmative Action and the Legislative History of the Fourteenth Amendment." *Virginia Law Review* 71:5 (1985): 753–798.

Schrecker, John. "'For the Equality of Men—For the Equality of Nations': Anson Burlingame and China's First Embassy to the United States, 1868." *Journal of American-East Asian Relations* 17 (2010): 9–34.

Scott, John Anthony. "Justice Bradley's Evolving Concept of the Fourteenth Amendment from the *Slaughterhouse Cases* to the *Civil Rights Cases*." *Rutgers Law Review* 25 (1970–1971): 552–570.

Scott, Rebecca. *Slave Emancipation in Cuba: The Transition to Free Labor, 1860–1899*. Princeton: Princeton University Press, 1985.

"Public Rights, Social Equality, and the Conceptual Roots of the *Plessy* Challenge." *Michigan Law Review* 106:5 (2008): 777–804.

Selingo, Jeffrey. "The Two Most Important College-Admissions Criteria Now Mean Less." *The Atlantic*, May 25, 2018.

Sexton, Jared. "Proprieties of Coalition: Blacks, Asians, and the Politics of Policing." *Critical Sociology* 36:1 (2010a): 87–108.

"People-of-Color-Blindness: Notes on the Afterlife of Slavery." *Social Text* 28:2 (Summer 2010b): 31–56.

Sharpe, Christina. *In the Wake: On Blackness and Being*. Durham, N.C.: Duke University Press, 2016.

Shih, Shu-Mei. "Race and Revolution: Blackness in China's Long Twentieth Century." *Proceedings of the Modern Language Association* 128:1 (January 2013): 156–162.

Shimazu, Naoko. "The Japanese Attempt to Secure Racial Equality in 1919." *Japan Forum* 1:1 (1989): 93–100.

"The Racial Equality Proposal at the 1919 Paris Peace Conference: Japanese Motivations and Anglo-American Responses." PhD diss., Magdalen College, University of Oxford, 1995.

Sinha, Manisha. *The Slave's Cause: A History of Abolition*. New Haven, Conn.: Yale University Press, 2017.

Sitkoff, Harvard. "Racial Militancy and Interracial Violence in the Second World War." *The Journal of American History* 58:3 (December 1971): 661–681.

Skrentny, John. "The Effect of the Cold War on African-American Civil Rights: America and the World Audience, 1945–1968." *Theory and Society* 27:2 (April 1998): 237–285.

Smallwood, Stephanie. *Saltwater Slavery: A Middle Passage from Africa to American Diaspora*. Cambridge, Mass.: Harvard University Press, 2008.

Smith, C. Calvin. "The Response of Arkansans to Prisoners of War and Japanese Americans in Arkansas, 1942–1945." *Arkansas Historical Quarterly* 53:3 (Autumn 1994): 340–366.

Smith, Rogers. *Civic Ideals: Conflicting Visions of Citizenship in U.S. History*. New Haven, Conn.: Yale University Press, 1997.

Smith, Stacey. *Freedom's Frontier: California and the Struggle over Unfree Labor, Emancipation, and Reconstruction*. Chapel Hill: University of North Carolina Press, 2013.

Solomon, Mark. *The Cry Was Unity: Communists and African Americans, 1917–36*. Jackson: University Press of Mississippi, 1998.

Song, Daeun. "The Asian American Division over Affirmative Action: Examining the Case of SCA5 and the Rise of Chinese American Conservatism." PhD diss., University of California, Irvine, December 2020.

Song, Min Hyoung. "*Sa-I-Gu* Revisited: Interview with Elaine Kim." *Amerasia Journal* 30:1 (2004): 229–242.

Strange Future: Pessimism and the 1992 Los Angeles Riots. Durham, N.C.: Duke University Press, 2005.

Specia, Megan. "Japanese Comedian Who Used Blackface Comes under Fire Online." *New York Times*, January 4, 2018.

Spillers, Hortense. "Mama's Baby, Papa's Maybe: An American Grammar Book." In *Black, White, and in Color: Essays on American Literature and Culture*, 203–229. Chicago: University of Chicago Press, 2003.

Stanley, Amy Dru. *From Bondage to Contract: Wage Labor, Marriage, and the Market in the Age of the Slave Emancipation*. Cambridge: Cambridge University Press, 1998.

Starr, M. B. *The Coming Struggle, Or, What the People on the Pacific Coast Think of the Coolie Invasion*. San Francisco: Excelsior Office, Bacon & Company, Book & Job Printers, 1873.

Stevenson, Brenda. *The Contested Murder of Latasha Harlins: Justice, Gender, and the Origins of the LA Riots*. New York: Oxford University Press, 2013.

Strickland, Arvarh. "Remembering Hattiesburg: Growing Up Black in Wartime Mississippi." In *Remaking Dixie: The Impact of World War II on the American South*, ed. Neil McMillen, 146–158. Jackson: University Press of Mississippi, 1997.

Sugrue, Thomas. "Crabgrass-Roots Politics: Race, Rights, and the Reaction against Liberalism in the Urban North, 1940–1964." *Journal of American History* 82:2 (September 1995): 551–578.

Sullivan, Michael. "The 1988–89 Nanjing Anti-African Protests: Racial Nationalism or National Racism?" *China Quarterly* 138 (June 1994): 438–457.

Tajima, Atsushi and Michael Thornton. "Strategic Solidarity: Japanese Imaginings of Blacks and Race in Popular Media." *Inter-Asia Cultural Studies* 13:3 (2012): 345–364.

Tajiri, Larry. "No Jap Crow." *Pacific Citizen*, February 19, 1944, 6.

Takagi, Dana. *The Retreat from Race: Asian-American Admissions and Racial Politics*. New Brunswick, N.J.: Rutgers University Press, 1992.

Tamura, Linda. *Nisei Soldiers Break Their Silence: Coming Home to Hood River*. Seattle: University of Washington Press, 2012.

Tang, Scott. "'Becoming the New Objects of Racial Scorn': Racial Politics and Racial Hierarchy in Postwar San Francisco, 1945–1960." In *The Political Culture of the New West*, ed. Jeff Roche, 219–245. Lawrence: University Press of Kansas, 2008.

Terkel, Studs. *Race: How Blacks and Whites Think and Feel about the American Obsession*. New York: The New Press, 1992.

"The Harvard Plan that Failed Asian Americans." *Harvard Law Review* 131:2 (December 2017): 604–625.

Thomas, Dorothy Swaine, and Richard Nishimoto. *The Spoilage: Japanese-American Evacuation and Resettlement During World War II*. Berkeley: University of California Press, 1969.

Thornton, Michael, and Atsushi Tajima. "Japan Times' Imagined Communities: Symbolic Boundaries with African Americans, 1998–2013." In *The Handbook on Japanese Media*, ed. Fabienne Darling-Wolf, 241–255. New York: Routledge, 2018.

Torok, John. "Reconstruction and Racial Nativism: Chinese Immigrants and the Debates on the Thirteenth, Fourteenth, and Fifteenth Amendments and Civil Rights Laws." *Asian American Law Journal* 3 (January 1996): 55–103.

Tupper, Eleanor, and George McReynolds. *Japan in American Public Opinion.* New York: Macmillan, 1937.

Uyeda, Clifford. "Rhetorics over Racial Discrimination." *Pacific Citizen*, November 10, 1961, 2.

"This Is Our Voice." *Pacific Citizen*, July 19, 1963, 2.

Uyeki, Eugene. "Process and Patterns of Nisei Adjustment to Chicago." PhD diss., University of Chicago, 1953.

Uyematsu, Amy. "The Emergence of Yellow Power in America." *Gidra*, October 1969. Excerpt reprinted in *Roots: An Asian American Reader*. Los Angeles: UCLA Asian American Studies Center, 1971, 9–13.

Van Volkenburg, Matthew. "Three Decades of Blackface in Korea." *Gusts of Popular Feeling* (blog), March 5, 2012., see at: https://populargusts.blogspot.com/2012/03/three-decades-of-black-face-in-korea.html.

"Blackface and Depictions of Indigenous People in South Korea in the 1960s, 1970s, and Today." *Gusts of Popular Feeling* (blog), July 22, 2020, see at: https://populargusts.blogspot.com/2020/07/blackface-and-depictions-of-indigenous.html.

Verdun, Vincene. "If the Shoe Fits, Wear It: An Analysis of Reparations to African Americans." *Tulane Law Review* 67:3 (February 1993): 597–668.

Von Eschen, Penny. *Race against Empire: Black Americans and Anticolonialism, 1937–1957.* Ithaca, N.Y.: Cornell University Press, 1997.

Wacquant, Loïc. "Deadly Symbiosis: When Ghetto and Prison Meet and Mesh." *Punishment and Society* 3:1 (2001): 95–134.

"From Slavery to Mass Incarceration: Rethinking the 'Race Question' in the US." *New Left Review* 13 (January–February 2002): 41–60.

Wagner, Bryan. *Disturbing the Peace: Black Culture and the Police Power after Slavery.* Cambridge, Mass.: Harvard University Press, 2009.

Walker, David. *Appeal to the Coloured Citizens of the World*, 3rd ed., repr. Eastford, Conn.: Martino Fine Books, 2015 [1830].

Walsh, Joan. "Can This Man Fix Our Schools?" *San Francisco Focus*, October 1993, 60–63, 134–136.

Wang, Esther. "The Counterculturalists: Alex Hing." *Asian American Writers' Workshop*, October 9, 2014, see at: https://aaww.org/counterculturalist-alex-hing.

Ward, Jason Morgan. "'No Jap Crow': Japanese Americans Encounter the World War II South." *Journal of Southern History* 73:1 (February 2007): 75–104.

Wareham, Roger. "The Popularization of the International Demand for Reparations for African People." In *Should America Pay? Slavery and the Raging Debate on Reparations*, ed. Raymond Winbush, 226–236. New York: HarperCollins 2003.

Warren, Jonathan, and France Winddance Twine. "White Americans, the New Minority? Non-Blacks and the Ever-Expanding Boundaries of Whiteness." *Journal of Black Studies* 28:2 (November 1997): 200–218.

Washburn, Patrick. "The Pittsburgh Courier's Double V Campaign in 1942." Paper presented at the Annual Meeting of the Association for Education in Journalism, East Lansing, Michigan State University, History Division, August 1981.

  A Question of Sedition: The Federal Government's Investigation of the Black Press during World War II. New York: Oxford University Press, 1986.

Weglyn, Michi. *Years of Infamy: The Untold Story of America's Concentration Camps.* New York: William Morrow, 1976.

Wells-Barnett, Ida. *On Lynchings.* With an introduction by Patricia Hill Collins. Amherst, New York: Humanity Books, 2002 [1892, 1895, 1900].

  Southern Horrors: Lynch Law in All Its Phases. Bristol: Read & Co. History, 2021 [1892].

Wenger, Kaimipono David. "The Unconscionable Impossibility of Reparations for Slavery; Or, Why the Master's Mules Will Never Dismantle the Master's House." In *Injury and Injustice*, eds. Anne Bloom, David M. Engel, and Michael McCann, 248–266. Cambridge: Cambridge University Press, 2018.

Wenzer, Kenneth, ed. *Henry George: Collected Journalistic Writings.* New York: Routledge, 2003.

West-Faulcon, Kimberly. "Obscuring Asian Penalty with Illusions of Black Bonus." *UCLA Law Review Discourse* 64 (2017): 590–646.

"What's behind China's 'Racist' Whitewashing Advert?" *BBC News*, May 27, 2016, see at: www.bbc.co.uk/news/world-asia-china-36394917.

Whitman, James. *Hitler's American Model: The United States and the Making of Nazi Race Law.* Princeton: Princeton University Press, 2017.

Wilderson, Frank. *Red, White, and Black: Cinema and the Structure of U.S. Antagonisms.* Durham, N.C.: Duke University Press, 2010.

  Afropessimism. New York: Liveright 2021.

Williams, Chad. *Torchbearers of Democracy: African American Soldiers in the World War I Era.* Chapel Hill: University of North Carolina Press, 2010.

Williamson, Elizabeth, and Vivian Wang. "'We Need Help': Coronavirus Fuels Racism against Black Americans in China." *The New York Times*, June 2, 2020.

Winbush, Raymond, ed. *Should America Pay? Slavery and the Raging Debate on Reparations.* New York: HarperCollins 2003.

Wolfe, Patrick. "Settler Colonialism and the Elimination of the Native." *Journal of Genocide Research* 8:4 (2006): 387–409.

Wollenberg, Charles. *All Deliberate Speed: Segregation and Exclusion in California Schools, 1855–1975.* Berkeley: University of California Press, 1976.

Wong, Edlie. *Racial Reconstruction: Black Inclusion, Chinese Exclusion, and the Fictions of Citizenship.* New York: New York University Press, 2015.

Wong, Janelle. "What the Media Gets Wrong about Anti-Asian Hate." *Medium*, June 23, 2021, see at: https://stopasianhate.medium.com/what-the-media-gets-wrong-about-anti-asian-hate-369656a98684.

Wong, Janelle, and David Silver. "Telling the Wrong Story about Racial Discrimination in Education." *The Boston Globe*, June 18, 2018.

Wong, Janelle, and Karthick Ramakrishnan. "New Survey from Momentive and AAPI Data Offers Important Correctives on Hate in America." *Data*

Bits (blog). *AAPI Data*, March 16, 2022, see at: http://aapidata.com/blog/discrimination-survey-2022.

Wong, Julia Carrie. "'Scapegoated?' The Police Killing that Left Asian Americans Angry—and Divided." *The Guardian*, April 18, 2016.

Wong, Vivian. "The Chinese in Mississippi: A Race In-Between." *Trotter Review* 7:2 (1993): 20–22.

Wood, Amy Louise. *Lynching and Spectacle: Witnessing Racial Violence in America, 1890–1940*. Chapel Hill: University of North Carolina Press, 2011.

Woodard, Vincent. *The Delectable Negro: Human Consumption and Homoeroticism within U.S. Slave Culture*. New York: New York University Press, 2014.

Woods, Jeff. *Black Struggle, Red Scare: Segregation and Anti-Communism in the South, 1848–1968*. Baton Rouge: Louisiana State University Press, 2004.

Wu, Ellen. *The Color of Success: Asian Americans and the Origins of the Model Minority*. Princeton: Princeton University Press, 2014.

Wu, Judy. *Radicals on the Road: Internationalism, Orientalism, and Feminism during the Vietnam Era*. Ithaca, N.Y.: Cornell University Press, 2013.

Yamamoto, Eric. "Friend, or Foe or Something Else: Social Meanings of Redress and Reparations." *Denver Journal of International Law and Policy* 20:2 (Winter 1992): 223–242.

"Racial Reparations: Japanese American Redress and African American Claims." *Boston College Third World Law Journal* 19 (1998): 477–523.

Interracial Justice: Conflict and Reconciliation in Post-Civil Rights America. New York: New York University Press, 1999.

Yamashita, Jeffrey. "Becoming 'Hawaiian': A Relational Racialization of Japanese American Soldiers from Hawai'i during World War II in the U.S. South." In *Relational Formations of Race: Theory, Method, and Practice*, eds. Natalia Molina, Daniel Martinez HoSang, and Ramón A. Gutiérrez, 185–202. Berkeley: University of California Press, 2019.

Yamashita, Robert, and Peter Park. "The Politics of Race: The Open Door, Ozawa and the Case of the Japanese in America." *Review of Radical Political Economics* 17:3 (1985): 135–156.

Yancey, George. *Who is White? Latinos, Asians, and the New Black/Nonblack Divide*. Boulder, Col.: Lynne Reiner, 2004.

Yang, Caroline. *The Peculiar Afterlife of Slavery: The Chinese Worker and the Minstrel Form*. Stanford: Stanford University Press, 2020.

Yoo, David. "'Read All About It': Race, Generation and the Japanese American Ethnic Press, 1925–41." *Amerasia Journal* 19:1 (1993): 69–92.

Yoon, So-Yeon. "Okyere Gains Support for His Objection to Blackface Photo." *Korea JoongAng Daily*, August 9, 2020.

Young, Elliott. *Alien Nation: Chinese Migration in the Americas from the Coolie Era Through World War II*. Chapel Hill: University of North Carolina Press, 2014.

Yun, Lisa. *The Coolie Speaks: Chinese Indentured Laborers and African Slaves in Cuba*. Philadelphia: Temple University Press, 2008.

Index

Introductory Note

References such as '178–179' indicate (not necessarily continuous) discussion of a topic across a range of pages. Wherever possible in the case of topics with many references, these have either been divided into sub-topics or only the most significant discussions of the topic are listed. Because the entire work is about 'Asian Americans', the use of this term (and certain others which occur constantly throughout the book) as an entry point has been restricted. Information will be found under the corresponding detailed topics.